THE IAN
NICOLSON
TRILOGY

THE IAN NICOLSON TRILOGY

IAN NICOLSON

C. ENG. FRINA HON. MIIMS

AMBERLEY

First published individually as *The Log of the* Maken
by Peter Davies Ltd in 1961, *Sea-Saint* by Peter Davies Ltd
in 1957 and *Building the* St Mary by Tileyard Press Ltd in 1963,
and together as *The Ian Nicolson Omnibus* by
Ashford Press Publishing in 1986.
This edition published by Amberley Publishing, 2015.

Amberley Publishing
The Hill, Stroud
Gloucestershire, GL5 4EP

www.amberley-books.com

British Library Cataloguing in Publication Data.
A catalogue record for this book is available from the British Library.

ISBN 978 1 4456 5196 5 (print)
ISBN 978 1 4456 5197 2 (ebook)

Typesetting and Origination by Amberley Publishing.
Printed in Great Britain.

Contents

The Log of the *Maken*

1952

Chapter One

A tiny car hurtles down the Dover Road. As it roars past policemen, they instinctively reach to their tunic pockets for notebook and pencil, muttering: '... causing a noise in excess of the legally permitted ... not fitted with adequate silencing device ... clear case of misuse of ...'

Long before they have read the car's number, it has gone – a half-ton of humanity and machinery zooming outrageously through town after town, the rackety engine making too much noise for conversation between driver and passenger. They are two of a kind, young men swathed in multiple layers of clothing; the September air is cold, and the open car lacks weather protection.

An oncoming bus is about to pass a limousine, but the wee black mass of noise is aimed through the narrow space by the driver. He takes time off to shout: 'That's the best of these Morgan three-wheelers. So narrow you can plunge through small gaps'.

'Yes,' comes the bellowed reply: 'and as they're triangle-shaped, you know that once the front wheels are through you're safe, even with a closing gap.' Which is almost true.

At Folkestone the driver eases his foot up a millimetre and the speedometer creeps back from the maximum, just a fraction. The uproar warns pedestrians well in advance; they leap for safety on to the pavement. Policemen continue to try and get the elusive noisebox's number. However, the owner has thought of their evil intentions and, when he last washed the car, he left a thick layer of mud on the number plate. This makes it hard to read in all but the best light.

All this haste is justified. The relentless speed caused trouble a few miles outside Folkestone. Burning was smelt and the car was stopped. The bonnet was lifted to reveal the engine gleaming, steaming, very hot and dripping oil, but not actually on fire. Further examination of the rest of the car showed that the floorboards were steadily smouldering under the carpet. This was put out with water from a nearby garage, and the radiator filled up. Then the drive went on, flat-out, a 1934 car driven to the limit and taking it well in spite of its age; for this was in 1953.

Later, two more stops were necessary to repair ignition failures. The tools in this car are bright with constant use, but the results are above average. Mile after mile is thrust behind, as are many bigger cars. At last the passenger is dropped at Folkestone. Then on up that long, winding hill along the Dover Road, the car cornering dead-upright like the race-bred machine she is, even if the single back wheel does skid all over the country, even if it takes sheer muscle-power to turn the steering wheel. This is the essence of an enthusiast's car, uncomfortable, a trifle noisy, battered but very brave and so willing. The driver huddles in his monstrous black leather motoring coat, jammed in the tiny driving seat, enjoying every minute of the journey.

Up to now the driver has been holding the car at its maximum of sixty whenever possible, but without the weight of the passenger and his luggage the speed is better. On a straight stretch of road the speedo creeps up and round till it points to 'Smiths, Made in England'. With a blissful smile the driver thinks: 'Wonderful. Right off the clock!' Then he notices sheep wandering across the unfenced road. For sickening seconds the car hurls onwards, all brakes making no apparent difference to its progress. The driver makes an effort to change direction. The back swings in skater's arcs all over the road, one way, the other, back the first way. The driver thinks it's going to be mutton for dinner. For breakfast, lunch, tea and supper, too, if he hits that big ram.

The sheep take a horrified look at the oncoming menace, slithering all ways, and decide that the butcher is kinder. They scatter and, by a series of rapid-fire miracles, the car misses all of them.

Down into Dover it goes, the long winding hills taken at wild speed; then on more sedately through the town towards the docks. Humping over the railway lines the little black monster putters and crackles, twin exhausts still rending the air, till the inner harbour is reached. The driver hardly looks where he is going now. With bright-eyed eagerness he's scanning every yacht. 'That's a Tumlare, that's one of Mylne's jobs; that looks like a copy of Freddy Parker's work, and that's a converted fishing boat.' He examines each boat, classifies it, and rejects it. He knows exactly what he's looking for – a boat so distinctive, so different from the normal run of yachts. He'll know her the instant he sees her.

There! Two massive masts are showing above the quayside; that must be her. The quay hides the hull, but in an instant the driver has applied the brakes and is out while the car is still moving. He moves across to the quay as fast as a mass of motoring clothes will allow. There she sits, massive, rotund, rugged, every part gigantically strong; there is no mistaking the genuine Colin Archer type of yacht. That was my first view of the *Maken* ...

Dammit! Now I've given myself away. All that shocking driving – what a disgrace it was. But at the time it seemed justified; I had to get from Southampton to Dover on a September Saturday afternoon before daylight faded, to see the *Maken*.

At the time I was working in a ship drawing office, getting in a rut, not learning much, not earning much. Quite by chance I happened to spend a day with a cousin who, by the merest fluke, glanced at the agony columns of *The Times* during breakfast, and in idle conversation said: 'Just listen to this; "Wanted, crew for ketch sailing to Vancouver. Reply Box No. –"

Within an hour I had a letter written, carefully worded, full of hope:

Dear Sir,

This letter is in reply to your advertisement in *The Times* of – August. I would like to apply to join your yacht to sail to Vancouver. I am free to join as soon as convenient to you, and can pay for my share of the food, canal fees, harbour dues, etc.

My age is 24, and I have been sailing since I was 17. My sister and I share a 4½-tonner and we previously cruised and raced in an old 6-metre. I have served an apprenticeship under the naval architect Frederick Parker at the Dorset Yacht Co. and have a little experience in shipbuilding, sail-repairs, etc., etc. We have navigated our boats all over the English Channel, and I am at present looking into the matter of celestial navigation. I have a book on the subject which makes the whole subject seem simple, and I think that I can manage to work out normal sights. I have my own sextant, and could also bring along a set of tools, various spares for your boat, and so on.

Any weekend I can meet you anywhere to suit you, and would be pleased to help fit out the boat before the voyage. If you should wish to exchange references, this is no problem.

Excuse all the trumpet-blowing, but I assume you want to know a bit about anyone keen to join you.

This letter is of course neatly loaded. It was intended to make me out as wildly experienced, a jack of all trades, a mighty useful crew. In those days I reckon I was a pretty dead handicap on any ocean cruiser. I omitted to state that I wore glasses, suffered chronically from seasickness, and had never actually used my sextant in 'battle conditions'. But I need not have worried. Mine was one of thirty-five replies to that advertisement. Many of the others were girls, nurses tired of nursing, typists tired of offices, lasses who thought it would be such fun to sail across the sea.

The upshot of my letter was the frantic drive to Dover to see the *Maken*. She had been sailed from Norway by four Canadians and was to go on from there, across the Atlantic, through the Panama Canal, up the Pacific, to Vancouver. About 14,000 miles. Under good conditions she would do 100 miles in 24 hours. In slow conditions? Nothing. With no wind she would make no progress. I realised that as I looked at her. She was no delicate yacht, capable of making a knot or two in the lightest of airs, a delightful toy for breathless summers. The *Maken* was the complete opposite to the modern idea of a yacht. She was built originally as a Rednigshoiter in 1910. These craft are the Norwegian seagoing lifeboats. Because Norway has a deeply indented coast, her lifeboats cannot be kept ashore and launched when a craft gets into trouble, as happens round the British Isles. The Norwegian craft used to put out to sea in September and lie around the North Sea till May. If one of the many Scandinavian fishing craft got into trouble, a Rednigshoiter was there to bring help.

Yachts tend to stay ashore from September to May. Rednigshoiters worked during that period, and were refitted during the summer. No wonder they were so toughly built and fitted out. The boats they were intended to help were rugged by most standards, so the Rednigshoiters had to be truly stupendous and virtually unbreakable, regardless of weather conditions.

I liked the *Maken* at first sight, but I never loved her. Of course she was against impossible competition, as some of my previous boats were such perfect creatures. The 6-metre for instance was the complete opposite of the *Maken*, a light, delicate, incredibly fast boat. A joy to sail, she would frighten me often, terrify me sometimes, wet me always, but every time she would win through the most impressively bumpy weather. The *Maken* was a carthorse compared to the polo pony that the 6-metre was. This is not intended as an unkind remark. Carthorses are sturdy, useful creatures, but they are not exciting. The *Maken* would always get you there, but there would seldom be any of that delicious heart-snatch when a shocking great sea threatens to blot out life in one wet watery wallop.

I stood gazing at her bluff hull for some minutes. The white paint was in new condition and the rail was a contrasting dark blue. Above the bulwark there was a double steel tube guard-rail so that it would be more than ordinary bad luck to get washed overboard. There was plenty of room on deck for a dinghy, but in defiance of this the dinghy was tiny. It looked rather too small to be safe except in a flat calm, and it had a very round bottom, promising exciting instability, and a ducking to anyone a trifle unsober when returning aboard after a party.

My eyes travelled along the deck to the main mast. If the whole boat was magnificently massive, the main mast outdid the rest. It stood about 45 feet high and was some 18 inches diameter at the deck. It needed no rigging, so mighty did it seem, yet the rigging was as prodigious in proportion as the mast. Great steel wires, ¾ inch diameter, lent support which no hurricane could defy. The rope running-rigging was in proportion, most of it being almost an inch in diameter.

A glance round the deck showed that there was very little to criticize; and that mast – my eye kept straying back to check that it was really as big as it had seemed at first sight. As I stood and weighed up the chances of a successful voyage half way round the world in this thickset craft, I saw a man approaching who matched the boat. He was not excessively tall, nor vastly broad, he was just big and tough and certainly Canadian. As he came near I said: 'You're Mike Fitz-James?'

'Yes. Are you Nicolson?'

At once we were summing each other up. I was thinking that in a gale all that muscle would be handy. He must have been wondering if I'd be the least use in a gale. His natural politeness prevented him from blurting out: 'You're too small to be much good on this massive ship'. Instead, he asked me to come aboard.

My politeness was not proof against an overwhelming curiosity, a professional interest burning bright. I walked round the deck fingering, examining, firing off a string of technical questions. At close quarters *Maken* was just as overwhelming. The windlass up forward was a crude, heavy but extremely strong mechanism, hand-driven and promising a lot of hard work. The glass in the skylights was protected with rows of stout bars, closer spaced than in a well-made prison. Everything the eye fell on was three times thicker, heavier, and more rugged than anything I'd experienced before on a yacht only 45 feet long.

We went below, an unsteady small-talk conversation gradually breaking down the barriers of reserve. Every so often we would get on to a technical subject and the conversation would burst into a bubbling flame. A sort of wary mental fencing was going on, each trying to decide if the other was a tolerable person to live in close company with for seven months.

As the dusk began to close in, I said, 'I haven't booked a hotel room for the night. I'd better do that, before it's too late'.

'You can sleep here,' said Mike, pointing to the empty bunks.

'Thanks. That's a few shillings more saved to spend on the boat.' Thus I admitted I'd very much like to join the *Maken*. But would Mike have me? By the time I left next day, he had told me I would be signed on.

Chapter Two

Mike Fitz-James bought the *Maken* in Norway with three other Canadians. Their idea was to sail it home to Vancouver via the Panama Canal, but, by the time the yacht had got as far as Dover, the other three had decided that the original plan was not a good one. They left, and Mike set about finding a new crew. While in Norway a young Norwegian artillery officer, Bjarne Thorbjarnsen, said he would like to make the voyage; so Mike contacted him, and he got long leave. He joined the *Maken* at Dover, and with Mike sailed along the south coast to Poole and then to Weymouth.

This was near my home and was convenient for victualling and overhauling the boat. She was hauled up on a slipway and various minor repairs were made. We stowed away the food I bought, enough for one person for seven months. There was already enough food for two people for about five months aboard, but the lockers on the *Maken* were so many and so numerous that stowage was no real problem.

In Norway, the lavatory had been taken out and the compartment made into a storage room. Under each bunk it was possible to stow something like a hundred tins of food. We had farinaceous food like macaroni and rice, oatmeal and flour, in bulk. Under the saloon table was a sack of rusk-like bread, a Norwegian seaman's food halfway between biscuit and bread. It never went mouldy or got too soft or too hard; it didn't need air-tight containers, and if it was relatively tasteless, it certainly went well with margarine and jam or treacle.

A case or two of tins of food were stowed beneath the floorboards. There was a cavernous space down in the bilge, for the *Maken* was full-bodied and roomy everywhere. Even the water tanks had a large surplus capacity. They were not interconnected, so if one leaked the loss of water was not too serious. There was one tank beneath the galley bench which was used for daily necessities. The big tanks under the floorboards had no piping. When the tank under the galley was getting low we waited for a calm spell, took up the floorboards, lifted the steel cover-plate from one of the tanks in the bilge, and, with a small hand pump, lifted the water up to the ready-use tank. This was admittedly inconvenient and a bit tedious, but it was safe. For this sort of voyage it pays to remember that a man can live literally for months on almost no food, but he will die swiftly if he has nothing to drink. As our route was well off the beaten track, we had to be entirely independent of help from other ships. Moreover, the tanks under the floorboards had been installed by Mike and the other Canadians; putting the extra tankage in without piping had saved a lot of lolly. The eternal cash shortage, which plagues all ocean-cruising people (with very few exceptions), was always with us.

After I had put aboard seven months' supply of food, plenty of clothes, books and the usual toilet gear, I reckoned that I would need to buy very little except stamps till I arrived at Vancouver. I took with me £20 in cash and earned less than £5 on the way. When I arrived in Vancouver I had $5 in my pocket, less than £2. We had very little to pay in the way of harbour dues but we did have the canal dues through the Panama, and fuel. All these expenses the whole crew shared.

The food occupied so much room aboard that there was not much left for clothes; as I was expecting a seven-month voyage with a period of impecuniosity in Canada, it was essential to take along plenty to wear. It can be cold at sea, and there are warmer places than Canada. I had made out of waterproof canvas several bags of different shapes. These I screwed up against the ship's side round my bunk.

The berths were of the 'pilot' type. They were almost totally enclosed, with just a short length of the inboard side open. Once inside, it was very snug. There was a blue cotton curtain to pull across the entrance, and this gave an air of privacy. It also worked up a soupy fug, especially in the warmer latitudes. We liked these berths on the whole, even if they were a bit difficult when it came to making up the bedclothes or cleaning out. At the height of a gale, as we each lay snugly tucked in and reading, a voice from the cavernous depths of a berth would say: 'Well, if we do sink now, I'm cosy in my coffin, all ready!' This remark, punctuated by the CRASSSSSSSSSSSHHH ... BOOOOOOOOOOM ... SPLOSSSSSSSSSHH of a wave breaking in solid tons of water against the side of the yacht, might or might not raise morale.

We each had a stout cotton sleeping bag. These were wonderfully warm when we set out, in November. By the time we were on the sunny seas they were a bit too hot. Then we used to go to sleep on top of them and crawl inside later on when it was cold, in the small hours of the morning. The big asset of these flea-bags was that they were easy to make up. With three men aboard, the domestic side of life was, shall we say, spasmodically efficient, and if we'd had blankets they might not have been very neat very often.

But, from the first, Mike insisted that each day whoever was doing the daily chores should at least sweep up and make sure that the boat was tidy. This was unpopular but sensible and we never descended into a 'spanner-in-the-jampot' existence. There was seldom a time when it was not easy to show someone over the boat with pride.

While we were fitting out, several people visited us and we received all sorts of farewell presents. There was a fire-extinguisher from my stepfather, who was a practical yachtsman himself and appreciated the horror of having the ship afire with the nearest land 500 miles away. My mother made up an air-tight tin with Christmas fare. This included an iced cake, a present for each of us, and so on. We put a selection of books aboard – not enough as it turned out – and innumerable other gear like spare torch batteries, primus prickers, my carpenter's tools, seizing wire, spare canvas, the hand bearing compass and big bilge pump from my little cruiser, and hundreds of other items. Even though the *Maken* had made the voyage from Norway and had been fitted out there, we found literally dozens of things were needed.

Day after day we made lists of things to do, to buy, to collect from hither and yon, to select, to stow aboard. By the early part of November we were ready. The yacht was relaunched after having some caulking done. The fuel tanks were full, the paraffin tank for the primus stove was topped up. We had remembered the matches, and had persuaded a firm of industrial chemists to sell us a drum of detergent – though from the way they carried on, one might have thought it was arsenic we were after. We'd made a couple of candle lanterns because they proved impossible to buy; and had organised a farewell party.

All the other yachts in Weymouth were laid up, and the swallows were far south, ahead of us. At nights it was frosty. We knew it was time to get going. The tension mounted. We decided to make the first stop Plymouth. If the weather was fine then, we would push straight on to Vigo, in Spain. But if it turned out rough when we were clear of Plymouth we could always go into Falmouth, thus gaining some ground and getting farther to the west. This would make the slant down to Vigo easier if the prevailing Westerlies blew.

Mike and I had discussed whether or not we should pull the long bowsprit inboard. If we did, the boat would be more snugly rigged. In the event of a hurricane this might have been an advantage. But the whole yacht was so strongly and safely rigged that I thought it quite unnecessary to take this extra precaution. If we did reef it in, we would be unable to set the jib, and our average speed would be badly reduced. As we were in a tearing hurry to get to Vancouver by May we wanted all the speed we could squeeze out of the old barge. The idea behind getting to Vancouver before the end of the spring was this: Mike and I would want jobs as soon as we arrived. You can't live without lolly, and short of a career of crime, which I personally would only contemplate in a country where I knew the lie of the land and would have a reasonable chance of making good, we had to have jobs. It so happens that Canada is much dependent on certain industries like logging, farming and fishing. These tend to be very slack in winter. The tremendous building boom also quietens down a lot during the cold weather. Consequently anyone emigrating should plan to arrive in the spring when there are plenty of jobs. To arrive in autumn and find that there are five men already waiting for any vacancy that might arise would be a piece of faulty planning such as no competent ocean-cruising yachtsman should commit. The sea does teach all but the truly dumb to look ahead.

So we decided that the bowsprit would be left standing out ahead of the boat, even though we were setting out very late in the year with every prospect of rough weather before we could get into the sunny seas. One of the arguments we used went like this: 'The jib has an outhaul, so it'll never be necessary to go out along the bowsprit at sea. It'd be wet and dangerous to crawl out along the spar when the yacht was plunging along in a wicked sea, but the occasion will never arise.' 'No. That's true. There's no likelihood of having to climb out there. If I thought there was, I'd be very much in favour of having it inboard. With frozen fingers and clothes sodden and heavy it would be ruddy frightening and more than ordinary hard work hanging on to that round, smooth spar. There's nothing to hold on to.'

Thus we agreed while, 14 fathoms down, old Neptune cooked up a little panic to shake us up.

It was necessary to leave early in the morning. We had to catch the tide round Portland Bill with its off-lying Race. The Race is a tumbling mess of outrageous waves boiling over underwater rocks. There is no danger of running aground, as the rocks are deep down, but they create such a shocking sea when the tide hurries over them that this is probably the most dangerous area in the English Channel, for yachtsmen.

The *Maken* lay moored fore and aft in Weymouth. Below, the three of us slept the deep sleep of the fairly just and moderately innocent. The alarm was set for 6.30 a.m., and freezing dawn crept over the sleeping town. It would be nice to say that the townspeople turned out in great numbers to watch the intrepid adventurers set out on their hazardous voyage to the uttermost corner of the globe. What in fact happened was that the alarm failed to go off.

Mike eventually awoke to see that we were about to miss our tide. In a tearing rush we scrambled out of our berths and hauled the dinghy on deck. The mooring line aft was taken in while Mike worked to get the engine going. Swiftly the tyers were whipped off the sails, and the engine throbbed into life. Shivering in the chilly morning air, we hurried about the boat getting ready for sea, watched only by a seagull on the railway shed roof. The bow line was let go and the *Maken* moved forward with that massive, ponderous, pushing motion she has, like a dowager undismayed by any external influence. The thump of the semi-diesel echoed between the harbour wall and the quay railway station. The only witness of our departure was a yawning porter who hardly gave us a second glance.

Outside there was very little wind. The main, staysail and mizzen were set quickly enough, considering the bulk and weight. One of us hooked the jib halliard on, another started to pull the outhaul along the bowsprit. The jib came off the outhaul hook within seconds. I don't think we saw the funny side of the situation at the time, but within minutes of our departure I was crawling along the bowsprit to rehook the jib on to the traveller. So much for our mutual assurances that it would never be necessary to go out along the 'sprit once we were at sea. Looking down from the insecure perch before slithering back inboard, I contemplated the chilly wetness below. If I fell in, just how cold would it be? People bathe in the Serpentine at Christmas, but they probably die young, or perhaps they have heaters in their bathing shorts. I remembered that in the North Sea it was possible for a man to fall overboard and be dead before he was picked up. That's the worst of setting out early on a frosty morning: thoughts tend to be consistently morbid, and morale touches unplumbed depths. Even Mike, who was going home, looked grim, and as for me, leaving home for a couple of years, I felt ghastly. Bjarne was his usual phlegmatic self. At the back of our minds there was the constant worry that we were setting out to cross the Bay of Biscay in the depths of winter in a very old boat, undermanned and with an engine that should long ago have been in a museum. And the Bay has such a shocking reputation.

We headed south to pass round the tip of Portland Bill with our primitive piece of machinery driving us more than the sails, for there was not much wind and we wanted to catch the tide.

Throughout the voyage we used the engine almost exclusively to get in and out of harbours, apart from calm patches well out at sea, when our patience was exhausted. Otherwise, we never used the engine unless there was a compelling reason. This was partly because we were keen to save fuel since it was not cheap, but also because the gigantic labour of starting the engine was not lightly undertaken.

Assuming that everything went right it took 20½ minutes to start the engine. If anything went amiss, we could slog away for 90 minutes before the single massive cylinder let forth the first deep boometyboometyboom.

In these days of universal self-starters, when the smallest and the largest engine is started by pressing a button, it is hard to convey the sheer physical labour of getting the machinery on the *Maken* turning. Even in temperate climates Mike, who bore the lion's share of the sweat and toil, would be running with sweat before success was achieved.

The procedure went like this: first the galley pressure-stove was lit. Yachtsmen will know the cursing, fiddling messing-about which that simple sentence sums up. Sometimes the stove behaved and roared into life quite quickly; at other times it was found, too late, to need refilling with paraffin. The pricker might be rusty, or the boat might roll just when the pricker was going into the hole, so that the pricker got broken.

Once the stove was going just right, the top of our blowlamp was held in the flame to heat. This was no ordinary blowlamp but a gigantic model, in keeping with everything else aboard; it stood about 18 inches high, a truly lethal weapon. Before heating its topknot in the cooker flame it was necessary to pump the blowlamp exactly fifty times. When the top was hot right through, the operator would turn the valve on the blowlamp. Three things might happen at this stage. A hot, vicious, blue flame should shoot out of the spout, a wicked flame full of power and noise. That is what the operator was trying to achieve. However, sometimes nothing happened. That meant the operator had either forgotten to fill the blowlamp with paraffin, or he had not held it right in the cooker flame and it was not hot enough. Or perhaps he had only pumped it forty-eight times instead of the statutory fifty. The third possibility was the most exciting of all: if the operator had negligently pumped fifty-two times, instead of a short hot blue flame, a long waggly yellow one would whip out of the nozzle. This long dragon's tongue of flame was laden with burning gouts of paraffin. It was completely uncontrollable and would lick with hot embrace anything and everything. Other crew members would find their trousers growing suddenly hot. The bunk curtains would smoulder, the cushions would turn yellow, there would be wild shouting and yelling, and patches of the white paint on the bulkheads would blister due partly to the flame, partly to the language. The wretched operator would have to rush up the steep ladder to the deck, bearing his frightening burden, to douse the flames as best he might. The obvious thing would have been to hurl the whole blazing mass into the quenching sea, but far offshore one cannot replace vital pieces of machinery.

Once extinguished, the process would start again at the pumping stage. Then, carrying the torch aloft, and without singeing more than the minimum amount of paintwork, the operator would go up on deck and climb down the slippery vertical ladder into our Black Hole of Calcutta, the engine room.

The engine room was not a pleasant place. It lacked both light and ventilation. In the centre stood the massive single cylinder, a tower of rusty steel coated with oil, grime and soot. Various pipes meandered about with disconcerting lack of straightness, and some sharp bends which were rank bad engineering. At the fore end of the engine was the flywheel. If everything else on the *Maken* was over-size, the flywheel outvied all the other gear. It lurked deep down in the bilge, a thick circle of steel so ponderous in appearance that at first glance one could be excused for wondering if any human hand could turn such a vast piece of ironware.

In practice even Mike, for all his strength, couldn't turn it; at best he could just rock it gently backwards and forwards. But we are getting ahead of ourselves.

Down the engine-room ladder our operator directs the blowlamp on to the top of the engine. The idea is to get the top of the cylinder thoroughly hot. Meanwhile a second victim has climbed into the pit of horrors and is oiling various points on the engine. There are, dotted about in the most remarkably inaccessible places, little brass bowls, like egg cups, which have to be filled with oil from a battered old can. Doing this in the dark, with the ship pitching in a seaway, it was not surprising that plenty of oil was spilled into the bilge. Naturally the risk of an engine seize-up was not to be considered, so we were liberal with the oil. This merely doubled the quantity which went into the bilge.

With the top of the cylinder almost glowing hot, one victim would pump the fuel into the cylinder while the other rocked the gargantuan flywheel backwards and forwards. If all went according to plan and prayer, there would be a thumpety-thumpety-thump and the engine would go at once and for ever till the fuel ran out. That was the chief virtue of this primitive old grinder. It was reliable to the point of embarrassment. There is a tale about a motor yacht, many years ago, which had one of these hot-bulb engines. Going into Ramsgate harbour the fuel was cut off but the engine refused to stop. It went on thumping away burning its own lubricating oil. The yacht refused to stop, and charged round the all-too-small harbour causing chaos and caustic language till at last it ran aground on a sandbank.

When the *Maken*'s engine was running it was necessary to go down to oil it once every hour or so. This was an exciting venture. The poor mutt who had the job would climb down into the darkness and smoke, holding the slippery oilcan in one hand. The other hand groped for something to hold on to. The oil in the bilge would be floating on the surging bilgewater, together with the rust, soot and grime from the engine. Every so often the bilgewater would be flung up as the yacht lurched over a wave. The noisome water in the bilge would splash against the whirling flywheel and be flung in swathes all over the engine room. Everything was plastered with a mucky, greasy mixture. The floorboards were dangerously slippery, so it was essential to hold on. Alas, there was only the engine to hold on to, and this consisted mainly of two parts, the whirling flywheel and the almost redhot cylinder.

We looked on the engine with a mixture of loathing and love. It would keep pushing the boat along even against a stiff breeze and tide. It was not temperamental once it was running. It would consume almost any grade of fuel. But it was a frightening thing to put in motion. Even the simple job of getting the fuel into the cylinder called for severe hard work for a brief spell, as the fuel had to be pumped against pressure, using a short lever. Working this pump was like cracking hard nuts in the palm of the hand, satisfying when it worked ... *when.*

We sailed steadily southwards towards the Portland Race. We had told each other the horror stories we had heard ninth-hand about craft being hurled skywards and thrown hither and yon by outrageous waves. The Channel Pilot book has a lot of depressing things to say about the Race, including some strong warnings, especially for small craft. Nicely keyed up, we approached the Race through mist and haze, expecting to be dashed to the ocean depths, hurled on our beam ends and thrown about every which way. We were disillusioned when we got to the tip of Portland Bill; the giant was asleep. Every so often it would snore, a hollow splash as a slick on the sea unexpectedly broke and bubbled, an erupting wave without apparent foundation or reason.

Before we knew we were in the Race we found ourselves clear of it. A quick navigation plot suggested that we went clean through the top end, and it was no more exciting than the tumble of water found off any headland. The rest of the day was quiet and progress was steady.

Long after nightfall we were off Plymouth. Of the three of us, I was the only one who had been into this harbour before, and my knowledge of it was very slight. However, I was navigator for the occasion. We were well offshore, and there to the northward was a single line of white lights. This row of lights was fairly evenly spaced and extended a long, long way. It looked queer, downright curious. However, like all the best navigators, I quickly fitted facts to the situation: 'There must be fog over the land. Those lights are along Plymouth Hoe. Being near the shore, they showed up while the rest of the town is enveloped in the mist'.

It sounded plausible; the others could think of nothing more convincing, so they didn't argue. Perhaps they were dumbfounded in the face of such inventiveness. We turned north to enter the harbour. The lights got closer and closer but there was absolutely no other sign of land or mankind. Quite suddenly we saw that the lights were moving very slightly in relation to each other. Also, as we approached, the lights were reflected on the sea, and soon we realised that it was a line of fishing boats.

Wireless warnings are often given out to shipping to beware of drift-net fishing boats near the Eddystone lighthouse. This is what we were peering at through the darkness. The line of light seemed to stretch for miles in both directions, athwart the entrance to Plymouth. We agreed it would be a very long detour to go round them to get into harbour, but to go through the line was a great risk since we might very easily get entangled in the nets. That would involve damage, compensation, litigation and a lot of paying out on our part. We had little enough money between us, and to start out with a big disbursement was not to be considered. At the time it was almost dead calm, so we had the engine going slowly, and that added to the danger since we might wind yards of net round the propeller and shaft. This would immobilise us, so that we might need a tow into harbour and have to be hauled up on the slipway to cut the net from the propeller. It looked like a difficult and expensive situation. We decided to go slowly and extremely cautiously towards the line of fishermen to see if we could find a gap between them. Perhaps we could approach one of the boats to ask them the best way through to Plymouth.

Mike was at the helm, I stood right forward, peering anxiously over the bow. Only the thump of our engine was heard in the chilly stillness. Visibility was very limited and moisture condensing on my glasses made life no easier. There! Suddenly right ahead I saw a row of white net floats.

'Hard a'starboard! Helm right over, Mike!' my worried shout went aft. The cork floats flapped to life as three startled seagulls flew out of our way. 'Sorry, Mike! False alarm. Only some seagulls – they looked like fishing-net floats.' The *Maken* was turned back on course and we resumed our vigil. Slow minutes dragged past, the cold bit through layers of clothing, nothing showed ahead except the approaching line of lights.

Then, there! Right in our path ...

'Look out, Mike! Hard over with the helm!' and again Mike leant desperately on the helm so that the lumbering boat swung off course, just as four indignant seagulls squawked and clattered off into the darkness. 'Sorry, Mike. Just another lot of seagulls. They must be hanging around waiting for the fishermen to haul in and provide a meal of fish guts.'

Mike muttered something in the darkness astern, as he brought the boat back on course. I felt a flaming fool and wished Bjarne would come forward to help look ahead. When a few seagulls appeared right under the bow a few minutes later I was cautiously wondering if they would float on the sea near the nets when:

'Look out Mike! It really is a net this time!'

Those dammed net floats looked just like seagulls bobbing up and down on the swell. With sickening mental agony I watched the line of corks come towards us. I could see the rope stretching between the corks. The *Maken* went straight towards the rope. She was too massive and ponderous to turn in time. Mike had the helm hard over, but it was no use. With deliberation and almost in slow motion we moved relentlessly towards our financial doom. The bow rode over the row of corks and their linking line. We leant over the side and watched the corks move aft down the ship's side, the tingling tension mounting as they approached the stern and the propeller. The engine never missed a beat. We were expecting that hesitation in the beat, possibly the complete cessation of the thumping as the rope wound tight round the propeller shaft and strangled the engine to a standstill. At least we expected to hear the engine note drop to a slow struggling beat as the shaft was forced round in spite of a throttling necklace of rope.

But none of these things happened. The devil looked after his own that night, though we'd rather overworked the old boy for a few hectic minutes. By a stroke of luck the *Maken* passed clean over the top of the nets without damaging them. We were clear of the fishing boats and motoring on towards Plymouth before we dared breathe again.

Out of the murk we picked up the breakwater lights, and dawn was coming up when we tied up in the Hamoaze, an inner harbour near the town.

Chapter Three

We spent a few days in Plymouth, topping up the fuel and water tanks, buying yet more odds and ends which we found were needed, and, most important of all, taking on board duty-free tobacco, cigarettes and liquor.

Long before this date I had given up smoking, preferring to spend every spare farthing on my boats and their gear. However, I was in agreement with the others that cigarettes were a good form of international currency, and they were both keen smokers, too. So we took on 10,000 cigarettes, and some tobacco in sealed tins. A case of whisky was also bought and, as events turned out, this proved a better international currency than cigarettes. In fact I've heard some remarkable tales of the exchange rate of a nip or bottle of whisky. This precious fluid will get repairs completed for very little money in great cities and tiny fishing villages. It will unearth vital spares reputed to be quite unavailable locally, and will find a snug berth in harbours where yachts are either unwelcome or uncomfortable due to a shocking swell or clouds of coal dust blowing off quay walls.

We only bought a dozen bottles of whisky, whereas subsequent experience suggests that a second case would have been worth having. A jar of rum was also bought. The jar was a magnificent receptacle; standing high and proud in its wickerwork casing, it weighed wondrous heavy. The actual jar was about 18 inches high and cost 17s 6d. The contents were, of course, tax-free, being in bond, and all that rum also cost 17s 6d. Never have the iniquities of taxation been so heavily underlined for me. The jar of rum was carefully lashed down by my bunk, which seemed to me an appropriate place for it.

Everything was ready for the final departure except the weather. It was typical November muck – rain, excessive winds and cold. We did not mind what the weather did, provided it did not blow too hard, or even moderately hard, from the sou'-west. The boat was to a large extent an unknown quantity. We were not sure of ourselves; the one thing I was sure about was that I should be heartily seasick on the first and second days of our initial bout of rough weather. Experience warned me that the seasickness would not lay me out helplessly, but I knew I should be weakened by it, and on the *Maken* all the toughness available was needed to handle the gear.

We went ashore daily to phone for a weather forecast and, on the third occasion, the local met. office at Mountbatten performed a remarkable feat of weather prediction. We told them we were sailing to Spain and asked for the longest time ahead they could predict the likely weather pattern. They told us what it was going to do for the next three days. We pressed them to look further into the future. They told us what was likely to happen for the coming five days. We tried to wheedle out their opinion of the possible weather for a whole week in advance. The fellow on the other end of the phone was thoroughly helpful and, without committing himself, told us the sort of weather one can expect in the Bay of Biscay during November. In the end he gave us a forecast for the coming seven days. In the event he was right, with only minor omissions.

The met. man was rather discouraging for that day, promising westerlies fresh to strong, decreasing slightly the next day. It was fine for us if the wind did decrease, but no good if the wind backed round to sou'-west, as it would have been a dead beat to windward. The shape of the *Maken* is such that she is a poor performer to windward. Added to this, a ketch rig is generally considered, with reason, as inefficient going into the wind. Gaff ketches are doubly slow on this point of sailing, and gaff ketches with gaff-rigged mizzens are exceptionally weak for close-hauled sailing. So the dear old tub had very little in her favour when it came to a slog to windward, and we were agreed that to set out with the wind on the nose was senseless even though we were impatient to be away.

At last the weather was right. It was raining intermittently, chilly, and inclined to be blustery, but without great weight in the wind. We got up with our usual reluctance, shaved and ate breakfast in the customary morose silence as sleep fought a rearguard action, and went up on deck to get ready. While Bjarne and I took the tyers off the staysail and mizzen, Mike sweated and slaved over the engine. It boomed into life, one of us jumped ashore, cast off the four lines, hopped back aboard again, and we were off.

Under power, with just the mizzen and staysail set, we chugged out into Plymouth Sound through the gap in the breakwater, and off to sea. It was a miserable departure, as romantic as cold porridge. Even with double thicknesses of sweaters, and oilskins over all to keep out the chill wind and drizzle, it was no fun on deck.

Visibility soon shut out all view of the land and, if the Navy had not chosen that moment to send along an escort, we would not have been very cheerful. With a right sense of the fitness of the occasion a great aircraft carrier loomed out of the murk about a mile away and steamed along on a parallel course. We looked smugly at each other, knowing perfectly well that this was the merest fluke; but there she was, a very fine warship to all appearances giving us a send-off. Aircraft took off and landed in quick succession, apparently practising deck landings. Soon enough she disappeared into the thickness ahead and we settled down to watches at sea.

It sounds fine, doesn't it: 'We settled down to watches at sea'. Brings up a mental picture of three bronzed stalwarts lounging in the sun while the yacht curtseys along o'er sunlit billows. Like hell! It was damned cold and uncomfortable. The watch from midnight to four in the morning was probably the worst, but the whole period of darkness was pretty unpleasant.

Three sweaters and a scarf with woolly pants, vest and trousers had seemed enough before we set out. In those days I was innocent enough to believe that just because I never wore a hat ashore, I would not need one afloat. Fortunately there was, among my gear, a woollen cap which was folded up all round when worn normally. How I blessed that hat! It just about saved my ears from frost-bite. I would come on watch with it worn in the normal fashion. As the hour grew later, the darkness ever colder, I pulled the hat down more and more till it met the scarf at the back and my glasses in front. Then I pulled the oilskin collar up high, rolled the sweater sleeves down over my hands as far as they would go, and cursed as hard as need be to keep warm. Luckily I'm not one of those people who notice the cold acutely. But, no joking: this was November, and we were going to windward. The wind cut clean and cold across the wastes of the Atlantic. It carried frigid spray over the weather rail to cut red weals on our cheeks.

Chapter Four

For 24 hours there was rather too much wind. We stayed under mizzen and staysail which was a modest sail plan, but we were breaking ourselves in. The wind headed us till we could only just lay the course we set, which was to take up well clear of that ultra-dangerous headland, Ushant. We were unanimous that Ushant was to be avoided by a very wide berth at all costs. We were not full of confidence yet. Our celestial, or deep sea, navigation had to be tested; so had we ourselves. The ship had lived through many gales in the past, no doubt, but she was getting on in years. Already she was leaking steadily as we plugged into the short, lumpy sea with the engine just ticking over. Time was getting short, so it seemed only common sense to use the engine to get us well out to the west and on our way. The engine would make sure we gave Ushant all the room we wanted and, running dead slow, it used very little fuel. We all felt vaguely annoyed that we should be using it. Although it was the seamanlike thing to do, it irked to have to motor when the weather was by no means calm. Also, the engine was one of the causes of leaking: where the propeller shaft passed through the hull the gland was worn, and the turning shaft let the sea trickle in.

Pumping was absolutely no fun. The pump was in the engine room, so to work the thing meant going down into that black hole to face the tumult of the banging engine, with seasick-making smells wafting up and grease with a layer of dirt transferring itself on to our clothes as we slithered about in the dark.

We all grew beards, as shaving would have been almost suicidal when the boat was heaving and throwing herself and us all over the place. The others were moderately immune from seasickness. Only once on the whole trip was Mike in an unsteady state because of it, and even then it was not much more than a passing annoyance. His time afloat in freighters and fishing boats stood him in good stead here. It had also taught him to swear in about seven languages, a most valuable accomplishment when dealing with varying emergencies in foreign parts. This ability also added interest to any of our own crises, and it was rather fun to pick up a useful vocabulary of positively devastating remarks which could later be used in drawing-rooms without offending the most maidenly aunt.

Bjarne was occasionally seasick, but never seriously. I had my usual thorough, complete, devastating bout which lasted all through the second and third day, and tailed off during the fourth, leaving me so weak that I could scarcely hoist the staysail. Thereafter I was quite immune till I tasted deep the fleshpots of San Francisco. (A period of ten days' high living there so jolted my stomach that it had its own back in no uncertain fashion. But that comes later).

If you've never been seasick, it's no good trying to describe it. The first stage is quite short: the sufferer thinks he's going to die; the second stage lasts sometimes for days, while the victim fears death may not come to bring release.

The real trouble, as far as the cruising yachtsman is concerned, is that the malady leaves him weak and helpless. It takes much more determination to walk forward and reef a mainsail when racked by seasickness than it does to climb the mast in a gale when fit. At least, that's my experience.

When we were finished with our seasickness the weather settled down, all sail went up, and we made steady if slow progress towards Vigo. It was often misty and navigation was by guess and by hope. After four days at sea it was calm with patches of haze all round. To make any progress we had to use the engine. The previous day we had passed a tanker fairly close and had signalled to it asking to be reported to Lloyds so that our families would know how we were progressing. As usual the signal was ignored, or perhaps not seen, though our flags were enormous for the size of our craft. I believe Mike got them from a ship ten times our length.

Now, as we chugged along over a glassy sea, a very old tramp was seen ahead and coming straight toward us. We wanted most of all to get the exact time as we had no great faith in the chronometer we were using. The radio time-signals from London were already getting faint, probably due to a weakening battery as well as the lengthening distance. Later on we got perfectly good time-signals from Washington, but at this stage we wanted a check to make sure we were getting the correct longitude. The method of signalling time by flags is a bit complex: the time is spelt out using numeral flags, and the instant the flags are hauled down is the precise time signalled. It takes some practice and skill to signal with flags in these circumstances. One glance at the decrepit old crate coming towards us convinced me that they would never be able to accomplish any feat of signalling, and I wanted Mike to signal something much simpler – just: 'Please report us to Lloyds,' and the yacht's name.

After discussion we ran that signal up. The tramp passed very close, a real old-timer she was, about contemporary with the Ark. There were long poles and fishing lines protruding from various points, and dirt competed with rust for the greatest prominence. No one on board appeared to take the least notice of our signal, though we were so close when we were abeam we could have heaved a dead fish right on to their deck. We gave them a hail and pointed to the flags. Even if they could not speak English they should be able to read the signal, since the international flag code is translated into all seafaring languages. Eventually someone realised that we had flags set. We saw the officer of the watch run into the captain's day cabin. The old man had evidently been having a sleep. He appeared, dishevelled, on the bridge, and studied us, by now receding in the distance, through his binoculars. Each ship proceeded relentlessly on its course, drawing farther and farther apart while on the tramp more and more of the crew gathered at the rail to look at us.

She was such a decrepit old barge, going so slowly, that if we had turned round and set out in pursuit we might have caught up and got our message over, but one doesn't dash about the ocean in that flippant style. With never a flicker the helm was held straight and we went on our way. Once more, flag signalling at sea from a yacht had proved unsuccessful. The number of times we were to experience the same frustration in failure to get a simple message across a short distance by flag convinced me that flags are a waste of time. Shouting is impractical, as it's dangerous to get close enough to be heard. It was not till my next ocean cruise that I found what is almost the complete answer, and I painted big notices to hold up.

A day or two after this, Mike showed us a horrid boil developing on his wrist, right on the projecting bone. It might have been a saltwater boil brought on by continuously wearing oilskins. It was often damp and usually cold on deck so we wore them over layers of other clothes very frequently. The chafe at the wrist could have been the cause of the trouble; the end result of it was that Mike was out of action for 48 hours. He was in a bad way, lying in his bunk for long periods and at times writhing with the pain, though he never complained, and only stopped standing his watch when we pressed him hard.

It was a time of some acute anxiety for me and I think Bjarne was worried, but he never showed the smallest trace of it. The *Maken* was designed to be handled by five experienced seamen. We were now down to two below-average-height men and, though we would know what to do in the event of bad weather, if we had been caught napping I doubted if there would be the necessary muscle-power to handle the sails in a severe squall. It was a fairly big strain, steering watch and watch, but the real stress was the vital importance of not being outwitted by the weather.

In theory we each had 12 hours a day out of the 24 off watch. This sounds ample to get plenty of sleep, cook meals and wash up. However, there is far more to cruising than just that. Working watch and watch meant that theoretically each of us had two periods of 4 hours' sleep each day. In practice it was impossible to tumble straight into a bunk after coming off watch. The log had to be written up, perhaps a drink heated, and sometimes there was a brief spell of pumping.

By the time oilskins had been peeled off, and the outer layer of clothing, it was probably 30 minutes since the change of watch. Then if the man on watch felt that the weather was threatening, he would call the watch below about 40 minutes early. Struggling into heavy clothes, fumbling and stumbling and stupid with sleep, the off-watch man would totter aft and up on deck. He'd screw his eyes up and look to windward, disgruntled and tired and wishing he were in a snug bed on a solid piece of ground at least 500 miles from the sea. The helmsman would say: 'Sorry I had to drag you out. Thought we better get the jib in before that lot comes down on us. Take the helm while I drop the sail.'

The chap who's just come up feels thoroughly mutinous by now, only half convinced that there is trouble windward. He sits down at the tiller. There's some sea running and the tiller is alive. It jolts across and back, telling the new helmsman that the *Maken* is very much awake, whatever anyone else may feel like. The boat transmits her vitality to the helmsman. He peers ahead into the darkness, hearing the rattle of blocks and the flap of canvas as the jib comes in. After a few minutes the other man lurches aft, one hand constantly on the handrail.

'It's quite lively up for'ard.'

'Just as well to be cautious, with Mike flat out.'

'Feel like a brew-up?'

'Uh-huh.'

'I'll make coffee.'

'Well, for the love of Allah let's have coffee, not that sugar with a small dash of coffee you usually make!'

'Make it yourself, then.'

'All right. Here, take the tiller.'

'No ruddy fear! It's your watch now. I'll brew up, and let you add your own sugar.'

'Right. And don't forget the cookies.'

'Cookies' is, of course, the Canadian for biscuits. The language on board was a mixture of English, Canadian and Norwegian; as the voyage progressed, other languages contributed their share. For instance 'pesates' (with a flat 'a') was used for money, being a corrupt form of 'pesetas'. This private language was the consequence of living in a tiny, cut-off world. We were fortunate that Bjarne spoke perfect English. In fact, the main language problems arose from the differences in meaning of words like 'cracker', 'bun', 'sloop', and 'gas', which are by no means the same in English and Canadian.

Cookies were the great standby. The *Maken* had been presented by the incredibly generous Norwegians with sixty-four big tins of biscuits. Whenever the weather was too hot, too rough, or otherwise inclement, we ate dozens of biscuits. There was never a day at sea when we missed our regular three cooked meals, or two hot meals and a good cold lunch, apart from the time we were hove-to in thoroughly bad weather. But at times like this, when Mike was in no state to do his share of the cooking, we had simple meals backed up by literally dozens of biscuits.

After two days in which he was completely incapacitated, Mike gradually came back into circulation. We had a good batch of drugs aboard, including the various 'wonder drugs', thanks to an understanding doctor. We fed Mike with the stated doses, feeling faintly daring because we had been warned so thoroughly about the dangers of overdosing. When we got ashore a few days later the boil was far from cured and Mike had to have it lanced. This hurt a lot and was a powerful inducement to eating proper regular meals to avoid getting run down. We found that in harbour it was often more convenient to miss meals till hunger could no longer be denied. Memories of Mike's pain and my own anxiety made me take on the job of cook every day in harbour when the others felt disinclined to tackle it.

We were aiming at Vigo, on the north-west coast of Spain. When we were well out to sea but level with this port, it was foggy. It was only sensible to sail onwards, keeping well offshore, with the general intention of making Lisbon. The fact that our mail was waiting at Vigo was just a minor detail. Half the fascination of cruising is that there is no certainty where the point of arrival will be until it's a fact.

The fog persisted and we sailed slowly through it, gradually closing the Iberian coast. One day we noticed that the lifebuoy flare was damaged. It was smoking in a very small way, so, looking carefully round to make sure that no one was near who might precipitately fly to our aid, we ditched the flare. A tiny wisp of smoke emerged; then there was nothing. So much for the flare that was intended to mark with smoke by day and flame by night the location of a luckless individual in the water. Clearly it was going to pay to avoid falling overboard, from now on, in the dark.

Actually it would often have been fatal to have fallen in even during daylight. In even moderately bumpy weather the waves would have concealed a man by the time he had dropped four or five boat's lengths astern. And the *Maken* could not be whipped round on a sixpence and taken quickly to windward to pick a man up. We sailed with the booms lashed out, often enough, to prevent chafe and to try and increase the drive of the sails. So to turn and go back would be a long, slow job, especially at night or when there was only one man left on deck. The booms and sails were so heavy that the lashings had to be heavy, and the odds were that if anyone had gone into the sea in anything but calm weather he would have been lost. However, all round the *Maken*, except right forward, there were two strong steel rails on top of the low wooden bulwark. Only a vicious sea combined with extreme bad luck or extra-special stupidity would have got a man overboard.

After eight nights at sea we closed the Portuguese coast and picked out a series of lighthouses in succession which enabled us to confirm our position. When dawn came up next day we saw the land clearly and had a delightful sail along the shore. We were now determined to go to Lisbon unless the weather made it impossible.

At this juncture Mike and I disagreed about taking a pilot up the Tagus. He was steeped in the rules and laws of the sea as applied to fishing boats and freighters. My own attitude was fairly typical of the yachting fraternity. This is another way of saying that I would never think of taking a pilot except under the most extreme emergencies. Mike's view was that if the navigation books said a pilot was compulsory it meant just that. I said that yachts were never subject to compulsory pilotage, and told him about the Thames, the Mersey, and all the other places I had sailed into and knew, which had compulsory pilotage, but for merchant ships only. It was unfortunate that Mike had far more sea-going hours to his credit than me, but almost all in commercial craft. Virtually all my sea time had been in yachts, and I had the yachtsman's slightly lawless attitude to harbour authorities in general. This is partly the result of the dislike which so many harbour authorities have for yachts. They look on them as nuisances which get in the way of commercial craft and add to the dangers of navigation in narrow water. We tend to resent that attitude since we feel we have the same right to use the sea as anyone else. Also, by the nature of things, yachtsmen are independent types and dislike being pushed around by officials.

On one point Mike and I agreed. We wanted to avoid spending money on pilots if at all possible. It so happens that there are two ways of going up the Tagus. The 'front door' is up the centre, but there is a 'side entrance' along the north shore. We thought that if we entered by this 'tradesmen's gate' we might not meet a pilot boat, so the problem of taking a compulsory pilot would not arise.

We sneaked in as dusk was falling, hugging the northern shore as close as we dared. Well inside the arms of the land it seemed more than unwise to go on, and we anchored for the night off a suburb. Next day we were delighted to find ourselves anchored off a townlet of brightly coloured villas and exotic-looking gardens, all most cheerful in the early morning sun. We hove the anchor up and hastened up the river under sail and engine and with a favourable tide before anyone could order us to take a pilot. After several miles we sighted a little dock off the river, with several yachts in it. There seemed to be room for one more and we slipped through the narrow entrance and moored up in the Doca de Belem. The first proper leg of the journey had taken a long time – ten full days.

Chapter Five

We spent a week in Lisbon and got away to a bad start. When we went to report to the immigration authorities in the correct fashion we took along our passports for them to stamp after inspection. They wanted to keep the passports while we were in Portugal. Mike was at once against this, and pretty soon both Bjarne and I saw how right he was. We were not ordinary tourists on a carefully planned itinerary. We had no idea of the exact day or time of our departure. We didn't want to trail all over Lisbon to pick up passports before leaving, just when there would be a great deal to do on the boat. We had no land transport and no money to waste on taxis or buses. Quite apart from this, government offices have a bad habit of closing from Saturday midday to Monday morning, which might delay our departure more. Finally Mike said that this was a land run by a dictator, and he had no intention of giving up his passport, and they could lump it. There was some official sullenness at this attitude, but we kept our papers and our independence to leave when we wanted.

When the time came to leave we wanted to buy fuel. At first one of the riverside refineries said we could load at their depot. Then when they heard the name of our ship they said they could not sell fuel, but declined to give a reason. We tried another refinery. They wouldn't sell us fuel either. There was an air of mystery and shiftiness about. In the end we left under sail, so I reckon we beat the dictatorship after all, though I admit they won the middle round.

Lisbon was mighty pleasant. Where the *Maken* lay she was surrounded by interesting and attractive yachts. The quay was the promenade of many pretty girls, and on the road close by there was a constant stream of all sorts of lovely and exciting cars. Altogether, the scenery was delightful. We bought food at the market and this turned out to be quite easy in spite of the language barrier. On one occasion I went with a seaman, the paid hand of a friend, who spoke English as well as Portuguese. This was not much fun, and after that I went foraging on my own. By pointing to what I fancied and then indicating the amount, I picked up a few words every day.

In Lisbon we met the first batch of ocean cruisers, those nomads like ourselves travelling to far places in small boats. There was the inevitable German bunch escaping from intolerable conditions at home. Most of them were heading for South America. They were sometimes brave and sometimes efficient, but all too often they were pathetic, still marked, mentally, by the war. There was a long, slim motor cruiser in the dock near us; good enough for summer cruising on semi-sheltered waters, she was no boat for offshore cruising. Aboard there was a family – or rather a collection of human beings possibly linked by consanguinity. They had got this far and were now short of money. Heaven knows how they fed! They could not afford to buy fuel for the next stage of the trip. Perhaps this was just as well: a proper gale would almost certainly have drowned the lot of them.

In contrast there was a big, able sailing yacht which lay just outside the dock, in the river. All sorts of rumours were circulating about her. Distilling these rumours, we came to the conclusion that the yacht was on a voyage to make films. But even on her I saw weaknesses in her gear which would have given me sleepless nights if I had been one of her crew. She was German-manned and there was an air of lavish opulence about her which one naturally associates with film-making.

In the dock there was an ocean-cruising yacht which in some ways typified the type simply because there is no mean or average in this extraordinary game. She and her crew cannot be considered unusual as ocean cruisers go, simply because the whole sphere is so completely removed from normal standards. For a start the yacht's crew consisted of more than ten souls, yet the overall length was less than 40 feet. We never discovered exactly how many people there were aboard; it was such a warren that counting heads was virtually impossible. Where they all slept was something of a mystery, though we did discover that at least two people and one of the children lived in the after end of the yacht, a mere sail-locker. It made us feel almost guilty on the *Maken* with our headroom, enough even for Mike's ample height, while these people cheerfully went to sea in such super-cramped conditions.

The skipper was a Swiss journalist. He was widely travelled and extremely well informed. He had been to the Far East and collected some superb wood carvings from a Buddhist temple far inland. The priests and worshippers of the temple took exception to this pillaging and chased the thief through the jungle to the sea. We thought that the carvings were rather wonderful but entirely unsuitable for use as interior decorations in a yacht. Also we thought it outrageous to pinch other people's objects of piety. On the whole Lisbon was not wildly interesting for us, and we were pleased to be on our way after a week. We had done a little work on the boat, a few hours' sightseeing and worked out a technique for the time we were in harbour.

As we saw so much of each other when at sea it seemed good sense to split up as soon as we went ashore. The disadvantage of this is that meals are liable to be a bit haphazard. None of us had enough cash to eat ashore, except on special occasions. In practice we all ate a large breakfast, those staying aboard to work on the boat had a good cold lunch with soup, and there was usually a substantial evening meal. We worked hard and had gigantic appetites which were encouraged because there was a fairly sharp rivalry between the three of us in the culinary arts.

Mike had been cook on a fishing boat and was a skilled hand with the galley gear. He was less adventurous than I was, but he had virtually no failures. One of the things that I had contributed to the boat was a 'duck oven'. This is just a double-thickness steel plate with a deep lid which fits over the top of the dish. The double base is put on the primus stove, the baking dish stands on the base, and the lid keeps the heat in. It worked well enough but was rather too hot. The primuses we had, like all their breed, tended to give out too much heat for slow cooking. As a result we could only bake fast.

Mike would regularly roast meat when we had it fresh. I favoured making various forms of bread when we were at sea, after the fresh bread had run out. Bjarne did not get any fun out of cooking but he liked to give us Norwegian dishes. One of the extraordinary features of our set-up was that, using identical ingredients and equipment, the three of us would produce quite different tastes and appearances, even when using the same processes. Mike made apple pie that was a miracle, whereas mine was insipid. But I reckoned he was wasting his time when he tried to produce a steamed pudding, since it had to stand comparison with what I immodestly thought was a miraculous confection which gave me endless pride, and no one any stomach-ache.

The day we left Lisbon was fine and sunny. Under all plain sail we were surging along out of the Tagus when we saw a fishing boat ahead. It was a typical local job, about 35 feet long, with a fair turn of speed and a truly enormous crew. We tried to count the number aboard, but there were so many that it was not possible to complete the count before the fishermen reshuffled positions and we had to start counting again. There were about thirty people on that 35-footer, and we got the impression that the skipper took with him all his male relatives unto the fourth generation and down to lads of twelve.

They were harpooning porpoises as these delightful creatures played and dived along the surface of the sea. A good-sized beast came gambolling along and they turned in pursuit. The porpoise seemed to think it was a game and kept surfacing every few seconds, going in a straight line. The boat followed, gaining fast. Pedro stood up in the bow, harpoon at the ready, and the younger members of the crew danced about with excitement. Pedro waved to Alfonso at the helm, ordering changes of course as the porpoise weaved about. When the launch was right up to the fish Pedro drew back his right arm, and down went the harpoon.

All this went on just ahead of us. If the performance had been staged for our benefit it couldn't have been better arranged. The harpoon found its mark and at once all hell broke loose. With a lash of tail and a wild flurry of foam the porpoise made off at right angles. Pedro was so excited at scoring a hit that he dashed aft to help Alfonso at the helm. Alfonso already had advice from twenty different throats hurled at him. The rope attached to the harpoon was in the hands of some eight stalwarts amidships. They heaved mightily, yelling and laughing and generally behaving in a disorganised way. The fish went off to starboard, the rope-handlers hauled like fury, everyone gave everyone else advice and tried to help. Alas, Alfonso steered the boat off to port instead of following the fish. The harpoon came adrift, and that was a hundredweight of good fresh fish lost. Still, a lot of people had a lot of fun for a few minutes, especially the crew of the *Maken*. We took note for future occasions and Mike decided to make a harpoon. When we reached our next port, Las Palmas, in the Canaries, he made a vicious weapon about 6 feet long.

Like the first proper leg of the journey, the voyage to the Canary Isles took ten days. This was partly due to being held up by bad weather. When we were well clear of land the wind rose steadily, and we matched its increasing power by reefing down. The gear for this was like everything else, tough, far stronger than normal use or abnormal weather demanded, and not easy to handle. If only we'd had a few modern winches on board, we would have done a lot with less effort and in half the time.

We used a ⁵⁄₁₆ inch diameter flexible wire pennant on the clew of the mainsail, with a simple three-part rope tackle. The wire was passed through a thimble on the sail and down to a block on the boom, then forward where its raw end was bent on to the hook of the tackle block. It was wonderfully simple, but then so is a caveman's axe. The wire was intractable and caused bloody hands. I will refrain from describing the language it induced. Even in daylight after we were practised, it often took well over an hour to shorten sail. When I built my next boat I made things just as simple, and correspondingly reliable; but on that new boat I reckoned I was becoming a dodderer if I took more than 10 minutes to tuck a reef single-handed. Even allowing for the difference in size, there is no doubt that the gear on the *Maken* was too massive and a shade too primitive in many ways.

The first concession to the rising wind was to take the jib off. This made a big difference to the speed, and the whole motion of the boat eased. It made a change comparable to changing from a fast sports car on a rough road to a smooth saloon passing over a smooth town road with mild undulations. It also made a lot of difference to the poor devil sweating and swearing in the galley.

The weather was obviously going to throw a lot of muck at us. The clouds got lower and harder every minute. The sea turned from blue to grey to green to black. The spray started to rattle hard as pebbles on the deck. We struggled into stiff, cold, rubbery oilskins and hauled ourselves up on to the deck.

'We'll take two reefs down in the main.'

'Is it worth heaving-to? Then three of us can do the job, otherwise one man has to stay at the helm.'

'No. You take the peak halliard, I'll do the throat.'

'We'll have to hurry. That mizzen looks as if it's being strained.'

Two of us scramble forward to the mast. The ropes are thrown off their cleats but the heavy gaff remains fixed aloft.

'Those damned blocks. The sheaves have rusted to the pins. I'll go aloft and stand on the gaff. That'll make it come down.'

Up aloft the scene is superb. Away to the windward horizon a mass of waves roll towards us. Domineering and overwhelming they look. Even the *Maken* shrinks in size before them. From halfway up the mast she looks like a toy, a plaything in a bath made turbulent by the fretful hand of an Olympian child. The mast and gaff creak and lurch and the motion is enough to unnerve and de-stomach anyone foolish enough to think of possibilities and consequences.

The gaff needs a firm thrusting foot to force it to start coming down, but, once started, its weight carries it down fast enough. The halliards are made fast and prevent it going all the way. Back on deck we haul and heave, tie and pull. The canvas has to be pummelled sometimes, it's so solid.

When the mainsail is subdued we go aft to the mizzen. This is a toy in comparison and, apart from one wild swing of the gaff before it's captured, there is no excitement. The helmsman has some fruity things to say about the gaff as it was his head that was nearest.

The cockpit is just abaft the mizzen mast. It is a watertight well. In extreme conditions it fills with water and stays that way, though some water will slop out when the boat rolls or heels a bit. It has high wooden sides and no seats and is tough, unyielding and rather uncomfortable. By especial good fortune we had a dumpy motor tyre aboard for use as a fender when passing through the Panama Canal. This tyre made a fine seat, though its shape and impression were reminiscent of a lavatory. But without it we would either have had to stand at the helm, which would have been very tiring in rough going, or perch on the sharp edge of the cockpit coaming. This was just like sitting on top of a fence. Fence-perching is fine with a blonde on a fine sunny day, but absolute hell if the fence is jumping and thumping about for four solid, dreary hours on end, and the scenery consists of nothing but dark grey waves which look cold and are just that, when they shower over the wretched helmsman every so often.

With all the sails snugly reefed, the *Maken* made slower progress but still went well enough. Steering was less hectic now that she was not over-canvassed, though the steel tiller with its thick wood end still swung about, however hard the helmsman tried to keep it still. As a wave chucked the stern of the yacht sideways the pressure on the rudder would start that mass of timber swinging. The tiller starts across, a live rigid thing which has no intention of obeying the helmsman's hand. The helmsman knows this beast and leans back to take the weight. Without warning the sea drops away on the other side of the rudder, the force is reversed and the tiller whips back to crack the helmsman a neat blow on the lower ribs. While he is expressing his feelings the boat starts to wander off course. After 4 hours' steering it was mighty pleasant to go below and get dry and fed.

There was no let-up in the weather. It got steadily, relentlessly worse. The mainsail was a tight arc of grey, wet canvas driving the boat along with dozens of horsepower sucked from the wind. The stage was reached when waves were breaking aboard regularly and the boat was obviously being strained unfairly. We decided to heave-to, and it was just a question of which was the best way. Mike favoured leaving some sail set. This is certainly what most of the books recommend. My experience was all against this. Sail tends to drive the boat forward, which is just the thing to avoid when hove-to. Moreover, if there is a sudden wind shift, or the boat is thrown round by a wave, the sail may flutter; in winds of gale force a few seconds' flogging does a great deal of harm to the sail. Constant flagging and whipping will soon destroy the stoutest canvas, quite apart from shaking up the whole ship and damaging the sheets and halliards.

Mike was just the weeniest bit sceptical about taking all sail down, but I was persuasive, having tried it with complete success so often. In the end we lowered all sail and lay ahull, just about as comfortably as possible considering it was by then a good full-blooded gale with seas which seemed to tower over us. In the troughs we had a range of vision which was limited to about 50 yards and it was like being in the bottom of a moving amphitheatre. We were the actors in a tense drama, while all round from the stalls and the circle the hostile audience looked down with grey frowns. Instead of throwing tomatoes this audience would hurl themselves at us, tons of roaring foaming water, breaking and thundering, then suddenly falling silent. This was worse than the noise. The moments of almost complete silence before the uproar returned, the pause which made us think, the eerie hush with the long, long hissssssssss in the background, a vicious reminder of the menace which was close all the time.

We went below and brewed up. In the cabin it was quite peaceful. Every movement from place to place had to be thought out first, and to move without holding on was dangerous. But the thick hull deadened the sound, the drink cheered, and it was satisfying to find ourselves in the middle of a gale with no trouble from the boat.

There was nothing to do now but wait. We all retired to our bunks and dug books out of our kitbags. My own choice was a semi-technical book, just complicated enough to need a small mental effort to understand, not so difficult that the interest would too easily flag. The tension died down a shade. Darkness came and we slept. Dawn came up and we slept on still, tired by the fight with the sails and the unremitting watch-keeping in steadily rising wind.

At mid-morning the wind was as hard as ever, and we were glad to stay warmly ensconced in our sleeping bags, dry and comfortable. Conversation was desultory; it's hard to talk under such conditions. I dozed off again, then woke with a jolt. A bang and crack, a truly frightening sound went off right over my bunk. Completely awake in an instant, I looked across to Bjarne's bunk. He was looking at the structure round my berth, as if expecting to see a great crack in the planking with torrents of water pouring through. Mike had heard the noise, too; he could hardly have helped it. I shouted through to him: 'There's no sign of damage here, Mike.'

'It sounded like something breaking.'

'That's what I thought.'

'Must have been on deck.'

We scrambled out of our sleeping bags and reeled, holding on all the time, to the companion steps. Mike stuck his head out of the hatch: 'It's the bulwark. Bashed right in.'

'Let's have a look.'

'It's forward, ahead of the mast, to starboard.'

I swapped places with him in the hatchway and looked where he had indicated. The thick planking of the low wood wall round the deck was shattered and splintered. The broken timber had already been washed away and the gap left was quite big enough for a man to crawl through, or be swept through by a wave on deck.

'Right over my bunk. No wonder it sounded so close.'

'Shows the power of the waves!'

''m. Thank heavens the planking is more than twice as thick as the bulwark!' and on that optimistic note we went back to our bunks to endure till the wind died down.

All that day the wind shrieked and whistled in the rigging, pressing the yacht over, piling the seas up till they toppled. We kept the sails lashed firmly down. It was not till well on into the next day that we got the reefed main and staysail set. Gradually the wind strength dropped, and we put on more sail at the change of each watch. 24 hours after the first sail was hoisted we were back to normal: on watch, below to cook and eat, sleep, rouse-up, struggle into warm clothes, on deck to take the watch. Round and round the clock, pleasant but not exciting, progress but not swiftness, hell when getting out of a warm bunk, but bliss when going below after a watch.

The chart table was a piece of ply hinged to the deck overhead in the saloon. Each day after the position had been worked out, this flap was lowered and a mark made on the chart. Sometimes there would be a good gap between the last mark and the new one, and we'd all be cheerful, making rash remarks about the number of days before landfall. On other days the distance run in the previous 24 hours would be a paltry figure. We would wonder if the underbody of the yacht was becoming foul with weed – or should we have taken that reef out earlier? Bjarne and I had done enough racing to be full of ideas for boosting the daily mileage.

'We ought to reef later.'

'You can't ocean race an old ship like this.'

'We should pump the bilge more often to keep the weight down.'

'Wouldn't make any ruddy difference! We've tons of stores and fresh water aboard.'

'Every little helps. We could try tightening the rigging.'

'Not at sea. Something might go wrong and we'd have a mast overboard.'

'I'd like to see that mainmast shift. It'd stand without any rigging in a hurricane.'

So the discussion would go on. It was always hard for Mike to run the ship because in many ways Bjarne and I had more experience than he had, and three skippers in one ship is always a potential source of trouble. Before he bought the *Maken*, Mike had only owned a small day-sailer.

Both Bjarne and I had had a variety of small craft, including cruisers. But there was no doubt that the *Maken* was not the sort of yacht that could be hustled.

Nine days out of Lisbon we should have seen the high ground of the first of the Canary Isles. Mike as chief navigator had some worrying hours as the day grew old without a sight of land. In the afternoon I was on watch and the others were below. Without warning land appeared very high and apparently only a mile or two away, dead ahead. Though we had not realised it, the horizon was obscured by fog.

'We're damn near running aground,' I shouted from the helm.

'Whereabouts?'

'Somewhere pretty mountainous, dead ahead.'

With proper restraint the others do not rush up on deck. Ocean-cruising etiquette calls for a blasé approach to a situation like this. True, it's our first difficult landfall, since we could hardly help finding our way into the Tagus, with the aid of the long coastline and ample lighthouses. But here we are seeking a lonely group of islands set in a vast ocean. It would be easy enough to sail right past them if the navigating department went awry. After some minutes the others amble up on deck and glance at the towering isle ahead.

'Shall I leave it to port or starboard?' I ask.

'We'll go a bit closer yet to identify it.'

'You mean you want to see what the local lovelies are like, before deciding whether to stop here or go on to Las Palmas.'

'We'll stand well clear of the land.'

'Spoilsport!'

'Dreadful what ten days at sea does to a young and innocent child like you!'

A sight of land always raises morale, and we expected to have a better time here, after the tameness of Lisbon. That afternoon saw us past the first island, then the wind went light and all night we crawled south-west, so that dawn found us abeam of the long island of Fuerteventura. We gazed and gazed at it. The land seemed entirely deserted and scarcely cultivated, or even tillable. It was a wild land, interesting but not inviting. Up to now we had not been so very hot on deck, but now the breeze off the land was a torrid draught. We lay on deck in the sweltering sun, turning browner every hour. At last we were proper ocean cruisers. The decks got warmer and warmer and the cabin became like a hothouse.

It was midnight when we eventually saw the lights of Las Palmas ahead. The wind was just a gentle zephyr easing us imperceptibly along. Foot by foot we slipped through the water. On the foredeck by the light of a single torch Bjarne and I tried to free the windlass so that we could drop the anchor. The spray had wet the mechanism again and again till now it was seized solid; an immovable mass of rust-bound ironware. Mike turned the helm over to me and tried to ease the shafts and cogs. I turned the helm over to Bjarne and tried to work paraffin into the rusted bearings. The windlass was a primitive job, tough, unbreakable, and totally without refinements. All the oil had been washed out of it in the gale. In turn we wrestled and cursed and tussled with the inanimate, obstinate, infuriating machine. We thought it would be impossible to let an anchor go without a working windlass because the anchors and chain were so heavy that we would never raise them without mechanical assistance. The darkness, and the weakness of our lighting, made the job doubly awkward.

The hours slipped by but no one slept. More and more oil and paraffin was poured on to the immovable joints of the windlass. A hammer was played with force and frustration on the joints. All our tools accumulated on the foredeck. We tried wilder and wilder ideas, but nothing would move the thing, and at last we prepared the lighter kedge anchor and broke out a long warp to use instead of a main anchor and chain. By this time we were scarcely moving through the silent, windless night.

The night was at the deepest point, that uttermost depth around 4 a.m., when we rounded the end of the stone breakwater and ghosted into the harbour. Crossing the big basin took another hour, so slow was our progress. Dawn was well up when we finally tied up to a buoy not far from the yacht club, among a small collection of yachts. Some of these were clearly ocean cruisers, and this did not surprise us, for Las Palmas, like Lisbon, the Panama Canal, Tahiti, Honolulu and Cape Town, is one of the main junctions of the ocean-cruising routes. It is unusual nowadays to be the sole ocean-wandering yacht in one of these harbours, as the sport has gained a lot in popularity since 1945.

There was a thick sprinkling of fishing boats near our moorings, and each one had aboard a fierce dog which barked most of the time. Some of the dogs would let up occasionally, but they would make up for their brief relaxation by crescendos of barking if any boat passed near their charge. These dogs were the all-important guardians against thieves, who are numerous and active in this region.

Soon after we had tied up we were visited by various bumboats. Each was rowed by a rough-looking fellow who wanted to be hired as watchman, and they all had bundles of letters of recommendation from yachts which had passed this way before us. We had already heard of one, called Johan, a rogue less dishonest than the others. I was able to recognise the writing on one of his letters, and the names of the yachts on several others were very familiar. We were too hard-up to hire Johan for long, but we took him on for the first day, to show us the best place to moor, the location of the best laundry, where to buy fresh food, and so on.

He had the sense to see that we were not a wealthy crew on pure pleasure bent. He explained that the thieving in the harbour was every bit as bad as its reputation and showed us how to take basic precautions against it. We tied all the running rigging up as high as we could and knotted it innumerable times. Anyone who wanted to steal a halliard would have to untie two dozen knots before he would get a reasonable length of rope. We took off the deck all movable gear, put a great number of lashings round the sails since they were too bulky to carry below decks, and generally prepared for a state of siege.

We discussed getting some barbed wire, wondered whether bird lime was available and whether it was costly, and talked over various defensive measures as we ate breakfast. Then we lowered our tiny dinghy over the side and I stayed aboard as watchman while the other two went ashore. With some envy I watched them rowing away in the horrid little death-trap that was our yacht's tender. It lacked stability athwartships and fore-and-aft. It had leaked like a baby when Mike first got it, so he'd coated it thickly with red lead and covered the outside with canvas. This kept the oggin out, but the inside of the boat was liberally smeared with tenacious orange paint. Also some of the nails holding the canvas on, which had been the only ones available, were just longer than the planking was thick. So the interior of the dinghy was like a fakir's bed, except that no fakir has the benefit of gluesome paint as well as the points of nails.

There was plenty to do on the boat, though I felt disinclined to work with the shore so tantalisingly close. Admittedly the harbour, which is called La Luz, is like so many harbours, unsalubrious and far less pleasant than the adjacent town, Las Palmas. As I pottered about doing the hundred and one jobs which had accumulated while we were at sea, the time passed fast enough, for it was sunny and hot on deck, and pleasantly warm but shaded below.

A dinghy came alongside and I was very much on the alert. The ruffian at the oars and his scruffy mate lounging aft surveyed the *Maken* in sullen silence for some time. Casing the joint, I thought, all suspicion at once. After a long pause, one of them spoke: 'You got any brass?'

'What sort of brass?'

'Brass. Any sort. We buy brass. You got any brass? We pay lots money for brass.'

'There's no scrap brass aboard,' I said, thinking that if there were any bits of brass in any of the lockers we should certainly keep them for making and repairing fittings. There was still a vast distance to travel and we had no wish to part with any of our emergency gear.

The conversation went on for a long time, getting no one anywhere, and at last they sheered off. When Mike and Bjarne finally returned I told them about the conversation. Mike said: 'Pity we never knew about this before we left Norway. The *Maken* was used for whaling before I bought her. She had a massive great brass whaling gun on a brass pedestal. I left that lot behind because it took up a lot of room on the foredeck, and we didn't seem likely to have any use for it.'

What's it like ashore?'

'Very poverty-stricken. No wonder they're scrounging for brass. They're all as poor as hell.'

'What goes on ashore?'

'Damn all, except lounging in the sun.'

'Did you bring any fresh food with you?'

'No. Did you want something?'

'Want something! You clueless coots! We've had nothing but tinned food for days and you come back without so much as a fresh loaf.'

'Well, what's wrong with that?'

'For a start, it's much cheaper to eat fresh food. Besides, you had one hell of a boil and were out of action for a couple of days. It's fresh food that keeps away that sort of trouble.'

In an instant one of those petty rows which breed on ocean cruisers flared up. I was thoroughly fed-up after a whole day aboard with the land so close. None of us had had a wink of sleep the night before. The others never seemed to care about food in harbour, and they did not have my determination to avoid getting run down and ill through poor food. As a result of this argument and some hard thinking, I took over most of the cooking in harbour, apart from breakfast which we continued to do in turn. We had no further trouble from boils and for the rest of the trip we avoided illness almost entirely. We also ate regularly in harbour, and were a lot better fed than many of the other offshore cruising yachts we came across.

The row settled down soon enough. Mike was wise enough early on during the voyage to discuss quite openly the all-important question of quarrelling. He said he thought we were bound to have arguments and they would probably be bitter at times. That was my view, too, so we started off with an intelligent attitude to the matter. It didn't stop us rowing, but it did keep most of the verbal collisions within bounds. Considering that we had vastly different backgrounds, did not truly have a common native tongue, and were all old enough to have well-rooted prejudices, we got on well together most of the time.

I went ashore alone that evening and wandered round rather disconsolately. The region round the harbour was not interesting. I was able to buy bread and fresh butter, but sheer fatigue drove me back aboard fairly early.

Chapter Six

Next day and for several days we worked on the boat. The next hop was a long one, across the Atlantic. We expected it to be very tough. Several parts of the yacht needed minor attention and we set about overhauling the craft. We needed a pair of staysail booms so that we could rig twin headsails for running downwind with the sheets led to the tiller. The idea of this is that the yacht will steer herself so all the crew have to do is eat, sleep, read, gaze at the horizon, navigate occasionally, and generally live the lives of leisured gentlemen.

Mike got hold of two fine balks of timber, which were fashioned into booms. The usual method is to pivot these booms on the mast, or on a special pillar on deck near the bow. We used much shorter booms than usual and cut a Y-fork in the inner end of each which fitted round the shroud. This idea is only successful on very heavily rigged craft, as otherwise the rigging is subject to strains that it could not stand for long. We fitted up our twin booms with sheets leading aft, joined to lengths of chain which passed through heavy blocks and then to the tiller.

Mike also made friends with a blacksmith and came aboard one day with a murderous-looking harpoon. We gathered that it had been difficult for Mike, who spoke no Spanish, to explain to the smith just what it was he wanted. In the end Mike made most of the weapon himself.

We made friends with the other ocean-cruising yachtsmen in the harbour, and a pretty fantastic bunch they were. There was one yacht whose crew were all American pipe-welders. These lads had been helping to build US airfields in North Africa. Their high wages and lack of amenities had built up good bank balances, so they decided to club together at the end of their contract and buy a yacht to sail home to Texas. They knew very little about cruising and in some ways their ignorance was frightening. For instance, they were not quite sure how to reef in bad conditions. They joked that they held on to full sail till the sails blew away. To date they had blown out one mainsail. They had used the second to complete their first hop to Las Palmas and there was still another mainsail in reserve. We wondered what would happen after the latter was blown out.

There were no lifelines round their yacht, and she was flush-decked with no cabin top, but only a skylight and two hatches to break up the big area of decking. As a result there was nothing to hold on to on deck. Going forward to change headsails at night in a rough sea would have been terrifying to anyone used to doing such a job on a properly equipped yacht. With this crew it seemed that ignorance was fairly blissful.

Then there was the *Harry*. This was a Morecambe Bay prawning boat converted to a yacht. She had a vast sail area for her size. We looked with awe at the length of her bowsprit and boom, and could well understand her owner's boast that she was very fast. He was Dutch and we gathered that his wordless crewman was Scandinavian. Neither was fully conversant with sextant navigation, and it was only in Lisbon that they had actually got a sextant, having travelled a long way without using anything more than their two compasses and charts.

The owner had an overwhelming pride in his boat. 'She knows the way,' he boasted. 'She will find Barbados herself. We will navigate there by dead reckoning.'

This was a pretty sweeping statement. It's about 2,900 miles from Las Palmas to Barbados. That island is some 30 miles across, so it was expecting a miracle to hit such a tiny target at such long range with only crude methods of navigation. They wanted to race us to San Francisco, but we had the sense to decline the challenge. In the end they missed Barbados and were wrecked on the South American shore. For months after we saw them I tried to find out what had happened to them, having a well-founded foreboding that they might get into trouble. It was several years after seeing them that I learnt quite by accident of their final fate, and they'd left behind them, wherever they went, an open-mouthed astonishment at their naïve approach to what is, after all, a game that can be dangerous.

They had already been in trouble when we met them. The *Harry* had no engine and one day, in good visibility, they were becalmed in the Bay of Biscay. A big tanker had come up over the horizon heading straight for them. Relentlessly it came on and on, never wavering from its course. Horrified and desperate, they tried everything to attract the attention of the tanker's crew. The watch on her must have been drunk or sleeping or both. She steamed straight at the tiny *Harry*, hit her and badly holed her. The owner and crew feverishly plugged the gaping hole, which was at waterline level, and pumped hard. The sea was calm at the moment of the accident, but within minutes a wind came up and the sea lapped into the hole. The tanker never paused, but just steamed on, leaving the crippled *Harry* to the mercy of the weather. For 18 hours solid hours the two men pumped and bailed. Their lives depended on the pump; if it had broken down, they would have drowned. The owner, telling us the story, said: 'At the end of 18 hours I was exhausted. I could not go on pumping any more. Then I looked out over the cold grey sea and didn't want to die, so I went on pumping more. We managed to plug the hole and got to harbour somehow. There we patched up the *Harry* and now she is fine.' But not for offshore cruising, I thought.

They had learnt one lesson from their fright. They carried a dinghy that was large for the size of their yacht. At each end and all down both sides of this craft there were buoyancy tanks, so that in the final emergency they had a miniature lifeboat. It might have got them to land, but it was a tiny dinghy and, though I like to go afloat in anything that floats, I would hate to be forced to travel far in a thing of that size, especially on the Atlantic.

The Swiss journalist who owned the overcrowded yacht turned up some days after us, having stopped at the Salvage Islands. These uninhabited isles lie north of the Canary group. They are heavily populated by rabbits and we were presented by the journalist with a fine specimen which we roasted in our duck oven.

Incredible conversations took place in our saloon. The *Maken* had by far the roomiest main cabin, so it was the best place to collect to yarn. Also, Bjarne was the best linguist of all the yachtsmen assembled. One night I remember hearing something like this:

'You reckon to be in San Francisco by April 1954?'

'May or June at the latest.'

'Why not push on from Panama across the Pacific? We'll rendezvous in September, in Cape Town.'

'I'd rather go up the Aleutians. Alaska looks a pretty interesting place, judging by the charts.'

'The Baltic's the place we want to do.'

'Me too, but not till we've seen some of the Pacific islands.'

'Well, let's make a date. Meet you at the Royal Danish Yacht Club, Copenhagen, three years from today?'

'Better make it later in the year. Say 15 May 1956.'

All this was perfectly serious, a sober conversation between two ocean wanderers who thought of time in terms of the number of miles their yachts could travel per month. They would plan these vast journeys without doubting that they would reach their goal, never worrying about such trifles as gales which might damage sails and rigging. They were sure that they could refit their yachts as and when the need arose. The weeks at sea made them self-reliant and indomitable to a degree that is hard for the landbound city-dweller to comprehend.

One night just before Christmas we turned in about eleven o'clock as usual, after a fairly strenuous day's work. We were quite sober; our shallow pockets made sure of that. Mike slept in the port bunk in the saloon; Bjarne and I were in the fore-cabin, just as always. It was a quiet night, and well after dawn I awoke. I looked across to Bjarne's bunk, but he lay motionless, apparently deeply asleep. There was no noise from the saloon, so Mike was either asleep, or still screwing up enough energy to crawl out of his cosy sleeping bag.

The cabin looked very neat, I mused. Very trim indeed. Too tidy. Far too tidy. Something's wrong! With a horrid sick-in-the stomach I woke the others up.

'Bjarne! Bjarne! Did you tidy up before turning in last night?'

'No, I did not.' We lived, when in port, in a state of pleasant, masculine disorder, knowing instinctively where everything was, without all the fuss and flap and eternal tidying up which always exists when women are about.

'Mike, did you tidy up last night?'

'No. Holy Saints! Where're my shore-going clothes?'

'Where're mine?'

'My suitcase has gone!'

'They must have come right into our cabins while we were asleep ...'

'How in Hades did they get that great suitcase out of here without making a racket?'

'My passport was in my jacket.'

'Most of my money was in my trousers-pocket. They've taken them and my reefer jacket!'

'My knife's gone. And my passport too.'

'My clean laundry's gone. And I hadn't even paid for it!' Cursing and searching we went through the two cabins, examined the little fo'c'sle, and looked in the engine room. The thieves had taken the special long warp which we kept coiled in the fo'c'sle, though to this day we cannot fathom how they extracted it from such a cramped storage space without making a great shindy. They took one of our metal buckets, and we had to admire the cheek of this, for nothing makes so much clanging and banging as a metal bucket.

Breakfast was a miserable meal. We felt thoroughly depressed because all our precautions had been so completely circumvented. Every few minutes the grim silence would be rent:

'They've taken my best sweater.'

'And my only good sea-going trousers.'

'If either of you see one of the locals wearing a blue reefer jacket with Parkstone Yacht Club buttons, carve him up on the spot!'

'We'd better go and see the consul right away.'

'Won't do much good. There was one yacht in here that had her anchor stolen, the very anchor she was moored to. It happened while the crew were ashore having a drink and they were asked by a couple of roughs if they needed anything. Their mates were doing the stealing at the same time.'

'I've heard they'll steal to order. One yacht's crew were told they could have the funnel of the harbour tug, if they paid enough.'

'Maybe we'll be able to buy our own gear back.'

'Using our own money that they've stolen?'

'At least the police will have to do something, as our passports have been whipped.' But the thieves thought of that one, too. When Mike and I were ashore seeing the consul and the police, Bjarne examined every inch of the yacht and found on deck a plain brown-paper parcel with our passports inside. The robbers had searched our clothes, put our vital documents into a parcel and returned with the parcel, thus ensuring that the police would not be forced out of their all-enveloping lethargy. When we visited the police station they just raised enough energy to shrug their shoulders, then sank back into somnolence. We decided to do our own detective work.

It was Mike who first had success. He was walking through the local second-hand clothes market when he saw a fawn duffel-coat. It was patched with black, so it was extremely easy to identify. It so happened that some months before, when I discovered my duffel-coat had a hole in it, there was no fawn material handy, so I patched it with black. Mike marched up to the stall-holder, seized hold of the coat and growled: 'This coat belongs to my friend. This my friend's! See? Stolen!'

The stocky Canary Island woman running the stall did not understand Canadian, and Mike spoke no Spanish, but he made his meaning pretty clear.

An argument developed. Soon the usual crowd collected, all and sundry joining in the discussion, except the police, who stood on the outskirts of the turmoil and merely watched. At last Mike stalked off with his trophy, followed by a diminishing crowd who maintained the argument *fortissimo* for a mile or so.

When Mike came back aboard we at once made a plan of action. With Bjarne as interpreter and reinforcement, he went back to the stall and cross-examined the stall-holder. I stayed on board as watchman, but I learned later that the crowd that gathered, the uproar and the chaos reached remarkable dimensions. But it was worth it, for the name of the people who sold the coat to the stall-holder was discovered, and the address where one of the thieves lived was also given to Bjarne. However, even with this evidence, the police refused to help. When Mike and Bjarne came back on board they were rather depressed, having got on so well, only to face what seemed to be a blank wall of bureaucratic obstinacy.

I was absolutely delighted with their success. 'You've done incredibly well. All we have to do is go to the thieves' address, barge in, and search the place.'

'Don't be a clot! You can't just search a private house.'

'We could if we had a search warrant.'

'How in Hades can we get a warrant? You know what the police are like.'

'Dead easy. Everyone here is vastly illiterate. They won't know whether a search warrant's real or faked. Why, even you couldn't tell me what a search warrant looked like. I'll write out the warrant in English, Bjarne can translate it into Spanish, I'll type it out in Spanish, and there you are.'

The others saw the force of the argument and we forged a search warrant on my typewriter there and then. When it came to the signature at the bottom of this document I paused. It was one thing to concoct a fictitious warrant, another thing to forge someone's signature. We didn't even know the name or rank of the local police chief. I got over the problem in the simplest way. I made up a very high-sounding title, which I there and then conferred on myself, and signed my own name over this imposing title. As no one has ever superseded me, I remain to this day the Grand and Most Illustrious Commander of those Oceans and Seas bounding the Shores of the Uttermost Isles and Domains Not Particularly Specified.

It was easy to fake a search warrant, but using it needed a little thought and cunning. First, who was to stay aboard to guard the yacht against further raids while the search was on? Bjarne alone of the three of us spoke Spanish, so he had to be in the search party. Mike was the skipper, and he'd spotted the duffel-coat, the vital clue. He would recognise the old woman again if she was in league with the thieves and living in their house. Also Mike, with his ample muscle-power and merchant-navy experience, had a lot to offer if it came to a rough house.

Sadly I watched the other two row ashore in our silly little dinghy. My work of art was in Mike's pocket. Gloomily I turned away and tried to get on with the work on the ship. There was so much to do, getting her ready for the big jump across the Atlantic. Distractedly I pottered about, unable to concentrate. I had visions of them breaking down a massive oak door to be confronted by a bunch of cutthroats, knives at the ready. Or perhaps they would not be able to bluff their way in, in spite of my so carefully contrived document. As the hours wore on I imagined myself going to the British Consul with a story that would cause international repercussions. The headlines would look pretty interesting: 'BRITISH YACHTSMEN JAILED. FORGERY CHARGE' 'THREE SAILORS SENTENCED. 20 YEARS' ... and so on.

Dusk settled over the harbour and I prepared the evening meal. It was well after dark when I decided to eat alone. I badly wanted to go ashore to see just what had happened, but as we had only one dinghy I was marooned aboard unless I could get a lift from a passing boat. I started to write a letter, tried to read, brewed up. It was no good. Concentration was just impossible. Eventually I turned in, but stayed awake. Long after midnight the others returned. I was bursting with a million questions, but they were strangely quiet. I never did get the full story. It seems that they went ashore and had no trouble finding the house. They knocked and a very beautiful señorita answered. Mike and Bjarne were invited in. The girl had a most alluring sister, and these two were the only people in the house. The lad who we thought was the thief had taken to the hills. I could get very little out of Mike and Bjarne, except that they had not retrieved any of the gear.

It was all rather melancholy, though Christmas did cheer us up. Mike and I went ashore to midnight Mass. The whole town was out celebrating with crackers, music, carousing and one hell of a lot of noise. Every drinking establishment was active and, as we approached the church, the crowds grew dense. There was a wonderful Christmas atmosphere in the church with innumerable candles, bright clothes, and overhead the bells ringing out their good news. As the Mass reached its climax, more and more people pressed into the church and the noise outside died away. At the consecration there was that perfect silence, tense and dramatic, which almost hurts. When the time came to go to the communion rails I found myself alongside one of the local police. His enormous pistol holster knocked against me, a reminder that 'Peace on Earth' is often broken.

After communion the noise outside started again as the revellers got into their stride. By the end of Mass the whole town was out and about celebrating.

Next morning we had a party aboard the *Maken*. We opened the sealed biscuit tin and found a fine Christmas cake inside and a present for each of us from my mother. The crews of other yachts came aboard, so that soon the saloon was full of yarning yachtsmen, each with glass in hand. As usual the main topic of conversation was long-range cruising. Who would get to Barbados first? Was it best to head due south from the Canary Isles to pick up the Trade Winds? How much water do you carry? Only half a gallon a day? That's enough if you don't wash. Well, do you? You shave? But how, without cutting yourself? An electric razor? Damned plutocrat! Will you swap five tins of spinach for five of carrots? Have you tried that American government-surplus beef hash in cans? It's good: swap three tins of it for peaches. Where do you get drinkable fresh water in this God-forsaken dump? The Yanks fill their drinking-water tanks with bug-killing pills. They put in more pills than water. Where shall we meet again? And so on and on. The endless yarn. The comfortable feeling in the stomach after one glass more of heavy local wine and rich cake. This is why people go ocean cruising. At least, it's one reason.

Chapter Seven

It makes me laugh when I read about trans-Atlantic crossings in the London daily papers. Every so often one of them serialises the voyage of some lunatic who floats across the oggin on a rough tub which he miscalls a yacht. The paper plays up the trip and tries to make readers believe it's all vastly difficult, dangerous, exciting and breath-taking.

The truth is that an actual trans-Atlantic is usually a very fine holiday. What is really hellish is the approach period. The nervous tension which builds up in the mind; the sudden awakening in the middle of the night with the blinding realisation that the voyage is now only five days off; the sick-making mental processes that go on before the determination is screwed up to just the right pitch – all these are extraordinary. This is what the newspapers never tell about, and this alone is something which is different. Other sports work up their own particular tensions, but only ocean cruising draws the strain out so long. Boxing is the nearest equivalent, since the preparation goes on for a long time, but here there are violent physical exercise and practice bouts to break the line of strain. In ocean cruising, all during the fitting out, there is in the back of the mind the rather frightening prospect. The work is seldom strenuous and every job underlines the need for thoroughness, complete preparation, the importance of leaving nothing to chance.

On the *Maken* we did not have to do any important refitting, just half a million little things, but each one took so much time for so many reasons. Taking on water was a typical job. The rumours about the Las Palmas water were many and wild. There was so much hair-raising talk about it that we agreed there must be some truth in the matter, and at the same time there must be a lot of untruth, since the stories conflicted so. We made a lot of enquiries to find out which water was the best, and ended up getting ours from a pipe on a nearby quay. We already had two tanks full, and we argued that if the water we put in our two empty tanks proved bad we had enough of the old water, which we knew was good, to get all the way to Barbados and beyond.

Getting to the quay and back again involved starting the engine. The anchor had to be hove in, fenders got out, and, what with the usual delays and lethargy on the parts of the waterman, it took hours just to fill those two tanks.

However, not all the locals were Mark I loafers. We met one exceptional lad, a real seaman and a first-rate mechanic. It was this way. One day Mike was ashore when he spotted a grizzled old seaman who had been bosun aboard one of the freighters that Mike had worked in. The bosun recognised Mike and they had a drink on the reunion. The old boy was most interested to hear what Mike was doing, and Mike invited him aboard. This old fellow was a Spaniard and he brought with him a fellow countryman, who may have been a relative; we never really learnt. The lad had recently left the Spanish navy. He had not been aboard more than 20 seconds before he was up on the foredeck looking at our windlass. This antediluvian lump of machinery was still immobile. Mike had had a try at freeing it. Bjarne had disagreed with Mike's method of approach because Mike had not had any success. Bjarne got no joy either. I naturally had to open my big mouth and explain why they had not got the wheels turning, and to prove my theories I had a crack at it. The heap of tools round the windlass made an impressive sight. Oil and paraffin, rags, blowlamps, levers and cans were gathered thickly about, when this young Spaniard approached the job. He spoke no English, I spoke about four words of Spanish, Bjarne was at this time ashore, and Mike was showing the ex-bosun round our yacht. By signs and mime the young Spaniard and I fell into conversation. I showed him that the windlass was seized solid. He said: 'Let's get cracking,' or words to that effect. I said: 'You try.' He did, while I passed tools and generally played the plumber's mate.

Little by little things began to move. Pieces were taken off. Nothing was broken; the components were of such proportions that a breakage was beyond the bounds of human endeavour. Oil was applied, gentle taps moved more pieces. Down below, Mike and the ex-bosun were yarning about old times with the aid of a bottle. All through the afternoon that lad worked away. When he finally stood up, the whole contrivance was running just as well as when it was first cut out of the solid so many years before.

My delight knew no limits, as I had forseen that we would have had to haul the anchor in by hand. Apart from the fact that I dislike unnecessary work, the job would have taken hours and been shockingly hard going. As it is axiomatic that an ocean cruise is only successful if everyone does an equal amount of work, and as the other two were both larger and tougher than me, I had forseen a day of extremely hard toil. I took my miracle-worker down into the cabin for a drink. He refused even a small glass.

'A cigarette?'

Another polite negative. We tactfully asked the ex-bosun if we could reward this brilliant lad in some way. After all the shiftiness of the locals, he was such a complete contrast: a truly remarkable fellow. With the aid of a few more words in Spanish which I got from the ex-bosun, and using an old envelope to sketch on, we carried on a prolonged conversation. He wanted to know about the engine. We inspected it and he saw the funny side of it. Where were we going? All that way? – expressed by a skyward sweep of the eyebrows. And so on.

After the two Spaniards left I rowed across the harbour to a big liner lying alongside a quay. With me I took a parcel containing a dress for my brand-new niece. If I had posted the parcel in Las Palmas it would have cost a fortune to send it to England, so I hit on the idea of asking the purser of this ship to post it for me when he got back to England. He would be in Southampton in five days, when we would be setting out across the Atlantic. For a moment I considered stowing away, and in the confusion aboard it would have been easy enough. There must be something about ocean cruising that breeds lawlessness in people. First forging search warrants, now stowing away. And that evening it was immigration evasion that we plotted.

All three of us aboard the *Maken* were mighty short of cash. We knew well that there was very little chance of earning anything as we sailed our way round the globe. We also knew that the journey was going to take longer than planned, what with the robbery and other delays; and the thieves had reduced our meagre cash supply. Now it so happened that there was a chronic shortage of work on the Canary Isles, whereas money was to be made in South America. All sorts of people wanted to get to South America, especially Venezuela, where the oil wells were pumping money and wealth into the country. However, most of the people who wanted to go to South America could not afford the steamship fare. Others could not get visas to land. Some could not obtain or afford passports.

All in all, we could have taken a crowd of passengers on the *Maken* if we had charged a modest fare and told them to bring their own food. Mike was very much in favour of at least two passengers. Bjarne was non-committal, I was against it. My main objection was that if we arrived somewhere and tried to unload passengers, we might be told that no one was allowed to stay without a visa. Then we should have to carry our passengers on to the next stop, while the word went ahead of us that we were carrying illegal immigrants. I knew that we would not be allowed to dump a couple of Canary Islanders at Barbados, I had strong doubts about Panama, and I was damn sure the United States wouldn't let them in. It seemed to me that we stood a chance of having to pay the passengers' fares back to the Canaries.

Then again, we could be run in for all manner of charges if it leaked out that we had charged for the trans-Atlantic passage. Mike pointed out that we would not actually receive any money. Our passengers would pay for their fares by bringing aboard food for all of us for the whole trip.

'What about landing them?'

'Easy. Stay offshore till it's dark, then sail in to a beach, lower the dinghy and row them ashore about 4 a.m., and beat it before daylight.'

'What if they refused to go under those conditions? If anyone sneezes 10 miles away, that damn dinghy will turn over.'

'We could sail into harbour at night, tie up alongside, and land the passengers quietly before the customs and immigration people came aboard.'

'You can't go into a strange harbour at night without the engine, and when it's running the whole country knows we've arrived.'

The discussion ranged back and forth. I had to admit that an extra hand might well be useful if the weather was bad, but it seemed more than unwise to take Mike's first proposed passengers. They were a Canary Islander and his wife, both well on in middle age. It was easy enough to be sorry for them, but it seemed wrong to me to dump these two people in the middle of a strange continent in the middle of the night, even if they were in favour of the idea when we set out.

In the end we decided to take a young German lad of about twenty. He was a fairly typical product of the times. He spoke English well, also Spanish, as well as his native German. His experience on yachts was limited but this did not appear to worry him. That hard mental shell, which youngsters from Germany had in the immediate post-war years, was clearly marked on this boy. It would not be fair to say that we three did not like him, for we hardly knew him before he joined the ship. It was just that he seemed so cynical, so completely devoid of any sort of emotion, high or low. Heaven knows, Bjarne was no softy! He had lived through the German occupation of his country; he never displayed any special joy or sorrow, but at least he was friendly, understandable, human. Mike had knocked around on Canadian fishing boats, starting from the bottom as cook's mate and working his way up. The company on these ships, the sheer hard labour when the fish are about, the mixture of races which make up the crews, ensure that anyone who spends any time aboard one of them gets case-hardened. But compared with Mike, the young German was in some subtle way grimly sophisticated.

Like so many Germans, he was keen to get to South America. He knew he would meet plenty of his countrymen, get a job that would pay well, and generally acquire the material security so lacking in his own country at that time. We arranged that he should join us 24 hours before we were due to leave. When he turned up, he brought with him only a small suitcase. He explained that he had to go ashore to get the rest of his gear and the sailing kit we had told him to bring. We were to lend him one of our spare suits of oilskins. His final job was to be a trifle complex. He had to change all his currency into dollars. This called for careful negotiation, since it had to be done unofficially. The rate of exchange was cruel and varied from one source to another. It also varied a lot according to which currency was being sold for dollars, as at the time in the Canaries there was one of those complex financial situations, rather like in Tangiers. The mixture of tight state control imposed by Franco, the constant arrival and departure of ships and yachts of all nations, the tourist trade and the black market all contributed to these complications. We of the *Maken* solved a lot of our problems by using whisky as a barter commodity. Indeed, if ever the urge to sail over the far horizon gets too strong to deny, I shall set out with the bilges solid with bottles of the best Scotch. It's the finest currency there is, quite apart from its 'medicinal' value.

The night before we were to leave, the German boy should have come back aboard, to help with the last-minute preparations. He did not turn up. Next morning we speculated on what had kept him, surmising that perhaps he had not been able to tear himself from the fond embrace of his señorita. As the morning wore on we began to get worried. Perhaps he had changed all his money and then been robbed. After all, he would have had to move around those shady localities where illegal money-dealers live, finding out who would give the best rate. Soon enough too many people would know that he was carrying a useful sum of cash. The lanes down to the harbour edge were dark enough.

Perhaps I give the impression that I consider the whole of Las Palmas solid with thieves just because we'd met some of them at close quarters. The fact is that a very large proportion of the yachts that go into that harbour are robbed by one means or another. When we reported our loss to the British consul he was not even slightly surprised. One owner, on a dark night, was hailed by a boat alongside, to ask if he wanted to buy some rope. The end of the rope was handed up for inspection. It seemed a fine warp. The owner asked how much. The price started high, as is the custom, to allow a margin for bargaining. Before the deal was completed the owner suddenly realised that the rope he was buying was his own kedge warp. While his attention was held by the rogues in the boat alongside the yacht aft, another boat was lying hidden up forward, paying the rope off the yacht's foredeck, along out of sight below her deck edge, into the boat from whence it was being sold.

While we were lying at Las Palmas, a German yacht came in. She was heading for South America with three men aboard who intended to settle there. One of these men went ashore the first evening for a drink. At a bar he met a charming pair of local lads. They yarned about this and that till it was time for the German to get back to his boat. He asked the way back to the landing stage. His two new friends offered to show him. They walked with him to his dinghy, and bid him a friendly goodnight as he rowed back aboard. It was not till he went to look at the time before going to sleep that he realised that his new friends had relieved him of his watch.

The continuous stream of incidents like this made us wonder if our new crew had been hit over the head during the night. By the time breakfast was over we were planning the best method of finding him. Mike went ashore, while Bjarne and I cleared up; after so many days in harbour, a lot of gear needed putting back into safe seagoing stowage places. Before lunch Mike came back, annoyed and without a clue. We hailed the German yacht, as they knew our man. We asked the crews of the other yachts. We began to get bad-tempered.

In the end we left without him. We put his little suitcase aboard the German yacht, explaining what had happened, and they promised to return it to the owner if he turned up. It was hard for Mike to make this decision, as we were already so far behind our schedule. However, we had not taken any payment from the German, and when we finally hove up the anchor he had been absent for more than 24 hours. The mystery of his disappearance remains to this day.

When at last we'd decided to go, Mike and I took the two handles of the windlass and started to wind in the heavy chain; he was in a flaming mood, and I was wildly impatient, as ever. We started off at a fool's pace, whirling the great handles round as if we were mincing butter. Soon the pace began to tell and, to make the pull harder, the chain came vertical. By the time the anchor was up, Mike was puffing and I was as tired as if I'd just finished three rounds of hard fighting.

There was very little wind and hoisting the sails was easy enough. We went out under power, past the German yacht to drop the suitcase, then out towards the harbour entrance, shouting farewells to the other yachts. Three of them were to set out soon after us, but we never saw them again.

Chapter Eight

Outside the breakwater there was a swell, but little wind. We made intermittent progress as the wind came and went and so it continued for two and a half days. Mostly we hardly moved through the water; sometimes we would get up to a respectable speed for a brief spell. As it was calm we were able to work on deck, and we finished and rigged the two booms for setting the two staysails, our downwind rig.

The soft weather gave us a chance to get back into seagoing routine, but, in fact, we never truly swung into the groove of it before we picked up the Trades. After that, it was wonderfully easy. Don't believe those yarns of shocking hardship on trans-Atlantics on the east-to-west southern route. With a properly organised yacht and experienced crew it's just the finest holiday.

As soon as the wind was fresh and in the right direction we assumed that this was the true Trades. We rigged our twin staysails with some difficulty, because the gear was not specially designed, but merely adapted for the job, and after a slight faltering we were off. Those two headsails did not take us the whole way across, but they did give us some fabulous runs. We rigged them in the conventional way, for'ard and boomed out with their sheets led aft to blocks at each quarter. The sheets passed through these blocks to the tiller. If the boat swung off to starboard the starboard head-sail would then pull harder, the port one less strongly. As a result the starboard sheet would tug at the tiller while the port one slackened. This would pull the tiller over and put the yacht back on course.

To see a pair of 'twins' (as these downwind headsails are universally known in ocean-cruising circles) at work is to watch a living miracle. Talk about something for nothing! It comes near to perpetual motion in the right direction, in a powerful and usable form. Consider this. After working on and off for some days we had a continuous spell of good following winds. We hoisted the twins and they drove us across the sea for seven days and nights without faltering. We never, in that full week, touched a sail, a sheet or a halliard. We just lived aboard while the yacht careered across the ocean, doing just about 100 miles every 24 hours. We literally did nothing to help our progress and, if we had all gone overboard, it would have made no difference to the yacht. This was the best run under twins, non-stop; but there were several other periods of three or more days during which we did not have to do a hand's turn to aid or guide the yacht.

Imagine the sheer luxury of it! Up to now, come rain, hail, gale or other form of hellishness, we had to steer, change sails, reef, unreef, and generally sweat to make the miles. And come what may, we each had to take the tiller for 4 hours in every 12. There was never the feeling: 'today is Sunday. No work.' Every day and every night, out of the 12 hours, 4 had to be spent by each of us in turn, steering. At times this could be very hard work, for the rudder was as large and as heavy as a barn door. It gave the nice feeling that it would never break, but it also swung about viciously in a rough sea, and sometimes threatened to stove in a rib or three. Sometimes these 4-hour spells were just purgatory, as the torrential rain sloshed down, chilling the body, killing the wind and cutting visibility to a dangerous few hundred feet.

In crossing the Atlantic, all this slavery and servitude to the tiller was taken away. We used to turn in, all three of us, and sleep the whole night through. Sometimes one or other would wake up and potter up on deck. A quick glance round to make sure all was well, a look round the horizon, nothing in sight ... so back to a nice warm bunk.

If it had not been for the rolling it would have been a perfect holiday. However, all things mortal have their disadvantages. On our flying carpet we had escaped the telephone, licensing laws, yapping dogs, and all the other disadvantages of civilisation. We could not escape the rolling. And what rolling it was! The dear old *Maken* was probably no worse in this respect than any other yacht. But we weren't worried about what other yachts might do. We had our own species of purgatory and, when it was going great guns, it was beyond purgatory and well on the way to Hades!

Bjarne seemed to find it worse than Mike or I did. Perhaps his army training made him less able to sway with the ship, perhaps he was less flexible in temperament. Anyway, he found it unpleasant till one night, with a suitable string of oaths, he humped his flea-bag out of his bunk and laid it down athwartships. It gives some idea of the great beam of the *Maken* to say that he was able to sleep diagonally athwartships in the fore cabin. There are few enough yachts with enough beam to make it possible to sleep on the sole of the for'ard cabin, let alone athwartships. Anyway, that was how Bjarne partly solved the problem of rolling. He found it easier to go to sleep rocking first head-down, then toes-down, than being rolled to and fro across his bunk.

The rolling at night scarcely worried me. I used to turn in and sleep almost at once, night after night. I must confess that on one yacht I used to crew aboard I was called the Dormouse, but I would counter this by saying that anyone who does a full day's crewing should be so tired that he will fall asleep at every spare moment. On the trans-Atlantic there was no work to do for long periods, but I used to fill every day with so much writing, reading, studying and drawing, that by nightfall I was tired enough. Also I used to chock myself off in my bunk with spare clothes, which effectively damped out any unsynchronised rolling between my carcass and the ship.

Waking up in the middle of the night, when the selfsteering was at work, was an uncanny experience. We always made it a rule that anyone waking would go on deck to check up that all was well. As sleep dropped away it was hard to resist the temptation to snuggle down in the cosy sleeping bag and fall asleep again. It was not particularly hot in these latitudes, especially at night and when the wind was blowing freshly; but good seamanship would prevail and a silent figure, barefooted, wearing nothing more than a pair of trousers, or perhaps shorts, would pad across the cabin. The other two are asleep, breathing steadily, dead to the world.

On deck it is a bit chilly with no shirt on. The boat surges and rolls steadily on, foaming through the moonlit waves. A glance round the horizon shows that no ships' lights are in sight. (We made the whole 2,900-mile crossing without seeing a single vessel, once we were clear of the Canaries.) The waves look gentle in the soft light, and it's almost a temptation to go for a swim; but to drop overboard now is certain death. The yacht is covering a relentless 5 miles every hour. She plunges on and on, and anyone who fell in the sea would never make the crew, sound asleep down below, hear his cries for help.

The ship is not silent. We could not lead ordinary rope sheets from the boom ends to the tiller. They would have chafed through in a day. Instead we had fixed those short lengths of chain to pass through the big blocks (pulleys, in landlubberese) on each quarter. These chains showed how much wear and strain there was; they became burnished bright in no time. As the tiller sawed back and forth, keeping the wandering yacht on course, the chains rattled and chattered to and fro. It was an almost unceasing noise, and in fact when the chains fell silent it was usually a sign that the wind had shifted suddenly and the twin headsails were aback, or that something else was awry.

The night prowler looks at the compass to check that we are still heading west, always west, towards the Spanish Main, the sunny Caribbean, lovely lasses and long, cool rums. He wanders forward to see that nothing is chafing, nothing coming loose. For a few moments he looks down at the gleaming bow as it chops the waves in half; a scutter and a splatter behind him tell of a flying fish, come aboard in a swift, graceful arc. No point in looking for it now, in the dark. It will still be there in time for breakfast in the morning.

All is well and so back to bed, with a final look round the deck, then round the horizon. Back in the warm bunk a brief prayer goes up for such thoroughly blissful conditions. While we three comfortably sleep the night away, our guardian angels keep the Trade Winds constant in strength and direction so that at breakfast time we can look at the log and see that the night has given us another 50 miles along the way.

Then there was the extra bonus, the one more 'something for nothing' that this Trade Wind joy-run gave us. Breakfast was provided free and gratis. We only had to go up on deck and hunt around under the bulwark, beneath the canvas cover over the windlass, and in other corners, and there were succulent flying fish. Chop off their wings and fins and fry them, and that's a breakfast as tasty as any ashore. Only here we met one snag. There were never more than two flying fish on the deck in any one morning. We never thought it a good idea to keep them from one day to the next, and there is no known method of dividing two flying fish among three people. This made for complications at breakfast time. But there's more to it than this. When we got to Barbados, we met other yachts which had done the trans-Atlantic; one of them had four people aboard, and every morning they would find up to three, but never more, flying fish on the deck. A yacht which had only two of a crew reported regularly finding one fish aboard, but never two. Clearly there is a conspiracy here, some sort of trade union agreement affecting the flights of fish.

After breakfast we would sit on deck and enjoy the sun. The other two, in Las Palmas, had discussed sunburn very seriously. They came to the conclusion that it would be best to get some olive oil and smear this on our torsos, to prevent excessive burning. So oil was duly ordered, with the groceries, as it was to have the secondary use of cooking fat. When the oil arrived, it was in old wine bottles, and there was no doubt that it was olive oil; it fairly stank of olives. Little bits of them, and big bits for that matter, floated in the thick slime. I was fool enough to laugh, which only made the others even more determined to anoint themselves thoroughly.

Neptune's beard! How that oil stank! It got on the settee cushions and on the clothes the other two were rash enough to wear in the evening after the anointing. It seeped into bedclothes and curtains, carrying its high smell with it. I wonder where the unfinished bottle finally disappeared to?

But on one count the others were always up on me. In the evenings we used to have regular card sessions, since after dark the illumination in the cabin was not really good enough for reading and writing. All through the voyage I tried everything I knew, but I could seldom beat Mike at cards. Bjarne usually beat me, too, but not always. It did not matter what we played, Mike would usually come out on top in the end. This used to infuriate me because I assumed that in the long run we would have an equal amount of luck; but the skill factor must have counted more. When it came to any job on board, Mike always went at it hammer and tongs, muscle-power-must-win-through, with seldom a thought for the best approach. That was fine for him, he had the strength to get clean through most brick walls without undue delay; but for me it was always a question of concentrated thought first, then a subtle application of just the right amount of force in just the right place. Which usually worked, just as Mike's standard formula usually brought success.

Very well, then: it was illogical that Mike regularly did best when it came to plotting the best course through a hand of cards. There's no way of bulldozing through cards. Not that it mattered much; we both enjoyed these games, if for no other reason (in my case) than the ever-present possibility that I might win.

The other amusement in the evening was the radio. This was a remarkable set, a portable battery type (for we had no wired electricity aboard) made in Norway. It had a wonderful range and clarity and apart from giving us the exact time for navigation it also had enormous value as a morale-booster and time-passer. For there were times when our ideal existence was boring: the library aboard was limited; it was impossible to do any work apart from perhaps some canvas sewing, when the boat was rolling; and there were occasions when we could have done with more occupations.

Sometimes, though, there was too much to do. For instance, soon after we left Las Palmas, and it was clear that the weather was going to be soft, we decided to change our tough new mainsail for the old lighter one. The idea was to save wear and tear on the good sail, since there was still a very long way to go, and we wanted the hard-weather sails to be in good fettle for the rigours of the Pacific. It took well over an hour of hard work to change the sails. Even the light one was mighty heavy, and it had to be humped up from below, pulled out of its bag (which, like sail bags the world over, fitted too tightly) and put on the boom and gaff. There was a long lashing to reeve through to keep the sail on to the boom, and another just as long on the gaff. Then the best sail was carefully folded up, stuffed into the sail bag, and wrestled below.

Within 10 minutes of being hoisted the light mainsail tore all along the foot. We lowered it, replaced it by the tough sail, and set about repairing the rent. We should have been suspicious that such a long rent should occur in the moderate wind then blowing. What with breaks for meals and knocking off at dusk, together with various other interruptions, it took Bjarne and me a day and a half of continuous sewing to repair that sail.

Then came the job of changing sails all over again. Within 5 minutes of getting the light mainsail hoisted it tore again, this time all the way along the head. So we lost that contest thoroughly. We lowered the sail and once more put up the big heavy brute. Hell's bells, and we were doing this for fun!

The light mainsail must have been rotten, though not so weak that we would notice till it was hoisted and tore. The mizzen was a different sail altogether. It had started life as the mainsail of the 4½-tonner which my family owned. When I converted to Bermudan rig this sail was a spare, and so I gave it to the *Maken*. We left that sail set for by far the greatest part of the voyage. All the time we had the twins set forward, the mizzen stayed up to help them along. It was a tanned sail, the only one aboard, and it certainly worked hard. We hauled it down when the wind really whistled in the rigging, but it was not reefed.

Around midday we would work out the daily position, lower the chart board to its working position, and add another cross to the row creeping across the chart. As the distance from Las Palmas to Barbados on the chart was only about 30 inches, it was a good day's run that was an inch long on the chart. When three or four of the position marks were close together, not spanning a couple of inches between them, we would feel morose. The old hooker seemed slower than a dray with a broken wheel. The wind was wrong, the current foul, it would be summer before we got anywhere; every other boat would be there before us, and so on. But when the little crosses strode out across the chart we soared off into rash predictions about dates of arrival, made up wild menus which were to be eaten with a devastating popsie on each knee (a well-nigh impossible feat, incidentally: even with one popsie, it's not a satisfactory way of dealing with a sumptuous meal) and morale would take a bound skywards.

All talk of popsies may seem a bit puerile, but just try a month at sea without setting eyes on anyone except a tough-looking, bearded, muscular man, wearing a battered pair of trousers (because most of his clothes have been stolen) and you will understand. Actually we were very proud of our beards. After about two weeks at sea a voice came from in front of the mirror: 'Who's got the best beard, and why have I?'

Fortunately we all had completely different growths, so we could each tell ourselves that our own was quite the best, without feeling self-delusive. Bjarne's hair is straight and raven-black. He matched it with a Captain Kettle beard, glossy and black and pointed, very naval and fine-looking under his yachting cap, on the very rare occasions when he wore it. Mike kept his hair short, and his beard was in keeping, short, curly and very trim without being trimmed. It made one think of one of the younger Biblical characters. Mine was blond, a very fine blond indeed. The only trouble is that it did not even nearly match my hair, which is a plain mousy shade.

We made it a regular habit to grow beards at sea, both to keep out the cold in the chilly latitudes and to save water. On arrival in harbour we always shaved, and this proved good tactics, because the hearty sailor types, who overemphasised their far-ranging over the windswept briny, were not so popular at some of the ocean-cruising junctions.

It was always a sign that we were getting near land when one or other of us took out shaving tackle and examined it with a critical air, wondering if the blade would do for just one more harvest. It's all very fine sailing 14,000 miles on £20 but when it comes to using a blunt blade because new ones cost money, then poverty is less amusing.

When there were only 700 miles to go, we began to think that we could be anchored within a week; ten days at the most. It is at this point that the daily tasks become a grind. Cooking, in particular, could be a grim struggle. It was not the heat – that came later in the Pacific – it was our old enemy, the constant and ferocious rolling.

Imagine that it is about six o'clock in the evening, and the cook is just getting down to the third meal of the day. He comes below and goes to the forward cabin. Holding on with one hand, he lifts the mattress and bedclothes on one of the bunks and pulls up a couple of bunk boards. He's looking for a tin of peaches. He plunges his hand into the locker under the bunk and pulls out the first tin at random. As the locker is pitch-black inside, he can't tell what tin will emerge till it has been examined. The cook wishes he had three hands, the extra one to hold a torch while he fumbles around in the Stygian locker. After three wrong selections, the fat, round tin of peaches emerges. He puts it on the cabin sole (floor) while the bunk boards and bedclothes are replaced.

All the time the constant rolling goes on and, when the cook turns round to look for the tin he put down just 30 seconds before – it's disappeared. It has rolled behind a kitbag, and it hides there while the cook hunts around. This caper is repeated two or three times more till the right batch of tins is assembled. Then potatoes are put into the washing-up bowl and the bowl is filled with water. Peeling spuds is easy enough generally, but it loses its fascination when the bowl has to be held between the knees to prevent it escaping, while at every roll the muddy water laps over and wets the trousers.

At last the potatoes are peeled, put into a pan of sea water and set on the stove. This is not gimballed, as in many yachts. If it were it would stay level as the yacht heeled first one way, then the other. Our stove performs the same antics as the yacht. The cook pours a measure of methylated spirits into the cup to heat the stove. He lights the meths, the yacht gives an extra deep roll, and the blazing liquid spills out of the cup and runs like a fiery blue dragon all over the galley bench.

When the stove is going well, the potatoes are soon boiling. Time to put on the stew. The tin is opened and the contents prised out into a saucepan. Now it is easy enough, with two hands, to strap the potato pan on to the stove. There are special springs which extend across the stove top and clutch the pans in place. But how do you fix two pans down? You need a hand for each pan, a hand to hold yourself against the swoop and surge of the boat, and two hands to fix the springs round the pans. It's not very funny if something goes wrong at this juncture, because the water in the potato pan is boiling, and when it spills it not only scalds the cook, but also puts the primus flame out so that in no time the whole cabin is filled with noxious paraffin fumes.

Dishing up is the real test of the cook's skill. The meal has to be served as well as cooked by the man on duty. To keep three plates steady, let alone three dishes of steaming hot food, calls for more than juggling expertise. It was Mike who produced one of the trump cards. He wetted a drying-up cloth and spread it on the table so that the plates stuck to its damp surface. It might seem to the fastidious that eating off a damp tablecloth is not pleasant. It's a damn sight nicer than eating off plates that have slid across the table, arrived at the fiddle with a whomp, and flung half their contents on to the settee. There is nothing so discouraging as to sit down to a delicious dinner, only to find that half of it has beaten you to the seat, so that you have a big proportion of your meal plastered on your behind. It is even less amusing when the plate remains quiet till the eater has sat down, then with a slither and a skid careers across the table and – splosho! Right into the lap of the diner.

The peak of gastronomical horrors is a tin of peaches running amuck. One day someone was rash enough to open such a tin before the meal began, instead of waiting till the peaches were immediately required. The results defy description. It was one of those days when the rolling was not too bad. No one noticed the creeping horror that was among us. First the boat rolled one way, and a driblet of juice escaped over one side of the tin. Then the roll corrected to go over the other way, and the opposite side of the tin started its dribble. As each roll followed, so the trickles down the two sides of the tin were fed with more and more juice. It so happens that the juice which surrounds the peaches, as they nestle inside their tin, is one of the ultimate achievements of mankind. Nowhere will you find a more sticky, more oozy substance. Also it is translucent, and nearly invisible. The damage which that one tin of peaches did went beyond the bounds of imagination. Days afterwards we found stickiness on charts and books, the backs of lockers would have an unexplainable tackiness, and socks would ooze a nauseous goo. Some of the errant fluid got on the settee, so that it was sat on, and this transferred the stickiness to the deck, the cockpit, the cabin top; if we had gone bathing and found the outside bottom of the ship tacky, it would not have surprised us. All this would be unpleasant enough in a house, where there is running hot water so that such a mess can fairly easily be cleared up. But on a boat there is very little water except the eternal salt stuff. And to wash anything in salt water is not successful unless hot water is used, with detergent. Using cold salt water just leaves a sticky mess – which is where we came in. Fortunately we had bought a 5-gallon drum of detergent, so there was plenty of it. But we would heat up some salt water, add the detergent, wipe up all the contaminated areas, throw away the water, and promptly discover more zones of stickiness. In spite of this, tinned peaches were extremely popular, in fact it is a universal law that an ocean cruiser does about 200 miles per tin of fruit.

Another popular thing was the nightly brew-up. We made our jar of rum stretch a very long way, taking a tot almost every night across the Atlantic. We eked it out by having it in hot water with sugar – to keep out the cold, you understand. The whisky we tended to keep for special occasions; but as there were twelve bottles, we sometimes decided that we had travelled, say, a third of the total distance to Vancouver, and had not used up one third of the dozen. So the cork would come out in the evening, under the swinging cabin lamp, as we sprawled round the table with a deck of cards laid out, and a mixed array of drinking vessels would each take its ration. It was in the drinking of whisky that we found one of the serious differences between our three nationalities. Mike and I favoured a glass or two, and then we would have put the bottle away for the next occasion. But Bjarne did not like to put the cork back once it was drawn. He reckoned that the right procedure was to finish the bottle at a sitting.

So the time came when we had to consider the nervy business of a landfall. The target was Barbados, only 30-odd miles long. The vast sea, nearly 3,000 miles across, made it easy enough to miss the island altogether. We were dependent on so many things. If our sextants had been inaccurate we might be getting poor sights. We guarded against this by using more than one sextant. Admittedly mine only cost £5, but it worked well enough. We were fairly sure that our chronometer was right, as we could check it by radio. We had reason to trust our calculations, as Mike had been taught how to do them and I learned them from a textbook. Thus we had a double check on everything. Nevertheless ...

On the day we should sight land I reckoned, soon after lunch, that if we were ahead of our plotted position, and if the weather was very clear and I went to the masthead, I might just see land. Looking very nonchalant I ambled down into the cabin and rummaged in my gear till I found my binoculars. I hung them round my neck inside my shirt (to prevent them swinging about, of course, not that I cared if the others saw) and, without any hurry, climbed up to the gaff. A glance all round showed nothing in sight. Earlier that day we had seen the smoke of a steamer on the horizon, the first sign of humanity since the Canaries dropped astern. With the binoculars I minutely examined every section of the horizon. More than one yacht has got the first sight of her goal broad on the beam, having almost sailed past it. After some time aloft I came below and decided that the only way to drag the land up over the horizon was a proper display of nonchalance. We had been up through the previous night steering as a precautionary measure, so I went below and slept.

2 hours later when I woke there was land close aboard. The others had shown the right spirit in not making sounds of disgusting exuberance and wakening me. It looked a slightly disappointing island at first, but the wind was fine and we bowled towards it at great speed. Not 50 miles away a tiny yacht, the *Felicity Ann* sailed by Ann Davison, the only woman (at that time) to do a trans-Atlantic single-handed, was finding the wind too much. But the rugged *Maken*, massive compared with Ann's wee boat, was just getting into her stride. I used to complain that we needed force 6 to move us, and had to heave-to in

force 7. As darkness fell the wind eased, apparently, though it was probably just that we were getting into the lee of the island. The lights on the shore attracted us so that we stared and stared. Here we were, across, without so much as a rope yard broken (apart from a rotten sail twice rent in a moderate breeze). It was all very wonderful, slightly mystifying, and highly satisfying. We should have been thin, grizzled and haggard from privation and danger, according to all the popular stories. We ought to be down to eating hair cream and leather belts, instead of only one-third of the way through our supplies. At least we should have had a couple of hurricanes behind us, three broken masts and innumerable torn sails blown out. Someone's been misleading some people more than somewhat, we thought. In fact we had had a pleasant, unexciting sail under almost perfect conditions. It was a good deal safer than cruising in the over-crowded English Channel.

By ten that night we were creeping in towards the beach off Bridgetown, the capital of the island. There was no noise from the sea except the distant breaking of the waves on shore, and that was intermittent, muted, not an angry thundering. A motor boat passed fairly close and we tried to see where it was going to anchor. Our chart showed no definite light, nothing we could get an exact position from, before putting the anchor down. We moved slowly nearer and nearer the shore. At last we saw other boats anchored. They seemed to be dancing about a lot, and we realised that there was a lot of swell. In that respect we were truly toughened: it had to be blowing freshly before we noticed that there was any vice in the sea.

As soon as the other yachts were in sight in the darkness ahead, we dropped the anchor, twenty-nine days and some 8 hours after clearing Las Palmas. Not a record by any means, but not too slow either, especially considering that we hardly moved the first two days, and the third was slow enough. We were just clearing up on deck when a rowing boat was discerned with difficulty in the darkness. We had come in with our side lights showing, so whoever was in that boat could see us clearly. We were at once very suspicious. The men in the boat were talking together, but in quiet tones. Our last contact with human beings in rowing boats had cost us dear, and we were surly towards these strangers who behaved in what seemed an underhand fashion. They asked us where we had come from. It was obvious as soon as they opened their mouths that they were natives, but how were we to guess that they were connected with the immigration authorities? We treated them as if they were about to case the joint, then come back later and rob us. They got short answers to their leading questions, till at last they said that the doctor and customs officials would come out to us soon after dawn. Even then we were not satisfied. At every other harbour we had visited, the minions of officialdom always came out in a launch, and at least had proper navigation lights. Muttering darkly together we went below to have a big brew-up, a proper celebration, before turning in, at anchor for the first time within a month.

Chapter Nine

The laugh was on us, because the locals in the rowing boat had promised that the immigration officials would be out at 6.30 a.m. and this was one of the most suspicious things they could have said. In our experience it is more like 10.30 a.m. before any sense or action is obtainable from bureaucracy.

But sure enough, at that unnatural hour a smart white launch, brasswork gleaming, crew turned out like naval ratings, ranged alongside. The formalities were extremely brief and we were free to go ashore. What a prospect it looked! There was a pure white beach, real palm trees, not imported, stunted jobs looking depressed, but lively, swaying trees clearly in their natural surroundings. And cars. For some curious reason the sight of a car is the most stirring thing under these circumstances. People are too far away to see clearly, so perhaps it is because vehicles are moving, alive, full of suggestions of the comforts of civilisation, that they are watched with such delight.

We went ashore in clean clothes, shaved and looking strange to each other. Once on land we split up, as agreed, and I went to collect mail, then to a newspaper office to see if they would take a story. The *Barbados Advocate* accepted a description of our trip from me, and this was one of the very few occasions when any of us earned anything on the whole trip. We met hopefuls who planned to work their way round the world and we could not help pitying them; they were on a dreary, well-nigh impossible mission unless favoured by phenomenal luck. The truth is that the places where casual work can be picked up are not on the good ocean-cruising routes, for the most part. Those places which are, and they are few indeed, tend to be separated by such big gaps that it is necessary to spend very long periods at each stopping place. The trouble is that in many places there is a surplus of labour. Other places have rigid trade union regulations and immigration laws which militate against the ocean wanderer who wants to earn a living. But if I could have got a job, I would have been very tempted to stay at Barbados.

I early established a high local reputation as a naval architect. I was invited to lunch by a man who owned a small sailing dinghy; this boat lay on a mooring off the beach by his house. The boat would not sail well; she had too much weather helm, so that she tugged at the tiller and was no great pleasure to sail. Would I suggest a cure for this trouble?

'Let's go and look at the boat.'

'There are three of us, and the dinghy'll only hold two.'

'That doesn't matter. It's so warm we can swim out.'

'Is it worth taking the dinghy?'

'Yes. I can't see well without my glasses, so we can put them in it, and push it ahead of us as we swim.'

And so it was. The water was just perfect for swimming and the wind was just grand for sailing. The owner was right, his sailing dinghy had too much weather helm. The dagger-board (a steel plate which drops in a case in the centre of the boat, and makes it possible to sail to windward) was D-shaped, and I cured the weather helm by lifting the plate out and dropping it back the other way round. Thus are reputations made.

To us Barbados was a paradise. The climate helped. Kitty told me that there was only one fireplace on the whole island and that was built in the very early days of the settlers, before they discovered just how wonderful their island was. I see I've blurted out a remark about Kitty pretty soon. But it's astonishing how many paragraphs have been written already without a murmur about her, because it was Kitty who really made Barbados all that it was. I saw her the second day we were there, and at once determined to introduce myself very, very soon. This called for the same initiative that forged the search warrant, but much more subtlety. Oh, much more!

She turned out to be just as fine as she looked. And how wonderful she was to gaze on! She had golden hair, not an uninteresting, uniform gold, but a shot-through-with-dark-waves gold, a gold that was molten and rich and gleaming and ... and ... well, just superb. She was tanned evenly and richly, and she always dressed very simply in cotton clothes that were somehow exactly right. I never saw her in a coat or sweater or any of those stodgy clothes that girls have to conceal their loveliness with in chilly climates. I asked her: 'Do you even have a coat or a mackintosh?'

'Oh no. We just dodge between the raindrops.'

'This is a perfect place to live. It's so peaceful, too.'

'On the lee side of the island it's quiet. But on the east side, with the waves sweeping in after gathering strength and size right across the Atlantic, it's terrific. The sea pounds and thunders and the beach is steep because the surf's so strong.'

'Pity we can't go there to bathe.'

'We can. Dad'll lend us the car.'

Clearly the perfect girl, she was even equipped with sensible parents. We went that afternoon. It was just as she said. Every wave arrived on that windward beach with the might and sheer force of 3,000 miles of rolling across the uninterrupted Atlantic. To swim offshore was a fight. It was necessary to dive under each breaker to avoid being hurled back up the beach. This was in complete contrast to the Bridgetown side of the island, where the land formed a lee and bathing was lazy, languorous, luxurious. We tried it there by moonlight.

One of the first things we had done on arrival was to go to the bank to get cash. In Bridgetown there are Canadian banks and it was here that I first noticed a most pleasant thing about them. Behind the counters, the tellers are girls. Not ordinary girls, but fantabulous ones. I can only infer that the directors wisely select with enormous care, from the pick of the available talent, all the prettiest girls they can employ. I like to think of these men, wise and learned, and constantly engaged in abstruse and lengthy calculations and negotiations, taking a special day off each week to select replacements and recruits for new branches of their banks. I can see them putting aside long columns of figures in order to scan long legs, and it gives me pleasure to think that such a dreary business as banking is, in one country at least, made a lot more interesting by the intelligent policy of the directors. It was not just in Barbados that I noticed the superlative standards in the Canadian banks, but in other countries as well.

When we three breezed into the bank we were struck by the pleasant sight at once. There was a groan from one of us which sounded like: 'Just *look* at that blonde!'

'Which?'

'Don't be a fool. That one.'

'She's probably married. Engaged, at least.'

'We'll see!'

'We're supposed to be sailing on, in a week ...'

'A lot can happen in a week.'

'Be careful it doesn't!'

We learnt later she was engaged.

One evening I went to dinner with Kitty and her parents. When I arrived she was wearing shoes, but within minutes she kicked them off. 'I hope you don't mind. I go everywhere without shoes,' she said.

'Everywhere?'

'Nearly. I even drive without them. It's much easier.' And that evening, when we went out in the car, she did indeed drive most competently without shoes. We stopped for a stroll in the moonlight, and she told me: 'This is the old wishing well. It goes back to the early days of the settlers.'

'Have you wished?'

''m. Long ago.'

'Long ago?'

'When you first came.'

'Will it come true?'

'That depends. Now you wish.'

It was very late when I got back aboard.

There are a lot of flying fish round Barbados and that dinner with Kitty and her parents included them as a main course. The natives go out after these fish in boats which look ill-shaped and poorly built. They sail out from the island almost over the horizon and it seems slightly miraculous that they get back with their catch. The ballast in the boats is just stones and, to improve the sailing qualities of the boats, these stones are humped up to the windward side. This is fine provided there is not a sudden change of wind, or someone makes a mess of tacking. The boats go out every day, so that the fish are eaten within a few hours of being caught.

One day our dinghy disappeared in the night. I never liked that boat: it lacked character. To chafe through a new painter was pure spitefulness, and to take off in the middle of the night was downright underhand. If you don't believe that dinghies, and ships of all sizes, have character and personality you must miss half the meaning of every sentence in all books about the sea. It's part of the background, the firm conviction of everyone who sails, that there is just as much personality in every craft that swims as in the people who make up the crews.

The dinghy incident is a case in point. We woke in the morning and we were marooned aboard. It was against all the chances. There was the dinghy painter, new, quite strong enough, leading well clear of the bulwark, yet chafed clean through. Did one of the native fisherman cut the rope, then pick the dinghy up later and claim salvage money? Perhaps, yet there was no evidence that this sort of thing happened regularly. No, I think it was just the contrariness of the dinghy, and I back this statement with the simple fact that she did exactly the same thing again, a month later. Again it was a new painter, again I would have passed the painter and the method of tying it as more than adequate (and it was not I that did the job, so this is not an excuse).

On this occasion we got ashore without having to swim for it, though this would have been no hardship as the water invited bathing at all hours of the day and night, and it was apparently quite safe. We went at once to the local police station and later, when we called a second time, they had news of our boat. While we were waiting in the 'cop-shop', a detective brought in a thief. Both parties thought the whole matter of arrest and statement-taking a huge joke, and certainly to us, the spectators, it was the nearest thing to comic opera in real life. The utter lack of formality or hostility was at once so cheerful and so naïve that we had to find out what it was all about. There was no hesitation in explaining the whole story. Lying in Bridgetown inner harbour was the big diesel motor yacht *Marsaltese III*, at that time owned by David Brown, the industrial magnate who rejuvenated and successfully raced Aston Martin cars. The thief had stolen some tools from the yacht. By a coincidence, several years later I had the job of finding a buyer for the *Marsaltese III*; I read through the inventory to see if there was a full set of tools aboard, and there wasn't.

Barbados was a true paradise, even to the many temptations. Having agreed to crew the *Maken* to Vancouver, I now found myself with two wonderful offers to change ships. Some years before this I had known a yacht called *Ling* at Poole. Here she was again, lying near us off Bridgetown, having been sailed out by her English owner and a Turk. The Turk had left and the owner did not feel inclined to go on alone, since his yacht was not light, and had a mainsail that took some handling. I was offered the berth and it was hard to resist the chance to sail on another yacht, to learn her whims and ways. She would have been a pleasanter yacht to handle than the *Maken* except in hard weather, by all appearances. Also she had a gadget I longed to play with. On her port crosstree a large two-bladed propeller whirled away whenever there was enough wind. This generated electricity and it seemed to be the finest toy in the world, because there was in those latitudes always enough wind to set that prop humming round at a great rate.

Not far away was another yacht built of steel in Holland. She had her masts in tabernacles and was a fairly typical Dutch ketch, with rather low freeboard.

Again she was a complete contrast to the *Maken*, and she was due to start back for Europe fairly soon. The owner and his wife had come out with a third hand, but he had left, so a replacement was needed. I still wanted to get to Vancouver, but we discussed sailing north to Bermuda, then turning west to the American shore, where I could have landed and then hitch-hiked across the American continent to Vancouver. This would have been quicker than going round by sea in the *Maken* and I would have made Vancouver by spring, whereas in the *Maken* we were already behind schedule. It's true it is illegal to hitch-hike in some forty-five of the fifty states of America, but a year later I found a way round that law and hitched from the northern border to the southern one, and then diagonally right across the continent.

In the end I put behind me these tempting chances to try out new craft, and we set off again in the *Maken*. The last outing with Kitty was to a sugar factory. Growing and processing sugar is by a long way the main industry on the island, and it is an economic process which the Almighty has worked out with singular cunning. The sugar cane is crushed and ground by steam-driven machinery. This machinery needs a given quantity of crushed cane burnt to process a ton of sugar. And the amount of cane that has to be crushed to produce that ton of sugar leaves enough husks to provide steam to process just 1 ton of sugar. So there is no need to bring in additional fuel to make the machinery work, nor is there any cane husk left over. And to cap this happy state of balance, the sugar is used to make the finest rum, the very finest, as my palate confirms.

It was a miserable day when we left Barbados. True, the sun still shone with the same brightness, the sea still sparkled gay and blue, flecked with silver and gold. But my heart stayed ashore and as we sailed away I stood looking, looking at the little island paradise sinking over the horizon. I was so sad that it was not until we had covered a good distance that I realised the others were solemn, too. So the *Maken* sailed on towards Curaçao, the crew all dismembered, as they had all left their hearts behind.

Our next port of call was to be the Dutch colony island which lies north of Venezuela. The reason for this next stop was simply to fill our fuel tanks. Curaçao is a big refining centre, so fuel is cheap. The crude oil is brought by small tankers from Venezuela and unloaded on the island, refined, and shipped all over the world. Politics in South America is an incendiary game, and so perhaps it does not mix with the inflammable pastime of petrol refining, and hence the need to ship the crude oil to the more staid Dutch colony.

The island was in sight soon after dawn a few days later, but it was well on in the morning before we were approaching Willemstad. This is the sort of harbour that occurs in novels but not in real life. The entrance is so narrow that, as big ships sail in, spectators on the shore have to crane their necks to look up at the decks of the ship. It is no exaggeration to say that a man standing admidships on a ship could throw two cricket balls ashore, one to port, one to starboard. Into this tiny entrance really big ships steam. Once inside there is plenty of room, the harbour widening out into acres of deep water. We were told by a pilot that the inner part of the harbour is a sunken volcano, or set of craters, and the job of getting a big ship in is so nerve racking that pilots tend to crack up in the first few months of working here. If they survive eighteen months piloting, and *turning* ships in these confined waters, they have no further worries, and remain immune from mental disturbances.

We had a good wind to help us, and we approached without the engine, a brave decision by Mike. As the land closed in round us we were sheltered from the fine westerly Trade Winds, and the boat slowed down. She still had steerage way, which was as well, since we had to slip over to one side of the channel to let a tanker in, then another out. Ahead we saw the bridge open for these two tankers.

This bridge crosses the narrow neck of water. It consists of a row of boats or pontoons over which the roadway runs. These boats are tethered together in a subtle way, so that when a ship wants to pass through the entrance, the whole bridge swings as if hinged at one end. We were now going quite slowly, the sails occasionally fluttering as the wind came and went in puffs and lulls. The bridge started to close, pushed by a little motorboat. We tried to speed up, but there was little we could do. The men in the launch did not see us, and our shouts were not heard above the roar of the launch's engine. Mike steered right over to the starboard bank, so that we would still be able to get into the harbour when the bridge was almost shut. If only we could have pressed a switch and started the engine! But the engine needed its full 20 minutes and more before it would burst into life. So we fiddled with the sails and crept in closer and closer to the starboard shore. At the last moment, when the great swinging gate-bridge was about to slam in our faces, the launchmen saw the *Maken* and stopped their boat. Even then the momentum of the roadway on its pontoons was enough to keep it moving relentlessly towards us. Worse still, we were now so close to the shore that we hardly felt the breeze. There was little enough we could do. Our boat would not respond much to those little tricks which work so well on racing machines.

We got in, but for some minutes there were dry mouths and pumping hearts aboard, because it could so easily have been a bashing match between us and the bridge. And on these occasions the ocean wanderer always remembers that harbour authorities have the law and the power and the upper hand in every way. So it behoves the crew of a cruiser to avoid collisions with authorities and their property.

There was a quay to starboard and we sailed up to it and took lines ashore. We intended to visit the harbour master to find the best place to tie up. No sooner were we alongside than a pair of typical American tourists came to gaze at us. 'Say, Mamie, jus' look at this cute li'l boat!'

'Why, Hiram, isn't she jus' sweet!'

'Say, boys, where've you come from?'

'Norway. Two of us joined the boat in England.'

'Well I do say. Mamie, d'you hear that? All the way from Eu-rope in that li'l boat!'

One of us: 'Do you know where the Harbour Master's office is?'

'Well, no. We're jus' tourists here.' (Bless you, we could tell that easily enough, by the uniform of multiple photographic paraphernalia, blinding bright clothes and crazy hats.)

'Jus' you try up thar. Some sort of Dutch office; this is a Dutch island, y'know?'

One of us: 'Thank you, we'll try there.'

'Say, you boys here for long?'

'Just while we get fuel aboard, and water. Maybe two or three days.'

'Would you care to come to lunch with us today?' The all-enveloping American hospitality burst out thus early.

We had been living on tinned food, and were not vastly enamoured of our own cooking after all these weeks.

'We'd like that very much. But we've got to find out where we can leave the boat, get her properly moored up, get cleaned up and shaved, and so on.'

'That's all right. Jus' you carry on! We'll meet you at the Sea Club. Bes' eating place on the island.' And so they departed, leaving us to rush through the business of getting ready for shore-going.

We had no idea which way to go to the Sea Club, but once ashore we hitch-hiked with success until we arrived at a pleasant shoreside building with a big veranda, bigger restaurant, and ample bars. Our hosts wanted to know all about the voyage and we found it peculiarly hard to describe. I think they took this for European reticence, but it was honestly a sort of mental tongue-tiedness, a reluctance to tempt the Gods with so much of the way still to go.

When we sat down to lunch we found that the menu was in Dutch. None of us understood more than a few odd words of it.

'You can always trust the chef's special … Bes' eatin' house on the island!' So we settled for the chef's special.

It is necessary to explain about the food on the *Maken*. Much of it was bought wholesale in Norway. As a result some of the tins, notably of wieners and margarine, were enormous containers. The wieners (or Vienna sausages) were in tins about 9 inches in diameter and 15 inches high. These wieners, which are nothing more than a good sausage ruined with sour spices, wrapped in a casing of tough skin, were packed in a thin, watery juice with lumps of yellow grease floating in it. If this sounds unappetising, consider what it must have been like in the sweltering heat! However, we were not in a position to be fussy. Nor could we waste a morsel, travelling as we were on such limited budgets, and with such long hops between harbours. There was no nonsense such as feeding the seagulls with scraps. There were precious few scraps after any meal. So when we opened one of these gargantuan tins of wieners we had to eat our way through them before they went bad. This meant wieners for breakfast, lunch, tea, dinner, late night snack, breakfast again, lunch again, and so on till the tin was at last, *deo gratis*, empty. In short we ate wieners from necessity, not from choice. We tried them boiled, fried, roasted, toasted, nearly raw, nearly burnt, peppered, salted, with vinegar, with curry, with potatoes, in a pie, in a casserole, in a hotpot; always they tasted just the same – sour, sad, and sodden.

You will have guessed the end of this story. For of course, when the 'chef's special' arrived, it was wieners. Fortunately the rest of the meal was wonderful and we almost enjoyed the chef's special, since it was a new approach to the old enemy, one we had not thought of. It was heavenly to be eating in civilised surroundings again, without the restless heave and lurch, creak and rattle of gear, which was part of every meal at sea. Half the fun of deepsea sailing is when it stops. The other half is when it starts again.

After lunch our hosts wanted to know if we had any friends on the island. We hadn't, so he insisted on introducing us to three stenographers from some American concern that had offices and works on the island. No doubt they were pretty and intelligent girls, but they were under an overwhelming disadvantage; they didn't come within a million miles of Kitty. Vivacious, gracious Kitty with the honey hair and lovely smile, I kept comparing you in every way to these lasses. Mike and Bjarne were labouring under a similar disappointment, for when we got back aboard that night they said:

'Pleasant enough, but very far from Barbados.'

'Not the same kind of girl. The only thing they have in common is that they wear skirts.' Perhaps distance lent enchantment, perhaps it was just that we reached Barbados after twenty-nine days at sea, whereas we got to Curaçao after only three.

Next day we had a rendezvous with these three at the bathing beach. The impression may have percolated through these pages that Barbados was pretty damn near perfect. It was the bathing beach of Curaçao that just about proved the point. In Barbados we bathed wherever we pleased, and it was all quite safe. Here we had to bathe inside a wire net fence, since there were sharks and other malicious fish in the area.

A little bay was cordoned off with big posts driven into the sea bed, and fixed to these posts from well above the high tide level down to the sea bed was wire netting. The water was beautifully warm and there were many people there, including little toddlers so young that they could scarcely walk. These nippers were fitted with life jackets, just pieces of cork sewn into canvas belts, and they were swimming far out of their depth with complete confidence. Rocks overhung the water at one point so that is was possible to dive in and plunge deep down. This was fascinating, as it was possible without effort to get to the sea bed and meet the little fish which were small enough to swim through the mesh in the wire. I was surprised how tame they were. This was in the days before skin-diving, aqualungs, snorkels and all that sort of paraphernalia were for sale in every seaside store. Like most people I had assumed that on the approach of a human being all fish whiffled off for the nearest horizon and kept going till after dark. These wee fishes had obviously never heard about the horrid habits of humans, such as eating poor harmless fishes. It was possible with care, to touch them. They were positively friendly.

It was quiet and peaceful down in the depths. I went languidly round the boundary fence, coming up for air frequently, then down again to explore the limits of safe territory. Without warning I came across the most enormous hole in the wire. There is on record the reputed fastest time for swimming 50 yards. This so-called record occurred with a battery of timekeepers at some international baths, with a vast crowd of spectators. Alas, that record-holder lives in a dream-world, believing that no one has ever swum as fast as he, no one in the whole wide world. I have news for him. That fine, sunny afternoon I made his record look like the aquatic amblings of a senile sea-tortoise. Up the beach I went at record velocity, smashing the running record, too.

'There's a ruddy great hole in that wire. Big enough for the grandfather of all sharks to swim through.'

'We know.'

'You know? You know?'

'Yes. There's more than one hole. Been there for ages.'

'What about the sharks?'

'They're not as bad as barracuda.'

'The holes are big enough for *shoals* of barracuda to swim through at one time!'

'They never do. The wire seems to keep them off.'

So I went back to the water; not, I must admit, wholly convinced. When we got to Panama we heard the story, apparently true, which was told to all the American troops when they were first posted to the Canal Zone. It goes like this. A soldier went down to the beach to bathe in spite of express orders not to do so. He waded into shallow water and a barracuda came and bit his foot off. He put his hand down to feel the damage, saying 'Ouch' (or something), and the barracuda, or its mate, came and took his hand off. Certainly in this part of the world the shark seems less feared by far than the barracuda. This fish is said to attack particularly in shallow, disturbed water. Men rowing have reported having oar blades bitten off. The barracuda has teeth that are real killers, rows of them, frightening just to look at.

One afternoon, wandering back to the ship alone, before dark, I came across a dry dock, tucked away in a corner of the harbour. The mental magnet in my cranium swung round with great promptness, as it always does when there is a ship or boat within a dozen miles. Here was indeed a special ship, lying in the dry dock. She was a freighter, yet she was slim and curvaceous, more like a yacht or warship than the usual bluff-ended vessel which is favoured for cargo work. Also she had twin screws, another fairly rare thing for a small freighter. The more I studied her, the more I liked her. Yet she did not fit in, somehow. She was under the Venezuelan flag and she was a real honey. I stood just gazing and delighting at that softly rounded shape, admiring and approving, and getting very curious. This was something I had to know more about, so I walked across the gang plank, to look for the skipper and talk about his ship. After climbing a ladder or two I reached what I took to be the captain's cabin. I knocked at the door and, as I did so, it occurred to me that in all the fiction about the sea the skipper of a South American tramp ship always wore mauve silk pyjamas, had black, greasy hair, and a great big paunch. Someone answered my knock, I opened the door, and there was the skipper, perfect down to the last detail. He wore mauve silk pyjamas, had black hair that was indeed greasy and curly, and his paunch was thoroughly noticeable.

However, he was charming in every way, not the villain he would surely have been in fiction. He invited me to lunch, which was a success in spite of the fact that we had so little language in common. Later I saw over his ship, and what stand out in my mind are the pin-ups in the crew's cabins. These little cubicles were off a passage, and as we walked down it several of the doors were open. I saw that each cabin had two bunks, a wardrobe and a complement of pin-ups the like of which I have never before or since beheld. In all my working years, and before that too, I've been in and out of hundreds of shipyards and boatyards. They all have this in common: each shed and shop has its own little group of pin-ups, and each department vies with other departments to have the best display, the finest gallery. As the shipwrights get hold of one or two special super-hot plates from a magazine, so the riggers are stimulated to add lustre to their collection, and they obtain some remarkable specimens from some of the newspapers which cater for this art-form. This in turn rouses the departmental pride of the joiners, who are not to be outdone by mere shipwrights, let alone riggers. So you see, I have beheld a wide and varied selection of pin-ups. Like all art, pin-up collecting knows no frontiers, and the choice in Cherbourg is rivalled by the selections to be seen in Dumbarton, which in turn are matched by the galleries to be seen in Long Beach, which are on a par with those in Lunenburg, and so on. Very well, then; having established my credentials, I say – with full realisation of the import of such a statement – that the pin-ups on that South American ship topped all collections I have ever seen. Later, when I broke into a US army camp, I was able to view the art galleries therein. I can only report that the North Americans, in my experience, cannot match the South Americans in this matter.

There was another feature of Willemstad that we liked – the floating market. One of the quays is a main road. All along this quay, bow into the wall, rows of sailing ships, small traders, are moored. They sell fruit and vegetables which they have brought over from the fertile mainland to the south. The island of Curaçao is very heavily populated and this influx of food is very important and very picturesque. The goods are sold straight off the deck so that stevedoring and middlemen are neatly circumvented.

Curaçao was a bit disappointing after Barbados. But then how could it match up? Heaven has no equal, nor peer. This Dutch island was certainly interesting, with its mixed inhabitants, some native, some Dutch, some tourist, some permanent, many in transit. The whole population appeared to speak Dutch, English and a local dialect of the most extraordinary complexity. We gained the impression that here prices were permanently high, whereas in Barbados they had price tickets for normal times, and tickets with much higher prices on for when the cruise ships came to anchor off Bridgetown.

Once we had our fuel aboard we were ready to push on. We left the harbour of Willemstad one afternoon and motored round to the bathing beach, to anchor for the night. It was a bit nerve-racking being anchored outside a haven, yet so close to the rocky shore; but we were on the lee side of the island and it was a quiet time. Next day we left for the last sea passage before we got into the Pacific. With all plain sail set, we rolled and dipped and pitched our way towards Colon, the Caribbean port of the Panama Canal.

It was one of those uneventful trips, the type of sail which typifies a good ocean cruise going well. No panics, no flaps, no breakages marred the easy passage of the days and nights. We were once more working all round the clock, steering night and day. The tyranny of the tiller was back with us. I didn't blame Bjarne for wanting to leave the ship. If I had not been completely determined to get to Vancouver at all costs, I might well have tried to find a substitute to take my place aboard the *Maken* to help Mike sail her the rest of the way. I knew that we should meet other ocean wanderers at Panama and I was thirsty for experience aboard more exciting, faster, less stolid yachts.

Bjarne had decided definitely to leave the *Maken* at Panama, though he had not made firm plans as how he was going to proceed from there on. He had no goal, and Vancouver was not any different from Vladivostock as far as he was concerned. He just wanted to sail and to write about it. Indeed, Vancouver was, for him, an unsatisfactory place to go to, since it meant long weeks at sea, on a great sweeping passage out of sight of land for months on end. This was not going to provide material for him to write about. So from his point of view it was common sense to leave at Panama, and try to get aboard a boat making fairly frequent stops. For Mike and me the problem was to get someone to take Bjarne's place. Three of us had found the *Maken* hard work in temperate climates when the wind was unkind. Two of us might not be able to cope in times of crisis.

So when Bjarne decided to leave we were a sombre crew, each chewing over in his mind the problems newly arisen. For relaxation I took to designing boats for sailing in the Arctic. The sun, day after day, hot and sometimes too hot, had satiated my appetite for warmth. I dreamed of sailing among fjords and along rocky coasts with Northern Lights as a backdrop, just as hungry men dream of great meals.

We arrived at Colon at night, going rather too fast, with the wind on our tail. We shot through the entrance and rounded up to look for a place to park for the rest of the night. The harbour seemed enormous, endless, an unfriendly place for a yacht. We sailed to port to look for a mooring berth; we sailed to starboard. We found great freighters anchored, but in water so deep that our anchor would have scarcely have reached the bottom, let alone held us fast. At long last a US Coastguard launch turned up to see what was going on and to find out who we were. They shouted at us, but our replies were drowned by the noise of their unsilenced engines. A futile situation developed, with us bellowing, them yelling, both parties shrieking in concert. It was no good. Eventually they went away and we hove-to till daylight, then anchored near the harbour mouth, but to one side so that if anyone came in we should not be run over.

Far too early in the morning, another launch turned up with the customs and immigration authorities aboard. We were just finishing breakfast and someone had started to shave. Someone else was trying to remember how to wash and had the necessary equipment spread out in the fore cabin. It was all a trifle untidy *before* the doctor, his assistant, three men from the US customs, a launchman or two (or maybe it was three), all came aboard and down into the cabin. The chaos was then rife. Forms were produced and they promptly got marmaladey. So the form-fillers went into the fore cabin and settled down with Mike. The boat was still in an open roadstead, so she rolled and water slopped out of the basin. Soapy water joined the marmalade on the forms. The doctor decided that we must be injected, and he added his gear to the paraphernalia on the table and on the galley bench. It was a cheerful mess. To add to their confusion, I decided that if we were injected we would have stiff arms and feel poorly, so I thought I would rather produce my certificates of inoculation; as these forms were at the bottom of one of my kitbags, more gear was thrown out when I burrowed down to get the papers. Then we remembered that success in many foreign lands depends first on pouring libations to the gods, and that these gods live in the tummies of the immigration and customs officials. So out came a bottle or two and glasses, mugs and so on. Two lots of officials were asking two sets of questions. Mike was answering questions about the ship, and his questioner was filling in a form the size of a newspaper, while Bjarne answered questions about his antecedents and intentions. There was so much confusion that we nearly forgot to ask where we should go, to leave the yacht for a day or two while we made arrangements to go through the canal. We were directed, at last, to the local yacht club.

Chapter Ten

The *Maken*'s engine disturbed some pelicans as we thumped through the backwater to the yacht club. These birds are most curiously designed, as if the Almighty decided, when planning them, to make a flying clown. When airborne, they lollop along so slowly that they give the impression they are staying up only by a miracle. Their landing is so clumsy that the first few times I saw it I thought the birds were injured or diseased. In fact, pelicans just don't seem to have a natural element: they look sad whatever they're doing.

The presence of these poor performers may have influenced us as we came alongside the jetty, and we made a mess of it. Instead of arriving at a stately glide, coming to a standstill just 2 inches from the piling, we gave it a firm nudge and made our fenders flatten. This of course was no worry to the *Maken*; indeed when describing her in letters I used to write that, if we ever hit a quay wall, the wall would come off worst. But this anecdote is mentioned because there is an impression, put out with wonderful aplomb and subtlety by some of the long-range cruising group, that such persons are superb sailors who never make a mistake. This is quite inaccurate and, in fact, it is the inshore sailing men who are often the best at yacht-handling. For there is no getting away from the principle that practice makes perfect, and on long-range cruises there are relatively few occasions when coming alongside and similar manoeuvres are practised.

We soon had the boat tied up, and hurried ashore for mail from the British consulate, our regular collecting centre. It was properly hot in Colon. Up to now we had seldom felt that oven-blast of enervating heat, the sort of temperature that takes away all desire to work or walk. But here the blinding sun soon made the decks too hot to touch.

Back on board later, I went aloft to grease the blocks on the mizzen mast. These blocks did not have the modern patent sheaves (pulleys, to a landsman) with roller bearings. Instead the sheaves ran on steel pins, and so rust was our constant enemy. Every time we were in harbour for a few days after a long passage at sea we had to grease all the blocks. It was a great waste of time, but it did ensure that we examined all the gear aloft at regular intervals.

Swinging aloft in the sweltering heat, my face was soon wet with sweat. I looked down to shout something to Mike and my glasses, slipping in the sweat, fell off and crashed to the deck. At home this would have been nothing. Out there, with money so very short, it was a tragedy. My spare pair of glasses was now my main pair, and I went about with a constantly worried feeling, like a nagging mental toothache. In the end I got a new pair of glasses from a Japanese oculiste (which is presumably the correct spelling for a female oculist).

One evening at a dance at the YMCA I met a young American soldier. We fell into conversation and found that we had something in common – impecuniosity. Between us we could raise the price of four drinks and, when all our change was spent, he said: 'I'll have to rush off now. Being broke, I'll have to get back to camp; I can't pay for a bed here in town.'

'But it's early, yet.'

'And it's a long way back to camp.'

'You can sleep in one of our spare bunks.'

So we stayed till the end of the dance, and that night Pete had the spare bunk in our fore cabin. At breakfast next morning I asked Pete what he was going to do all day. 'You don't work on Sundays, in the army?'

'No, I'll just go back to camp; plenty to do there. Why not come and see it?'

'Are visitors allowed? I'm not even an American citizen.'

'Doesn't matter. We can easily smuggle you in.'

'How?'

'You just walk in with me. You're dressed like any soldier at the weekend, in that cotton shirt and those lightweight trousers.'

'What about passes? And won't the guards realise they've not seen me before?'

'No. There's over 2,000 men in camp, and a lot only arrived a few days ago. You don't need a pass to get in, and we'll get you out easy enough.'

The camp was across a neck of the sea. With studied unconcern we walked down to the ferry. This was an army craft, with guards on the ramp, and it was solely for people going to the camp. I kept my mouth shut, knowing my accent would give me away in a trice. The guards hardly glanced at us as we ambled aboard and went into a quiet corner. When the ferry arrived at the far side of the water, there was another guard to pass, at the camp entrance; again we sauntered past, with a group of other men.

Once inside, there was nothing to worry about. Pete took me up to his barracks. This was a wonderfully spacious, airy and well-designed building. There were dozens of men about who knew Pete, and I was introduced all round. They wanted to hear about the *Maken* and I wanted to hear about life in the US Army. We yarned for some time, then I was shown round the camp. We carefully avoided officers and NCOs but there seemed to be very few signs of authority about. There was a big green where we practised golf, then I was taken to inspect the fast launches kept permanently afloat in a very fine boathouse. These launches were used for emergencies and were beautifully kept. In fact the whole camp was in superb condition. It was new, well-built, with every sort of amenity. But of course the soldiery had plenty of moans, as they have the world over.

I went with them to lunch. This was a bit worrying, as we had to pass several NCOs, and they knew many of the men, if not quite all of them in the camp. However, by keeping quiet and doing as everyone else did, I had no trouble. What a meal that was! It was just an ordinary Sunday dinner for the men, but the standard of cooking, the choice, the vast helpings with seconds for anyone who wanted it, rivalled a great many good restaurants I've tried. There was turkey and cranberry sauce as the main course, with a choice of vegetables, all the usual etceteras like gravy and stuffing, and as much as even an ocean-cruising man who's lived for weeks on tinned wieners could eat. There was a choice of sweets as well as iced coffee and iced tea to drink.

Pete thought I would give myself away, I was so delighted with all this plenty and luxury. He and his platoon did not think it was so very wonderful, so I told them a few hard facts. In the afternoon there was a free cinema show, which suited our finances well. We came out just in time for a tea which matched up to the lunch. Then there was a dance, again all laid on and with no gate. I've heard of people deserting from armies, but I began to wonder if it was not possible to reverse the process.

All good things come to an end and about midnight it was time for me to ease out of the camp. This was simply effected. To make the dance possible a goodly selection of American girls from Colon had come over to the camp by special arrangement. Naturally these lasses had to be escorted back home. Pete introduced me to Marilyn, during the dance, and after the party was over she and I wandered down to the ferry arm in arm, just like dozens of other couples. There was no reason why the guard at the gate or on the ferry slipway should single us out from the others, and it was conveniently dark. It was just as easy as it's made in all the best spy stories.

Bjarne was trying to make arrangements to leave the *Maken*. There was another ocean cruiser in by this time, and a fourth came in later. Neither of them was going back eastwards, and the Pacific is so vast that either would have taken too long to cross it, as far as Bjarne was concerned. So for a spell he tried to get a job ashore. However, only Americans could get jobs in Panama, and even those opportunities were few and far between. The big opening for ocean voyagers trying to raise cash was the Panamanian fire brigade. We were told that the locals were such an incendiary lot that they were more likely to start fires than put them out. It is apparently something to do with their politics, which involve revolts and insurrections to the accompaniment of fires and the overturning of vehicles.

The crew of one of the other ocean cruisers split up within a few days of arrival. This bunch had only come from one of the American harbours west of Florida, and Panama was their second stop. Their boat was well equipped and in many ways better suited to far-distance cruising than the *Maken*, but the crew did not realise that the first essential to making a cruise over a long period was a determination to get on with each other. One of the most insidious mental germs found on an ocean cruiser is the feeling that someone is not pulling his weight. It is very easy to get angry, living cooped up in a wooden box only 40 feet long and 12 feet wide, without enough space to stand upright. Add to this the infuriating habit of this box of not remaining still even for a blessed second. Most prisoners live in vastly more comfortable conditions. To get angry in this shaken, humid, cramped, sometimes smelly box is downright dangerous.

Anger so easily grows out of all proportions. It is so fatally easy to be quite sure that you are doing far more than your share of the work. Why, you've washed the dishes three times in the last 30 hours! And that bastard so-and-so was late taking over the watch, then he called you up to reef, the windy idiot, when a blind aunt could have seen the squall wouldn't come to anything. Then he ate what was left over of the tinned peaches, so you got no second helping. And how is it that his oilskin isn't torn when everyone else's has at least two rents by now? I bet he pinches someone else's, when he goes on watch at night. (It's those flaps in the middle of the night, the hurried tying of a reef while the wind whines up the octaves in the rigging, that causes torn oilskins ...) And so on and on and on. The difficulty is that there are the long night watches, alone with nothing to do, no one to talk to, just the furious thoughts tumbling round and round in the head. That's when the blistering hate boils up; that's when crew break-ups are germinated. And the greatest cause of these splits is the feeling that someone is not doing as much work as he should be doing. The only safe course is to make sure you are doing twice, no, three times as much work as you feel is your share. And keep on doing three times your share. That way, most of the time you are too busy to worry how much anyone else is doing.

It was sad to see this other crew divided, and sadder still that Bjarne was leaving us. One of the big assets of the *Maken*'s crew was a well-established *sang-froid*. We had gone through two gales and all sorts of excitements, not heretofore mentioned because they were of the conventional type, and very rarely had anyone raised his voice or rushed about in an unseemly fashion. What used to happen, when things got bad and the wind really howled a high shriek through the rigging, was something like this: the man on watch would either heave-to or get the boat to sail herself; he'd go below and wake the rest of the crew.

'Better get oilies on; it's blowing up.'

'Was'at?'

'Bit windsome on deck, chum.'

'Uh-huh. The old hearse is jumping about.'

'I'll put the primus on for a brew-up.'

'Seen my seaboots anywhere?'

'Under the table. ... I think we'll have to double reef.'

'Let's have a cigarette first.'

That was the key remark. Whatever the weather was doing, the other two always rolled and lit a cigarette apiece before dealing with the situation. By the time they had gathered together tobacco, paper, matches, performed the solemn ritual, and produced what they called 'Camels' (because these hand-rolled cigarettes had humps in the middle), there was plenty of time for thought. It's not pleasant to be woken up at 2 a.m. after doing the 8-to-12 watch, but the slow methodical manufacture of cigarettes, the long deep draw of smoke not just into the lungs but right down to the toes, all took time and gave the newly awakened ones a chance to get acclimatised. It also gave an opportunity to talk quietly about the noisy situation developing up on deck. By the time we climbed the steps to the deck we would be feeling a good deal less ghastly than in those horrid few seconds after the man on watch had woken us up.

On occasions like this Bjarne's deep voice muttering: 'Why in hell do we go yachting?' was a pleasant reminder of the funny side of the situation. He didn't say much as a rule; in all the months I knew him I never learnt much about his family, his job or his home; in fact the one thing we did talk about was the boats we had owned. And even here he was pretty reticent.

We tried hard enough to find a substitute for Bjarne, but it was a waste of time. Our next hop was likely to be well over two solid months at sea. Few people can face that sort of prospect with equanimity. It's fair to say that Americans least of all seek out and enjoy very long spells at sea, such as the run from Panama to Vancouver. And the vast majority of the people we met in Panama and the American-occupied land adjacent to the canal, known as the Canal Zone, were from the United States. To make our task all the more difficult, these men were either soldiers who could not get such a long leave, or civilians who were married and had families to consider.

There was one young tough who was keen to come with us. He was the sort of boy who spent his leisure in the jungle, shooting alligators and other fauna. He was a slight fellow, bronzed and lithe and very hardy indeed. He liked to sit in a tree all night and shoot the crocs by the light of a torch lashed to his rifle. It sounded rather fun, and we made plans to join him on one of these hunts. Then his sister heard that he intended to sail with us. These two were orphans and very close. The sister pleaded with her brother not to go. She turned her tear-filled eyes on Mike. The upshot of a heart-rending scene was that the brother said he wouldn't come with us. Worse still, the hunt was off.

Meanwhile Mike made arrangements for *Maken* to go through the canal. It cost us just over $7 (say £2.50). For this total sum we were provided with a skilled pilot for the whole day, taken up through gigantic locks which must have used many gallons of fuel just to open and shut, given help with our mooring warps, and generally looked after. As the charges are based on tonnage and our registered tonnage was tiny, we were lucky. There's a tale told of two ocean-cruising lads who arrived at the canal entrance. Frank went ashore to fix up the passage through the canal; Ben stayed aboard. Presently Frank came back and said: 'They won't take a cheque, Ben. We'll have to go round the Horn.' Which may not be true, but there are plenty of crews who would have done that.

When the morning came for us to go through the canal, the engine would not start. With most prime movers we would have known what to do. Like everyone born in the last forty years, all three of us have cleaned sparking plugs, cleaned filters, tested for spark, checked that the fuel tank was full, tested for compression, and generally gone through the standard gamut on dozens of occasions. But with our early Ark-age machinery, ordinary mechanics were no use. Some form of witch-doctoring might have been successful. We started in the conventional way and the lighting of the cooking stove and subsequent surge of life in the blowlamp were achieved without undue trouble. Then the setbacks flooded in. Down in the dark, dreary engine room we heated the engine top till it was damn near glowing. Mike swung the enormous flywheel while I tried to pump fuel into the cylinder. The heat in the engine room was so bad that we ran with perspiration, could hardly talk, and were weak with exhaustion within minutes. The engine gave off heat quite apart from the normal steaming atmosphere of the place. Working by torchlight seemed to make the effort and the stuffiness worse. Again and again we heated the top of the engine, each time raising the temperature in that tiny engine room. Never before have I seen anyone really running with sweat in the way Mike did that grim morning. His face became haggard in half an hour. We were due into the first lock at a definite time and here we were, still stuck alongside the pier as the minutes ticked away. There was no wind, so we could not sail to the lock. Anyway, sailing through the canal would not be practical even if it was allowed, which it most firmly is not. The Americans run the canal very well, as far as we could judge, with a reasonable tolerance towards the ocean-cruising fraternity, who are, after all, not always the most cooperative or straightforward characters.

We were already several weeks behind schedule, what with the robbery in the Canaries, the calms and gales we'd had, and trying to find a substitute for Bjarne. Now it looked as if we would miss at least another day. If only we could have swung the flywheel round and round, getting up momentum, the way one would with a small diesel engine! We might just as well have wished we could have slung the massive *Maken* over our shoulders and carried her across the Isthmus of Panama. That flywheel weighed about as much as the combined weight of the three crew.

At last, after repeating the starting ritual time and time again, the piston started its slow methodical dance up and down the cylinder. Once going, we knew that nothing would stop that steady heartbeat as long as the fuel lasted. We didn't have to stop the engine at all going through the canal. Even in the locks it kept hammering away. To make the boat start, stop and go astern we had a feathering propeller – one with blades that can be twisted. Twist them one way and the boat surges ahead; twist them the opposite way and she goes astern. Put them halfway between the full-ahead and the full-astern position, and the propeller rotates round and round but does not drive the boat forward or backwards. It was perfectly simple, with only one snag. The mechanism for twisting the blades was hand-operated. But naturally! And it was exceedingly hard work to shift. It was a wheel which had to be wound round, and this wheel was too small to give a good swing; working flat out, it took a long time to go from ahead to astern. So we would surge into a lock and then whoever was at the reversing wheel had to work like a mixture of mammoth and maniac to get the propeller working astern to stop us. Otherwise we would charge straight for the gates at the top of the lock, a most nerve-racking sensation.

Before we entered the first lock we had to lie alongside a quay wall. Large notices forbade crews of ships from landing, and soldiers patrolled to enforce this order. The crew of the *Maken* wanted to take photographs. The deck was too low, so it was necessary to climb up the rigging and jump ashore. Notices and soldiers notwithstanding, we got a big selection of photos, but the joke was on me. My camera had by this time succumbed to the damp heat and was so rusty that it gave poor photos.

The whole canal is a superb bit of engineering, and it is one of the sights which passengers on cruise ships are shown. While we were waiting in one of the locks, a sizeable party of these tourists appeared on the quay wall. There were enough cameras between them to start not just one shop, but a chain of photographic stores. There was nothing about worth snapping and when the *Maken* was observed she was hailed at once as something to photograph. They saw our Canadian Red Ensign flying and did not recognise it. Some loud-mouth said importantly: 'She's a Britisher,' the way a self-appointed spokesman always does on such occasions. Of course, this annoyed Mike.

'No, she's not. This is a Canadian ship.'

And so we fell into conversation with a bunch of tourists. Like so many we had met in the Caribbean, they were rather bored with the standard round, the stock routine, the well-worn sightseeing tours. In an aside to Mike I said: 'We ought to show them round the *Maken* and charge a quarter a head. It'd pay for our fresh vegetables for the next hop.'

This was not intended as a serious suggestion, but several people on the quay heard it. 'Say, that's a good idea! C'mon fellers – show us round your yacht!'

But their guide, sensing a mutiny brewing in the ranks of his mob, led them away to hear how many thousands of people died during the first attempt to cut the canal.

It took us all day to go through and even then we did not make the full length, but stopped on our way down the locks. We turned into a backwater where there were just a few yachts and boats and a small yacht club, and tied up alongside. The journey was almost uneventful. An iguana swam across the canal behind us, quite close, apparently not worried by the thump of our engine. It looked the essence of wickedness. Its very imperturbability seemed evil. Then, in one of the locks, going up, we had a lump of excitement flung at us unexpectedly. The gates were shut behind us, and we were as usual moored fore and aft to the quay wall on the port side. As the sluice gates on the uphill side of the lock are opened the water level naturally rises. That is the object of the exercise. As the water rises it is necessary to haul in on the warps, to keep the boat tightly alongside, otherwise she will wander all over the lock and damage herself. The water is let in at a rate which is nothing to a big ship, but to us it was dangerously fast; thousands of tons of water pouring through the sluice gates stirred up the lock, like a bath with all the taps running hard into it. The *Maken* came alive and tried to surge about, threatening to crash herself against the stone quay walls. I was tending the bow warp, which was round a bollard on the deck.

Now a bollard is a vertical steel post, and the rope led from it vertically upwards to the quay edge and on to another bollard on the lock side. The trouble was simply this: our warp had nothing to grip; it was just wrapped round a steel post which had nothing to prevent the rope pulling off the top. This is just what happened. Like a wild animal sensing her freedom, the *Maken* wrenched and slewed round. The rope bit and burned through my hands as I struggled to take a turn that would check the boat's movement. As is usual on these occasions, a lot of people did more shouting than the situation warranted.

'Take a turn. Take a turn!' they all bleated, as if I was standing watching the trouble grow, instead of sweating and struggling to take just one turn to stop the old tub. She really got the bit into her teeth and, as more and more water swirled into the lock, so she rose higher and higher, causing the warps to get slacker and slacker so that they had to be hauled in more and more. If some of the senseless shouters had taken a little useful action, such as shutting the sluice gates, at least a little, we might have had less of a fight. As it was we managed to check the old barge before she flung her great fat bulk against the stone walls.

We were inexperienced then. Now I realise that what we should have done was to take the bow warp through a fair-lead and aft to the windlass. Then, as the warps needed tightening in, all we would have had to do was wind on the windlass. Dead easy, when you know how.

Once out of the locks it was straight motoring through gorges and across lakes. The scenery was primeval, and anyone wanting to film prehistoric scenes might do worse than use this part of the world for background. Our pilot told us a lot about his job. In some situations, pilots have to give peculiar orders. For instance, going through a narrow gulch, a ship may get too near one bank. The thing to do then is to order the helm to be put towards the close shore. This builds up a cushion of water between ship and land, and edges her off. I've heard similar tales from other inland waterways. But here's the interesting point. Some helmsman do not obey the pilot, or hesitate, simply because he seems to be ordering them to run their ship into trouble.

Taking big warships through the canal is exciting. One pilot stands forward, another aft, and the senior one is up on the bridge. The banks are so close that if the senior pilot stands amidships he cannot see where water meets land on either side. So he goes over to one side, but then has to judge how much clearance there is on the other. Right down at the water's edge along the dangerous stretches there are red lights, and various leading lights mark certain sectors.

The place where we tied up that evening was quiet, apart from the little yacht club. This was a grand place, full of life and interest. Most of the members were servicemen or technicians connected with the running of the canal. One of the flag officers of the club was a senior NCO and in the American style he had batteries of stripes on his arm and ribbons on his chest. He seemed to me to be the complete antithesis of a warrior; he was just a pleasant, gregarious old fellow, very much in the American manner. We yarned about ocean cruising and he seemed extremely impressed with the voyage of the *Maken* up to now. I couldn't see anything special about the trip and he thought this, too, was vastly interesting.

'Gee! I've always heard you British were unasoomin! Now I c'n see it's really troo,' he said with a great beaming smile.

'You must come and look over the yacht. Anyone could go anywhere in her, given time.'

'I'd sure like that. Gee, it's the first time we've ever had real sailors in this club! Say, steward, I want you to see that this young man never has an empty glass. Mark it up to me.'

I did not take full note of this, and the significance was borne in on me next day. I was sitting alone in the club lounge, waiting for the others, carefully counting out the coins in my pocket. I decided that there were enough of them for one drink, which was more than a luxury in the sweltering heat.

'Devilled rum, please,' I said, and in no time that soul-strengthening liquor was glinting in a tall cool tumbler.

'How much?' I asked, as the steward made no move to collect payment.

'Nothing to you, sir. It's on the rear-commodore.'

'But he's not here! I must pay for this one.'

'No, Sirrr. It's on the rear-commodore. He said so.' And that seemed to settle the matter. When the rear-commodore is also a top sergeant, and old enough to be a grandfather, the combination is obviously powerful, and his word is law far beyond the range of his voice. I sat imbibing the liquid loveliness slowly, to make it stretch out, knowing to a cent how much money was left to see me through to Vancouver.

Deep in a yachting magazine, with the glass on a table beside me, I was completely absorbed, not taking the least note of what was going on around me. When I came to the end of the magazine article, I picked up the glass to drain the last precious drop. It was full! I was quite sure I had drunk nine-tenths of it. I vaguely remembered the steward wiping down the tables and emptying the ashtrays. I looked at the glass with delight; maybe I'd discovered a new Widow's Cruse? Three quarters of the way through the second glass I saw the steward coming towards me with the ingredients to make up a devilled rum.

'Thank you, no. I haven't paid for the first; you can't persuade me to have another.'

'Tha's right, sirrrr. The rear-commodore, he said that I was to see your glass was never empty.'

'Oh, yes, I remember that. But he didn't mean it literally.'

'He meant it, sirrrr. When the rear-commodore says something, why, it happens!'

This was a new and interesting situation. It seemed to me that there was no escape from a rather pleasant bondage. I was destined to remain trapped in the club till closing time, while an unending succession of devilled rums made life more than bearable. In some ways it was a typical ocean-cruising situation. One moment wondering if a drink, just one tiny drink, was justified out of the remaining cash resources; the next moment an infinity of drinks offering themselves, without even the effort of going to the bar to collect them. I drank the third devilled rum with calculated slowness; when the steward left the room for a moment, I swallowed the rest of the drink and left.

Chapter Eleven

We left that pleasant little haven next day, and chugged under power through the last bit of the canal and into the sea; the Pacific, at last. We got an inkling of what Magellan felt when he gazed for the first time on the long-sought-after ocean. Late at night we cautiously worked our way down to the yacht moorings off Balboa. These are really no moorings at all, just a moderately shallow place not well protected nor yet seriously exposed, but too far off shore, where passing yachts come to roost for a while, somewhat uneasily.

We saw that our neighbours were more than ordinarily interesting, when we came on deck next morning. There was *Beyond*, the lovely modern cutter owned by Tom Worth. She was on her way round the world, and I was shown over her. Only the most carping critic could find even minor faults on her. She was enough to make me wickedly envious, so well equipped was she, so easy to handle compared with the *Maken*. In fact, she was in almost every way the complete opposite to our craft. What I think I liked best of all were her two dinghies. We found it a constant nuisance that we had only one boat. With a crew of three, and all of us going our individual ways ashore, each of us wanting to return at different times, it was a great trial being handicapped with just one tiny tub. In the end we were dependent on launches and lifts, for our dinghy deserted us. As on the previous occasion, it was moored with a new painter, and as before it chafed its way through, unless someone cut the rope and left it feather-ended, to make it look as if the boat had gone adrift. We searched, but never found it, and it was a good job that before it went ashore we had scrubbed the *Maken* off.

Maken had been sailing since September, and when I joined her in Weymouth in November she had already done nearly 1,000 miles. With another 6,000 or so on the log dial, she was in need of a scrub to remove the weed and crustacea on her bottom; never a quick boat, she was getting sluggish, due to these growths. The tide at Balboa was sufficient to make beaching for scrubbing quite easy; and on the opposite side of the bay from the town there was an old steel barge lying on the sand. This craft was very much rusted away, but still offered a good support against which the *Maken* could be leant so that she'd stand on her keel when the tide dropped away. The story we were told, which seemed sensible at the time, was that the barge was one used by de Lesseps and his men during the first attempt to cut the Panama Canal.

We motored over in a glassy calm and tied up alongside the grounded hulk. The tide soon dropped enough to put the yacht's keel on the ground and we went overboard in the dinghy to scrape and brush the weeds off. Soon enough we could wade round the yacht, and then she was dry. Once the hull was scraped clean there was nothing to do but wait for the tide to come back, and I wandered off inland. As I climbed up off the beach to the jungle, the heat came at me like a disease. It was so bad that breathing became an effort. To walk was a labour and the heat played tricks with the imagination. Up to now we had never experienced real heat at sea and seldom ashore. This was something entirely different. It may have been the high humidity, but, whatever it was, I saw too clearly how de Lesseps' men must have suffered when slaving to cut the canal. No wonder the death and disease rate was so high.

Back aboard, we floated well before high tide and motored back to the moorings. We had got extra tinned food aboard, written final letters home, posted one of these airmail so that it arrived soon, and the other slow mail, so that it would arrive long after we were at sea and thus cut the waiting interval to the next letter from the next landfall; and we'd made lists of fresh food to buy. The water tanks were topped up, and I began to think that Bjarne was going to come with us after all on the long passage north and west. He still hadn't got a berth on a merchant ship, and he couldn't stay on at Balboa after we had left. He assured me he would not be coming with us, but we were getting more and more anxious to start, now it was clear that we would not be able to ship anyone new from Panama. Things were a bit tense on board, with the heat setting us all on edge. Then one night Bjarne came back aboard with Mike, in a tearing hurry. 'I'm leaving now. I've got a job on a merchant ship. She passes out of the canal at midnight.'

In a flurry of socks and shirts, knife and passport, books and a little reading lamp, all those precious belongings which make up a home in a bunk, Bjarne scrambled his gear into a suitcase and kitbag. It was a melancholy sight, and a sobering one. It meant that Mike and I were committed to two months at sea together, possibly three, working (and I mean working) watch and watch, day and night, through rain, hail and gale. It looked as if we were stretching our luck to the maximum.

Next day we pushed forward with preparations for leaving and by midday we were about ready. There was a launchman, a Scot who liked a drink, operating off the pier near where we were moored. He offered us a great deal of advice, made less effective by being slurred through a haze of alcohol. He boasted of the trips he had done years before, and said he'd have come with us if he'd been forty years younger. He also said he'd help us get underway, and we rashly did nothing to dissuade him. He saw us casting off the sail tiers, and with his assistant he came putt-putting out in the launch. A quick helm correction by the assistant prevented the old fellow from clobbering into us by bad driving. He clambered aboard with a big load of liquor, carried internally. By this time Mike and I had the anchor hove short.

'Hoish up the mishen,' our expert intoned. We could not obey this order, as the mizzen was already set.

'Roundly now on the thro' halliard, lads!' he shouted, 'Here, le'me help ya,' he shambled forward, grasped the peak halliard and would have had the gaff tilted up too high to hoist if Mike and I had not been contrastingly sober and swift on the throat halliard.

'Here, Jock, you go aft and take the helm,' said Mike in his quiet friendly way, urging the old oaf to get out of our way. We got the anchor hove right up, and gave it an offshore lashing so that it could not drop out of the hawse-hole, whatever happened. It meant that it could not be lowered quickly in an emergency, either, but then, 400 or 500 miles from land, quick demands on the anchor are not likely.

With all plain sail set and a fair tide, we made fast progress towards the open sea. The launch was still secured alongside, with the assistant aboard. This lad was by now anxious to cast off and motor home. He would have the wind and tide against him and his launch hadn't enough power to pull the skin off a rice pudding.

'Hey, boss, boss,' he wailed, 'c'mon back into the launch and let's go home!'

But Jock was steering the *Maken* and enjoying himself. He was remembering his youth and the voyages of long ago. He had a bottle in one fist and the tiller in the other, sometimes. We sailed a weaving course out towards the horizon with snatches of song and sentimental reminiscences coming from the helm. Mike and I were content to sit and rest after the labour of getting under way.

The cries from the launch grew louder and more plaintive: 'Boss, we ain't never goin' to get back if you don' come soon. C'mon, boss, we ain't got much gas in de tank. Leave tha' ol' boat and c'mon home.'

'Will you be all right getting back?' we asked, by now wondering if the little launch could make the journey to the pier.

'Course 'm all right, young feller,' Jock slurred. 'This reminds me o' the *Helen McCrea*. She were a four-masted barque as I sailed in a'fore you was born. Sailed her roun' the Horn, I did, and bloody miserable it were, too.' He paused for refreshment. 'Like you, I was, then. Young and foolish. No more sense than a hal'penny watch or I would've stayed ashore and been abed comfy every night.'

'You wanted to come with us, a minute ago,' we teased him.

'Aye, sure I do still. There's somethin' 'bout bein' at sea tha's better'n anythin' I know.'

The assistant in the launch did not share this feeling. 'Boss, 'f you don' come soon, Ah'll shove off and leave you!'

'Ah, shudd up, you ol' windbag! I'm comm' when I'm ready. Gotta show these youngsters how t' sail a ship.'

'The pier's 4 mile away, boss, maybe 6. We won't never get there unless we leave now.'

'All ri'. All ri', I'm coming. So long, lads, and remember al'ays reef when you see them black line squalls. Reef y'r tops'ls soon as you see them line squalls. Don' go crowdin' on sail like you was winnin' some damn race.' We didn't point out that the *Maken* had no topsails. The old fellow lurched to his feet and reeled to the yacht's side. By combined care on our part and with the help of the assistant we got him back into his launch; before we could say farewell, the assistant had loosed his ropes and was putt-putting back towards the town.

Thus we left the company of other men for eighty-one days. It was to be nearly three months before we set foot on land again, and seventy-five days before we spoke to anyone. For that period we had to rely on ourselves and our own resources. For conversation, for work, emergencies, problems, for cooking and cleaning, reefing and handling the sails, steering and repairing the gear, navigating and keeping track of the days and time, we had our two selves.

It turned out to be something of an endurance test. The physical effort was not so bad, since the human body has reserves far beyond expectation. When trouble arises and there is literally no living person within 500 miles, it's amazing what can be done, and with limited equipment. But the mental strain was something different. The body refreshes itself with sleep and food quite quickly and easily, even after long tiring spells of night watches. But the mind has a bad habit of not relaxing during sleep; and it will insist on picking up yesterday's problem the instant it wakes on the new day, to wrestle and worry over the difficulty without pause, hour after hour. Without outside distractions and interests, with a limited library and, above all, in the constant sweltering heat accentuated by weeks of windless weather, we were severely tested.

At first we went well and the wind pushed us smartly through the water. We began to wonder if the Bay of Panama was going to be kind to us. It had a reputation for prolonged calms which make sailing tedious and dreary. Before we set out we had filled the fuel tank and agreed to start the engine after a dead calm of more than 12 hours. We would use the engine till we were through that particular calm belt, or until the fuel was almost exhausted. We thought it would be sensible to keep a little fuel in the tank for entering harbour, our destination being Victoria, Vancouver Island.

Right away we found that having to steer the boat in alternate watches was trying. We had grown soft after the long spell in the Caribbean and passing through the Canal. Getting out of the bunk at 4 a.m. after being on watch till midnight was sheer misery (if it had been cold it would have been worse).

The land was still too near for us to get the yacht to steer herself; though there was little chance of running aground, there were fishing boats about which had to be watched. In practice we only saw three or four, and the last of these was ten days out. It was the last sign of humanity for sixty-five days, when we saw a merchant ship. Compared with the Pacific, the Atlantic is a tiny ocean seething with ships and aircraft; in fact the Atlantic has always seemed to me to be grossly overpopulated since that voyage diagonally across the most vast of all oceans.

After the first good day's run we made less progress each day. The heat grew more intense and we soon reached the stage when it was impossible to walk about on deck without shoes. Up to now we had always worn shirts and sweaters, often with a jacket too, during the night watches. In the Caribbean it was particularly chilly around 4 a.m. and at that hour a hot brew-up used to be welcome. Now it was so hot that we came on watch at all hours wearing nothing but a pair of shorts.

The second night out, and still fairly near land as we were sailing roughly parallel with the shore, I was on watch. I heard the splash and tumble of disturbed water and looked anxiously round trying to see if a boat was approaching us without lights. I could hear no engine beat so I thought it could hardly be a ship, and soon it was borne on me that the noise was horribly like the sound of waves on a rock. I tumbled down the companion steps and shook Mike: 'Mike! Come up on deck. There's a noise that could be surf on the shore. Can't understand it. We must be miles off the beach, surely?'

'Was'at? Oh!' and in a bound we were up on deck. The *Maken* was scarcely moving through the calm water. It was a dark, cloudy night without enough wind to give a full knot through the water. The noise got louder. We strained to see through the dark, and started imagining things.

'We'll start the engine,' Mike said and rushed down to the cabin to get the galley primus stove going. It was a horrid feeling sitting at the helm, unable to do a thing to reduce the time before that engine would burst into life and push us clear of ... of ... well – what was it out there in the darkness that made the sea rumble and grumble and hiss? Mike threw himself up on deck with the big blowlamp in hand roaring its head off. It drowned out the sound of the noises coming from just beyond our range of vision. I left the helm and went for'ard to see if there was anything in sight. The sea was disturbed, all right. Small waves were rolling hither and yon, without shape or purposeful direction. We glided into the middle of this jumbled water and I expected every second to feel the jolt as we grounded.

Now we were surrounded by the noise and the confusion of small waves. Nothing solid was to be seen and, little by little, I realised that it was just a tide rip. If I had been more experienced I should have realised from the beginning that we were near enough to the land to meet these tidal disturbances. But even today, when I'm sailing in the dark and we come across one of these races, it gives me a jolt, and I rush to the chart to confirm that we are not about to go aground. Sometimes it is possible to predict where they are going to be before meeting them. This is always true of the bigger ones, and then it's fun to sit quiet while the rest of the crew get restless, worried, and run for'ard to see what danger approaches. It is simply this: when a tidal stream runs over a submerged hill, the sea is disturbed. It's common sense, really. The bottom of the sea is far from being a flat, level plain. Where the ground is soft and muddy there are places where rocks (often a line of rocks such as a submerged reef) run across the path of the tidal stream. The tide carries along a given quantity of water; when it meets this barrier, the stream must speed up to pass over it. This speeding up causes the trouble and in certain cases, such as Portland Race in the English Channel, results can be serious.

Daily it got hotter as the wind came less and less. We rigged up that we called the Harem. It consisted of two bunk mattresses and a few cushions on the deck under the shade of a small awning. It was comfortable and cooler here, aft by the helm, but of course it lacked the essential ingredient of a harem. We tried washing the decks down with water every hour to keep the inside of the yacht cooler and make it possible to walk barefooted about on deck without pain, since we never wore shoes now. The decks scarcely seemed to notice the seawater we poured over them, so we tried a wash-down twice an hour. It made little difference, and we took to swilling buckets of seawater over the boat three times during every daylight hour. This didn't bring much improvement, either, and we gave up the effort.

Thanks to the *Maken*'s massive construction, she was well insulated below. The decks were so thick that it was generally not insufferable in the cabins. We used to sleep in our shorts, lying on top of our sleeping bags. I gave up using the coffin-like pilot's berth and had my fleabag spread out on the for'ard cabin sole (floor, in landsman's lingo: a floor in a yacht is a part of the framing which joins the keel and lower planks to the frames which are the ribs of the craft).

All through the voyage I kept an intermittently written journal. The section headed 'Four days out from Panama' reads:

> On the third night out and the fourth day we made so little progress that the engine was started just after dark since the general appearance of the sea and sky promised little wind. The engine ran reasonably well till one in the morning, when the after crankshaft bearing began to get hot, though not seriously so. My watch began at two, and at 2.30 the engine had to be oiled. By the feeble glimmer of a small torch I climbed down the vertical ladder into the black hole. There seemed to be a thicker atmosphere than usual and it was soon apparent that the fuel line was leaking, just where it joined the injector. As the fuel in the pipe at this point was under pressure the fuel was coming out of the tiny hole in a fine spray. It was just a hair-crack in the pipe, no doubt caused by the gigantic vibration of the machinery. Mike was asleep, but this was serious, so he had to be woken.

Unfortunately there were two leaks. The first, a tiny weep round the injector, was a relatively unimportant matter which Mike had noticed during his watch. The second, which had developed after I came on watch and steadily filled the black hole with fumes, was serious. My second visit to the pit of Hades was even less fun than usual. I oiled away industriously and repeated the process again at 4.30 when it was clear that the engine was in a bad way, and could not be run much more in its present state.

On deck again I cleaned my hands on a bit of waste, then rubbed as much as possible of the oil smudges from the rest of my anatomy before turning over the watch. As soon as Mike had grasped the tiller I hurried below to my mattress, to fall asleep at once. When Mike went to look at the engine at 5.30, he saw the extent of the trouble and stopped the machinery. All that day it was calm enough for us to use the engine, but we couldn't repair it. We had a complete set of spare pipes, but one of these had been trodden on and ruined. That one was, naturally, the vital one, and none of the others could be adapted to fit in place of the fractured pipe.

We tried to mend the broken pipe by winding adhesive tape round it backed with wire. This was not a success, nor was plastic metal. The first night that we were without a usable engine, a ship passed us. It was glassy calm, so we were helpless to get out of its way. We breathed more easily when we saw it pass us, about half a mile away.

As if the weather knew about the engine failure, we were now properly tortured. The wind came in fits and starts from all over the place. It became impossible to keep the *Maken* even pointing in the right direction in the dead lulls between the wisps of wind. When a zephyr did make a tiny ripple on the water, our sails were too thick and heavy to get much benefit from its gentle force. We would desperately urge the boat round on course, using all our cunning; then the wind would fail again completely.

The main and mizzen booms had to be tied out with tackles, otherwise their own weight would swing them inboard, and in the long, lazy swell the booms would swing about, killing what little driving power there was in the sagging sails. Even the headsails had to be tied exactly in position. As a result, when the wind came from the opposite direction – as it did with maddening frequency – we couldn't just put the helm over to tack. Each sail had to be freed and, when at last the boat was round on the new tack, all the tackles had to be set up again. The main boom, and indeed the mizzen boom, were too heavy for the sort of light lashings that one would normally use on a yacht. The tackles we used were necessarily stout because of the work they had to do. They had to be shackled on at each end and this in itself was a chore. The boom would flop about with futile little gestures while the wretch with the tackle in hand would vainly try to get the shackle through the small metal eye on the end of it.

It used to take 20 minutes to get the boat round and tidied up on the new tack, from the moment the helm was first put over, to the time when the last tackle was boused down. Doing all this in the blazing sun, knowing damn well that the job was a waste of time because, when it was done, the wind would change again, would try the patience of a placid angel. Mike and I, neither placid nor angelic, were now well behind schedule. We looked like arriving late in Vancouver, when all the jobs, certainly all the plum jobs, would be taken. We would arrive broke, and at this rate we would arrive with the yacht denuded of food. It was a grim outlook, and it is not surprising that we started to get irritable.

To keep up the morale we opened a big tin of orange juice, a wonderful luxury designed particularly for this sort of situation. In between the breezes we read and read – before we left Balboa we'd been given a great heap of back numbers of the magazine *Time*.

Another pleasant distraction in the middle of a dreary calm was a school of whales. They came to look at us, swimming to within 60 feet of the yacht. There were about seven of them, but they were not a cooperative bunch. I tried to photograph them from all angles, including from up the mast. But they would not rise together, nor would they do something interesting like lashing out with their tails. They blew continuously and looked beautifully cool, while we perched on coils of rope or lifejackets because the deck was too hot to stand on. They stayed with us for a long time and when they left we got a wonderful breeze out of an angry-looking cloud. But it was a kind cloud really; it sent us cooling rain which gave us an appetite for dinner and, when it left, it did not take the wind with it, but left us enough motive power to push us steadily all through the night.

The only concession we made to the sun, apart from rigging the harem, was wearing sunglasses. We never suffered from sunstroke or sunburn, though we wore nothing but shorts and stayed out in the full glare a great deal. It was perhaps because we had approached the hot latitudes slowly that we were unaffected by this constant exposure. We certainly had tough hides: I was cooking one day when I splashed boiling water down my leg. There was a stinging sensation, after a second or two, but nothing to get worried about. But I did worry, dreadfully. Being so far offshore, and so alone for so long, it was easy to imagine all sorts of things. This incident occurred after we had been several weeks at sea. I looked at the water in the pot, definitely boiling, and down at my leg. 'No feeling,' I thought; 'that must mean I've got leprosy. That's what happens when people have leprosy – they lose all sense of pain.' How I imagined I had caught leprosy in that secluded situation, I don't know. The mild lunacy passed after a few seconds when I realised that the truth was that we were baked hard on the outside by the gruelling sun.

On the evening of the eighth day out we caught a fish. After trailing every sort of bait for thousands of miles at every speed without anything happening apart from the loss of the bait, we hooked this fish by accident. We had tried everything from pieces of rag to bacon rind for bait. Polished spinners and even sausages (the hated wieners, if the truth must out) were no use, and our first victim fell to a hula-hula girl of the fish world. It was a metal plug with a skirt of nylon threads. Instead of concealing a pair of shapely legs, this skirt hid a hook, and it was snapped by a tuna 18 inches long when the lure was actually on the surface and abreast the rudder.

This was a fine addition to our diet, as fresh food was running low. We ate it for breakfast next morning, and it brought luck, for land hove in sight – the Isla del Cocos, or Cocos Island. We had not originally intended to visit this, the loneliest chip of land in the whole wide world. But when the engine fuel-pipe split we thought it might be worth going slightly out of our way to see if there was a chance of getting the pipe repaired at the island. Normally no one lives there, but over 700 expeditions have visited the spot to search for buried pirate treasure. We thought we might fall in with a party of diggers who would perhaps be equipped with tools for mending damaged pipes. After all, these days the best expeditions are equipped with everything from radio transmitters to geiger counters, so why not blowlamps and so on?

We sailed towards the island all day with a just perceptible breeze behind us. Cocos is all that it should be, for a treasure isle. It is high and precipitous, thickly covered with vegetation. It is the sort of place so frequently described in sea fiction. The western end rises to a peak which is at times covered by low clouds. At other times this is the best spot for shipwrecked mariners who wish to scan the horizon for a relief ship. Being unlit as well as uninhabited, the island is not popular with steamships, so that they keep well clear. The sailing-ship route from Panama to Cape Horn passes close by, but it is not exactly a crowded lane these days. You may ask how it was that we, who were going northwards, should be on the sailing-ship route leading to the south of the continent. The answer is that the sailing-ship routes, which we ourselves stuck to as far as possible, take note only of currents and prevailing winds. The latter change with the seasons of the year. It is often necessary to sail far to the west to get into a favourable north-going current and wind stream. We sailed far off the direct route to pick up the favourable influences; which explains why we were passing Cocos.

The sea all round this point was crowded with sharks and dolphins, and birds were very numerous. Off-lying there are islets, barren, but the homes of more birds. We could see no anchorage but there were several beaches which might have been suitable for landing. However, with no dinghy and with only two aboard, we were in no position to land. Even if we had had a boat, one of us would probably have had to stay aboard and sail up and down while the other went ashore.

The island seemed about a mile and a half long, and it had the appearance of a fine home for anyone seeking escape from the pressure of current civilisation. It is well clear of the danger zone of an atomic bomb attack on the nearest target – the Panama Canal. We looked at it intently, but there was no one there. We were condemned to days, maybe months, of dreary crawling across the steaming sea, drifting mostly, carrying the dead weight of the useless engine, all for the want of simple pipe-repair gear.

The gods relented, seeing our dejection, and sent a school of porpoises to amuse us. There had been diving and formation swimming displays all afternoon by these delightful creatures, but this latest was something special. The beasts were in a crowd and they came within inches of the yacht, zooming to the surface in twos, threes and even fours, in perfect formation. Their movements were beautifully synchronised, like fighter formations weaving about. The sight of all this fresh meat took our minds to the harpoon. We lashed the tiller so that the ship would sail herself and went to the bows to take turns with our spear. It was in Las Palmas that Mike made this weapon. He fashioned it from a long steel shaft with a rope attached at its after end and a removable length of pipe at the for'ard, or business end. This pipe was made effective by three barbed spikes protruding forwards. A length of chain was welded to the pipe, and joined to the chain was a piece of light, flexible rope. To keep the pipe on to the shaft during the hurling operation there was a pad of cotton waste inside the pipe's after end, and this jammed the shaft tight till a strike should be made.

The basic idea was to plunge the harpoon into the beast, whip out the shaft by the rope on its end, and bring in the carcass by the rope on the barbs which would remain, we hoped, embedded in the meat. For a time we had no luck, as we tried to spear the porpoises. They refused to cooperate, either swimming too deep when near the ship, or only surfacing for a brief instant and then some 12 feet away.

It was soon clear that to get any success we would have to get out on the end of the bowsprit. Mike climbed out along the spar and steadied himself by holding on to the jib. It was an unsteady platform to work from, with the boat gently heaving, sometimes rolling slightly. Also the bowsprit was, as is customary, a round spar, so that Mike had to keep exactly on the top to avoid sliding into the sea, among the porpoises.

I assembled the two parts and secured the ends of the two lines, so that if they were torn out of my hands they would not be lost. In a few minutes a likely specimen for our larder approached. Up went the harpoon, poised for an instant, so that Mike looked like the work of a Greek sculptor entitled 'Spearman Killing Snake' or 'Antiocles Slays the Gorgon'. Then down. It missed. Just an inch too far to the right. I coiled in the two lines and hauled the weapon aboard.

It was passed out to the end of the bowsprit again, neither of us mentioning the fact that if Mike fell in, it would be advisable for me to haul him out before sharks took an interest in the proceedings. Again the dramatic pose, but this time, as the steel slashed the water, we both yelled with triumph. The two coils of line swirled off the deck where I had carefully laid them and in a brief instant the line leading to the barbs was humming taut. It led aft.

Mike scrambled back to the deck and we rushed aft to where the water was being lashed by a writhing mass of blue and silver flesh. We flung ourselves into the fight and at once it was a battle royal, with shouting and swearing, sweating and struggling, fury and fear, lashing and crashing, taut ropes and tight muscles.

'Get its bloody tail out of the water!'

'Watch your hands!'

By now Mike had hauled the harpoon line in and was trying to get the beast's tail out of the water. He said later he thought that if he could get the tail above the surface the porpoise would not be able to struggle so, and would be unable to escape. This was a wrong guess. Meanwhile the porpoise was thrashing about against the ship's side so that if one of us had put a hand wrong we might have had a crushed paw – with the nearest doctor some weeks away.

We fought on, yelling at each other above the din and commotion: 'Get a rope round its tail!'

'Trying that. Damned harpoon's not in. It's just caught the rope round its tail.' That was true enough. Mike had not scored a direct hit, just a graze which had startled the porpoise. He leapt in the air, whirling thrice round. This wrapped the rope round his tail and made him fast for us. But now there was every chance the rope would unwind. We had to get a noose round the tail before he escaped, but it whipped back and forth with the speed of a lightweight boxer. I tried dropping the rope over, but that was hopeless. Next I tried to thrust the rope over, which was one degree better, and several times success seemed possible. But the beast was wet and slimy and a demon. We were working, I mean fighting, lying over the rails, in the most awkward position. It was like trying to drop a noose over the blade of a fan, a fan which didn't just whirl round, but changed direction every few seconds, twisted, jolted and lashed out fiercely.

Right from the start I was worried that the harpoon rope would snap. I had snatched a second to rush aft and fling off the tiller lashing, and thrust the helm down. We had been sailing along, and this put a great extra strain on the rope. By luffing, I got the boat to come to a standstill, and we were at least no longer towing that 5-foot mass of demented animation. When it was clear that our struggle was getting us nowhere, Mike thought we might play the beast like a game fish, to tire it out. He told me to get another bit of rope to attach to the harpoon line. This proved impossible. It was good foresight that had prompted me to tie the extreme inboard end of the harpoon line, for it was bar taut. We couldn't undo it to join on the extra rope; we would have lost the harpoon, fresh meat and all.

Mike continued to hold the line in against the side of the ship and the porpoise still did its best to get free, so that we were both splashed and sopping, while blood ran into the sea. The only remaining thing to do was to kill the porpoise quickly, in situ, if possible. I ran for the harpoon shaft. Fortunately I had hauled it aboard after the strike. It had a blunt end, but it was heavy. It seemed likely that, driven hard, it would give a *coup de grâce*, provided a vital spot could be touched. It was raised up and, just as I was preparing to put my whole weight behind it, I nearly lost my balance and all but fell overboard as the porpoise gave a terrific heave and freed itself, swimming quickly away a few feet. It jumped clear of the water with a defiant gesture, before disappearing with all the other porpoises.

That was the last we saw of a very gallant foe and a week's supply of delicious, fresh food. We went back to our rather dreary tinned diet. The whole battle only took a few minutes, but it left a vivid impression. I can remember noticing how beautiful the colouring of the whole scene was, especially of our fine antagonist. The red blood running down the shiny, silvery torso, with the foam catching the sun, made a wonderful sight. It would have been a pity to kill such a grand creature and, if we had succeeded in getting all that scrumptious meat, I'm not at all sure whether I would have been glad or sorry.

Next day we saw another performance. Again the actors were porpoises. This time they leapt clear of the water and crashed back with so much energy that we could hear the splashes above the noise of our own bow wave, though they were 300 or 400 yards away. The extraordinary thing was the precision of the act. How do twenty or thirty porpoises, swimming along head to tail, know when to jump so that they are all clear of the water at exactly the same instant? They did this several times just to prove that it was no fluke the first time.

This part of the sea was very much more interesting than any we had previously sailed through. One fairly common sight was a white bird, about the size of a gannet, standing on a piece of driftwood. There was a lot of this timber and many pieces had a group of little fish swimming in the shade beneath. Presumably when the white birds feel hungry they just reach overboard and snap up a local resident or two.

There were times during our long calms when the *Maken* looked like a domestic science college, with one member of the crew baking fancy pastry while the other cut out and sewed up a pair of shorts. These shorts were rather special and preceded by many years some of the more exotic beachwear now fashionable for gentlemen on Riviera beaches. We had some spare awning canvas aboard, lively stuff with broad red and white stripes down it. Then there was some rather less obtrusive canvas, a pleasant yellow shade. I made myself a pair of shorts for the beach (very short), another pair for afternoon wear (slightly longer), and an evening dress pair (longer still). The truth of the matter was that I was not satisfied with the first pair and went on to improve them, and then had a third try.

That was a feature of these hours of calms. We had so much time that we tended to elaborate anything we did with all the embellishments we could think of. Take that baked tart. It would start off as an unpretentious fruit tart, just a pastry casing with a layer of stewed fruit on top. Then a covering of custard would be added, with the edge of the pastry decorated. Next a sprinkling of raisins would be added. And so the cook's eye wanders over the stores, to see what further touches he could make.

Another example was my sailing jacket. Plenty of yachtsmen make their own canvas smocks and similar jackets, and in the past I had done so more than once. (All this is no longer true in 2015, but it was true in the early 1950s). But the jacket I made on the *Maken* was altogether a cut above the rather shapeless garments which go under the generic term 'sailing jacket'. My jacket did not have the parallel-sided sleeves, nor was it collarless, as are most of the breed. There were in fact no concessions to simplicity of construction and assembly. It was first carefully shaped and put together. Then after an initial fitting it was taken apart and rebuilt after some subtle cutting. It had tapered sleeves and a collar complete with padded lapels. The collar was difficult to make and, as no patterns were available, I adapted shipbuilding methods to tailoring. As a result I recommend that in future tailoring apprentices should be given a course in shipbuilding.

Before we took to making our shorts, we patched the garments we had. They had a rough life, being laundered with more vigour than skill. Their number was depleted both by the robbery and the rubber tyre we used as a helmsman's seat. This tyre, which was so useful as a fender in the Canal, was vicous on the seats of shorts, due to the constant motion of the boat. When there was any wind we each spent nearly 12 hours in 24 at the helm, so the chafing hours were long indeed.

From all this it will be gathered that we were not bored. The ship suffered little chafe and damage as by now she was well equipped with baggy wrinkles and anti-erosion measures, so there was not a great deal of maintenance to do. Navigation didn't take up much time; there was nothing to hit, and we had only to concentrate on getting clear of the calms as soon as possible. This only meant sailing well to the west to get into a region where we could expect favourable winds and no adverse current.

One recurring distraction was the lightning. Almost every night from when we left Panama, we saw frequent lightning flashes, but they were seldom accompanied by audible thunder, and we had little rain. One night, however, it was clear that a storm was coming our way. The lightning got brighter with each display, and instead of being low on the horizon it came closer and closer overhead. Thunder boomed away at irregular intervals, and the wind was capricious. Dawn was just an increasingly lighter greyness instead of the usually colourful sunrise. The first rain came quite gently and gave us plenty of warning to close the skylights and ports. After a few minutes the sky cleared slightly and the rain stopped. The *Maken* rolled sullenly as if her mood matched the weather. The whole atmosphere tingled with expectancy. A full-bodied rain squall came towards us, slowly, undeviating. It was easily discernible 2 or 3 miles away. The sea lapped listlessly against the ship's side. Grim silence between the rumbling thunder-crashes threatened a frightfulness to come. Then the rain was heard, hissing and lashing. Straight towards us it came. We felt a few preliminary drops, the vanguard of the horde; then it was on us. An outrageous mass of water, filling the air, pounded down on the sea and yacht. In a moment the visibility was reduced from miles to a few yards. Each wave had a white fur of rebounding raindrops on it. *Maken*'s decks were running thick with water; it swilled from side to side as she rolled, then poured off to leeward as a gust heeled her over.

At first the rain just overwhelmed us, even though we saw it coming. But we soon realised that we were wasting precious water, and we put buckets and saucepans in carefully chosen places such as under the boom ends, to catch as much rain as possible. We stripped off and washed, hoping that the rain wouldn't stop abruptly, leaving us lathered with soap. The first squall passed soon but was followed by another. We collected enough water to wash all our dirty clothes and still had some to spare. Afterwards, the sun came out and a gentle breeze stayed with us after the rain had passed, so we soon dried our clothes. The ocean all around was empty. No one, nothing, saw the transformation from yacht to mobile laundry, and after it was all over we made plans to collect even more water next time.

Chapter Twelve

The Pacific certainly gave us every sort of weather. We were bedevilled by calms, but one of these exceeded anything that Mike or I had ever encountered: it went on for three solid days and nights. We added up our total mileage every 24 hours. The first day and night in this calm we made 5 miles. The second 24-hour period gave us no mileage at all; the log never stirred the whole period. The third day and night we made just 3 miles. So in 72 hours we had covered only 8 miles, and that whole week, we made a paltry 135.

This trying period was a month out of Panama. Our diet was now bereft of fresh food. The heat was really unpleasant. To keep the decks from becoming impossible we were throwing fifteen buckets over them every 15 minutes. This was a chore which seemed to need a vast amount of energy. The sun was very high overhead at noon, and thirst began to nag us. We consumed more than our allotted half a gallon of water per man per day. Water was not rationed; we just kept a watchful eye on its use, and normally drank with restraint. I found two ways to ease my thirst: chewing something like a raisin or a malted milk tablet, and drinking warmed water. The latter seemed more satisfying than the tepid water in our tanks. We were thankful for the tins of fruit juice we'd bought in Panama.

This extra long calm was summed up in the log: 'No wind. No fish. No ships. No good.' Watches were not kept rigidly as there was nothing to do except wet the decks. For hours on end it was impossible to keep the ship headed the right way, since the rudder was ineffective. We both turned in for full nights of sleep, though Mike dragged his mattress on to the cabin top so that any breeze during the night would wake him. The second night I woke just after dawn and went on deck just as a breeze, a really cheerful, sparkling one, got up. But it lasted only a few seconds, hardly enough to get the yacht moving before it died right away. At the end of that week we knew that firm measures were needed to make progress. I stuck a knife in the mast (a sailor's superstition said to bring wind), Mike even whistled (another superstition, said to bring head winds), on the principle that even a head wind would be better than none. Finally we decided that strong medicine was essential: we would have to catch a shark. It is, of course, well established that a ship becalmed should nail a shark's tail to the bowsprit to bring wind. I put one of the hated wieners on a hook, a proper shark hook as big as my hand, with a chain trace so that the fish could not bite through it.

For some time a shark had been in attendance. It was not a very big one, not over 7 feet. But it was an annoying beast as it prevented us taking an occasional dip over the side. To the chain trace of the hook I tied some of that strong cotton-plaited rope that was so good on the harpoon. Gently, so as not to cause alarm, I lowered the baited hook down to the shark. He disdained it. I tried bringing it closer. The bait was not acceptable. Frankly, the shark had my sympathy; those wieners were pretty horrible on board, and soused in seawater they must have been disgusting. I hauled in the line and put on a piece of tinned steak.

The hook was again dangled where even a blind shark could hardly fail to see it. No reaction. I began to get impatient. I brought the hook closer to the shark's mouth. The beast was cooperative enough to lie right alongside the yacht, only a fathom or so below the surface. The bait was not taken. I was insistent, but the shark turned and swam away a few feet. I exercised patience. The shark came closer. I put the bait right in front of its nose. The shark was either not hungry, or blind. In the end I put the hook right up against his nose, and tweaked. I rather suspect that the sharp point of the hook, protruding through the bait, scratched his nose. Anyhow, the effect was immediate and he swallowed the bait.

The big fish was so lethargic that I just hauled away on the line, and not till he was near the surface did he begin to fight back. Then he twisted round and went down; but not very deep. I coaxed him back to the surface and he made a second run, less exciting even than the first. Soon I had him right alongside and hauled half out of the water. We lashed him alongside and pulled his tail up to bulwark level; when we were sure he was dead, I cut off the tail with the bread knife. This seemed the best implement by far, as shark skin is as tough and rough as a mixture of coarse sandpaper and the hardest leather. The serrated edge of the bread knife tackled the job well enough.

With the trophy I crawled out along the bowsprit, fixed it on the extreme end, and, sure enough, after that day we seldom wanted for wind. Which shows what a wonderful thing is science!

Apart from this shark we had a constant escort of albatrosses. They gathered in bigger and bigger numbers as the calms grew prolonged, and we thought of them as farmyard fowls. They would follow the *Maken* as she drifted and ambled along; then, as we threw overboard the galley refuse, they would all get up and chase each other to forage for food. Those furthest back would waddle and paddle, half flying as they skimmed along the surface, just like hens flapping and walloping along when the farmer's wife calls them at feeding time. Among our stores were massive tins of margarine and, as there were at this time only two mouths to feed, this stuff tended to go rancid before we had eaten more than half the contents of a tin. Also, some of the tins were defective, so we used to feed rancid marge to the albatrosses, and it was doubtful who enjoyed this the most, the feeders or the fed.

Taking a spoon we would scoop a great dollop of evil smelling fat out of a tin and flick it into the water. The birds, at least the old hands who had been with us for weeks, knew this special treat by sight, or perhaps by smell. At once there would be a great to-do. Those nearest the succulent morsels would lunge at the floating lumps with huge, vicious beaks. Those far away would arrive in a flurry of feathers and foam, coining in to land on the water with feet splayed out like water skis. These birds were wonderfully graceful on the wing, but even the adults never seemed to have mastered the art of landing properly. They would thump down in the most ungainly way, apparently unable to fix an exact point of contact with the sea. As a result they hurtled into the crowd of beaks, grabbing and snatching the lovely, stinking marge, causing chaos and confusion. Then the menacing fin of a shark would glide towards the squawking group, and they'd all sidle off. They didn't seem actually frightened of the sharks – just anxious not to be too near.

One reason why we had all this margarine on our hands, going bad, was that in the heat our appetites fell away. We didn't have much work to do, and we spent a lot of time in effortless occupations like reading and writing. When we set out from England, I had calculated our stores requirements on the customary basis of 2½ lb of food per man per day. This allows a little for waste and evaporation when cooking, and so on. At this time we were eating just a light two-course breakfast with coffee, and an afternoon meal which was also a two-course affair. Before turning in we had a brew-up and buttered (with marge) biscuits. We usually only had four biscuits in the evening, but at other times of the day we got through regular snacks.

As we worked slowly north we got into colder latitudes. Our appetites awakened. There was more sail-handling, and by the time we were actually finding it a bit cool we took to having hot soup in the middle of the day. As our appetites strengthened our thirsts dropped off, so that the daily quota of half a gallon of water per man per day for all purposes was enough. The water had a faintly unpleasant taste after seven or eight weeks, but this may have been due to the cement wash used on the insides of the tanks. We did not treat our water chemically, as we had been told that it was safe. Certainly one cannot conceive that drinking water in any region run by the Americans would have a single germ left alive in it.

It was inevitable that as week succeeded week, till we had been solid months at sea, and as it became clear that we were dropping further and further behind schedule, we became irritable and at times ferociously bad-tempered. The heat would have caused flare-ups of feeling under ideal living conditions. Cramped aboard a little world only 45 feet long and 15 feet wide, with no chance to go for a walk and never more than 45 feet from the same neighbour; never able to escape to a restaurant for a meal; knowing exactly what food there was in the store; worrying about such possibilities as running out of water before getting into harbour; chafed for hours on end both mentally and physically when steering through fickle wind patches; teased by squalls and calms – no wonder we quarrelled at times. The miracle is that we kept sane enough not to let our feelings boil over for more than a few lax moments.

We certainly had enough opportunities for misunderstandings, which are the quickest breeding ground for squabbles. For a start there was the ever-present problem of language. Mike spoke Canadian, admittedly with very little difference in accent to my English, but with a widely different vocabulary. Long before this period I realised that a difference in word usage could be dangerous. For instance, in the middle of a rainy, blustery night, when we were all tired and working in bad conditions – tying down a reef while the *Maken* tried to stand on her ear, then on her tail, with the wind shrieking enough to drown all but the loudest shouts – to misunderstand a word under those conditions could have serious consequences. As the *Maken* was a Canadian yacht, and as I was heading for Canada, I set about learning Mike's usage, and tried to adopt it. I took to saying kerosene for paraffin, can for tin, flashlight for torch, bumpers for fenders, and fenders for bumpers, gas for petrol (I never did discover what the Canadian for gas was), biscuit for bun, cookie for biscuit, and so on.

One day we found that the mizzen mast was moving subtly at the foot. When Mike bought the *Maken* she'd had her mizzen removed, as it was in the way for whaling. He and his friends replaced it, standing it on the after deck. It was supported by enormous beams. These beams were well in keeping with the rest of the boat, so there is no need to describe them in detail. But the constant motion – for even in a calm there was often a long rolling swell – settled the mizzen down a fraction of an inch. It was obvious that if we had a prolonged spell of bad weather we might be in trouble with the mizzen. So Mike went down into the nether regions, taking with him a balk of timber and a pencil. He marked the piece of wood and passed it up to me to be cut. I held the tiller until the job was passed up, then lashed the helm and quickly tackled the job before the boat could wander off course. I cut the timber the way it was marked and handed it down. A great dollop of swearwords came up from below. I had not cut the timber in the way Mike intended. I reckoned at the time, having been through the various shops in a yacht-building yard, that I knew more about shipwrighting than Mike. It was his fault for marking the timber wrongly. I told him so. And so we started. It was just a brief verbal squall, and the comic thing was we went on with the job, he measuring and fitting down below decks in the dark engine room while I steered and cut as directed, up on deck. This is a typical sample of the stupidities it is so easy to drop into.

On the other side, we had standard jokes. It was Bjarne who first said, when making the rum punch brew-up: 'Better put plenty of rum in, with water so short.' This became a nightly ritual, regardless of the fact that water was never short, nor ever seriously looked like running out.

It would be wrong to suggest that the diet was always dreary; we were not so naïve as to have set out without some luxuries aboard, and on this long hop we had a tin of chicken for every thousand miles. This was the result of a wonderful surprise. One day Mike decided to serve peas as a vegetable. He selected one of a batch of unlabelled tins lying in a remote locker, and it was like falling upon a miracle to discover the true contents. On this section of the trip the nightly cup of tea, drunk listening to the wireless, was the luxury we both looked forward to during the day.

One day we noticed that little fish were following the yacht. There was one the first day, then two, three and soon a small colony. They kept station by the rudder and, when we got into the 'sensible' latitudes, where the wind came continuously and progress was more or less constant, these wee fish swam along with us for hundreds of miles. At least, if they were different ones every few miles, we never actually caught them changing guard. And they were all dressed remarkably alike. It was uncanny at night to see the little wisp of phosphorescence trailing along behind us. There would be a little group of submarine-shaped bodies swimming in slight zigzags when the watch started, and 4 hours later the same little fellows would still be there; in that time we would have covered around 16 miles, maybe more. They certainly had stamina. One night Mike tried his harpoon on them and next morning we had three fish for breakfast. They were not as tasty as the tuna we'd caught by accident, and they had white flesh. The reduction in their ranks did not deter the rest of the escort, but we never speared any more.

When at last the wind came continuously, we found that it was exhausting work, steering alternate watches. Even limiting sail-changing to the change of watch, as one often can on a relatively insensitive yacht like the *Maken*, it was still tiring to get no continuous sleep for more than 3 to 4 hours day or night, for a fortnight on end. So when the wind went ahead and stayed there for long periods we took to sleeping all night, every night. Just before dark we would tuck a reef or two in the mainsail, substitute the small jib for the working one, and go below, leaving the ship to plod on through the hours of darkness. The reduction of sail took 30 minutes often enough, when the sea was lumpy, and it was seldom less than 20 minutes' labour. Then we would go below, peel off our oilskins, put the kettle on, tune in the radio and sit back in comfort to listen to one of several American stations which were in range. With the oil lamp throwing a weak light over the scene, a warm feeling inside and a noisy sea outside, it was very cosy.

A long way south we began to wonder if we could sail up to the position of the US Ocean Station Vessel, better known as the weather ship at 33°N 133°W. We did not want to tack to windward, as that would be a slow job. It is, in any case, poor ocean-cruising practice to so navigate the yacht that beating to windward is necessary for any length of time. Sailing to windward is a dreary, unprofitable pastime, all right for the racing fraternity who have never known the joys of downwind work with the self-steerer at work. The long-range sailor gladly leaves to them the head-bashing-against-a-brick-wall business of sailing to windward. It is incredibly tedious, and to cover a few miles it is necessary to wander about the ocean first on one tack, then on the other, while the wind dodges about so that 20 minutes after the yacht has been tacked the wind sidles round making the former tack the favourable one now. So the sad business of coming about has to be gone through all over again. This sort of game is grand in a dinghy, and that is the sort of craft which should play it.

We had the sense to plot our future course with care so that we would have long spells of beam and following winds. We decided that if our course tended towards the weather ship we would make no effort to steer away from it. But if the winds favoured a course clear of it we wouldn't worry. Even if we did sail near it, the weather might be murky, and we'd miss it. This was doubly possible, as we were given to understand that these weather ships are not stationary, but manoeuvre within a 10-mile circle. The idea of meeting this ship was not just to have a chat. We hoped that if the weather was fine, we might be able to manoeuvre alongside and pass our damaged engine fuel-pipe across for repair. This could only be done if the sea was calm, and, if it was so, the chances are that we would not have been able to sail into the 10-mile circle. A typical cruising dilemma.

In the end we found that to get to the weather ship we would have to sail to windward, possibly for a long spell, because the winds did not behave as predicted. So we gave up that idea and kept heading north. At one stage we were apparently going to pass within a few hundred miles of Honolulu, and we discussed going there. It must be explained that on this leg of the voyage, which was about 3,500 miles long, we were forced to deviate a good deal from the best route. Indeed the best route was a matter of opinion. Whereas on the first laps our course was in almost every case the direct one from departure to destination, on this leg we had to keep far off the curved line running parallel to the coast which was the 'power-driven' ships' route from Panama up towards Vancouver.

As the weeks wore on, we began to realise that it would be common sense to put in before Vancouver. We naturally looked at San Francisco on the chart. It is not difficult to enter, even for a stranger. Mike had been in before, though admittedly on a merchant ship, which is a different world to a yacht. On that occasion he was not an officer and had no access to the charts, no responsibility, no pilot books. However, we had a chart which gave ample information, a pilot book, which like many of their kind is not very much help, and a vast confidence in our own ability.

Soon enough it was clear that we were going to pass less than 500 miles to the west of San Francisco, so we altered course for this harbour. I was privately delighted. It was my ambition to see the three 'interesting towns' in the States: San Francisco, New York and St Louis. Here was the first coming up without effort. We had now been at sea for two and a half months. The fresh food had run out long before, apart from the onions and cheese. Now even they were finished. The water daily tasted more strongly, though it was apparently perfectly safe. We were going to need our engine for the narrows round Vancouver Island, so sense, seamanship and inclination all agreed that we should turn aside to San Francisco.

We reached a point less than a hundred miles from the port before seeing our first ship for some sixty-five days. It was a freighter and we saw it would pass fairly close. So out came the signal flags, though by now we did not expect to get any answer from any ship to this method of sending messages. We decided that the trouble might stem from the ship's officers being unable to read the flags. In this case the flags would have been blowing straight away from the ship, so we hit on the idea of draping the flags along our rail, in the correct order to spell out 'Please report us to Lloyd's'.

Mike and I stood watching the ship steam diagonally towards us. She came fairly near, perhaps a quarter of a mile, before we saw that she was altering course to pass within hailing distance. We pointed to our signal, and saw binoculars on the bridge scan us. The whole incident turned out to be a farce. Both sides yelled at the same time so that no one heard anyone.

'Please report us to Lloyd's. Yacht *Maken*,' Mike's bellow went across to them.

'Where're you bound?' they yelled back. Mike did not hear their hail, and I got it indistinctly because he was shouting near at hand.

'They asked us where we're going, Mike,' I told him.

'Damn them! Why can't they read a simple signal?'

Already they were abeam and beginning to be separated by distance.

'San Francisco, our next port,' Mike yelled.

'We'll radio them you're coming,' came back the reply.

'Yacht *Maken*!' I shouted.

'What yacht?'

'*Maken*. M.A.K.E.N.'

Their reply was unintelligible. This was just another proof that the use of flags at sea only works if both parties know all about the game.

The night after this unsuccessful attempt to signal I came off watch at 2 a.m. Instead of going to my bunk I turned on the radio and listened to the crowning of the Queen. The voice of the commentator came from the other side of the world, describing the scene inside Westminster Abbey. He told of the superb clothes, the luxury and sparkle, the glitter and sumptuousness of the array. I looked round our cabin and considered the contrast. My woollen shirt was a nondescript grey after innumerable washings in seawater. My jacket was cut from a piece of old sail canvas – the bottom of my five-tonner's mainsail, which we had reduced in area to fit our mizzen. My sea boots were worn and scuffed, and my trousers had a patch in the seat the size of a dinner plate. Instead of a diamond-studded sword at my waist I had a rough sheath knife in a homemade leather sheath held together by big stitches of sailmaker's twine. Instead of a coronet I had on a woolly cap that lacked shape or decoration, but it did have the outstanding virtue that it kept me warm during the night watches. It was hard to tell from the description of the coronation whether anyone, apart from the crowd of spectators, was enjoying the occasion. Without hesitation and most wholeheartedly I was sure I would not have swapped places with anyone in London then. The *Maken* was stolid and slow, but she was always taking us to new excitements, new places, new interests.

When we got to San Francisco we found everything was in profusion. The scenery, the entrance, the tide are all on a grand scale. It was morning when we sighted land, and we crept past the off-lying Farallon Isles with a light beam breeze. This haphazard collection of rocks is inhabited and has a lighthouse, so we signalled by flag to get tidal information. There was no one in sight and the watch (if any) on the light either could not read our signal, or didn't know the answer.

As the day grew older we passed more and more shipping. There were freighters with war cargoes (for this was during the fighting in Korea) and fishing boats, including one which was a converted assault landing craft. A trooper passed, a salvage ship was next, then a tug towing a barge well laden with lumber. We stared and stared, feasting our eyes on all this after so long looking at the empty ocean.

The Golden Gate Bridge which spans the entrance is so large that it can be seen many miles away, provided the weather is clear. But there's the rub; this region is pestered with fogs. We saw the bridge quite 8 miles away, but had difficulty in sighting the lightship marking the main channel. By mid morning the visibility was perfect, and as we came up to the lightship it was all too obvious that the tide was in our favour. Mike was most anxious about the tide, fearing that it would turn before we got through the narrows.

By the time we reached the lightship the wind was a moderate breeze so that we were moving fast over the ground. We shouted to the lightship crew to find out the time of high water. One of them scrambled into the wheelhouse to look up the tide tables. As the distance between the two vessels increased we saw him emerge, book in hand, quickly turning the pages to find the place. Evidently he didn't know how to read the tide tables, because he passed them on to another man. By then the tide had whirled us too far away to hear what they said when they shouted.

Astern of the lightship was a pilot vessel, vying with it in smartness. We went through the same procedure again to get the tide data, but no one aboard the pilot boat appeared to know offhand, which we thought was rather extraordinary. A hand hurried into the wheelhouse and a few seconds later came out with the tidal calendar. This time we had more luck, for they found the place before we were whisked out of earshot.

'High tide one-thirty!' they yelled. It turned out to be wrong, but at least they'd tried. As it was now well past midday Mike was truly worried, but I've spent so many hours waiting for tides in engineless yachts, and on other occasions long periods creeping inshore to dodge the force of a contrary tide, that I've learnt some stoicism in this matter. I was inclined to think that all this shouting to and fro was altogether too amateurish. Actually the tide was 5.29, so when we came to the narrows we roared through them. As we went under the bridge the painters high above shouted down to us. They were so far above our mast that we couldn't hear what they were saying, and for a moment there was some confusion. Mike had been into other harbours where the port authority had a hailing box on the bridge. They give berthing instructions from this hailing station, and Mike thought we were being given instructions, till we discerned the painting equipment.

Next a coastguard launch approached, attracted no doubt by the yellow flag in our rigging, requesting customs and immigration clearance. More shouting ensued. Altogether it was a vociferous entrance, rounded off with a lunatic conversation with this launch. Its engine was virtually unsilenced and had enough power to thrust it along at a good pace, so anything we said was quite drowned by the roar from many cylinders. But we managed to ask them for directions to a yacht anchorage. They told us to follow them, and promptly set off at five times our maximum speed.

As we entered the vast bay, we saw no obvious parking place. The bay is so large that it stretches to the horizon in two directions, and the absence of easily seen yacht moorings confuses the visitor. The coastguard cutter set off towards the St Francis Yacht Club marina, and we turned to follow them. This brought the wind on the beam and we found ourselves over-canvassed. Mike ordered the mainsail down and for 20 minutes we struggled with the thick, unyielding canvas, fighting it, forcing the intractable mass to obey us. The blocks of the main throat and peak halliards were rusty after the long period at sea and in the end it was necessary to go aloft and jump up and down on the gaff to force it down. As I had run a splinter up under a nail when handling the jib sheets, I found this battle uncongenial. To cap it all, we found the wind and tide thrusting us towards Alcatraz Island at a great pace. It is on this island that the worst criminals from the whole of the United States were lodged. Mike had heard that any vessel approaching within 200 yards of the island was automatically looked upon with more than ordinary suspicion. Someone had told him that the guards immediately assume that an expedition to free one of the prisoners is aboard the approaching craft, and, so the yarn went, they would without fail open fire as soon as the ship was within the 200-yard offshore zone. It all sounded rather far-fetched, yet just sufficiently plausible to cause a fair old flap on the *Maken.* Alcatraz seemed to be rolling towards us at a shocking rate when the mainsail was stuck.

At last we had the sail down, but Mike didn't like the way it was furled, so we wrestled with it till it was in a neat bundle. By this time the coastguard launch was either bored with waiting or had been called away on urgent business. Looking round for a place to anchor, we saw that the marina was now far upwind and tide; but there was another possible place, a small harbour enclosed by two jetties. We learned later it was the Aquatic Park. The tide sluiced past the entrance and we approached at a fast, foaming pace with the jib, staysail and mizzen pulling hard. In through the narrow entrance we shot, a quick luff, the roar of the anchor chain pouring up out of the locker, and we were brought up, after eighty days at sea.

Chapter Thirteen

Soon after the last of the sails were furled and we had gone below, a launch came alongside with the customs authorities. This was the beginning of a thoroughly efficient and highly successful campaign by the people of San Francisco to make our stay the acme of enjoyment. Within the hour a dinghy came alongside, and the owner said: 'I wondered if you fellows would like to come for a sail tomorrow?'

'We've just *had* a pleasant sail, thanks!'

'Well – I'm a bit stuck for a crew, for tomorrow's race. That's my schooner, over there.'

Now this was too much of a temptation. There are very few schooners in Britain, and I had never sailed aboard one; so I fell for the offer. 'I'd love to crew for you. What time tomorrow?' And so it was fixed up that our first day in I would spend racing in the Bay.

As usual in America, the news of our arrival soon spread. Newspaper reporters came aboard in force and most of the papers gave us accurate write-ups which were good. They ought to have been; we wrote some of them ourselves. This was partly in self-defence, as on previous occasions we had been bothered by the consequences of almost wholly fictitious descriptions of our trip. To give an example: in one place, which shall be nameless, of the six or seven descriptions of the yacht, not one included the fact that the rig was ketch, though the poor old *Maken* was called everything from a 'trim little schooner,' to a 'fine fast yawl'!

The editor of one of the leading local newspapers in San Francisco was a fanatically keen sailing man. He sent down a reporter and photographer, chafed at his desk for 10 minutes, leapt up, ran to his car, and drove down to the dock at such a speed that he arrived at the same time as his henchmen. After the usual crossfire of questions and answers, photographs all over the place, and the usual strictly non-committal statements by us about future plans, we were taken ashore by this editor to his home for dinner.

He heard we had read everything on board, so he took two cardboard packing cases and filled them with paperback books for us to take back on board. While we sent cables homewards, his wife whipped up a fine dinner. We stayed and yarned late and then realised that we had not bought any fresh food for next morning's breakfast. We piled into his car and he took us to an all-night self-service grocers, where we got all the usual edibles which make up a breakfast. It was the editor who whipped round the store filling a big paper basket with all these good things; then he paid for the bag of food and drove us back to the ship.

Next morning, after a fabulous breakfast with fresh bread, bacon, eggs and fresh milk, I was collected by the owner of the schooner in his dinghy. We rowed back to his yacht and soon had her under way. As we dropped her mooring I looked back at the *Maken* with some affection. There she was, courageous, reliable, safe, a bit weatherbeaten now, with the white paint chipped and scarred, greenery beginning to show on the water-line, patches of grey on the furled sails. But these were honourable scars, and I saw her with new eyes and greater appreciation. Then, suddenly – what is *this* I see? A launch going alongside, and in it the most fabulous blonde, a veritable humdinger, a peachsome pearl; in short, a Girl, Mark One. The only other person in the launch was the boatman and I saw him leave his passenger and motor back to the shore. My eyebrows went up two storeys. Mike alone with *THAT*, after three months at sea!

It was a grand race. We threshed round the course, having a wonderful time. I thoroughly enjoyed the beat to windward, simply because we were racing. The crew were all very young and wildly enthusiastic. We sweated and slaved and came in well up the fleet. Afterwards we sailed back to the moorings and my host rowed me back to the *Maken*. I thought Mike looked as if he was harbouring a host of secrets and the conversation opened on a studiedly casual level.

'We had a visitor, just after you left,' he drawled.

'Oh, yes?' say I, not giving away a millimetre.

'Some woman from a television studio. We're going on television, on Sunday.'

'Sounds fun. How did that come about?'

'Remember that article you wrote in one of the newspapers? You said, and I quote: "I'd even go on television for a dozen cans of different food, to get a change from wieners."'

'She's taken us up on that remark?'

'Uh-huh. It's some sort of quiz show. They're sending a taxi down to the dockside for us.'

'What'll we wear? My shoregoing gear's pretty tatty.'

'She said we were to wear sailing gear.'

'Hell! She can't have any idea what we do wear at sea!'

'She wants us to wear yachting caps.'

'What are they?'

When Sunday came, we were nervous. To make matters worse, the taxi didn't arrive on schedule and we were late at the television studio, which was a big semi-country house on the edge of the city. We walked into the hall and there she was. At close quarters she was just as lovely as I thought. More so. Her figure was like a film star's, and her dress was one of those deceptively simple jobs with nothing to it except a gigantic bill for the buyer. Her legs were a naval architect's dream, because naval architects are much concerned with smooth fair curves, since all good ships, and particularly good yachts, are created by applying a system of perfect curves to paper, later to be wrought in the solid. She held out a hand with long slender fingers, a perfect hand in a country celebrated the world over for the lovely hands of its womenfolk.

I expect I just stared and stared and stared. It's only very seldom even in a well travelled lifetime that you meet a girl like this. Her voice matched the rest of her.

'You must be Mr Nicolson, and my name's Marcia,' she said, 'Mike says you're the brave one.'

'Me? Brave? How do you mean?' I managed to find my voice, even if my manners were wanting before this apparition.

'Mike says you'll love being on television.'

I looked round for Mike to ask him; no, damn it, to knife him! He'd fled.

I asked her: 'You mean he's not going on? Just me?'

'That's right. We can only have one of you, I'm afraid. But there's nothing to worry about. It's quite easy. The producer will explain how it all works.' She took me into the studio and showed me to a seat among the eight other contestants. Our seats were out in front of a goodly gathering. Behind us were rows and rows of the audience. We faced an open space in this biggish room, a sort of arena where the action would take place.

The producer walked into the arena and called for silence: 'Quiet, please, everybody. Now tonight we have some very famous contestants, and I'll just introduce you before we go on the air. First of all you all know Johnny Stadler, the Question Master.' A dapper young man walked forward so that everyone could see him. He was made up for television, but none of us contestants were.

'We are very honoured to have here tonight the crew of the *Maken*. You will all have read in the newspapers how these boys sailed their little yacht all those thousands of miles ...' and more in this vein, so that I began to blush.

'Then we have Miss San Francisco 1953,' the producer went on. I turned to look at my neighbour. She was one of those petite brunettes that look so scrumptious as pin-ups. She had on a topless, strapless, backless dress. She had a striking figure, well displayed by this dress which was a dark red, rich brocade material, as lovely as the girl it partially contained.

My pulse changed into top gear and I knew that this was my evening. Plenty of men go through a whole life never getting nearer than the front row of the stalls to this sort of girl, and here I was sitting in the front row almost on top of one. Following so soon after meeting Marcia, I began to think maybe I had journeyed far enough and should look for a job here in San Francisco.

The producer was going on: 'Now you'll each come up in turn and stand here, in front of the camera, beside Johnny. He'll pick the first card from his pile and ask you the question on it. But the first question will be an easy one, just to get you relaxed. It might be something like "Where do German sausages come from?" Well, of course, you don't have to be very bright to say "Germany."'(I thought of wieners).

The producer continued: 'If you answer five questions right, you stand on Johnny's left side, here, and you wear this little blackboard, with 5 chalked on it.' He picked up a miniature blackboard with a chain attached so that it could be worn as a necklace. The idea was, of course, to let the television viewers see what the maximum score was, even if they tuned in after the beginning of the programme.

'Now, if you answer less than the highest score to date,' the producer explained, 'you drop out. But if you answer more than the person standing by Johnny with the blackboard on, then you take the position on Johnny's left and you wear the blackboard till someone does better than you.'

It all sounded dead easy, provided of course the questions were not too tough. Here I was at a great disadvantage, because every other competitor had watched this programme often, whereas I had never seen it before. Also, I was sitting next to Miss S.F. '53, which made it difficult to concentrate on anything except her.

This was of course a commercial programme, and there was now a brief pause while the commercial jingles were put on the screen. Then the producer came forward again.

'Now you people in the audience, pay attention please. When I clap [here he held his hands high so that everyone could see], I want you to clap too, good and brisk. But when I hold up my hands [here was another wildly exaggerated gesture, like his clapping, which would easily be interpreted by the most moronic person in the studio audience] then STOP! You hear? That's most important.' This was the only bogus part of the programme. American television programmes have been slated hard for swindling, and in particular some of their quiz programmes have been shown up as phoney. But there was absolutely no dishonesty in this one.

It was now fast approaching the moment when we would be on the air. The audience was told to be quiet, the camera teams became active, there was that tense bustle that precedes any show. Then the atmosphere fairly tingled because the professionals there, Johnny, the producer, Marcia, and the cameramen, were all very much on edge. The previous week had been unsatisfactory, and there'd been murmurings from the programme sponsors about stopping the series. I would have been as nervous as any of them, but I was too busy whispering to Miss S.F. '53, 'Will you ...' On second thoughts, we'll omit what I whispered and get on with the show. The red light went on. A silence that hurt throttled the whole roomful of people. The silent electric clock with its big second-hand held every eye. The red light went out, the green one was on. We were on the air.

'Good evening, ladies and gentlemen. Once again the Sunnyvale Supreme Canned Food Company presents its Amazing Quiz Program ...' the commercial blurb was rattled off with a gigantic smile by the ultra-nervous announcer who had spent the whole evening going around muttering 'Good-evening-ladies-and-gentlemen-tonight-once-again ... No, that's wrong. Good-evening-ladies-and-gentlemen-once-again-tonight-we-present ... No, that's wrong, too ...'

Then the first contestant was on. Poor lad, he was so nervous that he was chewing his fingernails up to the elbow. He advanced towards Johnny, on whom the camera was concentrated.

'Good evening. Mr Efelbaker. Welcome to the Sunnyvale Supreme Canned Food Company's quiz. No need to be nervous, eh? Ha-ha-ha!' This was Johnny's way of breezing anyone out of stage fright. It worked like a candle in a gale of wind.

Gggggg-ggggg-ggggood eee-eee-evening, sir,' the poor fellow managed to
get out, glancing surreptitiously at the camera as if he expected it to bite him.

'Now what do you do? That is, when you're not appearing on television.
Ha-ha-ha!' cackled the dreadful Johnny, working hard to put the first victim at
his ease. The miserable wretch managed to blurt out his profession and a few
other facts about himself, with a lot of help and ha-ha-haing from Johnny.

'Right now, Mr Efelbaker. Here's the first question. What's onion soup made
from?'

'Onions,' says Efelbaker, with a sigh of relief that pushed the mobile camera
back 4 feet. The poor fellow had been so worried that he might drop out on
the first question, not realising that the first one was purposely simple. But the
show was going on.

'How many eggs in a dozen?' asked Johnny.

'Twelve!'

'Dead right. What colour is a bison?'

'Brown. Dark black. No, dark browny black, sort of ...'

'That's it: you've got it! Dark brown. You're doing fine ...'

'What is a stethoscope?' That beat our hero, and amid much clapping from
the audience the number 3 was boldly chalked on the little blackboard and
this lad went round behind Johnny and stood on the left. In front of these two
there was a raised desk and on it were placed, between each turn, a variety of
goods. The producer would advance, spouting something like 'And before the
next contestant, here we have a pair of Boudoire nylons, the stockings that
REALLY LAST,' and he would go off, allowing the game to proceed. Which it
did to some effect when the second contestant came up, that top-class honey
Miss San Francisco 1953. Johnny really enjoyed himself, but the show couldn't
be delayed and soon enough this piece of floosum was doing her stuff. She was
bright, too. In no time she whipped up to seven questions correctly answered;
then stuck on the next. So the little blackboard was taken off the first poor
clot's neck and the number 7 written on it. Then it was hung round that lovely
neck and laid, rather gingerly, on that full front by Johnny, who turned out to
be more voice than courage when the chips were down. So it was my turn and
I breezed up thinking the whole thing was highly amusing, and determined to
have a good run for my money.

'And you're Mr Nicolson, aren't you?' said Johnny, knowing damn well I was
because we had spent 5 minutes in conversation before the show started.

'Yes, that's right.' No need to admit too much; must play this cool, think I.

'Aren't you one of the boys that sailed that yacht all the way from England,
I read about in the newspapers?'

'Yes. Two of us sailed the *Maken* into the harbour a couple of days ago. We
left England six months ago.' I thought I might as well give the audience a run
for their money. Besides, it'd be pretty dull for all hands if I just went on saying
'Yes, that's right.' Then Johnny shot off a lot of nonsense about it being brave
and courageous to sail such a small ship so far, and so on. All of which was way
off beam, because it took five times as much nerve to go in front of a television
camera. Then we began the business of the evening.

'What was Washington's Christian name?' asked Johnny.

'George,' I whip out, full of confidence by now.

'Right. Where do Chow dogs come from?'

'China.' This is easy enough.

'Right. Where was King Tutankhamen the king of?'

'Ancient Egypt.' Tally-ho, we're still batting!

'Right. Is the present Queen of England Elizabeth the first or second?'

'The second.' Dead easy, that one; but then these questions were really prepared for Americans, not people like me.

'Right. Good gracious, the next question's an easy one for you! What is the kitchen called on a ship?'

'The galley.'

'Right. How many in a gross?'

'A hundred and forty-four.' Heaven bless a British education; it's streets ahead of the American brand!

'Right. Which side of the road do they drive on in Sweden?'

'The left, as in Britain.' Must get in a bit of propaganda for the Old Country. That was a tricky one, though, as Sweden is about the only country outside the British Empire to drive on the sensible side.

'Right! If you plant an oak apple, will an oak tree grow?'

'No. The seed of an oak tree's an acorn, not an oak apple.' Keep going, boy!

'Right! That makes eight questions right. So you're ahead of Miss San Francisco here,' Johnny pointed out.

'Oh, NO! Oh, I AM sorry! Why, I wouldn't have spoilt your chance if I ... I must say. I'm most terribly sorry!' I was thoroughly put out. I'd rushed through question after question without thinking that this sweet little Whomfle was going to lose the prize if I overtook her. And I had. With brutal callousness I had crashed past her, so that I was now one question ahead. Without taking the least notice of the camera I turned to the girl and apologised profusely, with my broad English accent. The producer just leapt in. The cameramen loved it. They lunged forward to get a close-up of the scene. The girl was charming and said something nice, I tried to soften her disappointment; it was all vastly good fun, with the camera now breathing down our necks. We had a brief chat and then got on with the job, but the scene had made the whole programme, and the producer was delighted. Next day wherever I went, in lifts and in the street, I was accosted.

'SAY! Weren't you the boy on television last night? Say, that was real great. You sure did liven things up ...' and so on. It's rather fun being a star of the screen, just for one day.

But to get on with the nonstop questioning, Johnny was back on the job.

'What is the capital of Nevada?' Now that was a killer. Plenty of Americans couldn't tell you the answer. I know: later, I tried them. I said 'Las Vegas,' which caused a mild laugh.

'No. Try again.'

Desperately I racked my brains. I could think of a dozen cities in all the surrounding states, but not one in Nevada, which is largely desert anyhow. So I was gonged out, but I had the top total to date, and Miss San Francisco gave me the little blackboard with a terrific smile; a figure 8 was put on the board and it was hung round my neck.

Now it was me standing on Johnny's left, permanently in front of the camera, while the fourth and subsequent contestants came up for their grilling. Meanwhile the producer kept adding to the pile of trophies on the desk in front of us. Now there was a lighter, a streamlined tin-opener the size of a large lobster, a powder compact, a bottle of hair oil, a leather belt.

One after another the remaining contestants were beaten, all with scores below mine. The producer never seemed to sit still for a second. He was either doing his absurdly exaggerated clapping act, leading the audience in their crisp, quickly cut-off applause, or he was adding to the pile in front of us, or organising the camera. I had plenty of time to think, now. All these products in front of me; what are they all doing there? It dawned on me: these were the prizes. I was busy winning this lot. Just let a few more ignorant people come up for questioning, and I would totter back to the *Maken* with enough booty to start a shop. And that is how it happened! No one else scored as much as I had, so I found myself acclaimed the winner, amid much celebrating. But the climax was to come.

The producer was in front of the cameras: 'This week, ladies and gentlemen, is the special week of the month! It's JACKPOT week! And here is the jackpot prize! This Supreme refrigerator, the 11.7 cubic foot, all-electric, all automatic with its extra SPACIOUS shelves, EASILY cleaned interior, LUXURIOUS finish, SUPER-SOFT door-catch, NO-NOISE motor, which normally costs $280 at any appliance dealer, this lovely machine is our special prize. Come and receive it, Mr Nicolson!'

This, of course, was just grand. The only trouble was that there was no room for a refrigerator the size of a sentry box on the *Maken*. She didn't even have electricity aboard. Never mind. The programme was still going on, so I went up for my prize, feeling that life was slightly fantastic and that this was a fair distance from reefing in a rising gale. I had to be ceremonially crowned on a tinsel-covered throne, as top dog of the week. There was the usual signing-off blurb from the sponsors of the programme, and then we were off the air.

Naturally I was at once thoroughly pleased and a trifle embarrassed. It's all very fine breezing into a hospitable port and having a good time with the citizens, but to go and whip their monthly prize from under their noses struck me as approaching piracy. But one and all were delighted. The producer was nearly crying with relief. His programme, his precious programme – it was a peach, a pearl, a hit! Already the telephone was ringing: Wonderful! Terrific! A grand laugh!

I went up to apologise for winning. He roared with laughter and relief. 'Delighted you won. Just *delighted*. Can you use the fridge? No? Well, never mind, Marcia will arrange to sell it for you.' And eventually she did, bless her. But that evening there was no point in wasting time selling fridges; we went off and celebrated. With Marcia.

Before all this happened, the day after our story came out in the papers, a woman of about fifty, a doctor, came down the pier and waited till we came ashore. She introduced herself and her family and said: 'I've read about your voyage. I think it's wonderful and we would be very pleased if you would come and use our flat as your home while you are in San Francisco. Just drop in when you want to, have a bath, a meal, bring any friends. There's a spare bedroom, if you want to sleep ashore.' And so on, in that vein. She was perhaps the most generous of these kindly people, but she was by no means unique.

There was the lawyer who owned a lovely yacht. He introduced himself, and without further ado said: 'It's time to eat; come and have dinner with me.'

'We'd love to, but we're not dressed for the yacht club.'(This was when we had moved to a mooring of the San Francisco Corinthian Yacht Club).

'Of course you are! Besides, everyone knows who you are, and they all know you've had your clothes stolen by a bunch of dagoes.' So we went and had a round or three of drinks, then into the dining room. There were just three of us round the table: the lawyer, Mike and me. A waiter put a basket of garlic bread on the table, between Mike and me. We took a piece each and started to nibble, while we finished our drink. Somehow the whole basket of garlic bread disappeared before we'd finished our drinks or ordered the meal. The waiter brought a second basket of garlic bread before bringing the first course. The room was full and the waiters were few, so that the first course was some time a-coming. When he brought it, the second basket of garlic bread had been eaten. Mike and I were a trifle embarrassed. Neither of us had noticed that, as we were yarning, we were munching away at this ambrosia. The long weeks without bread gave us an appetite for it that was scarcely satiable. Admittedly these were small loaves of garlic bread, but even so we did fairly well; in the end we ate, apart from the rest of the excellent meal, three complete baskets of this delightful food. In case it's never come your way, they made it like this: A Vienna loaf, that is a cigar-shaped crusty affair, new and warm, is cut into sections about 2 inches thick, and melted butter that has been swirled round a dish previously rubbed with garlic is poured into the innards of the loaf.

This lunch party was just one of a string of incidents in a continuous stream of invitations and other acts of generosity. There was the problem of getting the fuel-pipe repaired: the coastguards did this in their workshop, and refused payment. We needed jacks to push the mizzen mast up a fraction before fitting new shores beneath it: a lorry owner lent us a pair.

We also fitted a new bilge-pump to the boat at this time, because the old one was getting beyond its work. The boat leaked quite a bit in bad weather when she was stressed, and I believe that the stern gland was also responsible for letting some of the ocean come inboard.

We made it generally known that we would welcome two men as additional crew for the final lap of the cruise. The newspapers jumped in with both feet, and we had a number of applicants. In the end we asked two of these to join us. The eldest was Bill, a very tough individual who had fought with the American Marines during the war, and had the sort of square features, robust good humour and all round ability which one associates with the US Marines. The second fellow was a complete contrast. Harry was slight, younger than any of us, a schoolteacher and a quietly competent person, with one outstanding feature: he had only one arm. In spite of this, he was one of the best crews I've ever sailed with – he would tackle anything and make a good job of it. He'd learnt to use his one hand with remarkable dexterity. For instance, we continued the practice aboard of taking it in turns to cook; Harry never missed his turn, nor did he offer meals below our standard. This alone was a display of sheer guts and determination, because cooking in a rough sea called for a good deal of hard work. It meant holding on when a big wave passed under and the *Maken* threw herself upwards, over and sideways down the slope with a lurch that would unseat a doubtful set of dentures. Harry had taken up mountaineering, he drove a car with every bit as much skill and verve as the next man, and he was extremely good fun aboard. In fact, the whole tempo of the yacht suddenly changed into top gear when these two cheerful types joined us, which they did just before we left.

Meanwhile there was plenty to do. The yacht was beginning to feel the effects of the continuous thrusting. During the two or three weeks immediately before we arrived at San Francisco, we'd had some spells of hard winds and choppy seas, and this buffeting had found the weak places which had been caused by constant rolling and flopping about in the calms. At sea a yacht is seldom motionless even for a minute, so every part is constantly wearing and working loose. We found that two of the chain plates (steel straps which attach the wire rigging to the hull) were coming loose. The basic trouble is that three months' ocean cruising is equivalent to two seasons of normal yachting, with corresponding wear and tear.

What with invitations hither and yon, it took a whole day to do a job like regreasing the blocks. Normally one would take them all down in an hour or two, knock out the pins, slosh grease all round them, hammer them back again and get the blocks back in place before lunch. What was liable to happen was something like this. Some blocks are aloft, so it's necessary to go up the mast for them. From this vantage point there is a fine view – in fact, just look at that blonde going afloat over there! Back to work, man, or this job will never be done by teatime. Teatime! Good heavens, I'm due to have a meal with those two lads who have a 2-tonner, and all my shirts are dirty! Down on deck quickly, seize the cleanest shirt, boil water, wash hands, wash shirt, hang it up, and back aloft on to the job again. Mike is off on some other job ashore, so each block had to be lowered to the deck or carried down. In the middle of greasing, when my hands are really filthy, the wind changes and the clean shirt starts to blow against the rigging. To wash it, some more water has to be heated, hands washed, shirt washed, then back on the job. Blonde passes in sailing dinghy. I pause to admire dinghy. Blonde sails close and asks: 'Is this the yacht that sailed from England?'

'Yes. Would you like to come aboard?'

One hour later, work is resumed on the blocks. Putting them back, I notice a chafe in the main peak halliard. This calls for repairs and a method has to be devised to stop the trouble recurring. With interruptions and distractions it can take two days to complete a minor job like this.

We moved the yacht to the St Francis yacht marina for the final loading up, and this was quite the most luxurious berth we'd struck to date. The acme of high living was seen in the toilets. In those days it was rare to find tastefully coloured toilet paper such as is now common enough. The St F. marina not only had coloured paper, but paper seat-covers to match!

There was a bit of a scramble getting the boat ready for departure. We had a lot of fresh food to stow (always a difficult job) because we were well and truly stocked for the last lap. Bill and Harry had chipped in with cash for the kitty. The kitty didn't know itself, it bulged like a bank, and we had a food-buying spree. Then there were the many tins of food I'd won on the television show. These went under the bunks easily enough, but of course we couldn't stow fresh food in those dark, dank holes.

Harry took over Bjarne's bunk, and Bill was in the starboard bunk in the saloon. They came aboard the night before we left and there was a whirl of parties and ones-for-the-road and 'Heavens-I've-forgotten-films-for-my-camera' and suchlike exclamations, usually followed by a hectic rush to the shops. Fortunately these are not fettered by inane regulations, as in Britain, and many commodities can be bought at any hour of the day or night. This shows how things have changed in Britain over the past sixty-plus years.

It was all rather hilarious and confused, just as if we were off on the first lap, and I've no very clear recollections of the last 24 hours ashore. I managed to get the usual long slow-mail letter off to my mother, and at the last moment a short airmail one saying we were just clearing. She would get the first within the week, by which time we would be well on our way, and the second in three weeks, when we were almost in harbour. So she would only have a few days to wait till the cable arrived saying: 'Arrived Victoria. All well.'

It may have been noticed that this narrative falls down in one respect. As the tale unfolds, no hero or heroine has been thrown up, which is a prerequisite of all the best stories. Actually the heroine is in the background all the time. Imagine what it is like to carry on life normally while your family wander about the sea's surface in a boat built at the beginning of the century, with a few pounds sterling in the pocket, remaining at sea for weeks and months on end, miles, hundreds of miles off the beaten track, without wireless or lifeboat. My mother never suggested that it would be better if I did not go, or made worried noises, and every time we got into harbour there would be a little bundle of cheerful letters waiting. She ran the 'shore base,' which is an essential requirement for trouble-free ocean cruising. She'd have loved to have sailed with us; but, being unable to, she just made sure we had a good time with the minimum of trouble from shore sources.

Chapter Fourteen

We sailed out of San Francisco heading due west to get a good offing. The current and prevailing winds are down the coast, so instead of turning north into them we made a run straight out to sea for 700 miles. That brought us clear of the foul current and in line for a favourable wind slant to give us a reach up to the straits of Juan de Fuca (pronounced Waaan-di-Foookah).

It was grey and chilly as we left and we sailed slap into a gale. It was a full-blooded stiff one, a real wave-piler. The wind started off in a noisy basso, booming and roaring. Then it went up an octave and my heart went down in proportion. The sea was grey and thoroughly horrid. The waves piled up as steep as hills big enough for skiing; only they were wet, unsolid masses which burst in solid gouts of flying foam when they reached us. The wind went up another octave. Heart responded as before. All that soft living had its effect and it was like being a beginner all over again. But then, every gale is always frightening from the low deck of a yacht, so in some ways this was no different from the others; only this time there was no inclination in me to feel exultant and climb the mast. Maybe it was the grim, wet sky; the cloud-ceiling was somewhere the height of our mainmast, it seemed. The *Maken* seemed old and tired. Gear that had been stowed well the whole trip had got moved in the ten days in San Francisco, so that odds and ends came adrift and clattered about.

The new crew were wonderful, but both Mike and I were on edge. It was perhaps the thought that we were close inshore with the gale on us. Never before had we been caught by bad weather with any land near, and I'd said more than once to Mike that I didn't think the *Maken* could claw off a lee shore in a real gale, if there was danger of her being driven on to it. He hadn't liked being told this, naturally. Every owner likes to think his yacht is as near perfect as makes no difference, but he was bound to see that there was probably some truth in my remarks, and it was doubly forceful coming from someone who had ridden out gales in other yachts. As a naval architect I was supposed to know about these things, so Mike was pretty worried ... and that made two of us.

The second day out we were hove-to hour after dreary hour, with the constant thought that we could have been enjoying the fleshpots only a few miles away. We felt thoroughly cheated because somehow one associates California with sunshine and fine weather. We had not, in fact, seen the sun from the time we left, and it was to be eight days before we got a proper view of it again.

We had one great consolation, though. Our friend the newspaper editor had given us such a stack of paperback books that we had enough for all tastes and moods. So there was nothing but the flickering of eyes over page after page as we lay in our bunks and waited for the wind to moderate.

When the wind had first piped up, we had reefed. It was sheer luxury with four of us. Mike and I between us had found it a pretty grim struggle with a strong wind in the sails and no one at the helm. Now we had Harry at the tiller and Bill's powerful muscles to help us subdue the unruly canvas. The *Maken* had a wire clew pennant to haul down the reef cringle. This had to be passed through the eye on the sail, which was liable to flap about and be well out of reach, then through a bee-block on the boom before being taken for'ard to a great, long tackle. The wire had no eye in the end, otherwise it would not have passed through the cringle on the sail. So this wire had to be bent on to the hook of the tackle with a Blackwall hitch. This is the sort of thing met occasionally in Nelson's day, but seldom (thank God!) encountered these days. To get the hitch right, with the boat jumping about and the wire as recalcitrant as a steel cobra, called for more than ordinary cunning. Then when the hitch was on, the tackle had to be kept taut all the time or the cursed thing would come adrift. And of course the tackle was just made for tying knots in itself and generally behaving with all the perversity which inanimate objects can command. Admittedly the gear was simple, so that there was no chance of mechanical breakdown; but there were moments when human breakdown would have been entirely excusable. Still, it was all good experience, and boats which I have since had under my care have never had unruly reefing gear.

With an extra hand on the sails, with Harry at the tiller, and with Mike and me by now working in concert, we made short work of handling the sail. We went below, leaving one man on watch. Not long afterwards we put in the second reef. By now the wind and sea looked as if this was the real thing. From the deck it was impossible to see more than a few hundred yards, and often only a few hundred feet; the seas broke with that hiss and roar that is so sinister, so suggestive of gigantic ruthless power just waiting to deliver the *coup de grâce*. Below, it was fairly peaceful, but this merely accentuated the noise when a wave broke with a thunderous torrent of sound and a shuddering thump of solid tons of water against the ship's side.

We ended up with a fully reefed mainsail and reefed staysail. Under this tiny area of sail the yacht lay over at a small angle on the crests. The rest of the time she took up whatever angle the dominating sea dictated. Being so heavy and yet with ample reserve buoyancy, the motion was in fact not too bad. Most of the time it was possible to work one's way about the ship holding on with just one hand. By midday of the second day of the gale we were all pretty fed up, and Mike said: 'I'm going to do a roast. That always ends a gale.'

This was in fact true. On other occasions when we had been hove-to and the weather had started to ease, but refused to moderate enough to get sailing again, Mike had cooked a big meal, and promptly the weather had relented. By now it was no longer blowing the bats from Hades, but it was certainly no weather to start hoisting up a lot of canvas. Mike took our joint of meat, our precious fresh joint, and put it in the little duck oven, which sat on the primus. Presently the boat was suffused with a luscious odour. Mike worked away on the galley by the hour; every so often we would notice another succulent odour waft through to join the others which already tantalised our nostrils. At last he said: 'Come and get it. But hold on to everything all the time.'

What a triumph that was! He had cooked a four-course dinner in a galley that was lurching and rolling, thudding and gyrating every moment. It certainly was the finest culinary feat I've ever witnessed.

We fell to with sharp appetites, for we had eaten little all the long hours of the gale. It was necessary to hold on to the plates all the time, and ordinary knife-and-fork transactions were quite out of the question. I felt ill after the first course and had to go on deck to be seasick. That made me feel fine again, and I went back to the table to eat the second course. I'd thought that seasickness was cured, at least for that cruise, but the high life in San Francisco had brought it back again. After the second course I again felt sick and had to go on deck to waste a second lot of food. The third course I tried to eat very slowly, hoping that my stomach would realise that all this waste was profiting no one. It was no good, and a third time I had to leave the table. The others by now were beginning to feel full, but I was getting annoyed, as well as being still hungry. I concocted a plan. I ate the fourth course quite quickly and then made a dive for my bunk. I lay horizontal and read with concentration and so won the last round.

In the end we had to lie-to for four days and three nights. This was a pretty lousy introduction to ocean cruising for the others, especially as the decks leaked and the bunks were wetted. Even mine felt the effects of the deluged decks, so I moved my sleeping bag on to the floor.

At long last we were able to give up reading novels and get on with the job. We set sail little by little, and soon started making useful progress, but by now our position was more than doubtful. Day after day we sailed under grey skies with never a proper view of the sun, except for perhaps a few minutes, when the horizon would be completely blurred. We couldn't get a sextant fix, and had only a rough idea of how far or in what direction we had moved when hove-to. Nine days out we were all below because it was cold and the boat was sailing herself quite well. I went up on deck and there was the first ship we had seen since we left San Francisco. In the properly bored voice I called down the hatch: 'If anyone's interested in looking at ships, there's a fairly good specimen going to pass close.'

Of course, this brought a scramble of bodies from below. It was clear that the freighter would pass usefully close on a reciprocal course, so Mike decided to hoist the International code pennant followed by LFF which means 'Position Doubtful'. This was, after all, true. We knew we were in the Eastern Pacific; all we wanted to know was which part. Both he and I felt more than doubtful that the freighter would take any notice, and we were also rather shy about asking the way like a lost motorist.

Nothing visible happened except that the freighter continued on her way at a good pace. She flew no flag but her build proclaimed her to be very American. Her name confirmed this; it was *Keystone Mariner*. She seemed to go almost to the horizon before we saw her shape lengthen. She was turning. She made a big circle and we held up a board with the yacht's name painted on it, as she was too far away when she passed for us to shout. She stopped and we sailed towards her, but rather slowly as there was not much wind and anyhow the *Maken* wasn't going to rush about for some flighty young freighter only a quarter of her age. The ship's skipper must have thought we'd never get within hailing distance, and no doubt he had a schedule to keep, so he circled round us and stopped engines close downwind, pointing straight at us. The top of that ship's bow was higher than our mainmast, and the steel plates, glistening wet, looked dangerously unresilient. For several horrible seconds it looked as if we would be run down, because although the freighter had stopped her engine she was still moving at a firm pace through the water.

We yelled up to a figure on the fo'c'sle head: 'What is our position?' He might have shouted back: 'Ruddy dangerous,' but in fact he replied: 'Our engine is stopped,' which was a relief to know.

We just squeezed past that juggernaut of steel, and then Mike gybed round under her lee, whereupon she drifted down on to us. So we were no sooner clear of one danger than another was on us. It looked as if we would bump badly alongside, for though there was little wind there was ample sea – more than ample, we thought, as we lurched and lolloped on the swell.

Coming out of San Francisco we had not had a pilot, but we had expected to see the pilot boat; so we had written letters to post aboard it. These letters had been sandwiched between two wooden boards, all ready to throw, because it is absolute madness to get close alongside another ship at sea. Damage and very serious breakages are almost inevitable. Bill took this double slab of wood, which had in big letters on both sides 'PLEASE POST THESE LETTERS,' and with a fine baseball throw heaved it well and truly on to the freighter's deck. The letters subsequently got to their destinations, having originally been 'posted' a good 400 miles offshore.

Meanwhile we were on tenterhooks. We got closer and closer to that steel cliff. We put out fenders and prayed hard. We were gradually moving past the ship, and at one moment it seemed that we'd be all right; but the next moment the situation looked really grim. We were almost certainly going to crash. The two vessels seemed to heave up and down dozens of feet on the towering Pacific swell.

From above someone yelled out our latitude and longitude and I whipped out the pencil I always kept in my leather sheath with a knife and shifting-spanner, and scrawled the vital figures down on the white-painted hatch top (It would have to be painted again soon anyway, so no damage was done). It was as well I did this, because after the uproar was over no one had the vaguest remembrance of what the position was that had been shouted down.

There was some yelling to and fro about ports of departure and destination; it was cut short when we hit. We had drifted towards the stern of the *Keystone Mariner* and our main shrouds took the first blow. Then the mizzen started to take punishment and we got a glimmering of what it was like to be in a sea battle in the days of sail. Blocks, rigging, flags and spars rained down from aloft. Pieces of metal hurtling down to bury themselves in the wood deck between the feet are slightly disconcerting.

In a moment we seemed to be knee-deep in gear, though actually the total of our damage was a broken topping-lift block, broken mizzen gaff, and the top 2 feet of the mizzen snapped off. Of course, the signal flags came down, to add a touch of colour to the proceedings.

Meanwhile a new danger loomed, worse than all the others put together. Someone aft on the *Maken* shouted something about getting way on the freighter. She was in ballast, with her propeller standing way out of the water. To Bill and me, for'ard, it was a hideous sight, very sharp and close; if the suggestion to start the freighter's engine had been acted on, we should all have been minced into small pieces. The moment that propeller started we were as good as dead, because its power would be enormous. It would suck a great stream of water to itself, and on this stream the *Maken* would be just like a scrap of driftwood. The whole yacht would be drawn relentlessly into the maelstrom, the blade would chop the hull into firewood …

Bill and I yelled aft in no uncertain manner. The others aft realised that a mistake had been made, and we all bellowed to the freighter to keep their engine stationary. They had the good sense to do that. Up for'ard we grabbed a spare spinnaker boom to shove the *Maken* away from the freighter. The ship's side rose above us, a vertical wall of steel, smooth and without anything we could push the pole against. It was no good trying to push horizontally; the two craft were rolling and plunging about far too much. Then we spotted a small pipe outlet on the ship's side. With desperate haste, for the *Maken* was still taking an awful battering, we lodged the end of the pole into this cranny and shoved as if our lives depended on it – as well they might! Then we paused. Bill looked at me. I looked at him. Simultaneously we both realised that if anyone on the freighter pulled the chain of the toilet, we were standing directly in line of fire. So, circumspectly, ready to leap out of the way, we shoved all the harder.

It worked. The yacht moved slightly. Bill's great strength forced the two craft apart, though I feared he might blister the paint all round with his choice of language. After what seemed like hours but was in fact less than 5 minutes we got the bowsprit out clear of the stern of the freighter. The jib, which had been hanging limp and useless, caught a draught of wind round the ship's stern. The sail flapped once, twice, then settled down to pull us clear. The staysail cleared the ship's stern and it, too, started to draw us forward, then the main. The mizzen finally felt the wind, but it had a shattered boom, and it flapped and clattered like a bird with a broken wing till we lowered it. From the freighter someone shouted: 'You all right?'

'Yes, thanks. No serious damage. Report us to Lloyd's, please.' We drew away from the ship, to the accompaniment of the hollow slosh – slosh of her propeller, still stationary but pounding and splashing as the waves washed round and over it. It was the most eerie sound. Those last few moments alongside the freighter were by a long way the most dangerous of the whole cruise. Once we were past her pipe outlet we could no longer effectively push ourselves off. This was not very serious, as the bumping had eased, but every detail on the freighter's stern stood out with blinding clearness. The zinc sacrificial plates which are riveted on to prevent propeller corrosion, the places where the paint had flaked off, the rudder with its barnacles – these were milestones we painfully inched by. When we were beginning to draw clear, someone threw a light rope down from above. In the heat of the moment I couldn't for the life of me see what the blazes it was for. We certainly had no wish to remain tethered to this frightful steel monster. Then sense reasserted itself and I tore aft with the rope in hand and took a quick turn round the aft bollard: up on the freighter they took their end of the rope as far aft as they could, and helped to pull us clear.

In all this, Mike stood by our tiller, unhurt while lumps of this and that hurtled down around him. We started at once to clear up the deck while the freighter made a half circle back on course and steamed away. The mizzen was lowered, removed from the broken gaff, taken off the boom and bundled away. The ropes and flags lying about the deck were tidied away, with the usual care and cross-referencing to get the flags into their correct pigeon-holes so as to avoid future trouble, should the useless things ever have to be dragged out again.

A new topping-lift block was prepared and sent up the mainmast first, because if the weather had turned sour we could not have reefed comfortably without it. One of the steel bands round the mainmast had been forced down the mast in spite of the metal dogs holding it up: the retainers had been forced downwards through the grain of the wood. An ordinary yacht's mast would have given up the struggle for survival long before. We tightened the bottlescrews to stop the shrouds flapping in the breeze, then turned to see about the mizzen gaff.

The first attempt to repair this spar was a failure. We lashed flat steel straps along the two pieces of spar as splints, with the two broken parts butted together. Metal mast bands were put round the join, a rope wound round and the whole lot made tight by driving wooden wedges in under the rope and the mast bands. It made an imposing repair but it was not rigid. The second try was a success. A long scarf was made in the for'ard end of the old boom and it was married to that valiant spinnaker boom which Bill and I had used as a fend-off. The main reason for using the end of the old gaff was that it had the gaff jaws. These were strong, and had not suffered in the collision. To make a new set of jaws would have been a big job, and to take the old ones off the gaff would have been a titanic task. They were fixed on there to stay, come what may, in the manner of the general construction of the yacht.

As we worked on deck the sea got up a little, the wind blew colder and conditions became miserable, so repairs were completed in the cabin in comfort. A hot dinner followed soon after. Next day Mike spent some time aloft in a bosun's chair, fixing a new peak halliard for the mizzen. Before the afternoon was over the mizzen was set and there was scarcely a sign of damage to be seen.

So the *Maken* sailed on. We soon turned northwards towards Vancouver and were then right off shipping lanes. We sailed the boat day and night when we could not get her to self-steer well, but if the wind was kind we set her to sail herself and retired below at night thankfully, for it was uncomfortably cold in these latitudes. We even took to using the self-steering during the day, when the weather was foul. It was very cosy below, especially after darkness had fallen. We would play cards by the dim light of a little paraffin lamp and a candle, every so often going up on deck to check that all was well. One rather hectic poker session lasted till three in the morning, so that when we did eventually get to our bunks we slept long and deep. Something about the ship's motion woke me and I went on deck to find she had hove herself to. Close round us were several seals playing. We were 550 miles from the nearest dry land, and even the ocean bed was 2.5 miles below us. One seal put its head out of the water and barked cheerfully at me, like a dog asking for a biscuit; it was close enough for me to have thrown one right into its mouth. I brought the *Maken* round on the correct course, relashed the tiller and went below to cook breakfast. The seals didn't follow us for long.

That day was typical of others at this period. After breakfast, washing-up and tidying the cabin came first, regardless of other activities. Then one would read, another write, a third might play solitaire or darn socks, or start a discussion on anything from drowning at sea to the best way of making coffee. Each day was a pleasant holiday; only the *Maken* doing any real work, as she carried us onwards, 60, 80, or 100 miles a day. About midday someone would suggest a snack.

Various alternatives would be discussed.

'Let's have soup, for a change.'

'We had soup yesterday. You like soup damn near as much as beer.'

'Well, I thought, since it's a cold day …'

'Let's have coffee.'

'You damned Yankees, you *live* on coffee! And the stupid part is it's about the only thing you don't grow.'

On hot days we would have fruit juice or wine. Our rum jar was now full of wine, because by the time we reached San Francisco it was well and truly empty, and as Bill lived in the wine-growing part of California he filled the jar with it when he joined the yacht.

While one person was preparing sandwiches or hamburgers, someone else would be navigating.

'Good day's run, yesterday.'

'Look who set the tiller!'

'Look who cooked last night's dinner. It's the cuisine that makes the ship go.'

'You mean because an army marches on its stomach …?'

'When Napoleon said that, he was thinking of the Marines. I reckon I've; crawled several hundred miles on my stomach through every sort of swamp, jungle, mud-hole and dirty water.' This from Bill.

'Isn't it damn difficult to keep your rifle out of the water under those conditions?'

'You've been seeing too many films. I can tell you about some rifles that have been underwater for hours at a time.' And in no time we would be off on a discussion about the war, or guns, or girls, or food. One great advantage of an international crew is that the variety of experience was vast, and ideas were most diverse. For instance, we drank a truly fantastic amount of coffee, and when I mentioned one day that I had calculated our average daily consumption, Bill told us about his life during the 1930s slump in America. He was an orphan, to all intents and purposes. He lived with his brother in one room. They were youngsters in their teens and, apart from the clothes they wore, they owned practically nothing except an electric coffee pot. When they got up in the morning they cooked some beans in the coffee pot, then made coffee, before going out to work – if they were working at that juncture. Lunch would be soup warmed up in the coffee pot, followed by more coffee. The evening meal was on the same lines. The two boys tried every sort of job and I asked Bill how on earth he had learnt the various trades at the young age he was then.

'We used to learn as we went along. For instance I'd see there was a job for a turner, and I'd apply for it even though I couldn't tell the bow from the stern of a lathe. But in the slump there was a different attitude to now. Everyone would help everyone else. As soon as I got to the lathe I'd tell the chap on the next machine I couldn't work it. He'd show me, and help me along till I got the hang of it.'

For this last part of the voyage we were a very well matched crew. There was so much experience, in such diverse fields, between the four of us that we had the feeling we could tackle anything without effort. Also the big volume of stores purchased by Harry and Bill in San Francisco made our diet much more interesting and varied. From many points of view this was the best part of the journey. Only the long absence of sun was a cause of complaint. The cold made us gigantic eaters and, whereas before there had been only occasional enthusiasm for cooking (as, for instance, when someone tried out something new), now there was not even a need for a cooking rota. Whoever was free and felt inclined took on the job.

Harry produced, one night, a fine dish which he called an 'Original Joe Special'. As I remember the story of this dish, it goes like this. One night a fellow called Joe was just clearing up in his cafe when a drunk staggered in.

'Gimme shummat t'eat,' said the drunk.

'Sorry, we're closed,' Joe replied.

'Musht've somefink t'eat,' the drunk reiterated, in the childish way they have.

'Look,' said Joe with a great sigh, 'Even if I wanted to give you something to eat, I can't. We've sold everything, darn nearly.'

'Musht've somefink t'eat. Musht've. Drink on n'empty stummick's bad. I'll be drunk 'f'm not careful. Gimme somefink t'eat.'

'I can't. All we've got left is an egg, a hamburger, a bit of rice and some spinach. See for yourself.'

'Thad'll do. Tha's just fine. Jus' you gimme that. Why didn't you gimme that right away?'

So Joe served up this mixture. The drunk thought it was fine. The tale of this unusual recipe spread. People came to try it at Joe's cafe. They told their friends. Now Joe's cafe is celebrated for miles around, and Joe's getting rich.

On the *Maken* Harry did not have all the necessary ingredients but he used a can of asparagus tips instead of spinach and for the hamburger he substituted dried beef hash, reconstituted. Like all the meals aboard in grim weather, this one seemed a feast. There were never any scraps to feed the fishes.

Chapter Fifteen

We were by this stage slanting in towards the coast. We had been at sea over two weeks, a relatively short hop, but in some ways a tense one. The shore hereabouts is as treacherous as any in the world, because of the fog. It is easy to forget the hazards of the sea, these days, because so few ships get lost. But the sea is as dangerous as ever it was, and small craft are wrecked just as thoroughly, and quite as devastatingly, as they were in centuries past.

We could not get good radio position fixes, and the constant absence of sun made sextant navigation difficult – for long periods impossible. Among other excitements there was the possibility of being run down in the fog, because this is a fairly well used bit of the ocean, with ships going to Seattle, Vancouver, New Westminster, as well as the ports of the Portland coast.

This coast is as discouraging as any I've met anywhere. It's built like a row of sharks' teeth, rocky and rough and no place to go aground. Also, it's a lee shore. All this added up to a feeling that we had to keep on our toes. Mike and I had the subconscious feeling that we had got thus far without serious trouble, and we were bloody well damned if we were going to be defeated by anything at this stage. Anyone who has struggled to near the top of a difficult mountain after a long and rather grim climb, only to find the last 500 feet the worst, will know the feeling.

We hung around the companion steps, sextant in hand, trying to get a sight between breaks in the mist. When the horizon showed and the sun, too, we would whip up the instrument, only to find that the lenses had misted up in the last few minutes. Frantic drying and cleaning with a not-so-clean handkerchief followed. Then up to the eye again with the sextant. Hell's bells! The sun has slipped into a watery blur. Pause, allowing more than enough time for suitably caustic comments. The sun slides out into clearer air, a gentle breeze swings the yacht a trifle off course, she heels a fraction just to make sure that the sight will be anything but straightforward. The sextant is up to the eye now, the sun dead-clear in the telescope but where in the name of Neptune is the horizon? Oh, Allah give us patience! There is no mist at all now except right beneath the sun, where the horizon has melted into a smudge of nothingness.

While this lark was going on, a timber freighter emerged from the murk and passed close by. Very close. We shouted up to them. It might have been a ghost ship. We shouted again. The crew turned slowly towards us, like people afflicted by some plague which has sapped all but the last dram of energy. We shouted for a position check (how we hated doing that! But feelings are less important than safety). They stared at us, dully, as if we spoke a foreign language which it was too much effort to try and understand. The freighter continued on her way without even an answering hail. She looked as if she would steam on relentlessly till she met the coast, and even then would not have the stimulus to alter course or stop. Unswervingly, she plodded out of our lives.

We went back to chasing the sun. At last Mike got a position fix. It put us far enough offshore to be safe, but the coast was only just over the horizon. This was confirmed by the big logs we saw floating menacingly, every few miles. Sometimes there would be a whole batch of them, great grey-brown monsters, lying well down in the water, waiting for a dark, windy night. Then, going flat out, we might hurl our yacht into a group without seeing them, and smash in a plank, making a hole far too big to plug. We had no dinghy at this stage. Not that the little matchbox we had lost would have carried four of us, even in a calm. Some of these logs floated so low in the water that even in daylight the only way we could tell they were there was by watching the seabirds. They would stand on the logs, perching just a millimetre above the sea's surface, their white plumage standing out sharply against the grey water.

After Mike had shot the sun and plotted the position, I thought I would confirm his sight. The essence of navigation is constant checking, and now was a very good time to make sure we were right. I used the spare sextant instead of my own, for a change. How stupid can you be? We had a note of the error of the spare sextant, but were not certain that it was right up to date. On a yacht all the gear is subject to constant rattling, jolting, bumping. The sextant could have been wildly inaccurate.

It took an age to get the sight. The horizon was so indistinct that I was never sure I could see it truly. At last I got what I thought was a good shot and confirmed it. Down the companionway, and forward to my bunk. Drag out the little notebook, the textbook, a blunt pencil, the tables. Scribble, add, scrawl, subtract. Don't forget the sextant error. Look up the date, correct the chronometer, add again, more hieroglyphics. Consult the tables once more, add, subtract, squiggle, scribble, one more addition, and there is the answer. Now check carefully. Right through the whole calculation impartially, as if this was the first time it had ever been done. Yes, that's right: that is, too. So's that. And that. And so down to the last line. Dead right. Now to plot it on the chart. Mark the spot here. Measure off at this angle, this distance. Oh! That's not where Mike reckoned we are. Even allowing for the fact that we've shifted a bit in the interval. It makes us much further inshore, within sight of the coast, even in this weather.

Without saying anything, I decided that either my position was wrong, or the coast must be within sight. Either way, the sensible thing was to go on deck with the sextant. Another sight or a good look for the coast was the obvious course. But by now there was no horizon; the sun fought to pierce a limp mass of wetness which hung over everything. If the coast had been within a mile we would not have seen it. I hung around on deck, indecision stirring my innards into a pudding. After drying my glasses till the lenses were almost worn out, I gave up the struggle and went below. There was not a sound anywhere and, in the prevailing conditions, I thought we would probably hear the surf on the beach before we actually hit. I hoped so.

'Where do you make us?' asked Mike.

'Dunno. I made a hash of that sight, I think.'

'You're getting careless.'

'No I'm not.' We were on edge, and a row threatened within seconds. 'How are you so damn sure your sight is accurate?'

'Just because it's different to yours, that doesn't mean to say mine's wrong.'

'I never said mine was right. I at least admitted that I was wrong. If we stick to yours and go on sailing on a slant towards the coast, you'll look stupid if we get thrown up on your own back doorstep.'

'We'll go on sailing this course.'

Before the row could get going properly there was a booming hoot outside and we grabbed the fog-horn to go on deck and reply. A big ship was somewhere in the vicinity. Every time it sounded its fog-horn, we replied. It seemed to get closer, but we couldn't hear the beat of its engines. Perhaps it was a steam turbine, and so almost noiseless. Then the first thing we would hear, apart from the horn, would be the menacing hiss of the bow-wave. Under conditions like this it is pleasant to have an engine that will start at once, so that as a ship looms up out of the fog a press of the button starts the motor and the yacht is taken out of danger. This steamer never came close and, when its hooter was no longer audible, we went below and resumed our normal life; reading, writing, cooking, cleaning (sometimes) and yarning.

We discussed ocean cruising a good deal. We all looked forward to the next voyage and planned rather over-hopefully. Mike was the least enthusiastic when it came to making future voyages, but then he had been on this trip far longer than the rest of us. The other two were just whetting their appetites and I was plotting all sorts of trips – such as in motor boats or right inland – in strong contrast to the present one. I had even worked out some of the details of a trip home, but had the good sense to tell no one about this. Not so long afterwards this pipe-dream became a reality. Which is another story (see the next book in this trilogy).

Next evening the mist was as persistent as ever and we were quite close to a fishing boat before we saw it. We were on a course to pass close, so stood on, watching carefully to make sure we didn't cross the fishing lines she had out astern. She was trolling for salmon, with long wire traces leading out from the ends of poles. When she saw our red ensign, she turned and came towards us. One of the crew of two – for she was only a small boat, well under 40 feet long – picked up a very fine salmon and held it aloft. We waved. He bent down, found a big steel drum, tied a piece of line to the fish and to the can, and dropped it overboard.

The two ships couldn't get close, as we would have fouled their lines and probably have got their fishing poles mixed up in our rigging; but it was easy for us to manoeuvre to pick up this fish. To me, not used to the size or quantity of salmon in this part of the world, our present looked quite fabulous. We undid the lashing and dropped the canister back into the sea for the fisherman to pick up. It was probably one of the drums he used for spare fuel.

Mike had worked aboard salmon-fishing boats and he had the fish cleaned within seconds, with that professional flick of the knife which looks so easy.

We'd already had our evening meal, so the fish was put aside. When I came up on deck for my watch at 3 a.m., the whole saloon smelt of fried fish: the others had had a late night snack. They'd taken thick steaks from the fish and fried them in deep butter. I got the boat to steer herself and went below to see if the fish was as good as it looked. It seemed slightly pagan to eat great chunks of the finest salmon before dawn, without any supplementary dish or even bread. The method of cooking, using deep melted butter, heightened the effect. Having been brought up in wartime Britain, where a tin of salmon, if ever it found its way into the house, would be looked upon with considerable reverence and almost locked in the safe, I enjoyed my snack with triple relish.

When the coast did come in sight, it was the high mountains we saw, and they looked fairly close. The fog thinned and there they were, after almost three weeks at sea. This was our last landfall, yet it was as exciting as the others. But, as usual, it was only the beginning of a new set of problems. We lost the fog only temporarily and were now approaching the Strait of Juan de Fuca. The entrance to this long narrow belt of water is a well-stocked graveyard of ships. Not only is the wind variable, but there are tides, thick weather and other ships a'plenty to make life hectic.

Now we foamed along with a roaring bow-wave, sails taut and straining to rush us through the water, rigging to windward tight and rigid, to leeward the wires slack and just slightly swaying as the ship plunged, thumping into a trough, a downward swoop with the sea climbing almost to the decks – then a swinging change of direction up towards the bright sky, crashing through the next crest, on and on and on, marking up the miles on the log, 14,000 astern and not so very many more to go.

Near the entrance to the long Strait of Juan de Fuca is a fjord on the northern side. It is a perfect natural harbour called Port Renfrew. There is no proper town, just an embryo village with a long pier, a rough road leading through the few houses and then off into the deep forest. It is a logging centre and occasionally fishing boats call there. This was our first port of call. There were no customs or immigration authorities stationed here, but that was their lookout.

We sailed in late in the afternoon after a long day, during which the shore seemed to take an interminable time to get close. The air was so pure, the colours were so true and intense, that distances were very deceptive. As we tied up amidst much cheerful banter, I looked up to a nearby pine tree and saw an eagle perched near the top. It was astonishingly close, yet seemed undisturbed by the noise we made.

Mike went over to a nearby fishing boat to use their radio-telephone to let his parents know we had arrived. The fishermen were extremely kind, and the loggers, too. They came down the pier to see who we were, yarned, went away to get some beer and then came back to see the yacht. Some of us went up the single rough-hewn road to the store to buy cans of beer, and soon the whole boat was solid with men from the shore. They filled the saloon and the fore-cabin, so two of us moved out on to the pier to make room. The evening wore on and the empties mounted up. After a time there was no room on the table for more, and then the floor became packed. It was a very fine party indeed.

Next morning it was bright and sunny, but I would have preferred a dull day. I had a headache which cut like a stone hatchet. There was no wind, so we motored up the Strait of Juan de Fuca, taking most of the day to reach Victoria. This was civilisation with all its trappings: customs and immigration, reporters and sightseers, all the usual ballyhoo.

Some months before, Mike had promised our story to a friend of his who worked for a Vancouver newspaper; but Vancouver was still a good few miles away and, for us, several days distant. So we were in something of a dilemma when reporters came aboard. Being reporters, especially Canadian reporters, they were not easily put off. Indeed they were not to be put off at all: they naturally sensed a story. For a start the dear old *Maken* was beginning to look a little sea-worn. The paint had been renewed at times, but the continuous scour of the waves had taken its toll. Then there were plenty of other details to excite the interest of anyone observant. Mike and I wore home-made canvas jackets and home-made knife sheaths, and generally looked as if we had been out of touch with civilisation for several years. There was my flat British accent; rumours from San Francisco had gone ahead of us; and, to cap all, Mike was more than anxious to keep the story till his friend could have it. This made it look as if we had something to hide, so of course the reporters went all out to find out what it was.

The result was a battle of wits. The reporters would hope to draw some comment from us by saying something like: 'This'll be a wonderful yacht in bad weather?' To this they hoped we would reply: 'Holy smoke, yes! There was that time when it was blowing the bats out of Hades, with the seas piling high as Niagara, and the wind shrieking hideous horrishendos, and we took four waves in a row, deep, green and solid over the bow …'

Only we didn't. We just said: 'Uh-huh,' which is about as noncommittal as can be. Then the reporters would relapse into silence for a minute, and try another tack:

'You fellows all live in Canada?'

'No.'

'Staying long?'

'Couldn't really say.'

'Maybe you've got a job here?'

'Maybe.' And so on. Which was all a bit rough on the reporters, who were no doubt trying to earn their bread and butter, or rye and soda, or whatever it is that reporters live on.

As usual we planned to split up on going ashore. Mike thought of Victoria as a very quiet town, compared with Vancouver: 'They roll up the sidewalks at ten o'clock,' was his way of putting it. The others were soon through customs and immigration, but as a prospective immigrant I had to go through much more in the way of cross-examination, form-filling and the bureaucratic rigmarole. Harry and Bill were made officially welcome swiftly enough, being US visitors, and Mike was merely returning home. But my immigration papers were out of date, as it had taken us more than six months to sail from England; so there was a lot of walking from office to office, before I was legally allowed to settle in Canada. This took me all the morning of the second day we were in Victoria.

The first night, when we split up, I found myself with a bunch of Canadians, all inviting me to spend the evening with them, spend the night at their homes, spend the week. 'Dammit man, why go on to Vancouver? Settle here in Victoria. It's the most like Britain of any city in Canada.'

'I'd love to stay,' I said, honestly enough, for the hospitality was terrific. 'But what about a job?'

'You'll find a job, easy enough.'

I did shop around as much as time allowed, but there were no jobs of the sort I wanted. So, when the *Maken* motored thumpily out of Victoria harbour after her brief stay, I was aboard with the others. We steamed through the maze of perfectly lovely islands and islets, over a flat calm sea. Among these rock-strewn waters the tide runs strongly, in places ferociously. There are innumerable back eddies and, as the land all round has been heavily logged, ships have to contend with the added danger of great tree trunks, floating almost submerged.

It was just as well that Mike knew the way, because the navigational hazards are numerous, and there is in this region an ever-present risk of fog. We had plenty to look at, what with fishing boats, yachts and the inter-island packet boats. The islands are little paradises, mostly with rocky shores which make the sandy beaches all the more beautiful. From the shore the land sometimes rises steeply, wooded, dark and suggestive of bear, moose and other venturesome beasts. In other places the land is more gently undulating, with green fields, and everywhere the few houses seemed exactly designed to fit in with the scenery, as if every builder and architect had signed a solemn pledge to erect no eyesores. Over the whole scene there was a great quietness, and an eagle or two hovered high.

We motored all day. Part of the route was through the notorious Active Pass. It has a double bend, it is narrow enough to give the most experienced seaman thorough heart-snatch, and the shores are rocky, besides being very steep-to. It was at the turn of the tide when we went through, but even so we had only partial control over the *Maken*. Close by was a troller, one of the very numerous local salmon-fishing boats, about 35 feet long. The two boats would be moving on a parallel course; then one would enter an eddy while the other remained in the main stream, and, though neither helmsman had altered course, the two craft would swirl apart on diverging tracks. 10 seconds or perhaps 10 minutes later their courses would converge, again without any movement of rudder. Massive logs were gliding about in a crazy dance, moving endways, sideways, gyrating. It is easy to imagine the place as the ultimate maritime hell when it is snowing, at night, with a spring tide at full flood.

We turned aside into a little bay and went alongside a pier. Mike went ashore to make a few inquiries and buy some food. The inevitable small crowd gathered, for now everyone knew about us. At least they knew as much as the newspapers had published. This was Galliano Island, a favourite place for holidays. It was just as well that the atmosphere was so informal, because our clothes were as wild and unconventional as anything in sartorial history.

Our plan was to find a quiet corner to anchor for a day or two to paint and smarten up the battered *Maken*, and make her fit for a homecoming. After some discussion with the local inhabitants it was decided to go to the other side of the island. This was only 20 minutes' steaming, so a crowd came aboard for the ride. Close under the shore we went – with the pine trees almost touching the rigging in places – to another pier. Many of the houses hereabouts have their own jetties because boats are used in the area much as cars are used elsewhere. After our passengers had gone ashore we anchored off, as there was not enough water to lie alongside at low tide. The fjord we were in is called Whalers' Bay, though it is too small for a whaler, so far as we could judge.

After so much motion at sea for so long, the stillness and quiet seemed almost tangible. We stood on deck, bemused by the beauty. Among the silent pines a dove cooed. Then, close by, a seaplane taxi landed. It motored up to the pier, its engine making a shattering roar of sound which echoed back and forth, thrown from one hard rock shore to the other till the land and sea seemed to shimmer in layers of noise.

We went below to change and become more civilised. Dressing, I looked towards the land. It seemed such a mixture of the ancient and the ultra-modern. The latest pattern outboard motor was fixed to an Indian wooden dugout canoe. The log cabin by the pier might have been taken from a page of early Canadian history, only it had a television aerial on top. In a borrowed dinghy we went ashore, and found the rough ground peculiarly unresistant. Instead of giving as we walked, the way the deck seemed to, it gave the feeling of rising up to meet the foot about to be put down.

It was hard for Mike to remember the way, as he had not been here for twelve years. We were looking for a small hotel, with the idea of getting a meal ashore. When we came to a farmhouse, Mike was sure it was the hotel, so we knocked on the door. A pretty girl answered. She was flustered when we asked about a meal, and went for her mother. The mother explained that she had at one time run her farm as a hotel in summer, but did not do so any more. She was very apologetic about not being able to give us a meal. All there was in the house, she said as we were leaving, was ham and eggs. As a man, we stopped in our tracks.

'Did you say "Ham and eggs"?' we exclaimed in a chorus.

'Yes,' she seemed surprised.

'Lead us to it!'

She showed us into a dining-room and in a few minutes another pretty girl came to lay the table. She left, and presently a third pretty girl came into the room to ask: 'Mother says, one egg or two each?'

We all said, 'Three eggs each please,' but we all thought, 'That's three pretty girls, and there are four of us. Surely, oh surely there couldn't be just one more?'

In silence we sat, the atmosphere tingling with curiosity. Minutes ticked past. Culinary clatter came from the kitchen. At last footsteps came towards the door. It opened and a laden tray came first into sight. It was carried by – yes! – a fourth pretty daughter!

We fell on the meal – such a scrumptious one, with mountains of newlaid eggs, home-cured bacon, home-baked bread. The joy of eating off a steady table instead of *Maken*'s pitching platform! The solid delight of clean napery, lashings of butter, real butter after months of tinned margarine! On top of it all, there were four girls, and we were four …

After the meal the eight of us walked back to the boat, intent on having a party. It started off badly. We only had whisky on board, as the Californian wine had long ago been finished; so we politely asked the girls if they would have some Scotch.

'What is Scotch?' they all asked.

Astounded, we introduced them to the lord of all liquors, but they were not much impressed, and we consoled ourselves with the thought that there would be all the more for us.

Next day we worked on the boat, but not with much enthusiasm. Vancouver was so near; the radio programmes from the city came through with solid strength. We all wanted to get there. Suddenly, in our minds, the voyage was over. No more struggling through the black, raging night. No more risk, heart-snatch as the big sea roared up astern, thundering dreadfully, intimidating, a wild, whirling wall of water, promising annihilation in a tumbling confusion of dark sea. All I wanted was to get on to land. To get a job and work, work, work, wildly, furiously, 23 hours a day, flat out. To amass a wadge of money, a fat wad of notes, then get another boat, a better one, faster, slimmer, lighter, easier to handle. Then off again. Off on another flight across the oceans. Perhaps alone, this time … That's it! Suddenly I knew that was the next move. To hell with this trip! It's been fun, but now it's over: let's get ashore. In a surge of unrest and impatience, I wanted to get to Vancouver; the two Americans were keen to finish the last stretch, but their hurry was like a tortoise's compared with mine. In a burst of eagerness I rushed through my share of ship-cleaning. Mike was annoyed at my flurry. With thoroughness which nearly drove me to drink he carefully cleaned and washed the cabin paintwork. I could settle to nothing. Bill and Harry caught up with my restlessness, and at last we left Whalers' Bay.

This at last was the final lap. We hoisted the sails as we motored out of the bay and were soon in the Strait of Georgia, with the land round Vancouver in sight. None of us could settle. We wandered about the ship like caged animals. I knew I ought to be writing letters to post when I got ashore; ought to be finishing off my journal, taking photographs. I could do nothing except think of the next trip. The next yacht – oh, she'd be a beauty, a honey! She'd sail like a witch; laugh at the gales; have a snug little cockpit, deep, but not too deep, and safe as houses. All the gear would be light and she'd have … I was away on the daydream that lived with me for nine months and then became a reality.

Meanwhile we were approaching the river. We shortened sail and the land closed in on either side. The jib was off her now, and bundled up, thrust down the hatch into the fo'c'sle. Next the mainsail was lowered. True to form, it resisted to the last, that solid, unyielding mass of canvas. We fought it into some semblance of a stow. The landing stage was in sight now. Mike's parents were there, with his brother. In a scramble we lowered the mizzen and staysail. 50 yards to go, and Mike's urgent voice hurried us to get the sails stowed neatly before we arrive alongside. Fenders, now, are hung from the rail. Mike winds the propeller feathering handle and the *Maken* slows, nudges the quay … stops. The voyage is over. And, for me, the next voyage is just beginning.

Sea-Saint
1954

Chapter One

A skier slid off the chair-lift at the top of the run and without a pause started down the slope. The wide lane he skied on was cut through cedars and pine and these made shadows on the snow, for the afternoon sun was low. At first the trail was a series of sharp undulations. The skier twisted and turned in a number of joyous swoops, but he tended to keep in the shadows, where the snow had melted during the day but was now frozen to ice in the cool of the dying day. At each turn his skis rattled and juddered on the ice, the steel edges of the skis screeched and complained, fighting to bite into the ice-covered snow with its hard treacherous surface; instead of trying to check the side-slipping at each turn, the skier deliberately let himself skid flamboyantly, rejoicing in the wild flight-like motion. He came towards a small crowd of skiers standing around 'Hell's Gate'. This is the point where the run changes from a trail not seriously steep, into a wide ski-run, like a meadow, with a greater slope.

At Hell's Gate the beginners, the cautious, the aged and the lazy pause to consider the main part of the run. They stand around talking, weighing up the difficulties. Our skier approached the gate with a steadily straightening course, gaining speed. He knows the gate. It looks hard, but is merely exciting. Skis parallel, he gains speed every moment. Down into a small hollow and up in a wild swoop on to a hillock, then a quick small spin of a turn, and he's into the Gate. First there's a well-banked sharp left turn. Heeled over, skis hissing on the solid packed snow, he makes the corner and is instantly into a hard right turn with a snow bank at just the right angle to take him round the curve. Skiing fast, the wind roaring in his ears, he's out in the open, a white plain spreads down before him, with the city of Vancouver and the sea glinting in the sun far below. Now he no longer has to do the short zig-zags as on the upper part of the trail. He makes long diagonal runs down the hill, with wild, half-controlled, skidding turns; he picks out the shadows where the snow has frozen and makes the skiing faster. He gains speed all the time till his clothes are pressed against his body, trouser-legs flap like flags in a gale. He makes another turn, skiing with more enthusiasm than skill, and half turns his head to see if the other skiers are likely to collide with him.

A girl is coming down fast on a converging course. If either fail to turn, and at once, they will crash. Both start to swing out. Skis chattering, rattling on the

hard uneven snow, they slide, skid, turning wide; they are running parallel for a
brief instant, their ski poles touch lightly. The skier says 'Sorry' into the rushing
wind, and they tear off on different tacks. The girl smiles to herself, thinking,
'English obviously; Canadians are polite but they don't apologise on the slopes.
Besides, no Canadian would ski quite so badly. Seems to be enjoying himself,
though.' Meanwhile the skier is getting worried. He scarcely has control over
his hectic progress. He turns more frequently, dodges between two fallen,
laughing beginners struggling to stand up, dives down between the steel posts
that carry the chair-lift, and up a ridge. From the top he sees a tree-stump, a
black obstruction in the snow right in front of him. He does a quick spin turn
on the ridge summit, and squeezes past the danger in a breathless hopeful rush.
Then he is at the bottom of the run, stopping by turning up the hill. He stands
looking up at the slope, panting with exertion and excitement.

That was my last run of the season. When the tense thrill died away I
thought of the approaching summer. It looked as if it would be mighty dull in
comparison with the sort of devilment I enjoyed at weekends during the winter,
unless I could carry out the plan.

This plan was born during the night watches, as I sat at the tiller of the
yacht *Maken*, while sailing from England to Vancouver. The *Maken* is a 45-foot
ketch, comfortable but slow. She was plagued with calms, so I had plenty of
time to think about the plan. It was a very flexible thing, with four or five
alternatives for every stage; but the basis was to sail home across the Atlantic,
if and when I left Canada.

There were one or two outstanding problems connected with the idea of
sailing home. First, I knew of no yacht owner who was planning the trip;
secondly, I did not know for certain when or even whether I should be leaving
Canada; thirdly, I was on the wrong side of the country (which is about 4,000
miles wide); and then there was the question of finance. When I stepped ashore
from the *Maken* in Vancouver I had 5 dollars in my pocket, and no job. This
is, of course, the traditional way of emigrating, but it is inconvenient. We
arrived on a Saturday afternoon, and the Skipper, whose home is in Vancouver,
organised a party which started off round a fire on the beach that evening, and
went on till Sunday night, with small interruptions for sleep and so on. This
is a good way to celebrate the completion of a 14,000-mile sail, and it was an
excellent, typical introduction to life in British Columbia.

It was impossible to find a job till after the weekend, of course, but within
10 hours of starting on a hunt for work I was lucky – very lucky. The drawing
office where I started work looked north. The big windows were right over the
drawing-board, and the view was across the harbour, with the mountains and
ski slopes beyond. It was mid-July, but there was still some snow on the peaks.
Yachts and fishing boats were plentiful in the harbour. I was working with a
very good naval architect. The situation generally was well in hand. When I
received my first pay-cheque I examined a large number of shop windows,
decided I needed nothing except a pair of shoes, and so started a savings
account. The plan took a big step forward.

Vancouver was at once the best and the worst place for me to develop the
plan. There was plenty of work available and I plunged into it, putting in as

many hours as possible. At one time I worked 85 hours a week for several weeks, but most of the time 65 was the average. I wrote magazine articles; built a dinghy, originally with the idea of racing it, but shortage of time forced me to sell it without trying it; designed and helped a friend build a little cruising ketch; worked overtime at my job when the need arose, and dabbled in a very small way in the stock market, with success. But the distractions were many and strong; there was skiing at weekends, on four different mountains, each with special attractions and distinctive runs. During the summer and autumn the swimming and fishing were good. The motoring was most interesting, especially in the mountains. There was one brief moment when it became positively exciting too, as we skidded thoroughly out of control, on the snow-covered road up Mount Baker. On one side of the road the cliff rose almost vertically, the other side dropped down to a raging torrent below. The car went into a series of slides on a down-slope, till it crashed into a timber barrier built to keep vehicles on the road. The timber had rotted, and it tumbled down into the rugged Hades below, but the car bounced back and rolled over, fortunately only on its side, as our skis were lashed on top. I had been sitting next to the driver, but when we sorted ourselves out I found myself in his seat, and he in mine. We crawled out unharmed, but annoyed; the car was new and had only done 500 miles. On another occasion four of us decided to see the interior of the province and took a hired car through mountain and valley, through scenery that made driving a trifle difficult, for it was distractingly beautiful. This car also was new, but we wanted to cover as much ground as possible, so thrust on hard, till the brakes faded on a most interesting bend. Then we stopped to let them cool, and stood on the edge of the road trying to estimate how far we would have dropped if we had failed to negotiate the corner.

Besides all this there were pleasant evenings with the Royal Canadian Engineers. I joined their Reserve, which reminded me of a fine club. One weekend we enjoyed ourselves blowing up a timber bridge 130 feet long, after a riotous party the night before. The explosion was a great success; in fact, it split the ceiling of a brand-new house half a mile away. This was in spite of the fact that quite a few sappers were laying charges while suffering from hangovers, or with dreamy faraway looks, for we were far from home and the girls at the party the night before were typically Canadian in their high standard of hospitality.

In all I worked nine months in Vancouver, and towards the end of that time I wrote far and wide, to yacht clubs and associations, to friends and relatives, trying to learn of any yachts sailing eastwards across the Atlantic in the summer. Every other year there is an ocean race from Newport in the United States to Bermuda. This is a very well-supported event, and might well be described as the Derby of ocean racing. British yachts sometimes take part, and if there are several they often race home across the Atlantic. 1954 was a Bermuda race year, so I tried to join a British yacht taking part, but none sailed in the race; the only one that was entered got dismasted while sailing across to America. Another alternative I had in mind was to try and join one of the Portuguese fishing schooners that sail from their homeland to the fishing grounds around Newfoundland, where they work till they are loaded, and then return home. These ships occasionally put into port on the Canadian side. Another branch of the plan was to try and join a trawler from Europe. In fact I wanted to sail on any small craft that could be relied upon to float all the way across. One of the many reasons for this was that I wanted to get experience in small craft, to make me a better designer.

As time went on it became increasingly clear that very little activity was being planned in the yachting world as far as transatlantic sailing was concerned; more and more my attention was directed to the idea of buying a boat. Maps of Nova Scotia and Newfoundland were studied. A small black note-book was acquired, and an alphabetical thumb-index made on its pages, so that every time a thought, a piece of information, or an idea came to me, it was noted. For instance, under 'E' there is a heading 'Essentials': matches, torch, batteries, primus prickers, can-opener, etc., and lower, 'Emergencies': dismasting, holing, flooding, sickness, appendix, loss of food or water, broken bones, loss of navigational instruments, and the appropriate action for each trouble is briefly noted. Without this booklet, the cruise would probably have been uncomfortable and dangerous; as it was I had a large and increasing store of knowledge and information always with me, for the booklet was in my pocket continuously for weeks. Previous experience helped, new books on all related subjects were read, old ones re-read. Various people were consulted, about medical matters, living conditions in Eastern Canada, about hitch-hiking, about ship and boat building and repairing conditions in the Maritime Provinces. All this was done without telling more than one person about the plan, and she said:

'Don't do it, Ian.' And later: 'If you must, don't go alone.'

I never intended to sail alone if it was avoidable, but always kept the plan flexible, and made every preparation with the thought in mind that I might be single-handed, or might have to handle a ship alone if my crew became ill, deserted in the Azores, or fell overboard.

By the end of April it seemed as if I would have to cross in my own boat. The immediate problems were three in number. First, how to visit some relations in California; second, how to get to Nova Scotia, 4,000 miles from Vancouver; and third, how to get a boat, and fit it out ready to sail and be back in England by early August, all on the savings of nine months' work. I decided to hitch-hike fast from Vancouver to Los Angeles, then double back to Halifax. The pattern of travel was based on the idea that sitting in a car is not very tiring, so I hoped to stop for sleep every other night only.

A letter was sent to a yacht broker in Halifax, describing the kind of boat I wanted and how much I was prepared to pay, giving my approximate date of arrival in the city, but saying nothing about trans-Atlantic crossings. Farewell parties made the end of April pleasantly hectic. I had the pleasure of working for a man whose hobby was giving parties, and who not only took pride in organising them but was invariably highly successful. Canadians are a particularly talented race when it comes to throwing parties anyway, so an outstanding party-thrower in a nation of them made me wonder if I was wise to leave Vancouver. It is such a pleasant city; in one day it is possible to ski, sail and fish, leaving home after breakfast and getting back in time for dinner.

I did leave though, and hitch-hiking southwards, soon reached the US border. I planned to walk across the border, take a bus through the state of Washington, and then hitch-hike on. This was necessary because hitch-hiking is illegal in forty-five of the fifty United States, though the law is honoured in the breach rather than the observance, except in the border states. After some delay caused by the immigration regulations, which do no credit to the American people and are in strong contrast to their personal hospitality, I got myself onto American soil. I found it necessary to come close to breaking the law in order to gain access to the US, but it would be a very helpless person who could not sneak into the States from Canada somehow.

Hitch-hiking conditions were not good. So many crimes have been committed by thugs who pretend to be hitch-hikers that the motoring public is rather loath to offer lifts, except to servicemen in uniform, hitching alone. Needless to say, the thugs have taken to wearing uniforms and operating single-handed; but motorists have either not found this out or are prepared to take the risk, or most likely are too kind to refuse. Without much trouble I got to Northern California, just in time for a record heat wave. Here I could not get a long ride, just a series of lifts from one town to the next. Each vehicle dropped me at the entrance to a town, so that it was necessary to walk the long dusty main street to the far side to await the next lift, for it is rarely possible to get picked up at the beginning or in the middle of a town. All this walking with a heavy pack was not pleasant, but was actually a blessing in disguise, as I got toughened up.

My destination in California was Long Beach. Two things happened here. The Californians showed hospitality rivalling the Canadian efforts, which made me glad of a robust constitution and the good training I was in; also I got my first volunteer crew. In the public library I was gathering data, and making up a condensed tide atlas and lighthouse list, for I did not expect to be able to afford to buy all the navigational books containing this information. I was also finding out what I could about Sable Island, which lies about 150 miles off-shore from Halifax. A glance at the North Atlantic chart showed that this island was right on my route, and initially I planned to sail there, as the first part of the crossing, so that if any teething troubles arose in the boat, I could put them right at Sable Island. However, the pilot book was discouraging. I learned that it had no harbour or moorings, being, indeed, a serious hazard to navigation. After working on the voyage all afternoon I relaxed, reading an American yachting magazine. It occurred to me that someone might be advertising for a crew to help take a vessel eastwards to Europe, so I scanned the columns and instead came across a possible crew to accompany me if I sailed my own boat. He advertised for a berth, giving an outline of his experience and an address in Toronto. This was convenient as I intended to visit relations in Toronto on my way to Halifax. I wrote arranging an appointment.

From California I drove with an acquaintance to Detroit, motoring for 91 hours, stopping only for fuel and food. We arrived after midnight and I must confess that I have never been more glad to fall into bed. By nine next morning I was across the Canadian border and hitch-hiking to Toronto. Here I met Crew No. 1 as arranged. He had crossed to America from England in a 112-foot motor cruiser and had had several thousand miles' general sailing experience. I outlined my plans, and he agreed to crew for me provided he liked the boat; we arranged that he would leave his job and follow me to Nova Scotia as soon as possible. I was to provide a boat and all her gear, while he paid for the food for both of us. We set a definite limit as to how much he would have to spend, and discussed the financial aspects of the trip at some length. We both realised that any serious disagreement would ruin the voyage; even if we succeeded in doing the crossing it would be hellish if either thought the other had not paid a reasonable share. He was to look after the secretarial side of the organisation, much of which could be done from his office in Toronto. We hoped to do trials on food and equipment for the Canadian government, so he undertook to deal with that matter too. The whole meeting was a complete success. It was no worry to me that he lacked experience. If he could steer a boat, I could handle every other job comfortably, and only a very brainless oaf cannot be taught to steer a small yacht. So if he was overrating his own talents it did not matter. His name was Arthur.

Next day I hitch-hiked on, through French Canada, to Montreal, Quebec, along the St Lawrence, through the Maritime Provinces, hitching as long as there was daylight and often well after dark, relentlessly, without break for meals, walking when my impatience overcame me and I had stood too long on one corner. Occasionally a local bus was used to get past a bad area, in order to keep the best speed possible. The calendar was against me and I did not regret the stiff pace. It seemed desirable to get as fit as possible for the coming jaunt. My halting French was not much good in the French-speaking regions, for the patois there is unique and complicated, but I did learn the slang for a girlfriend is 'une blonde'.

On a Friday night I arrived in Halifax and was in the yacht brokers' office early next morning. Fortunately these people work at the weekends. This particular firm consisted of two young men who had recently set up in business together. We discussed the matter of buying a boat for a few minutes, each sizing the other up. They were obviously curious about this British youth (I was accused of being nineteen by more than one Canadian and it is true that British people under twenty-seven or thereabouts do as a rule look younger than their Canadian counterparts); they wondered, quite justifiably, what I intended to do with my boat, why I came across Canada to buy; in fact, the whole set-up looked peculiar, if not actually suspicious. My problem was simple: should I let anyone know my future plans, and if so, whom?

Various files and dossiers were produced. We talked over the qualities of a number of boats, and just as the conversation began to flag, I said:

'The boat must be really good. I want to sail her across to England, possibly alone.'

Chapter Two

Buying a yacht is usually a heart-stirring experience. Most people have a dream ship, which is based on their reading and experience, and this is what they set out to find. Every boat inspected causes a fresh burst of excitement. Sometimes she looks perfect, better than the vague vision the mind has cherished, and then turns out to have rot in every timber or the owner wants four times her value and the cash available. Other times the first sight is disappointing: the hull appears to be held together by rusty nails and chipped paint; but a close inspection reveals a teak cabin-top, bronze deck-fittings and an intelligent layout below, so she is bought, refastened and lives a long happy life, winning races, exploring new harbours and teaching a new generation the taste of salt spray.

In the few years I had been sailing I had bought several boats; as I outgrew my first dinghy a half-decker took her place, then a day cruiser, then a better cruiser, and so on. With each, the thrill of the search was renewed. This time things were slightly different. The almost choking excitement was there, but there was also a suspicion of grimness. This time there was no room for sentiment, and no time to search to the end of the country. This time, too, the boat in mind was of no particular length, width or sail plan. She had to be small enough for one person to handle, for even at that early stage I was taking precautions about being deserted by my crew, and besides, on an ocean cruise it is highly desirable for the watch on deck to be able to do all sail-handling and manoeuvring without waking the watch below. So I decided on a boat between 23 feet and 42 feet overall, preferably with no sails bigger than 500 square feet. I was not worried about the internal accommodation, nor the deck arrangement, nor the rig, nor whether she had an engine; I knew that I could easily change rig or cabin plan, and could fit a self-draining cockpit, move cleats, shorten spars and do any alterations needed. The boat did not even have to be thoroughly sound (I was quite prepared to put on a new deck); but she had to be seaworthy, to have a seakindly shape; she had to be cheap and if she needed alterations or repairs they must not cost much or take long. Even the construction did not have to be extra strong as I was willing and able to put in extra frames, knees, floors, diagonal straps or whatever she needed, provided the hull was well made. If I had any prejudice it was that I hoped to get a yawl or schooner, these being the only two common rigs I had never owned.

It was not a strong bias, but a sound one, for these two rigs are traditionally considered good for offshore work.

The Atlantic seaboard of Canada and the nearby States of America have for a long time sent schooners to sea, trading and fishing. These boats developed till they reached an unusually high standard of speed and load-carrying ability. They were good sea boats and they earned money. My own view is that the shortage of tall trees in Nova Scotia influenced the designers and builders, forcing them to make ships with two short masts rather than one long one. Other factors, such as riding out gales, come into this matter, but it is hard to see why even the very small fishing boats were and still are schooner-rigged. I had high hopes of getting one of these fishing boats, or a yacht of the same sort. With the yacht brokers I motored up and down the coast. We drove down some very rough roads to remote houses perched on rocky promontories. One or two boats would be moored in the lee of the land, or up some nearby fjord, with another boat or three hauled up on the stony beach. We visited tiny boatyards where lone boat builders worked with few or no mechanical tools. We went on wild goose chases, followed up rumours, asked a million questions, and saw dozens of craft. Very quickly the position became clear. The boat building industry was not thriving. Most boats were built of soft wood and given hard continuous use, so their lives were short. Not one schooner over 32 feet long of the traditional type was to be found. There were plenty of small schooners between 24 and 32 feet long, and many were for sale, as the fishing season had been bad. Most of them had one- or two-cylinder engines in, and these craft were called lobster boats. The type was going out of favour; the fishermen were turning to the so-called Cape boats, which are pure motorboats, without even steadying sails, and with powerful six- or eight-cylinder engines.

We examined dozens of lobster boats. As a last resort I would have bought one, but they all had several faults, namely, they were all old, all needed new decks, rudder, rigging and sails, none had much accommodation, and though their first cost was low, the finished conversion would not be cheap. Furthermore they were mostly of shoal draft, because many of them were kept in harbours where there was not much depth of water, or fished very close inshore. This meant that they would not have sailed well to windward, especially with a schooner rig. Adding a deep ballast keel would have improved their performance, but the hulls were not designed to take such strains as a deep keel imposes, so internal strengthening would be needed, which called for more work, more time and more money.

It is true that I intended to do very little sailing to windward, but there is always the possibility of getting caught on a lee shore in a gale. Every sailing yacht should be able to fight its way to windward in winds of gale force if properly handled. With an ocean cruiser there is the possibility that land may be reached after a long, exhausting passage, with gear badly worn, with the crew tired, discouraged and careless because of damp clothes and bedding, with the ship's position uncertain due to soggy charts and navigational books, grey sunless skies (which prevent sextant sights) and unknown ocean current; and perhaps some poor devil moaning in his bunk, an arm broken ten days before. If an on-shore gale strikes then … Cheerful game, this ocean cruising.

The search went on from Saturday morning to Tuesday night. At the end of that time the position was thus: the yacht brokers' car could not stand much more rock-climbing along unsurfaced roads; we had seen no boat that inspired me with confidence; we had seen not one yacht that was suitable for the job and at the same time cheap enough; there were two fishing boats that might do, but one was old and the other smelt strongly, both suffered from the usual defects in deck, rudder, rig and keel. More than one person had told me not to bother searching beyond the area bounded by Halifax and Lunenburg, and as we had covered more than that territory the situation was not satisfactory. The last two days of the search merely confirmed what we learnt on the first two.

A rather unhappy conference was held in the brokers' office. They could not spend all their time with me, it was the busiest time of their year, and they had great faith in the local type of fishing boat. As neither of them had done a great deal of cruising, and none of it off-shore in small boats, they wondered at my reluctance to buy. Perhaps they thought the whole project was based on an inflated ego. At a time like this it pays to remember what happened in some particularly vicious gale, so as to avoid buying an unsuitable craft. On their office wall there was a plan of a 30-foot 6-inch cruiser, with two alternative sail plans and three alternative cabin layouts. The plan did not include a set of lines, and the profile of the boat did not much appeal to me. This yacht was based on the Tancook schooner type. Big and Little Tancook are two islands in Mahone Bay, near the small town of Chester, 40 miles south of Halifax. The plan was signed by Gerald Stevens, designer of Chester Seacraft Ltd, and the brokers had told me that this yard had a hull lying in their shed, built as a speculation. Chester is a yachting centre, but we had not visited it in our search because the brokers knew that there were no boats there for sale except this unfinished hull, which was, they thought, both too expensive and too far from completion for me. Having practically no further ideas or clues we rang Chester Seacraft. They were interested, the price was not as high as I had been told, and I badly wanted a boat. So the next day I visited the yard.

Like most other boatyards it is a collection of sheds and huts of different vintage, at the end of a rough road, with boats and gear lying about. There are heaps of timber seasoning; various notices indicate the store, the office and the oil shed. The pier runs a short distance off-shore with a fuel pump and a floating stage at the end. Depending on the time of year, a few or a lot of boats are moored in the harbour, which is a fjord with steep rocky shores. The yard lies on a stony beach and is pressed in all round by the low but quickly rising hills, covered with coniferous trees.

The office is like every other boatyard office. It is a room that is too small for its job. There are two large desks, a drawing-board, various chairs, a big stove and a chest of drawers, which means that there is very little floor unoccupied. Nor is there much wall space, for plans, calendars, charts, pictures, photographs and lists cover most of it. Everywhere there are heaps of papers. Files and catalogues are stacked on the desks. Books of reference, books on sailing, and books that have nothing to do with ships are in profusion. Pigeon-holes full of letters, receipts and envelopes old and new, extend along the long edge of one desk. There is the usual filing cabinet, and inevitable too, in Canada, one or two empty Coke bottles. It is a fine place for working. Without rising from his seat the secretary, Emery Stevens, can reach almost any book, form or paper he may need. This office is Emery's domain, here he organises the clerical side of the yard, helped by the youngest of two brothers, Pete. Gerald, the yard manager, is in and out frequently. He is the middle one of the three, and is the designer.

When I entered all the brothers were there, also their father, Perry. I made myself and my business known. Gerald took me to see the hull. It lay in the big building-shed, planked, framed, but without ballast keel, rudder, decking or cabin; in fact, about one-third a complete yacht. The moulds had been removed, but the bow and stern were braced up to the roof, and supports reached across from the shed pillars to hold the boat upright. The length was 30 feet 6 inches, and the beam 7 feet 11 inches. Internally she was an ugly green, showing that she had been painted with wood preservative; externally she had a single thin coat of white paint.

I did not fall in love with her at once. After a glance at her from the side I went round to look at her from the stern. It was not encouraging. She was too full-bodied in the quarters and in the garboard to suit me. There was no point in saying anything, so I walked slowly round to the bow. This was better, indeed, it was positively lovely. Days later I told Gerald how much I admired the bow, and he admitted he had spent a very long time designing it. Meanwhile there was the problem of how she would handle at sea. The sheer was delightful, and the profile without ballast keel, fine for my purpose. This I noticed as I went round to get another look at the stern. Above water she was good. The counter was neat, and not long or flat, so that she would not pound out her heart and mine when we got into a nasty sea. But she was full, so full, below. We went back to the office. I explained that I wanted a boat, at once, for extensive cruising. There was no point in blurting out plans for a trans-Atlantic crossing at this stage, because I hoped to slip away without anyone except a few friends knowing about the crossing. We discussed the finishing of the ship from every angle. No one doubted that the hull could be made into a good yacht, no one knew exactly how much it would cost; we all agreed that I was the only person who could make a decision, and that the matter should be very carefully examined before the hull was bought. With Gerald I made a very detailed list of all the material and equipment needed, with prices, then we made another list of all the work to be done with the time it would take. Riding back to Halifax that evening in the bus, with these two lists, I balanced time and costs against available cash and the calendar. It seemed just possible to succeed, but the margins were dreadfully small and the risk correspondingly great. One thing was now certain, wild sea-horses would not prevent me from sailing across.

I do not remember all my motives; in fact, I probably never consciously thought of them. I wanted to get home, and without flying. I do not love the sea, on the other hand small boats are my passionate interest, which is paradoxical because I am neither a good helmsman nor crew. I have always had my own boat since first I took up sailing, but have sailed in many others, making it an almost invariable rule never to refuse a chance to go afloat. I like to have a crew with me when sailing, and even in my own boat spend comparatively little time at the helm. On long passages I stand watch like the rest, but do not claim it is the owner's prerogative always to handle the boat in the difficult and therefore interesting places. As a result I get all-round experience, sail-handling, navigating, cooking, as well as steering. This is the best way to learn designing. Designers who have sailed through a gale or two do not provide unseaworthy ships; their conscience and memory forbid it.

The next day I returned to Chester, after a discussion with the brokers in Halifax. They pointed out that the fishing schooners I had seen up and down the shore were cheaper and almost as good as the hull at Chester. That was not my opinion. Nearly as much work would be needed on a fishing boat as on the hull, besides which I would have to take off the existing deck of a fishing boat, and remove the internal accommodation. Again I looked at the boat, liking her more, for in the interval since I had last seen her, it occurred to me that the full stern would make her rise well to a following sea. As I expected to have a stern wind most of the time the fullness aft was not so disappointing. Furthermore, if the boat did tend to carry rather a lot of weather helm, at least she would stop quickly if I fell overboard. Some boats will sail away from the unhappy single-hander who gets into the sea.

We forgathered in the office and I posed a question:

'Do I pay tax on the hull?'

'Yes.'

So we added another item to the list, and the predicted cost was greater than the available cash. (This incident shows the falseness of ill-considered taxes. The boat building industry in Nova Scotia badly needed work at the time; many intending buyers must be stopped by the crippling 10 per cent extra.) However, I had the bit in my teeth now. Nothing short of the grave would stop that boat going afloat and setting out for England. Gerald was behind me. As her designer he had faith in the boat and wanted to see her sailing. Perry, too, thought it could be managed.

'If you work on her yourself,' he declared, 'the way you say you will, it can be done. I know where there is a complete schooner rig, spars, sails and rigging, which you should be able to get cheap ...'

Emery, on the other hand, was the devil's advocate. The typical 'finance-man' of a company, he pointed out the risks, and the penalties of failure:

'You'll be broke, without a job, with no way of getting back to England, at a time when jobs are hard to find, especially in this part of the world.'

This was what I needed. His caution and opposition were as valuable as Perry's advice (based on enormous experience) and support, or Gerald's quiet enthusiasm. Most of that evening I talked the matter over with Gerald. We had tea together, went down and painted his boat, then visited the tavern; the estimates were edited and revised till at last we were satisfied. By cutting out everything not absolutely vital, there ought to be 49 dollars left in the kitty by the time we sailed. The Stevens family had done all they could with advice; there was only one person who could make the vital decision, as all agreed. Alone that night, before I fell asleep in the spare room in Gerald's house, the decision was made, though actually this was merely a mental confirmation of a steadily growing determination. After breakfast I went with Gerald to the boatyard. His house, alongside Emery's, overlooks the harbour; both houses were built in the evenings and weekends by their owners, and were as comfortable and convenient as any in Canada, where houses are particularly strong in these qualities.

The shipwrights were sitting on logs around the entrance to the main shed. It was a scene I got to know very well. At exactly eight o'clock, Gerald gave each man his job for the day:

'Albert, will you paint the black schooner. Reuben, you had better finish the decking on the outboard cruiser. Tom, how's that dinghy coming on? OK, you may as well give her another coat of varnish while the weather's fine.'

At this time there were about twelve men and boys, apart from the Stevenses, working in the yard. I went to the office with Gerald and Emery.

'Have you made up your mind?'

'I'll buy her. Here's the deposit.' And I took a wad of notes out of my wallet. 'I'd like to start work right away.'

The worst part of the trip was over. Much of the strong mental tension relaxed. Perry came in and went to the store-room next door. He returned in a few minutes with some putty and a putty knife on a board. We went into the main shed and he showed me his way of stopping-in the seams of the hull. The whole family constantly made suggestions, demonstrated Nova Scotia methods, and were forever ready to overcome the current crisis, ship building being a series of linked crises. Their ways of building varied quite a bit from mine but we always found a good compromise, and only once was there annoyance, over the matter of the top of the stem. Even that was finally settled to everyone's satisfaction.

The work began on Friday morning. By Saturday evening the hull was stopped-in; as this entailed working along every seam, both sides, then going over the whole hull again, with a stiffer putty, to plug the nail holes, I got to know the shape of the boat thoroughly. The fullness in her quarters seemed less pronounced, and I began to like my ship more and more. On Saturday evening, I cut two wooden plugs on a lathe and bunged up from inside and out the hole which had been drilled for the propeller shaft. I decided not to fit an engine in order to save weight, to keep down the resistance of the yacht, to save time, but most of all to save money. Many times I was asked, particularly by local fishermen, whether I was fitting a motor. They were genuinely surprised when I said no.

'What will you do if you get in a calm?'

'Calms are inevitable,' I answered. 'They will be nothing like as bad in the North Atlantic as we had them in Mid-Pacific. Once in a 45-foot ketch in three successive days' sailing we logged 5 miles, 0 miles, 3 miles; that's 8 miles in 72 hours. In a whole week I've drifted as little as 135 miles. An engine is no good under far-offshore conditions. This little 30-footer couldn't carry fuel for more than two days, with all the other stores on board. Two days at an economical 3 knots is only 144 miles, which is negligible compared with the 2,800 that I have to do.' After this over-long speech I would get back to work.

Loafers were a problem. They wandered in, yarned at length, all too often displayed their own profound ignorance, and eventually drifted off. I preferred the children who came, asked to help, questioned me because they really wanted to know about sailing, and knew how to talk and work on the boat at the same time. When I eventually sailed, one of the biggest regrets was that I left behind half a dozen keen young sailors who were just beginning to learn the infinite art of messing about in boats.

Chapter Three

On Sunday the boatyard was closed. Borrowing a dinghy, an axe, a chart, and with a pocket compass, I set out in pouring rain to find myself a mast. Several of the islands nearby were uninhabited and heavily wooded. It is permissible to fell timber on them, or so I was told. By good fortune the dinghy rowed easily, and I revelled in the long, sweeping strokes, pulling for an hour with occasional pauses to check my position, for the fog that is never far away in this part of the world closed in when the rain eased. Ashore on the island I had picked on, the trees were too numerous. It was hard to see which were exactly straight. Every time I looked up rain blurred my glasses. Eventually I found one, marked it with a cut on the bark, and moved on to see if there were any better. The bush was so thick that I blazed a trail, lest I should not be able to find the first selection again. There seemed to be none better, so I cut it down. Or at least I cut it through, close to the ground. It did not fall, but stood almost upright, with branches entangled. Perhaps it would have been best to climb up and cut off the branches first, but when Gerald had offered to lend me an axe, I found he had only two large, double-bitted ones, and I took his reserve one, which was old, retired and in need of sharpening. An axe suffers easily from rusting, and is hard to keep dry whether in a boat or a dripping wood, which explains why I took the second best.

It seemed that my tree was supported by one other tree in particular, so I cut through that too. Mine moved a trifle. I peered upwards. There were several holding up the two severed ones, but I thought a certain quite small tree was the king pin. I hacked it through. Mine tilted a little more. A rough estimate suggested that I should have to cut down hundreds of trees to get my one. Changing tactics, I climbed one of the supporting trees and tried to haul or push mine down, but without success. Cutting with the over-large axe was merely dangerous, being quite unprofitable because the higher branches were too springy. Down on the ground once more, I tried pulling the bottom down, along, tried twisting it, shaking it; all without gaining anything. Those trees were very close together. All this time I did not know if mine was long enough, but there were very few longer, and none straighter, that I could find on that island. Eventually a successful technique was developed. I climbed up my tree, clutching the axe with one hand, or passing it from branch to branch, hanging it there, while I kept one hand or foot on the branch of one of the nearby trees. Every few inches I jumped, swayed or bounced on my own tree. It was possible to cut through a few of the obstructing branches. I worked my way up with several prayers and many bounces. This gradually coaxed my tree earthwards in a series of lurches. At last I had it nearly horizontal, though not lying on the ground. After hacking off a few more branches I measured up the trunk; it was just over 31 feet, whereas I needed one at least 35 feet. There were no trees 4 feet longer on that island. Evening was approaching. I left the tree and rowed home, getting a tow part of the way from a fisherman. Several days later I bought a long-felled tree from Perry, which was much better because it was seasoned.

Next day, Monday, I was woken very early in the morning by Pete Stevens, whose room was next to mine in Perry's house. We joined Emery on the boatyard pier, and went aboard the yard launch. Its engine roared into life, then settled to a steady rumble. We cast off, went astern, turned and steamed out of the harbour, leaving a pattern of waves behind on the still, clear water. As we passed through the moorings, each boat bobbed a greeting, then settled back for a few minutes' more sleep, as our wash moved on. In the early morning sun the coast and the many little islands were enchantingly, beautifully Nova Scotian. The dark green firs and the pines were everywhere, with the fields of contrasting light green grass between. Little beaches, mostly pebble, and low cliffs basked in the sharp sunlight.

We searched the water ahead, after running off-shore for a quarter of an hour, and spotted the first lobster-pot buoy.

The engine quietened, we slid alongside the buoy, a boathook grappled the rope, and we hauled away on the wet line. The heavy wooden lobster-pot, weighted with rocks to keep it in place in spite of tides and gales, came into view in the clear, cool water. Emery and Pete grabbed it expertly, hoisted it onto the gunwale, opened the trap door at the top, took out the piece of fish that served as bait, seized the little lobster that gambolled and snapped in the cage, and put him in a barrel, then lugged the trap to the forward end of the cockpit. We pulled up all the fifteen traps and stowed them in the boat, for this was the last day of the season and they could not be relaid. It was a lucky day, the best of the year. There were ten useable lobsters; two we threw back because they were undersize and one because it was a seed lobster.

The launch was back at the yard soon after eight, where I was introduced to Reuben Hiesler. Reuben had worked on the planking and framing of the hull, and, as I hope to show, is a fine all-round shipwright, so Gerry assigned him to help me finish the boat. Without any delay or pause for discussion we set to work. On each side two legs were built to support the boat from below, and prevent her tipping over. These legs were braced rigidly, because during the finishing of the yacht there would be a great deal of vibration, hammering, jolting and other activity, like heavy-footed visitors clambering aboard. Next, the overhead supports were taken down, so that we could put the deck on. Releasing these braces gave the hull more freedom. It began to come to life, giving tiny movements and little shudders as we moved about on board; it was like a child's first stirrings in the womb, and the boat became more and more alive, till the launching, like a birth, made her an active living creature.

The beam shelf had first to be put in. Taking a rough, weathered plank of oak, we lugged it into the top part of the main shed, where the power saws and planers were. The plank was passed through the planer twice, which reduced it to ⅞ inches' thickness and left it clean and smooth on both sides. How I loved that screaming planer!

It did in 10 minutes work that would take a man half a day, sweating and toiling. It had two partners, the bandsaw and the circular saw. These three were my very good friends.

Offer them a rough baulk of timber, indicate the requirements with a steady guiding hand, and they would serve up a set of beams, a mast or a rudder without any trouble, and not too much noise. More than once my heart missed a beat when a rumour went round the yard that the bandsaw had broken down, or the planer blades would have to be sent for regrinding. These happy three had spare sets of teeth, so that when one lot became dull, a renewed set could be inserted. Sometimes, as I notice some wretch try to masticate a tough steak, I think that human beings might do well to keep a spare set of extra sharp teeth.

When the beam shelf was fastened in place we cut the main beams, from spruce. This is a lovely wood, kind to the tools, clean, smooth-grained, easy to work, so that by the end of the first day real progress had been made. We stopped work at twelve and started again at one. In the evening, after tea, the yard was deserted. I splashed wood-preservative on my hull with a big paint brush, then took my hand-plane, sharpened it, and worked on the deck beams, trimming them to shape and cleaning up the rough spots which the planing machine had left here and there. At last it was too dark to work longer. I put the plane down on the bench, took a long look at the boat, saw a lot more than was there, then walked home to bed.

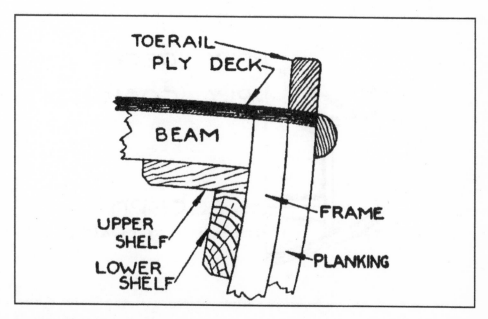

Beam shelf and deck edge arrangement.

We made and fitted beams all next day, till Reuben went home to tea; in the evening I put in the cabin sole-bearers, because it is awkward to stand and work inside a boat that has no flat floor. Again it was dark as I trudged along the rocky road to Perry's house, and blessed sleep. The following morning we had to deal with the problem of the cockpit. When a gale stirs the sea into a raging, surging chaos of waves it is most desirable to have a watertight cockpit.

Then the sea, roaring aboard in a deluge, tumbles along the deck, fills the cockpit up like a bath and drains away through the scupper in the bottom of the cockpit, back to where it belongs. But if the cockpit is an open hole in the deck, the sea runs into the bilge of the ship and soon fills her, especially when the crew has become too tired to pump fast. Even when the weather is just moderately lousy, the occasional sea that comes into the open cockpit can make things unpleasant below, for the bilge water splashes about as the boat rollicks along, and soon bedding, food and gear get damp, if not drenched. So we had to build a watertight cockpit, and we kept it down to a size that called for only one sheet of 8-foot by 4-foot by half-inch plywood for bottom, sides and end. Plywood is expensive, and a whole sheet has to be bought, even if only a small part of it is used, so we effected a saving here by not having to cut into a second sheet. The cockpit was made the same length as I am from heel to tail, so that I can sit comfortably in the bottom, steering in this well-protected position. The view from the bottom of the pit is limited, but this is sometimes a blessing, for the sight of a big wave, a lump of hell, surging unchecked and invincible down onto a little boat, is mighty disconcerting. Which reminds me that several people have said:

'Weren't you frightened?'

And on reflection I think the answer is:

'About twice weekly on the average.'

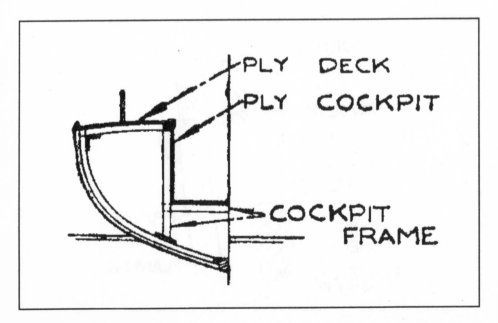

Cockpit is well above waterline.

I bought a second-hand iron ballast keel from the boatyard close by, run by Reuben's brother Ben. This neat casting weighed 900 lbs and lay down by the water's edge, surrounded by soft ground, close by a shed. No vehicle could get at it, there was no crane or lifting tackle available, rollers would not work on that terrain. Manpower in large quantities was needed to shift that keel, and manpower is expensive. Gerald, as usual, knew a sensible way to get the keel from its resting place into the building shed. First I went with the yard lorry to the town liquor store, at lunch time, and bought a case of beer. Then during the lunch break I collected crow-bars, several heavy wooden rods, and some stout pieces of steel pipe, and carted them along to the keel. That afternoon, as the men stopped work and were leaving the shop, Gerald said: 'Who's going to help lift Ian's iron keel on to the truck? There may be a bottle of beer in it.' Every man in the place trooped down to the beach, the tools were coaxed under the keel, and with 'Up now', and many witticisms, the load was lifted and carried up the steep slope to the truck. The beer bottles were handed out. Gerald drove the truck along the few dozen paces to the Chester Seacraft main shed, where two of us easily levered the keel off the truck. May I take this opportunity of apologising to the wives of the men that helped me? If they arrived home a little late for tea that evening it was entirely my fault.

The next day I prised up the keel, slid rollers under it, tied a tackle to it, and hauled it across the main shed till it lay beside my hull. On the shed's wooden floor it was no effort to manoeuvre the keel single-handed. As soon as that job was finished, the mast-step occupied my attention. This was rather a massive piece of straight-grained oak. It was cut to shape by machinery, but the job of making the slot, to take the foot of the mast, was done by hand. This is one of those satisfying jobs, involving a large mallet, a broad sharp chisel, plenty of big chips and shavings besides a lot of noise. The end product is put into the boat with particularly big fastenings, and when the thing is in place, there is something to see for the effort expended.

Boat building goes ahead in jumps; some days nothing seems to have been accomplished, others show a great and visible advance. There is, for instance, the making and fitting of the side-deck tie bolts, which are important, but quite insignificant to look at. I was working away on these bolts when a telegram and letter arrived for me. First I had cut lengths of galvanised iron rod, and was grooving a thread on one end to make them into long bolts. Swinging the stock and die round and back, round and back was a pleasant, relaxing job. It gave me opportunity to survey progress to date.

How well things were going! Every crisis, small and large, had been efficiently overcome; the troubles ahead were not too numerous, soon Arthur would join me from Toronto, and with two of us working, my burden would be halved, and the working rate would rise. Even the finances were nicely under control, with Arthur's contribution. Pete Stevens came up to the work-bench: 'Mail for you, Ian, including a telegram.' I mumbled thanks and tore it open; it read: 'Very sorry. Unfavourable medical. Doctor strongly advises not to make trip. Arthur.' The letter too was from Arthur. He had been x-rayed, and there was every indication that he had a cracked skull.

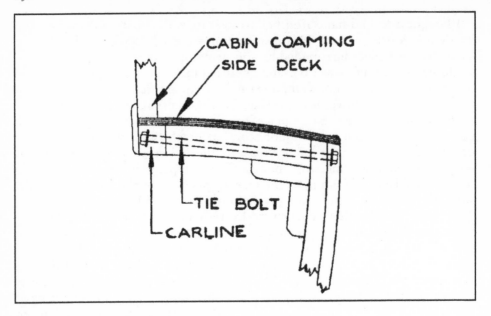

Side-deck tie-bolts, hidden but important.

This was such a devastating setback that I felt sick. I was saddled with a boat which I did not think I could afford to provision, my careful timetable was shattered, there was bleakness in all my thoughts. The stock and die went on rotating, back and on, the soothing labour was pleasant. I did a lot of hard thinking. By the time the bolts were complete the timetable was remade, also finances set up soundly by eliminating every luxury from the programme and by working out a few more schemes to reduce labour and material in the ship. But best of all, I had convinced myself that I was keen and able to make the trip alone. This complete *volte-face* required a severe mental effort. It was probably the major crisis of the whole expedition; it never seriously occurred to me to sell the boat (though there was an auxiliary plan available for that if needed), but this set-back had me seriously worried for an hour; in fact, I fell physically sick for a time. Later I remembered to be sorry for Arthur, and annoyed too. He had gone to great trouble and expense, with advertisements and letters, to find a berth on a trans-Atlantic yacht, before having the vital medical, which was doing things the wrong way round with a vengeance. It must have been a shock for him to learn that he had been living for weeks with a cracked skull, which was the result of a motor smash. That night I wrote letters to likely sources of crew and retired to bed mildly exhilarated by the thought that a completely new kind of voyage, definitely more exciting, was unfolding.

More trouble occurred the following day, and involved the rudder shaft. Gerald had found a piece of bronze propeller shafting that would make a superb fitting for the rudder. It was wonderfully cheap. Dave, the yard fitter, was working on the rudder (he was the only person, apart from Reuben and myself, to work on the actual construction of the ship). We found the shaft was too short, by the smallest amount. No amount of ingenuity could devise a means of making it long enough. Even Gerald had only one solution, namely to get a longer shaft. The local foundry was telephoned. They agreed to take the short shaft in part exchange for a longer one. Once again the kindness of a Nova Scotian saved the day. God bless them. Even so, bronze is most expensive and I ended the week feeling, and probably looking, depressed. Perry Stevens noticed this. He suggested a day's holiday. Sunday, anyhow, was a day of rest, so why not accompany him to Halifax in one of the yard motor boats? He had to make the journey to tow a hull back. I thought it would be a good idea to try and renew my sea-legs, get a view of the coast from off-shore in case I had to turn back, enjoy some experience in the typical Nova Scotian type of power boat, and take the opportunity to bring back some gear from Halifax.

We left on Sunday afternoon, four of us, including Perry's eldest grandson. Perry had six grandchildren, who were always playing around the boats, falling into the water, rowing the dinghies away just when they were wanted, and generally behaving the way small children do. Perry was one of the busiest men in the yard, but he found time to carve model boats for the youngest generation. When I first went to Chester, I thought Perry was wonderfully active for his age. I still do, but later I met his father-in-law (Reuben's uncle, incidentally) who was a good deal older than Perry; he was building a boat the same size as mine, single-handed. And this man's mother had only just died, so that for several years there had been five generations of the family alive simultaneously.

The motor boat we took to Halifax was powerful and seaworthy. It rollicked over the brightly glistening sea, biting into the waves and leaving them bleeding with white foam. It blew freshly, so that the motion became more and more lively as we worked our way off-shore, past one island after another. It was pleasant to find that Perry, besides being an accomplished shipwright, knew how to handle a boat at sea. This confirmed my choice of ship and shipyard, for I have always been strongly in favour of ship designers and builders being experienced seamen. The drawing office and various shops in a shipyard are altogether too comfortable, too remote from the weather and the outrageous Hades and desperate battle that is a gale at sea.

We put into a little harbour for tea. As we lay alongside the stone breakwater the bottom of the sea bed was clearly visible below, though the swell made our boat stir uneasily, as we went below into the snug cabin. A fire was soon made using chips and shavings from the yard, and in a very few minutes the tea was brewed. We had to make Halifax that day, weather permitting, so we pushed on, up the coast, bounced through a narrow winding channel with the sea breaking on rocks all round, and up the steadily calming waters of the harbour. We spent the night at anchor and next day, early, we put a heavy line aboard the boat we were to tow back, and set off. We got back to Chester harbour soon after lunch, and in a few minutes I was back on my hull, making and fitting the toerail, which is like a tiny bulwark all round the ship, to prevent the crew sliding overboard.

That evening I took four galvanised metal straps; I cut and filed them, then drilled various holes, till they were a strong set of chain plates. I liked making this sort of fitting myself. I knew exactly how strong the finished product was, whereas the bought article might be faulty and would certainly be more expensive. The penalty for fitting a dud chain plate would be dismasting. Working away in the dying light with my boat standing close by in the deserted, silent shed, I had plenty of time to consider the significance of being dismasted. If the stick came down on top of me I should probably get dented quite noticeably. If the mast toppled into the sea during bad weather (the most likely time, of course) it might lie alongside, battering in the planks as every wave hurled it at the ship. If the ship could not be sailed under jury rig, just how long could I survive? Would the drinking water run out before I was sighted by another ship? In spite of my restful trip to Halifax these rather morbid thoughts occurred to my depressed mind. Probably it was a good thing. I reviewed the action to be taken in a whole series of emergencies, until I felt I would do the right thing quickly and automatically even if badly stunned. The immediate result of all this was a very stout set of chain plates which some of my friends scoffed at; but then it was not their neck, so to speak, and criticism stopped when I pointed out the pertinent facts.

About this time I was adopted by the Gray family. Jack Gray, his wife Shirley and their eighteen-month-old son John lived aboard a 35-foot motor cruiser in the Back Harbour. Jack is a marine artist. The first time I saw his work I gasped; the thrilling hiss and roar of breaking waves came from that painting, and the helmsman lived. I commissioned a picture there and then, to be paid for when finances revived at a later date. I received an open invitation to have all my meals in their boat. As Shirley cooks divinely I became a regular member of the crew of the *Cheerio*. Wonderful meals, prepared on a small two-burner stove, were produced daily. Once a week we all piled into Jack's enormous Pontiac and went to Halifax, my object being to buy gear, equipment and provisions. We had lunch and dinner together in town, which was important to me, for their conversation distracted me from my absurd battles in Halifax. For some reason I had difficulty in persuading the merchants of this capital of the province to transact business. I paid cash, using the genuine currency of the country, but I got the impression they did not want to sell anything. I tried several different strategies, each without success. In the end I was forceful almost to a point of rudeness.

The incident of the pressure lantern is typical. At the ship's chandler's I asked for a kerosene Colman lantern. The salesman said it did not exist, only gasolene Colmans were made. I showed him a kerosene one in his own catalogue. The manager was consulted. He said they had never existed; again I showed him his own catalogue. He said nobody ever used them. I departed before I lost my temper. How I hate damn-fool remarks by ignorant stay-at-homes. I wonder how many millions of those lamps are used? Several other shops and warehouses had gasolene lanterns, but I was adamant. No dangerous fire hazard was going to sail on my little wooden boat, far from the shore. I insisted on kerosene. Then in a big department store I sighted my quarry; unfortunately there were no shop assistants about. It was a quarter past five. The store was due to close at half past. I waited 10 minutes, with Jack. We went off in search of an assistant. We ought to have stolen the lantern, I see now that would have been the sensible thing to do. Eventually I went behind the counter, took one of the four lanterns from the shelf and examined it closely. Just the job. A girl appeared.

'I'd like to buy this lantern. It does burn kerosene?'

'No, they all burn gasolene.'

'But they are not all alike. See this one. It has a little cup for the methylated spirits, and bigger vapour pipes.'

'Oh! I don't know about that. I'm sure they all burn gasolene.'

'Well, it's got a different number from the others.'

'It must be an older model.'

'What's the cup for, then?'

'I don't know. I'll get the Colman catalogue.'

Meanwhile the manager arrives, and displays a profound ignorance of his wares while we await the catalogue. The girl returns.

'Here we are. Why yes, you're right.' Chorus of surprised exclamations from the manager and his various minions, who have collected from somewhere in a small herd.

'How much is it?' from me. This causes chaos and consternation, so I throw in another verbal bomb to keep things interesting. 'Have you got the filler, mantle, and instruction leaflet?' Uproar. The manager and all assistants depart in a perfect frenzy of 'alarums and excursions', except the girl who went to get the catalogue. I stand squarely in front of her, blocking her escape. She looks small and rather crest-fallen. I feel a pang of remorse. Poor little thing. Just stop bullying her. She's only doing her job. She's probably frightened to death. I smile. She does too, a bit coyly. We get things going on a friendly basis. I admit I know a bit about the lamp, so the instructions are not needed. She agrees to include one mantle in the price of the lantern. I buy a spare. She promises to send the filler on by post. Alas, she forgot, or is she having her revenge? That evening the tension is slightly relaxed and at dinner I prattle garrulously. Jack eyes me anew. These Scots are fierce when they are roused, he thinks. I try to remember what the girl looked like.

When people were helpful, they went to great lengths. I experienced unstinted kindness from so many. For instance, Jack and Shirley painted the yacht almost entirely. Perry found time to paint in a trim dark blue boot-top which made the boat look smart and valuable. On the other hand there was the incident of the rigging screws. These always tend to be a weak link in the rigging. I was determined to have mine strong enough to stand a hurricane, even after they had suffered a lot of abuse. At the yacht chandler's the choice in the catalogue was good, but the stock on the shelves was poor. I gathered a selection, and worked out how they would fit. These two were alike, and really tough, so they would do for the main shrouds; this one was slightly different from all the others but it was a stout job, it would do for the jibstay. Some were missing the bolt that goes across the jaws even though they were not second-hand. When the manager saw my selection he asked how big the yacht was.

'30½ feet,' I told him.

'You're mad, they're far too big.'

'Yes? This boat has got to cross oceans.'

'Then I want nothing more to do with it.'

There are two interesting points here. First, the manager never asked the sail area of the boat, nor how she was rigged, and consequently had no means of knowing the correct size of rigging screws to fit. Secondly, he was as ignorant of naval architecture as an antediluvian ape. Subsequent events have proved the correctness of my calculation, and these fittings do not even look over-size. (Forgive my self-righteousness.) This and one or two other events taught me to be mighty careful about listening to advice. For instance, there was the incident of the potatoes. It was when I was loading provisions aboard. Carrying my 25-lb net of potatoes down the pier I met an acquaintance.

'Are those all the potatoes you are taking?'

'Yes.'

I grew worried. No one likes to think too closely about starvation at sea. Then, considering further, I remembered that my acquaintance did not know the quantity of other food I had aboard; he did not even know if I was going alone or with a crew, and finally he had no experience of ocean cruising, nor any idea how long the crossing should take. In the event, I used less than half the potatoes I took on the voyage.

The work on the ship went on at maximum pressure day after day. We had serious trouble with the keel. The casting I had bought was fine. It was cheap and the right shape, but not nearly heavy enough. Several schemes to increase its weight were considered. First we planned to weld a steel box on top of the keel and fill it with scrap iron, pouring in molten lead to make a solid finish. This was abandoned because it is not satisfactory to weld steel to cast iron. The local foundry were very loath to try. We thought of making a separate steel box to fit over the keel, filled with iron and lead. Calculating the cost gave me a severe shock. It was obviously too expensive. I decided to fill the box with scrap iron and cement. This was cheaper, but still came to more than we had allowed for the keel. We thought it would be cheaper to have a separate iron casting made. There followed another setback. The foundry in Chester would not be casting iron for three weeks, by which time I hoped to be well off-shore. So I wrote to a foundry in Halifax. I gave the size but not the weight of the keel I wanted cast. I had only a rough idea what the cost would be, and thought it might in fact be so high as to wreck the whole venture now that Arthur was not going to be with me, and buy all the food. For the first and only time I seriously tried to commercialise the trip. I asked for a special low rate in casting, in exchange for the use of the name of my boat for advertising purposes after I had completed the crossing. I received a very curt note in reply. The firm were not interested in advertisement (so I will carefully avoid mentioning their name, though they eventually did quite a good job). Furthermore they said they had never heard of me. So what? All I wanted was a modest little casting. They said my casting would weigh 3,200 lbs and cost 8¾ cents per pound. This was staggering. Gerry and I had very carefully checked my figures. We did so once more. The final casting would only weigh 900 lbs. Their calculations were as peculiar as their correspondence. I wrote to them again, gently pointing out the error of their mathematics, and received a more civil reply. They admitted their fault and they said that for castings below 1,000 lbs the price was 10½ cents per pound but in view of their earlier quotation, I could have mine at 8¾ cents per pound. Truly the devil looks after his own. A few more strokes of luck like that, thought I, and I'll live to be hanged in my old age. Reuben and I made a wooden mould of the correct size and shape and despatched it to Halifax. When it arrived it became the subject of another letter. It was not rectangular or true, the foundry said. This was just a trifle galling. With much sweat and labour Reuben and I had carefully shaped the mould so that its top was narrower than its bottom, as required by the design of the ship and keel. We knew it was not rectangular. It was not intended to be. But it was supposed to be true. Could it have warped? It was made of a single large baulk of well-seasoned timber. If it had lain long in the foundry near a furnace it might well distort. Already the building schedule was being upset by the keel. I rang up the foundry. They agreed to true it up if necessary, and admitted any warping was very slight. Meanwhile one day was a special holiday, the furnace would be cold the next, then what with weekends and so on, I could have the keel by Friday. Friday? But they had promised it on Tuesday originally, or Wednesday morning at least. This sort of thing cultivates duodenal ulcers in naval architects, and is quite usual in shipbuilding.

Chapter Four

On one of our weekly trips to Halifax we parked Jack's car near a quay. As we got out Shirley said: 'There's Dave, he might sail with you.' At this time I was looking for a crew to replace Arthur, but was still keeping the whole venture very quiet, so that I was handicapped in the search. While I went to see about my freshwater supply for the voyage, Jack and Shirley talked to Dave. When I returned they introduced me to him. 'Dave would like to sail with you,' said Jack. I looked at him; he appeared tough, weatherbeaten, with a pleasant open face. 'Have you much sea experience?' I asked.

'A good many years, mostly in small stuff. Fishing boats, trawlers and so on.'

'What about sail?'

'I've done a bit. Know how to handle a sailing boat. I'd like to come.'

'I'd like to have you. It's a very small boat. It'll be damned uncomfortable. Can you pay for your own food and tobacco if you come?'

'I don't smoke and I can afford my own grub. It should be an interesting trip. I would like to try it for the adventure.'

'There shouldn't be much excitement. I intend to stay out of trouble, so it ought to be just a quiet sail.'

We summed each other up. I wrote his address in the little black notebook, then we came across a snag. I wanted to depart in ten days' time, but Dave had agreed to crew on a trawler and would not be back for a fortnight. I said I would go back to Chester, examine the schedule and the hydrographic charts, and see if I could afford the extra delay. By the time we got back to Chester I had discussed Dave with Jack and Shirley. They had confidence in him, I thought I could live with him in the confined quarters of the boat for six weeks, and his presence aboard would definitely put up the average speed. So I wrote and asked him to come and have a look at the boat, before making his final decision. Several days passed. The letter was returned with 'Not known at this address' stamped on it. We had to buy most of the gear and stores in Halifax and next time we were there we tried to contact Dave. We visited the address he had given. It was a sailors' boarding house. Dave was unknown there, so we went to the trawler office, but they did not know the names and addresses of their crews as the men were different each voyage. We scoured the highways and byways.

My growing circle of friends insisted on my finding a crew. The idea of being alone at sea for six weeks did worry me; at times, when I woke up in the middle of the night, it appalled me. Besides, the constant drive of work was beginning to tell. Time was running short. The obvious thing was to sacrifice the secrecy I so much cherished. It seemed most unsatisfactory to noise abroad such a trip before it was complete. It was tempting fate. It was giving a valuable hostage to fortune. It would probably mean being plagued by sightseers, journalists and loafers.

I put an advertisement in the papers. From then on the troubles of publicity grew, but not as badly as I had feared, for though the Nova Scotian is truly of the New World he has a quiet courtesy of manner that is old-worldly. As for the journalists, I had found previously they can best be dealt with by giving them pre-planned, precise statements and this worked fairly well this time. The sightseers were more difficult to deal with. They were often people on holiday. I had no time to answer their questions, and was often very tired late in the afternoon when they ambled into the boatshop. Reuben used to get a lot of enjoyment out of the way I tried to get rid of these hindrances. He would just roll a cigarette, and smile, while I went on planing, sawing or whatever job was in hand. Naturally I welcomed the intelligent, sensibly minded people, like Jack for instance, who yarned with me all one afternoon but at the same time put on a complete coat of anti-fouling paint. Or the children who came, asked to help first, got down to the job, and once the work was well in hand used to talk about sailing.

The work went on. We were held up for suitable timber for the cabin sides. For these we needed extra wide, thick planks. There were none in the yard, nor in any of the lumber piles in the region round Chester. All the wood we used was local and Nova Scotia is short of large trees. In the end we edge-glued two pieces together, holding them in place, while the glue set, with many large clamps. When the glue was thoroughly set, two ports were cut in each side. It is usual to have more and bigger windows than we made, but this yacht had to be stronger and more seaworthy than the average. Apart from the hole they make in the cabin side, thus weakening it, windows are liable to crack or burst in when a heavy sea crashes aboard, especially while the boat is hove-to in a gale. I remember lying in my bunk in a gale in the Pacific, in a stout, heavy yacht. We lay a'hull fairly peacefully, heaving up and down. I heard the menacing hiss of tumbling foam that often precedes a wave breaking aboard. Then the awful brief, breathless silence, and with a bang and a sustained roar, an extra big wave piled over us. The ship winced at the blow. The crew looked anxiously at each other. A few seconds later we cautiously stuck our heads out of the hatch. The half-inch wooden bulwark was broken in for a couple of feet. We thanked God that the planking was four times as thick, and ducked below, to resume our reading.

I still had to find a mast. Perry had a suitable felled tree, but it was still in the rough, and much too large. Reuben and I carried it from the timber stack where it lay, to a pair of trestles near the main shed. It was enormously heavy for two people, though Reuben scarcely seemed to notice it.

I consoled myself with the thought that by the time the boat was ready I should be very strong and horny-handed. The idea of moving the spar was to make it possible to reduce its girth with an electric power-plane. After leading the electric wire through one of the shed windows to a plug, I set to work. The power-plane weighed 20 lbs. It grew blisteringly hot as it worked. The sun beat down and I peeled off all the clothes decency permitted. The whirling blade tore off great chips of wood. A spray of shavings flew from the nose of the machine, a rain of perspiration streamed off me. I had a healthy respect for that tool. It fairly tore chunks off the timber. It occurred to me that an injudicious move would find it planing pieces off me. Nevertheless it was a joy to use. Like all wood-working tools, it only requires guiding for a start, soon the wood takes charge, and the job is done in no time. It is much easier to handle wood than metal, though supreme skill in working it is no easier to acquire. When the spar was sufficiently reduced in size and squared up, we lugged it into the main shed. Until I power-planed it, it could not have been put through the planing machine. Now we whipped it through several times, reducing the spar still further and giving it the required taper. With no little profanity it was carried up the stairs to the spar bench, on the upper floor of the shed. Here it was planed by hand till its shape pleased me, then painted and fitted with track, cross-trees and other fittings. Local opinion took one look at the mast and prophesied disaster. When it was seen how I intended to rig it the disaster was placed 2 miles from the point of departure, if not closer. Actually the rigging is rather satisfactory. It is a blend of science and art; the science holds the mast up, the art kept its cost down. Because the mast is not hollow, like the vast majority of modern ones, I need not worry much about it bending. The usual way to design a modern yacht's mast is to treat it as a straight vertical tube. It is a tube, but in practice it is seldom vertical, or precisely straight. This may explain some mast breakages. On an ocean cruise a mast failure is not fatal, merely vastly inconvenient. I would in fact have preferred to have a hollow mast, of aluminium alloy for choice, but I could not afford it. My mast is probably the cheapest one ever to sail on an ocean cruise. Like a natural grown tree, it has much resilience and the same sort of reserve strength found in a fishing rod. As we shall see later, it may whip, in certain emergencies, but better a wriggle than a break any day.

Late one evening, while yarning and supping aboard the *Cheerio*, I was turning the pages of an old yachting magazine. Suddenly I came across a wonderful idea. There was a sail plan of that successful 12-metre *Vim*. Of course this is a quite different ship from mine, much bigger, built for in-shore racing instead of off-shore cruising, but one can learn from these delicate beauties. The *Vim* had an inner, low forestay. I saw a whole host of advantages in fitting such a piece of rigging. First, it could replace the two lower fore shrouds, and by putting one piece of rigging in the place of two I would save wire, two splices, two shackles, two thimbles, two chain plates, a bit of money, labour and time. Secondly, I would save weight and windage aloft, which delights both the designer and the sailor. Thirdly, I should be able to set the little storm jib on this stay, thus giving the boat more canvas in light airs, while on the other hand in a high wind this little sail, so nearly amidships, would make a good working sail plan by itself, or with the main well reefed. In fact, it would vastly increase the flexibility of the rig. It was rather like fitting an extra gear to a car.

However, one of the biggest advantages of this stay I only discovered during trials. It is so positioned that it can be reached by the outstretched hand while the other hand is still holding the main shrouds, and from this 'inner shroud' one can reach the jib stay. Even though I fitted a guard rail right up to the bow, it was still a terrific advantage to be able to swing, monkey-like, from shroud to stay, for there is nothing more exposed than the fore deck of a small boat in a gale. Sitting on that narrow triangular platform as it dropped into the hollows between those mobile mountains of water, wrestling with a flapping headsail, I have been reminded of other exposed positions, on mountains, in front of a runaway rugger scrum bearing down with the ball at its feet, in the ring against an opponent with the advantage of weight and reach, on a hunter that has got the bit in his teeth and is heading for a high hedge with the hounds giving tongue out in front. The fore deck in a storm is like these. It gives a wonderful thrill, especially to the single-hander. It is a fight where muscle counts, but the brain usually turns the scale, and the best brain is one that has been taught to work under adverse conditions. If the battle is lost, the headsail flaps itself to tatters, the crew get torn finger nails and sometimes get swept off the deck into the sea, on which occasion it is to be hoped they have a lifeline round their waist.

The cabin top was put on the ship, with strong bolts to hold it down, and without pausing, except to roll one of Reuben's inevitable cigarettes, we cut, planed and fitted the cabin top beams. These were of spruce, for, being high in the ship, it was important to make them as light as possible. While the main work went ahead a lot of minor jobs were done. In a lunch-hour I would make a pair of cleats, or put fiddles round the shelves. The interior work, the cabin furniture, was kept as simple as possible, and was done parallel to the main structure; because it is easier to put in the bunks and galley before the

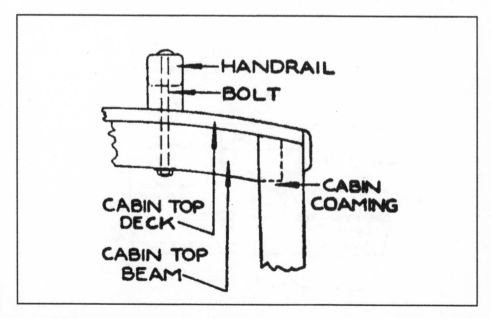

Extra-thick cabin coamings.

decking cramps the headroom. A lot of stowage space was necessary, since I had to provide for packing in food, water, clothes and bedding for two people, however doubtful it might be whether there would actually be a second person. In the end there were more shelves and lockers than were strictly needed, which was a great blessing and comfort. One very good feature of the boat is the total absence of doors or drawers. This means that everything in the boat is accessible with one hand. While holding on firmly the crew can grab a tin of stew, the emergency flares, or a piece of toilet paper, whereas a locker with a hinged door needs one hand to open the door and hold it open, while the second rummages inside.

Moreover, what so often happens is that the locker is stowed full while the boat is at anchor, upright, so that when the ship heels to a breeze, out at sea, opening the locker produces a cascade of its contents. And then, too, even well-made drawers and doors tend to stick, due to paint, warping or the swelling of the wood when damp. We made open-fronted lockers beneath the settee-berths, the galley and the chart-table; even an inexperienced person can stow these properly so that nothing spills out when the lee rail is awash and the boat is thrashing to windward. It must be admitted that these lockers are not quite so neat in harbour, but what particularly biased me in their favour is their cost. Another way that expenses were kept down was by doing without cushions or mattresses. Instead, the settee-berths and forward bunks were made with canvas bottoms. These proved to be most comfortable and never kept the crew awake, in fact they are something like hammocks.

A very large galley and chart-table were made, just inside the cabin, with the idea that cooking and navigating could be done without leaving the helm. Also, by putting them near the hatch, the steps down can be used as seats, for either

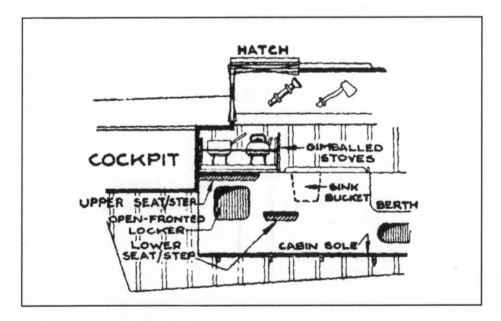

Looking to port at aft end of cabin.

cook or navigator. From the upper step one's head is just out in the open, which is so nice when waves of nausea and seasickness filter about, besides being a good lookout position, both warm and dry. On the lower step the operator is beautifully positioned, in a fine working stance, firmly ensconced regardless of the antics of the ship, while all instruments and much of the food is within arm's reach. This may not mean much to anyone who has never tried to cook in a boat that prances about, but a well-arranged galley is a priceless asset on any boat, particularly a sailing yacht, and especially for the single-hander, and it makes a vast difference to life when the morale is battered by bad weather.

Perhaps it seems that this boat was built with gales and storms constantly in my mind! That is almost the case, for a boat that can gambol joyfully through the rough will be all right in the smooth. Any boat, almost, will sail fairly fast, moderately comfortably, under ideal conditions; but these conditions are rarely met with, especially in the North Atlantic. Consider the galley. It has three main features: the stove, the sink and the work bench. Each was designed to be used under the worst conditions that could be visualised. Being a Scot, I am cursed with a sharp imagination, which when coupled with the experience of some interesting gales means that I can visualise mighty powerfully. There are several tales of yachts getting rolled over (and of course mine was designed to right itself if this happened), so I did at times consider the faintly fabulous sort of galley that would work upside down. But this was just a bit too aerodynamic. One must draw the line somewhere. Probably the worst conditions would be a struggle to windward off a lee shore in a very strong wind. Normally the boat would be hove-to in a gale, when she would be fairly tranquil. So the stoves were fixed on a long wooden tray, gimballed athwart-ships, so that as the boat heels, the tray swings and the two primuses remain upright. Two bars keep the pans on the stoves. The tray is much larger than needed for two heaters, so that there is always a horizontal surface on which to put a full pan or mug.

The usual yacht sink has a few disadvantages. It is too shallow, so that it spills when the boat heels. It either chips, cracks or dents easily, or it is plastic, in which case it melts when someone puts a hot pan on it. It is inevitably expensive, as all yacht gear must be, because the demand is limited. My sink is an oval bucket. It has very few faults, it is cheap and resilient. The work bench is large by normal yacht standards, and of plywood with a high fiddle to stop things sliding off. A covering of unburnable, unbreakable plastic is what I would have liked, but that was not obtainable at the time.

On the starboard side the long chart-table balances the galley. It is long enough to make a berth for my nieces and nephews for several years to come. It is also big enough to take a large chart fully opened. A book rack runs along the back. At the forward end is a circular hole, which takes the handle of the hand-bearing compass. When this is in place it can be seen by anyone sitting up in the settee-berths, so that the course can be checked without going on deck: an asset much appreciated in the depth of the night. The chart-table also has a fiddle round it, and can be used as an extension to the galley if some elaborate, expansive cooking is under way. There was no time to draw detailed plans, but this did not matter, because the designer had worked out his ideas months ago, and the designer was the builder.

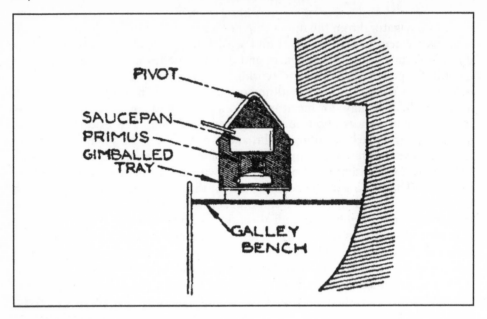

Gimballed galley stove for all-weather cooking.

About this time I bought my anchor. I decided to carry only one, and no anchor chain, because the plan was to sail out of Chester Harbour across 2,600 miles of water and into Weymouth Harbour, non-stop. This would mean that an anchor was just a piece of emergency equipment, and one of the least likely to be used. The only likely stopping place in the Atlantic was the Azores, and there it would be a question of going into a harbour, where I would probably find a quay or mooring buoy. It would have been unseaman-like to have set out anchorless, because I might have to turn back and go into some bay, or I might have got into the English Channel and been dismasted, or otherwise embarrassed. The main advantage of having one, instead of the more usual two anchors and chain, was the big saving of weight. I was offered an anchor for 17.5 dollars by a shark in Halifax. It was too heavy and a bad shape besides being outrageously expensive and second-hand, as I pointed out to this shameless dealer. He challenged me to find a cheaper one, which I did a few days later. This was identical, except that it cost 11.5 dollars. Still not satisfied I searched further and eventually acquired a good model for 2 dollars, which doubly pleased me, because the shark looked so disconcerted when he heard about it. Most of the gear was new, however, in particular the stoves, flares, torches and main compass. The original plan had been for Arthur to go to Halifax to search around and buy these things. When he defaulted I had to spend the time myself, which meant working all the harder, though even so I fell behind schedule. The equipment took a very long time to find. For example, to get just the right fire extinguisher I visited three shops, and never did discover where to buy good oilskins.

On the fourth Monday, arriving at the boatyard in the morning I found Reuben was not in the small crowd yarning outside the main shed. At eight o'clock we dispersed to work. The yachting season was just beginning, every man was feverishly busy getting the boats fitted out and launched in time for the first race. This meant that if Reuben was ill, there was no one to replace him. Besides this he knew the boat, knew me, and most important of all worked very fast, without making mistakes or getting held up by any difficulty. He was irreplaceable in every sense. The loss of crew had upset the all-important time schedule, and if Reuben were ill I might not get away until the hurricane season started. This would send the risks rocketing up. A gale is not much to worry about, but a hurricane is to be avoided at all costs. It makes a fearful mess of a boat, and sometimes ruins her for life, assuming she survives. If there are any rules to ocean crossing, the first is: 'Stay away from hurricane areas during the bad season.' I brooded on all this while working away, painting the boat and cleaning up the handrails ready for bolting on.

By lunch-time I was thoroughly depressed and had made up my mind to take the evening off to visit Reuben. It was a problem to know what to take him. Somehow he did not seem the person to take flowers to; the things I knew he really liked were his cigarettes and his beer. Was beer bad for any illness? Wasn't it supposed to be a liquid food? Or is that a convenient drunkard's tale? Damned if I knew. Meanwhile I must work extra fast all afternoon. Musing in this way, I returned to the boat and there was Reuben. Just as usual at lunch-time he was sitting on a wooden box, with a larger box in front of him, and two or three other men, playing a hilarious game of cards. His cap was well back, home-made cigarette aglow, and his face eager as he slapped his cards down exuberantly. So that crisis passed off. He explained that he had just been coming to work in the morning when his cow started to calve. This naturally called for his attention and assistance. He had eight children, each of whom consumed a great deal of milk daily (we had once calculated his weekly household needs, and they came to well over 10 gallons!). Not that Reuben's family could be considered particularly large: he was one of twenty-one himself, and his father had twenty brothers and sisters.

When Reuben started work on the boat with me, one of his first remarks had been, 'Will there be some beer at the launching?' This was not so much a question as a gentle reminder that it would be as bad as slapping Neptune's face to launch without celebrating. I explained: 'The boat has to be built on a very small budget. We must save everywhere possible. But by hook or by crook we'll have to set aside something to buy beer.' So every time we made some extra cunning move, like omitting the forehatch, we nodded contentedly. 'That's a few more cents towards the beer fund.' (Forehatches are no asset anyway: they invariably leak).

We wanted the cockpit coamings to curve, but they were too thick to bend by hand. So we lit a fire under the steam-box, and thrust the coamings into the box, stoking the fire to a great heat. This is, of course, the traditional and entirely satisfactory way of putting a big permanent bend into a piece of wood. While the coamings cooked we rigged up a jig. After half an hour we opened the steam-box, hauled the coamings out, clamped them into the jig and left them to cool and set. The next day we released the clamps, and there were two tough boards with lots of curvature, just as required. While Reuben cut them to the exact length needed, and planed off the top edges, I made a set of bolts. We took a long bit, put it in an electric drill, made holes down through the coaming and deck, drove the bolts down those holes, then I wriggled in under the deck, put the nuts and washers on, tightened them up, and there was another job done. Reuben rolled a fresh cigarette.

But one little job went less smoothly. Reuben asked me how I wanted the head of the stempiece cut. This still stuck several inches clear of the deck, rough and unfinished, like a neck without a head. I said 'Just cut it off flush with the deck. That will keep the weight off the bow and make it easier to pick up moorings, besides being neat and modern.' Reuben was aghast. 'What! You're not going to ruin her like that?' It must have been around lunch or tea time, for there were a lot of other men in the main shed. They heard Reuben. I was faced with a crescendo of protest.

'You'll spoil her looks!'

'You'll make a rat trap!'

'That won't look modern!'

'Good grief, not straight across?'

It was incredible, they all joined in. I might be the owner, but it was their craftmanship, their efforts, their reputation. They might not say anything in the ordinary course of events, but no one was going to sail an ugly boat anywhere, certainly not to England, and then say the boat was built in Chester. Every Chester boat, in fact all good Nova Scotians, had a high Viking prow. Gerald, with a few tactful words, brought the discussion to a quieter level. We ended up with a compromise which I personally liked very much. It looks just right, yet it is typical of the Chester marque. I hope Chester likes it.

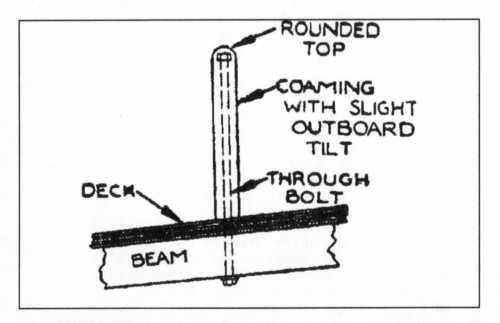

Fixing cockpit coamings.

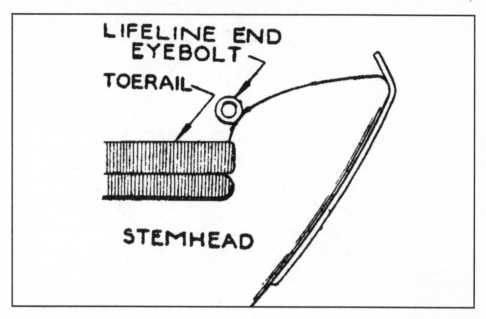

The controversial stemhead.

The boat was now nearly ready for launching except for the ballast keel. To get the two pieces of iron on to the boat, we devised and carried out the following scheme. A very strong bed was made, using baulks of timber, with its top surface at a slight angle, and padded with an old flock mattress. This bed was under one side of the boat. Then, after lunch, before the men dispersed to their several jobs, we all gathered round the hull, knocked out the side supports and the boat was then lifted by hand and laid on its side, at about 45 degrees on the bed.

The remainder of the job was left to Reuben and me. First we had to raise the boat and tip it further (after Reuben had rolled and lit another cigarette). With two lorry jacks we eased the boat into position. We propped it in place, so that no amount of energetic hammering, drilling or coaxing of the keel would move the hull. A pair of timbers were then put under the lower part of the hull, to act as guides and rests so that we could slide the two slabs of iron into place and bolt them there. Each piece of iron weighed nearly half a ton, and would have needed ten men to lift it, if no mechanical aids were used. We levered up one end of the upper section of ballast, put two or three lengths of iron pipe under it and rolled it as close as possible to the hull. A hardwood wedge was driven under one end of the block of iron, then a piece of wood inserted, the wedge was withdrawn, driven under the other end, which in turn was blocked up, and the wedge was returned to the first end. Soon we had raised the mass well off the ground; it was encouraged onto two horizontal baulks, slid across them and onto the angled baulks. Using the two jacks we worked the iron up the slope, till it lay in place beneath the wood keel. Every move had to be pre-planned, and done circumspectly, especially once the iron was on the last lap, up the slope, for then it was necessary for us to work crouched below the iron. Retaining blocks held

Fitting the keel.

the top piece of iron in place while we worked the second piece into place. This was more difficult because the surface that we put the jacks against, and which would be the bottom of the keel when the boat was upright, was not flat. This meant that the jacks had a strong tendency to slip, which was exciting. At last, the two slabs of iron nestled in place under the wood keel, exactly in line both in a fore and aft and in an arthwartships direction. The whole reason for laying the boat over was so that we could drill holes for the keel bolts. The electric machine and the large drill were a long combination. The drill had to extend through the two pieces of iron ballast, through the wood keel and, where needed, through a wooden floor. We could have simply raised the boat up vertically instead of laying it over, to get enough ground clearance for the drill, but it would have involved raising the hull absurdly and even dangerously high.

The five keel-bolts took a lot of making; it requires very little effort to cut the little ⅜-inch bolts we used for the cabin top, side decks and so on, but using a hand stock and die on the 1-inch bolts for the keel made the sweat run freely. There was another short sharp crisis, moreover, when I went to the store for the nuts to go on these bolts. The store supply had run out. There were none nearer than Halifax, it was thought, which meant more delays, and would hold up the launching. Fortunately the local foundry saved the situation.

This foundry also made the mast metalwork, the stem-head fitting, and the rudder gear. With the manager, Gerald and I discussed each piece of equipment, reducing it to the simplest possible arrangement. It was going to be a race with time to get the boat finished before the available money dried up. It was perfectly clear that I could not afford to let the least trouble linger or grow. We had to find the answer, at once, and be right first time.

With the keel bolted on, the boat was lifted upright by the same concerted effort that had laid her down. We put temporary supports under the bilge, for she would not be long in the main shed. With monstrous spanners the keel-bolt nuts were screwed as tight as we knew how. I turned my attention to the wire rigging, and discovered a curious thing. Whereas almost every man in the yard was an allround shipwright, capable of doing anything from planking a dinghy to launching a coaster, no one in the yard could do wire splicing. This did not worry me because I could do my own without difficulty, though by no means neatly. In fact I have always done my own wire splicing and wonder why it is comparatively rare to find an amateur doing so. The problem in splicing is to make a tidy job; practice is required for this, and plenty of time. As I had not done any wire splicing for months, and was in a tearing hurry, my first efforts looked a bit woolly. So about seven times the following conversation occurred. Someone, passing the bench:

'Do you think that splice will hold?'

Me: 'Mine always have done.'

'It doesn't look very neat.'

'You ever done any splicing?'

'Well, no, never actually tried it myself, but …'

'You should try it some time. 'Course, it cuts the hands to hell, as the ends of wire are like fish-hook barbs, and it raises blisters because of the unusual tools, but it toughens the hands wonderfully. Here, have a shot …'

'Well, not just now, I'm pretty busy.'

It was about two days after I had wrestled the last strand into place that I met a Dane who told me he would have been delighted to do the splicing.

'Have you had much experience?' I asked him.

'Yes, I was bos'un on the *Passant*, one of the last of the square-rigged sailing ships. At home I have a big chest full of splicing tools.'

I saw the joke was on me.

Sundays were no longer completely work-free. There was so much to do that even on these days at least a little painting, varnishing or other light work was tackled, besides the week's correspondence. Letters in quest of a crew went out to friends, yacht club secretaries and universities; other correspondence dealt with signalling at sea, my port and date of arrival, food, water, radio, and tests for the Canadian government of bad-weather clothing. Tactful, very carefully worded epistles were sent to my family, with no mention of a single-handed journey.

But there was still time for picnics and parties. The Nova Scotians have a liking for a single-screw motorboat about 35 feet long with a large single forward cabin, and big cockpit. They use this type for fishing and yachting; there were two at the yard, besides others belonging to friends. They make fine mobile party vehicles. We went on fishing expeditions, and visited friends who lived on the coast, parking the boat in the nearest bay. Once, on one of these jaunts, I fell asleep sitting in the cockpit with the clamour and uproar of the party going on all round, but 10 minutes later we had moored up in a cove and I was hurtling round on a boat's table converted into a surf-board, behind a high speed launch. If there was anything missing at those happy sessions it was the presence of other ocean-cruising people.

I missed those valuable conversations which recall to mind important details. They have a way of inquiring about a boat's halliard arrangements, or making suggestions for better ways of lighting the compass at night, which sometimes bring up some vital forgotten fact, or change the ship from an uncomfortable box that threatens to become a coffin, into a delightful wandering home.

It was a happy time, but occasionally I was worried by the thought that no single person can think of every detail. In books some authors claim to do so, but later on they or their craft get into some sort of difficulty that was not foreseen. I tried to recall some of those conversations that took place in Seattle, in Balboa, or the Canary Isles. It was easiest just before falling asleep; the voices of half-remembered people, strong voices, tired ones coming through teeth that clenched a pipe, from sun-burnt faces, from pretty girls or stubbly-chinned men.

'We were run down in the Bay by a tanker, pumped for 18 hours ...'

'Never reef, old boy, just wait till the bloody sail blows away ...'

'That water tasted foul, but then you can live on 10 per cent salt, or is it 30 per cent, mixed with fresh.'

'Dr Bombard did, but he's wrong.'

'The Canadian government says it gives you liver trouble.'

'My pump would never stand 8 hours ...'

'Give me some soda in this, please.'

'What, you never needed oilskins?'

'He's hellish tough.'

'I wish we had a squaresail.'

'Pretty good idea, well, what about rendezvousing in Iceland?'

'Say the year after next. You could do the Antilles some other time.'

'Holy mackerel! Where did you get this rum? Ours we keep confusing for stove oil ...'

'You should have seen her, long and lovely. Beautiful in every way, colour, shape ... No, not you, angel, that cutter we saw coming from Aruba.'

Then sleep and in the morning a quick scanning of the pages of the little black book to check details.

There was one man who knew a lot more about his side of the game than me, and it was a joy to be able to leave it to him. This was the sailmaker. We yarned for half an hour, and the next time I saw him he delivered the sails. He wanted me to have the best Egyptian cotton, but it was too dear; in fact, it cost twice as much as the Yarmouth duck material I selected. We agreed on three deep reefs in the main, and I asked for a single reef in the jib. We agreed that the sails must be strong, but not too heavy or they would be useless in very light breezes. Because the trip was not a very long one, and the boat would be used afterwards as a family cruiser, we decided on conventional yacht sails, instead of special ocean-cruising ones, which have the cloths cut vertically down instead of across.

Though there was no ocean-cruising experience around Chester, people like Jack and Gerald often helped with sensible suggestions. One of Jack's strongest arguments was in favour of a self-draining cockpit. The cockpit I had made was a watertight one; to make it self-draining it was necessary to put a metal flange pipe end in the bottom, another in the ship, and connect up with a piece of flexible pipe. The two metal fittings and the pipe did not cost much, but were not absolutely essential; so I retained the watertight cockpit till the following conversation occurred:

'Your cockpit has no outlet,' said Jack. 'How is the water supposed to run out?'

And I confessed: 'It will have to be bailed dry; admittedly a cursed nuisance, but to drain is too expensive.'

'You can't do that! In bad weather you'll have to sit for hours, even days, up to the knees in water.'

'I know. It's a bleak prospect, but given luck the wind ought to be astern most of the time. The cockpit shouldn't take in much.'

'How much would the fittings cost?'

'Lots, they have to be bronze. I'll buy a pair of rubber boots next time we're in Halifax. Remind me.'

'You can have my boots, I never wear them.' And he went off to find out how much cockpit fittings cost. Later he returned to the subject, and as things were going well at the time, I was persuaded. Days afterwards I blessed Jack and his insistence. The self-draining cockpit was a great success, whereas a plain watertight one would have been exceedingly uncomfortable on some occasions.

With the fitting of the drain, the boat was ready for launching. By this time a lot of people knew about the ship and her purpose, also I had a large circle of friends in Nova Scotia, though I had known no one when I arrived there. The Stevens family agreed that we should have a proper launching, with the full tradition, so there was an extra rush of work, to get the boat as far advanced as possible, and particularly smart. About now, too, the fourth of the seven separate girls who asked to sail with me made her request. She was much the most persistent. Later, when the newspapers and radio stations got the story, they looked eagerly round for the sex angle, inevitably, and pounced joyously on the fact that, while no man would sail the stormy seas in my frail barque, all sorts of fair damsels were keen. Only, of course, they got the facts wrong, giving the number as four instead of seven. Still this is better than their usual exaggeration. I often wonder what would happen if engineers and scientists were as careless as journalists. There would be a dozen plagues running concurrently, with bridges falling down, engines blowing up and chaos round every corner.

Chapter Five

To launch the yacht we first opened the massive doors at the end of the shed, and cleared away heaps of timber, shavings, paint cans, sawing horses and other assorted paraphernalia. Then skids were laid down behind the boat. These skids are flat-topped wooden baulks, on which the boat's cradle slides. As the boat came nearer to completion, it kept giving bigger and bigger movements, as if it was restless. Now it wobbled quite noticeably when anyone moved about on it, for only the two cradle supports on each side held it up. A fire was lit in one of the big stoves that are used in winter to warm the main shed, and a bucket of slippery, greasy substance, containing much tallow, was heated till it became liquid. This muck is known as crab-fat, when there are visitors in the yard, and by a less delicate term when no one is about. It smells, it gets on to everything, it causes innocent shipwrights to slip over more shatteringly than if they had trodden on the traditional banana skin. Finally it makes a horrible mess of decks. It works well on skids, though, so we slopped it on them. The boat had been built on a cradle, to which we fastened a long, thick rope. This rope was passed through two large blocks or pulleys, so that we could prevent the cradle from sliding uncontrolled down the skids. The two chocks holding the cradle in place were knocked away. With long bars we prised the cradle free; then pushing and levering, sweating and heaving, we got the cradle moving along the skids. At first it was the most back-breaking work, till the ground became steeper, when the cradle slid almost unaided. We had to check it frequently, because we had only four skids, so that once the boat was clear of one pair, they had to be lugged around in front of the boat, which was moved on to them, then the next pair were humped into place. The skids, of course, became greasy all over. So did we. In the middle of this slavery I was called to the phone.

'Yes?'

'Is that Ian Nicolson speaking?'

'Yes.'

'Well, sir, I was just driving through Chester; we stopped for lunch, and I heard you're looking for a crew to help sail the Atlantic.'

'That's right.'

'Well, I'd like to come.'

'You'd better come and see me if you can spare the time right away.'

'OK. I will, sir.'

I went back to work. About half an hour later I saw a pleasant-looking lad walk down the jetty and make some enquiries, then walk towards me. By the time he had reached me I decided that, if appearances were anything to go by, he would do. He looked about twenty-five but, as usual with Canadians, he was younger than his looks. Later I learned that he was twenty. He saw in me a very dishevelled person, covered in grime, crab-fat and sweat, with hair awry, trousers torn and shirt hanging out. Also, as usual with Canadians, he underestimated my age, and took me for the same age as himself. He introduced himself.

'There's the boat,' I said, 'have a look at her. Remember it's a long way to England. If you think she'll make it and you still want to come, we'll discuss the matter.'

He went over to the boat, while I resumed work. Shortly afterwards:

'I'd like to join you.' He was keener than before.

'What experience have you had?'

'I've done a little sailing, but not much. But I've been two years in the Merchant Navy.'

'Can you get away soon? Have you enough money to pay for your own food? What will you do when we get to England?'

He rattled out the answers just as promptly:

'I can join you in two days. I've got to drive my mother home to New Brunswick. I've plenty of money.' Here he produced evidence of 1,000 dollars. 'I can get permission to land in England, here's my passport and Merchant Navy discharge.'

'OK. You collect your clothes and get back to Chester as soon as possible.'

I gave him a list of gear to bring. One wants rather different clothes on a small yacht and on a freighter. We discussed a few outstanding points, and he left. I was delighted. A crew, at the eleventh hour, true, but what the hell! We seemed to get on well, too. Things seemed roseate, but I was being tantalised by fate, for he backed out later.

I hurried back to Perry's house to clean up and change for the ceremony. Returning to the yard, I found a cheerful crowd was collecting. It was Dominion Day, so most people were on holiday. The sun shone down on a happy scene. The girls' bright dresses made a splash of colour on the pier. Across the harbour, under the dark pine trees, the wooden staging where the *Cheerio* was moored was a hive of activity. Various friends had come to see the launching in their own boats. Just when we thought we would be late and miss the best of the tide, the *Cheerio* left the quay and motored across the little fjord, escorted by a small convoy of other boats. Jack brought his boat alongside with a swift neat manoeuvre, the engine roaring as the propeller raced to stop the boat. Shirley stepped ashore like Cleopatra from her barge. She looked positively regal, and the whole tableau was somehow most fitting.

I confess I said flippantly: 'My goodness, I've never seen you wearing a hat before.'

But she was equal to the occasion.

'You look unusually smart yourself. But why the sun glasses? Trying to disguise yourself?'

'Wish I could. Those blasted news-dogs are sniffing around.' We walked up the pier, and on to a specially rigged platform, out over the edge of the rising tide, in front of the bow of the boat.

Shirley, a little nervously: 'All right, can I begin?'

'Yes, you look fine. Just take it steady, let everyone hear.' Then, like a queen proclaiming a victory, she said:

'I name this ship *St Elizabeth*. May God protect her, those who built her, and those who sail in her.'

Bomp! She swung the champagne bottle, but it did not break.

Bomp! Still it did not break.

'Try a real swipe,' from me, *sotto voce*.

CRASH! The bottle shattered. Reuben, in his Sunday best, was at the helm of the yard launch, as was right and proper. Two other shipwrights were on the yacht, three more in the launch with Reuben. As the bottle smashed Reuben moved the launch's throttle full open. It surged forward with foam whirling in vortexes from the propeller. The line between the launch and the *St Elizabeth* came taut, humming, vibrating and dripping. With a slight jolt, then a tiny wriggle, the yacht slid afloat. She was born.

Reuben stopped the launch. The line was transferred to the *St Elizabeth*'s bow (for she was launched stern first as is usual) and the launch towed her to the pier. I noticed she floated just right, not too deep, and trimmed well. By the time I reached her, half the shipwrights were aboard. They had the floorboards up to see if she was leaking. Perry looked down the hatch, then at me, with a solemn face. 'Better get buckets to bail!'

'What! *Sacri bleu*! She's not leaking that fast?'

I thrust my way through the crowd and peered into my ship. She was as dry inside as my mouth in that moment of shock. Amid roars of laughter we moored her up. Already she was stirring beneath my feet. Look out, Neptune! We'll be sailing soon.

Shirley, Jack and a girlfriend piled aboard the *Cheerio* and recrossed the harbour to complete the last-minute preparations for the party. The rest of us dealt with the beer. Reuben looked happy. The subsequent party was terrific. Shirley had made a lovely cake with one candle on. Jack decorated the cake with icing, drawing a picture of the yacht and writing *St E*. It was at this party that we conceived the idea of hoisting the church pennant over the interrogative flag if I got lost at sea. The meaning? 'Where in the name of Heaven am I?'

The day after the launching I spent splicing wire, so that we were ready to step the mast the following morning. I rowed across the narrow harbour with the *St Elizabeth* in tow. Her mast was lashed on deck. We brought her alongside a quay where there was a high derrick. In 5 minutes the mast was lifted up, tipped on end and lowered into place. Reuben looked around the boat.

'I guess there's nothing more for me to do.'

'No. Thanks for helping. I'll soon finish the wire splices.' He rowed back to the yard while I set to work feverishly putting the bottom splices in the rigging, for until that was done the mast was very insecurely held up.

Like every harbour in the world, Chester has a speed limit that is ignored. At any time a launch might hurry past, leaving the *St Elizabeth* bobbing in the wake, with her unsupported mast whipping till it broke. On occasions like these, I envy the ship captains of old who could always take the law into their own hands and fire a few rounds of grape-shot. What would it matter if the aim was a little haphazard, the intention would be clear. On this occasion there were one or two alarms, but the job was safely completed.

The next notable event was the blessing of the ship. This took place on another perfect day. The crowd was bigger than at the launching, the press better represented, and we made it an excuse for another party. Before the blessing, the ship was presented with a Nova Scotian flag, the yard employees gave me an unspillable seagoing ash-tray with the Nova Scotian crest on it, and Perry handed me the bill of sale and customs documents of the boat. There were speeches, drinking and general festivities. This was rather far removed from the original secretive plan, but everyone was having a fine time, so what did it matter?

Gear was taken aboard in the next few days, and work on the ship continued. Mast wedges were made and driven home. A canvas jacket was put round the mast where it passes through the deck, after a heavy smearing of bedding compound had been put on the wedges. This was a place where I expected leaks, particularly during rain. Another important job was cleaning the sawdust and shavings out of the ship. These are so easily neglected, and they soon clog up the pump, usually when the weather is rough, for then the bilge water is thrown about, stirring up the sawdust and washing shavings out of inaccessible corners. And of course the pump is much more difficult to clear when the boat is dancing about.

Once the bilge was spotless I could put in the inside ballast. First it had to be burned clean, because it was coated with a thick oily black muck. I built a fire of scrap wood, on the beach, around the pigs of iron. It was not a very hot fire, and it seemed to me that the ballast would take a long time to burn clean.

'Why don't you use a bucket of gas? It would get things going,' suggested Perry.

I got some petrol and, still holding the bucket heaved the contents onto the fire, which promptly went skywards with an aggressive roar. I dodged out of the way and no damage resulted, but it was a foolish and thoughtless thing to do. I was distinctly startled by this, and worried. Tending the fire for the rest of the morning, I did some hard thinking. There was no doubt that the pace of work had been very fast. I was correspondingly tired. But this incident showed me that I was tired enough to be capable of dangerous unplanned actions which might get me into all sorts of trouble. This was no state to be in at the outset of a trans-Atlantic sail. After that I eased down. Jack helped me lug the ballast aboard. It was carefully fastened down, so that should the boat roll over at the height of a gale, the ballast would not crash out through the cabin roof, denting the crew on the way.

Having worked on the boat energetically all the afternoon Jack wanted to try sailing it in the evening.

'Look at the fine breeze,' he said. But I was discouraging.

'It's blowing far too hard for the first try-out of brand new sails. We must take them out in very light airs first, gradually working up to this sort of wind.

We might try the trysail though.' And this we did. The trysail was an unusual one. It had slides up the luff, and hanks on the leach, so that it could either be set aft of the mast as a main trysail in the conventional manner, or it could be set on one of the forestays as a storm jib. In light airs it could be used as a staysail, set on the inner forestay while the normal jib was set on the outer one. This versatile sail was not made of excessively heavy canvas, but was strongly flat-taped all round, which gave it the same strength as the more usual all-round roping, without making it so baggy or aerodynamically inefficient. It was quite small, but had one deep reef. Using Jack's boat, the *Cheerio*, as escort we took the *St Elizabeth* out for a brief run. There was not much to learn from sailing her in a moderately fresh breeze with so little canvas, but no faults showed up.

Next day we were out with full sail up. She handled beautifully. There was just a gentle touch of helm, so that helmsman and boat were comfortably attuned. The wind and sea were too light for a thorough appreciation, but we began to see great possibilities. It was thrilling for me to hand over the helm, climb aboard the *Cheerio* as she ranged alongside and then watch the *St Elizabeth* from afar. I visualised her in deep water, thrashing along, lee gunwale under, spray flying. I could see no alterations or improvements necessary.

There were still a lot of small jobs to be done and I was helped by quite a crowd of children. One of them was hoisted up the mast to reeve the second jib halyard and the topping lift, which doubled as emergency main halyard. Another served many of the rigging splices, which is a time-consuming job that requires very little skill. Another painted. They helped bolt down the stanchions, fit the ventilator, and in the evenings we went for trial sails. In some ways this was the pleasantest part of the time of preparation. It is true, departure day was drawing near, but the almost grim, relentless pressure was now relaxed. I began to regret having to leave so soon. My assistants were shaping into a good crew. They were proud of the boat. There were no races in or near Chester for a boat like the *St Elizabeth*, or I should have been tempted to try her in competition.

Jack gave me a sword-fishing platform from his previous boat. It was made of galvanised piping, which I cut up and had welded on to base plates, the result being a fine set of stanchions, four a side. The ventilator was a great problem. I did not want any holes in the boat at all other than the main hatch. But would that alone be enough for ventilation? Probably not, for without the draught of air, condensation would take place, and the whole of the inside of the ship would soon be running with moisture. Furthermore, in a gale one cannot leave the main hatch open, not even a crack sometimes. So I put a 2½ inch ventilator on the cabin top, for the voyage only, fitting much more extensive ventilators when England was reached. Even this single vent had a wooden plug, so that if necessary we could batten down and be safely submerged. All we needed was a periscope.

About this time I made two wooden spoons. There was no point in buying a single thing that could be made. For some time I hesitated about a dinghy. Reuben and I could have built a simple one between us in two days. A dinghy would have been extra weight and windage, both of which slow a boat, besides handicapping her in a tight spot, to some extent at least. There would be no chance to use the dinghy as a shore boat, for I intended to leave from the

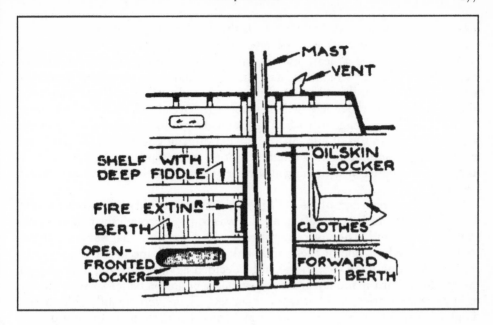

Looking to port at fore end of cabin, in way of mast.

Chester Seacraft pier and head for Weymouth quay, nonstop. Remains the question of a life-boat. Yachtsmen generally consider a dinghy quite useless for lifesaving at sea. The popular theory is that if the weather is so bad that it wrecks a yacht, then a dinghy would have no hope. The only exception given is in the case of fire during calm weather. My own view is strongly opposed to this, but there is so little evidence either way that I feel some experiments ought to be carried out. While I agree that very many yachts have dinghies which would not hold all the crew or even two-thirds, in anything but calm water, a dinghy properly equipped with lifelines or hand rails and buoyancy gear makes an excellent communal life-ring. It will probably fill, but if all the crew hang on to it they can keep up each other's morale, and they are bunched together, making a much more easily seen object than widely separated heads bobbing about. Now suppose a yacht runs foul of a heavy piece of driftwood, gets holed, and sinks; the crew cut the dinghy lashings, so that the dinghy floats clear. Some of the crew sit in the dinghy bailing as necessary, others hang on the outside, doubtless with chattering teeth. After an hour or two, those in the dinghy strip off their dry clothes, and change places with those in the water. This change takes place regularly till the crew begin to die off, or are rescued. A man has been known to survive 30 hours continuously in the sea, after falling overboard, so our hypothetical crew should last two days. A high morale is important. This is one way that a dinghy can be used as a life-boat. It is not a fanciful suggestion. Among other evidence two men, each in separate dories, rowed across the Atlantic and they had to get out and bail at one stage. Another point is this. The two main causes of loss of small craft are fire (from galley or engine) and grounding. In the first case, everyone piles into the dinghy or hangs on to it, and with luck the conflagration attracts rescuers. In the second case, the crew may be few enough not to overcrowd the dinghy, and in any case some, at least, may be saved by surf-riding ashore in it. Clearly we ought to find out whether a man has more chance of survival if he comes ashore on to a rock-bound coast unprotected, or huddled in the bottom of a dinghy. Admittedly the dinghy will probably turn over, but it might get him over the first and worst fangs of rock. Then it might get picked up by a following wave and drop on top of him. So you have a difficult choice. But I know from experience in handling rowing dinghies among rocks that if, in an emergency, I had to choose between swimming ashore or getting there in the dinghy, I should try the dinghy.

For the maiden voyage of the *St Elizabeth* a dinghy would not be overcrowded as a life-boat, since I was single-handed. I was to pass through the region where icebergs are found. They were reported to be numerous that summer. If the yacht impinged on one of these and sank, I might escape in the dinghy, and row to Newfoundland. But in the end I decided against carrying a dinghy on the grounds that the money and time available could be better spent. I did try to buy a small Carley float but without success. There were no inflatable rubber dinghies available locally either, so far as I could learn, though I did not pursue my search for one of these very far, due to the shortage of cash.

The only alteration made in the course of construction was in the position of the compass. It was first put on the after end of the cabin top. Fortunately I remembered that there were two concealed galvanised iron bolts inside the cabin coaming, close by the compass. The new position was in the cockpit, just below the seat level. Perry pointed out that this was not a good position, 'It is well below eye level,' he said, 'so you have to look down to see it. That will make it harder to keep awake at night.'

'That's true,' I agreed, 'but I have no intention of sitting up all night and every night. Besides, there is no alternative position.' The big advantage of the final site was apparent when I got to sea. Then I found that I could watch the compass while ensconced in the cooking-navigation position and thus steer a course from below. One of the last items I made was an extension for the tiller, for this type of steering.

Chapter Six

There was no sense of approaching climax, no last minute rush. The provisions arrived one wet morning and were taken aboard after sorting as soon as the rain stopped. The boat was provisioned as she was built, with a good deal of planning and no inessentials. Assuming that the most difficult conditions might exist the whole way across, with stiff head winds, horrendous seas and frequent trouble with gear, I decided not to do much more than heat food. Admittedly real cooking, such as baking, is a very satisfying experience. There is as much pleasure in laying a three-course dinner complete with trimmings on a pitching yacht's table, as in getting an accurate position fix or a quick, neatly executed change of sails. But elaborate cooking is too complex at sea, in a 6-tonner. With a 10-tonner, or in harbour, or with two people, things are different.

The four basic foods on the *St Elizabeth* were oatmeal, rice, macaroni, and potatoes, which last kept fresh in a net, though they sprouted. Spaghetti would have been taken as a substitute for macaroni if the latter had been unobtainable, but spaghetti is less easily handled.

The Stevens family produced a lot of glass jars with screw tops in which to stow the rice, macaroni and oats, which all arrived from the provisioners in paper packets. These packets are an unmitigated curse; they do not weigh heavily like glass jars, it is true, but they soon get soggy, then burst, causing misery and their contents to spread through the cabin. Glass jars are so beautifully watertight, clean, they allow their contents to be visible so easily, they cost nothing, and when they are empty overboard they go, perhaps with a message inside. This was many years before it became illegal to throw rubbish overboard.

Sugar (which is cheap and supposed to provide quick energy) was also slowed in glass jars in large quantities, likewise tea; jam arrived already jarred. Fresh carrots and onions were brought, packed in transparent plastic bags, as is usual throughout North America, and were quite fresh at the end of the voyage. These two vegetables are much better than most others in a small boat; they stand up to innumerable dampings and bruises, and seem to survive for a long time in the most uncomfortable stowage places (like the chain locker). Fresh green vegetables get soggy, smelly and then disintegrate. So many of them are just water standing up anyway; moreover, the outer leaves are all wasted and they take up too much stowage space, necessarily in the best lockers, by which I mean the light airy ones well clear of the bilge. Hence no fresh greens were aboard the *St Elizabeth*. But there were beans, peas and spinach, all nicely canned, involving no waste and no preparation; these tins were stowed low in the lockers below the chart-table and galley, so that the cook, wedged in his seat, could reach them without effort. Here also were slowed the bully beef and Irish stew, the tinned soup and the tinned milk. On the starboard shelf behind the settee was the tinned fruit, a tin a day being an important prop to morale. Here also was the bottle of lime juice, the tins of fruit and the five large loaves; the bread was expected to last ten days but did in fact last sixteen. The fifth loaf was still fresh at the end of that time, perhaps owing to its being a brown currant one. These loaves were bought cut and wrapped in wax paper, which saved buying that menace to all cooks at sea, a bread-knife. Tinned butter or margarine was unobtainable in Halifax, as seems to be the case in many parts of the world, but the fresh margarine remained good throughout the trip and was used for frying, in thick layers on the life-boat biscuits, in blobs on the vegetables by way of garnishing, and beaten into mashed potatoes, but not stirred into porridge as the Tibetans do.

Although I ordered all small tins, the wholesaler could not in all cases supply them. The milk, however, was in baby tins, which particularly pleased me. The usual way of opening a milk tin at sea is to pierce a hole in the top; the tin is shaken upside down, and the milk emerges at a slow, controlled rate. This is all very economical and makes the milk go a long way, besides making the can semi-spillproof, but it also means that the milk can easily go bad undetected. Tiny details like this make the difference between Hades and heaven on a small boat. It was a note in the little black pocket-book that reminded me to order the small size of milk cans; in fact, the whole diet was written out in detail weeks before the food was bought; the result was that the food taken was just about right, with a nice balance of staples and luxuries. The latter are the most important since they are a simple means of raising morale.

It is easy to order a balanced diet; the problem is to get easily handled food in the right form. For instance, jam was bought in 1-lb jars because a single-hander will get tired of a particular kind of jam if he has to eat through a 2-lb jar. Besides, the loss of a 1-lb jar through breakage is less important than a two-pounder. Then the jars should have screw lids, as these keep out drips, stay on when the jar falls over and are fairly easy to remove and replace, unlike some patent covers. The narrow-based jam jars fall over too easily. And so on. Innumerable details like this go into the buying of every item, which makes it a fascinating game.

Meals developed as planned, namely one hot meal on rising in the morning, and a second before turning in, with a cold picnic lunch on deck. Occasionally an extra meal was eaten. The morning meal was considered particularly important, so that provided the ship was behaving well and on the course, I cooked breakfast in comfort before going on deck. The stove was lit, and the pan put on to cook, while the cabin was tidied and the bedding rolled up. In the evening I often stood or sat in the hatchway, steering with one hand on the tiller extension while stirring with the other. The morning meal was usually porridge and tinned fruit, sometimes scrambled eggs. Eggs served any other way are so liable to end up scrambled that it seems a good idea to cooperate with fate and hash them up initially.

Few women who have cooked at sea will complain about their domestic duties in the house, for the effort required to cook in a wildly bucking yacht is awful.

I never try to cook things that need accurate measurements, when at sea in a small boat. The morning porridge was made thus-wise: from a secure position wedged in the cook's seat, a can of water is seized from beneath the berth, given a swift jab with the opener, then a second jab, to make the contents flow out easily. Most of the can is emptied into the saucepan and boiled. Oatmeal is heaved into the boiling water, the amount being impossible to determine because it is shaken straight from the packet and steam fills the air. Salt is added, and by some alchemy and much stirring the result never failed to please. The only reason for stirring is that it prevents the brew from sticking to the pan as this makes washing up so tedious.

By the end of the trip all morning chores, including making, eating and cleaning up after breakfast, could be completed in 35 minutes, and in a couple of minutes more the reefs would be shaken out and the owner comfortably seated at the helm deep in a book, while the *St Elizabeth* rolled and pitched, reeling off the miles with a joyous, cheerful gurgling.

The evening meal was often made of 'White Stew'. To make one of these successfully some art must be used. First either rice, macaroni, or spaghetti is boiled till soft, and until most of the water has been evaporated, then a can of stew, or beef or pilchards or beans or peas or several of these may be added. More stirring follows, then a sauce of tomatoes or Worcestershire may be included, or curry powder. Sometimes a hard-boiled egg or some raisins or, especially with curry, a few small blue plums should be put in. This sort of stew needs constant stirring, for it does not improve with burning. However, almost anything else is worth trying, and the variations are numerous, even with so limited a larder as there was on the *St Elizabeth*. Perhaps luck has favoured me or one of my ancestors has passed down a touch of culinary culture, but I have never made an unpalatable 'White Stew'. Frankly, I believe they are both foolproof and stormproof. They can be made sweet for a second course. In this instance dried fruit of any sort is put in at the same time as the basic farinaceous material, and all boiled soft together. Milk, dried, evaporated or condensed, and sugar are added at the end. For the small boat chef these dishes are a multiple blessing, as only one stove burner is used, and there is only one pan to clean afterwards.

Washing dishes is quite as unpopular afloat as ashore, but on the *St Elizabeth* great care was taken to keep up a high standard of living. It is so easy to drop into accepting a 'spanner in the jampot' attitude and soon the morale slumps. Gale or calm, washing up was carried out at least once every 24 hours except during the last run up the Channel, when I was too impatient to waste a second.

Chapter Seven

Having been so dogmatic in the last chapter, I will now return to the narrative, excusing myself by saying that it would be super-human, having made the crossing, not to put one's feet up on the table, raise a supercilious eyebrow, and lay down the law on one or other aspect of ocean cruising.

Before departing I made one more item of equipment, namely a sea-anchor. This is one of the most controversial pieces of gear connected with the sea. Most cruising yachts used to carry them, but the chances of using them are few, and they are gradually dying out of favour. A sea-anchor may take many forms, but is usually a conical canvas bag, which is trailed out ahead or astern of a yacht on the end of a stout line, to keep her end on to the waves in heavy weather. The difficulties are many, so are the theories and theorists. I spent an energetic afternoon making one. It was simpler than the usual cone bag, and was based on various drawings and sketches I had seen in technical books. It is a piece of canvas stout as steel, fastened along the top long edge to a wooden beam, and along the bottom to a galvanised iron bar. The two short vertical sides have pockets which hold strong battens when the anchor is in use; the whole job rolls up into a small stowable sausage, and only requires the insertion of the wood battens to put it in working order. Wires lead from all four corners to a common point 5 feet from the canvas where they are attached to a warp. The idea is that the anchor floats vertically, like a curtain, the beam pulling upwards, the bar downwards. It looks strong. As it turned out, I never had occasion to put it to the test; but in single-handed cruising it is a sound plan to leave no stone unturned.

The crew position had a variety of fluctuations. The boy who had so enthusiastically asked to join me on the day of the launching failed to appear at the time arranged. Two days later, while I was irritably wrestling with iron pigs of ballast, fitting them in place in the bilge, a finger-wrecking job, someone passed a postcard down the hatchway. The boy's mother wrote to say that she was very sorry, but she could not let him go. She hoped I had not been inconvenienced. Ye gods! I was beyond swearing. It was too amazing. The boy was twenty, he had been two years in the Merchant Navy. On the postcard his mother conveniently gave no address, so I could not invite her to examine the ship and meet the owner. She had never seen either. It was quite extraordinary.

That any mother of a Canadian boy should behave so, disconcerted me enough; when I realised he was from the Maritime Provinces I was doubly dumbfounded. Anyway, let some good come of this incident. I hereby warn all Canadian girls east of the Rockies. Look out! That young and handsome fellow with crinkly fair hair and blue eyes (just the sort you will fall for): Avoid him! He's inseparably tied to his mother's apron strings.

A few days later another crew offered his services, then another. One wanted to be paid and to have his passage paid home and was not prepared to help with any of the expenses. He had had experience in Merchant Ships, but not in sail. I explained that the crossing was a holiday, a comfortable sailing trip, and that I wanted someone to share the pleasure and the trouble, not a paid hand, so he lost interest. The other was almost broke, but prepared to join, to throw in almost his last dollar, and to risk not finding a job in England, also to risk being deported when we arrived. The last point seemed more of a gamble for me, as I might be charged his fare back across the Atlantic. I thought we ought to meet, let him see the boat and discuss the matter together before committing ourselves, so I sent him a telegram to that effect. He replied with another. He had changed his mind, he was no longer interested. That made the fifth let-down. It seemed bad at the time to have five failures, but a friend of mine, gathering a crew for a much bigger yacht, had forty-seven reneguers in two months, including the navigator who backed out half an hour before the ship sailed.

After that telegram I decided to give the matter no further thought, and asked Emery to complete the yacht's papers for an early departure.

Chapter Eight

The start of an ocean voyage is often hard. There are almost certainly dangers and discomforts ahead, perhaps not many, but almost inevitable. Then, too, there is the parting from friends. While fitting out I had met so many new friends, extra good people, whose kindness made their hospitality doubly pleasant. And Chester is such a pretty, happy little place. Fortunately I have a well-tried scheme which usually seems to make the omens propitious. It consists of an extra good dinner, followed by a visit to the cinema. On this occasion the trailer of *The Cruel Sea* was shown. Behind me, one boy said to another as the stormiest of waves rolled across the screen: 'I'll bet he wishes he wasn't going'. On the contrary, I considered the *St Elizabeth* dispassionately, saw that she was good, and stopped worrying.

On the last morning, with Emery in the shipyard truck we made a tour of the town. I paid a last visit to the little white Catholic church on the hill. Next we visited customs, where I got documents. One of the cardinal rules of ocean-cruising is to carry a thick wad of documents, of every description and in every language, covering all possible subjects and contingencies together with the maximum number of letters starting: 'To whom it may concern' – with big crests at the top and correspondingly big (but quite illegible) signatures at the bottom. The reason for all this is that the yachtsman is more likely to have trouble ashore than afloat, and these forms are insurance against such afflictions. With them officials can be placated or awed or entertained. It is true that I intended to stop nowhere, but the Azores were roughly on my route, Ireland was not far off it, France I like, the end of a gale might see me tired and near a Spanish harbour. In fact, ocean cruising is so uncertain, I was once more leaving no stone unturned.

There was 'Form B13 Customs Canada Export entry' in quadruplicate. There was 'C8 Customs Canada' which though only in duplicate (one for me, one for the government) had the encouraging phrase 'Clearance of yacht *St Elizabeth* of (Not Regd) approx. 7 tons burthen official No. None with 1 men I. M. Nicholson (spelt wrong dammit) Master from this Port to the Port of Weymouth, England with the undermentioned cargo viz. ... Ballast ... and the necessary sea stores for the voyage. Given under my hand at the Customs House Chester Nova Scotia this 16th day of July 1954. (Here follows the customary illegible signature.) Note Collector will issue no clearance except the same has been numbered in its consecutive order.'

There are two things I like about this form. First, the government seem quite certain I shall get to England, and Weymouth too. Mighty encouraging, even if they have not seen the boat. Secondly, I like the phrase 'Given under my hand'. It sounds as though some surreptitious palming has been going on, more suggestive of smuggling than of customs. Then there is the Bill of Health. Not one of these forms had been issued since 1939 from Chester, so my form was yellowing with age even before I got it. It had a red seal stuck on, and so it ought, too, considering I had to pay a dollar for the thing. I had from Emery the bill of sale of the ship in triplicate.

All this is not an imposing collection, but there was no time to get more. However, I had a trump card up my sleeve. I could always put into a harbour and insist on asylum for 24 hours, to repair storm damage. If there was no storm damage, it is but the work of a moment to sabotage the bilge pump, say, or a halyard in such a way that the trouble can be righted in an instant. If 24 hours is not sufficient one can plead that it is blowing too hard to go out, or alternatively that there is insufficient wind, and without an engine, well ... I am so sorry M'sieu, but what can one do? Here the shoulders are shrugged with a magnificent Latin gesture – and a bottle of wine broached. This gambit is a useful standby in an emergency, but it is very rarely necessary. Just occasionally though, one meets an intractable official, in some remote harbour where none but an ocean-cruiser would go. Of course if one travels in such places, the almost universal bribe is a bottle of Scotch. This is more of a worldwide currency than food, dollars or cigarettes. I confess I have never tried gold. What fun it would be to pass a glinting golden doubloon to some recalcitrant official and watch the change of attitude. Especially if it were really a lead coin gilt. There are so many varied pleasures to this game.

After the customs house, Emery and I went to the post office. There was one letter for me, from the Royal Nova Scotia Yacht Squadron, enclosing a letter which Arthur had written to them before I contacted him. In this letter Arthur asked the Squadron secretary if he knew of any boats sailing east to Europe. The secretary had heard that I was seeking a crew, hence his letter. Clearly fate had no intention of letting up with the crew game, but I was beyond taunting. Emery visited a grocer's and was given two transparent plastic bags such as are used a great deal in North America for food packages. We put my documents into one of these to keep them dry. I bought some boiled sweets and chewing gum. I am not particularly fond of the former, the latter disgusts me, but they are both great assets in a small boat, for they stretch the water supply. Chewing gum in particular keeps the saliva circulating and can make all the difference if it becomes necessary to ration water. Besides, there is no one to witness the ghastly gesticulations of the jaw once the coast has dropped behind.

Back to the yard we rattled in the faithful much abused lorry.

I made a round of the sheds. There were few men about because the majority had gone off to lunch. But the most important was there. Reuben was in his usual place, with the customary grin, the hand of cards, and the home-made cigarette.

'Just off. I've come to say goodbye, and thanks for doing so much.'

'Goodbye, Ian, and good luck.'

He looked serious. I thought: 'What's he worried about? He made a good job of the boat, I think and hope.' Then I realised that it was absurd to read what was not there in people's glances. Some of the other men looked a tiny bit anxious. Finally there was Gerald. He had done more than anyone, on the technical side; the difficult decisions I had made were often a thousand times easier because of his backing, but much more, he had made all sorts of amendments, put in ideas, he had been the only person with responsibility in the building apart from myself. We said goodbye with just a slight hesitation. So this is it. Now we shall see if we know how to build boats or not.

'Why not wait till a bit later, when there'll be more people here?' he asked.

'No, I'm on schedule, and I want to slip away quietly. We'll make a noise when I come back.'

I walked down to the pier. No more worries now, just a slight exhilaration. The *St Elizabeth* looked very trim, her white paint gleamed, and was smartly picked out with the dark blue boot-top, dark blue rail and dark blue line round the cabin top. The sails had been bent on by Ben and Alberta, Reuben's nephew and niece. A young friend of theirs was also aboard. I hoisted the mainsail and examined it critically. It had to set well to get the best out of its small area. Ben was on the jib. The crew of three knew their job, as a result of the few trial sails. I hopped back on to the pier for a final examination. Halyards free and neat. Ship trimmed just right. Decks clean, thank you, Alberta. Deck gear lashed well down. Back on board, I stood at the tiller.

'Let her go, Ben, throw the mooring-rope ashore, it belongs to the yard.' The wind caught her sails. I pulled the tiller over. 'Harden in the jib sheet. Make sure the weather sheet is free and ready.' The *St Elizabeth* heeled a tiny fraction, and slid forward. The wind in the harbour was light and fluky. One moment the boat went well, then the wind died, to return from quite another direction. Maddening. We fiddled with the sails, tacked and tacked again. She was well loaded, with all her stores and four people, even if we were all lightweights, so she was a little sluggish in light airs. At last we got clear of the Back Harbour, and the wind came free and fast. We had a slashing sail across Mahone Bay, past the lovely islands. The other three took the tiller, while I studied the chart, and later brewed some soup for lunch. It was a rattling good sail, cheerful and swift. The boat would have been reefed if I had been alone, but with a strong crew I could make good time without risk. If only the crew could have stayed aboard the whole way across, we would have made wonderful time, for they liked to press on hard, and they learnt quickly. They all wanted to come, too.

2 hours after leaving the pier, we were sailing into New Harbour. This is a long cleft in the rocky shore, narrower even than the Back Harbour. We moved on down this fjord, our momentum and the wind on the top of the sail pushing us. Jack and Shirley had left Chester some days previously to start on a painting and sketching tour. We had agreed to rendezvous at New Harbour, and there they were. Their dark blue *Cheerio* was moored alongside a staging. We shouted, and they yelled back 'Pick up that mooring with the dory on it.' We did so, and after stowing the sails, piled into the dory and rowed ashore.

Here was Canada, the real, wild Canada. Everywhere the pine and spruce trees grew, dark and silent. The light grey rock came straight down to the sea, which was clear and cold. Staging along one side of the fjord stood drunkenly in the water and on the rocky shore. Huts for fishing gear huddled on the staging; beneath in the water was a white mass of fish entrails and heads, for the fishermen clean their catch as they land it, and drop the refuse straight into the sea. Alongside the staging a fishing boat rises and falls on the swell. It is dark green, and sweetly curvaceous like most Nova Scotian boats. Overhead, billowy white clouds chase across a blue sky. I feel slightly sick, leaving all this.

Jack and Shirley look cheerful and sun-burnt. I think: 'I'm probably tanned too, but it has come on unnoticed in the hectic days'. We chat for a minute, then my young crew depart to catch a bus home. When I tell Jack and Shirley that I am off they try to dissuade me. 'Stay a month, or a week at least. We can cruise together. You might get a crew.' I have to quiet them. I must go, and refuse to be tortured by their kindness. I am leaving Canada just as soon as I have learnt to love it. The sea pounds and foams outside the harbour. Through the entrance I can see the islands stretching away to the horizon, some inhabited by friendly folk, some silent, unpeopled, inviting. In my cabin there is a chart of the coast showing a thousand scarcely accessible places to explore, quiet moorings, lonely bays and wide rivers. The sun beats down, but I feel vaguely chilled.

'Jack, will you give me a tow clear of the harbour? It's rather narrow to beat out of.'

'You're definitely going, then?' And, more quietly: 'Yes, we'll give you a tow.' He climbs down the ladder to *Cheerio*. Her engine breaks into a roar, then settles into a rumble, as he lets it warm up. I row the dory back out to the moorings and tie a single reef in *St Elizabeth*'s mainsail. It is like the start of a rugger match, or a race, or just before getting a pair of boxing gloves tied on. The faintly sick feeling and the awkwardness of the hands. It is like the few moments when the hounds are giving tongue but are not clear of cover, or that ghastly, chilly wait before a cross-country run. The whole of the body is tense for a start, helplessly unable to relax just when repose is so helpful.

The *Cheerio* ranges alongside. Shirley passes me an extra loaf, a packet of biscuits and some of the special cream cheese I like. They hand across a rope, which is passed through the bow fairlead, and on to the cleat. A quick look round to make sure all's well, then off with the mooring line and I'm away, severed from Canada. The tow line is taut. As we are heading straight into the wind I run up the mainsail, jump back to the tiller to steady the boat on its course behind the *Cheerio*, then forward again to coil the halyard. We clear the harbour and start pitching into the waves. In a second the jib is up, flapping wildly till I get back to the helm and haul in the sheet. Now we are well outside, and so for a third time I run forward, check the halyards, then slip the tow line.

Jack circles the *Cheerio* round and they come past. 'Keep well off that headland.' They point to the boulders and rocks running into the sea under my lee. The sheets are hard in and the *St Elizabeth* plunges eagerly forward. Gone now the tenseness; the fight has begun. Jack circles once more, then turns away. He waves goodbye, Shirley, with little John sitting on her knee, blows a kiss as they turn homewards. On the transom is the appropriate name *Cheerio*.

My knuckles stand out white, gripping the tiller unnecessarily hard. For a long, long minute I look astern. God knows, partings are no fun.

Chapter Nine

Once clear of the headland the wind is aft, as I set a course for England. The boat fairly tears along, in a wild, exultant, free flight, slashing at waves, happy and cheerful and thoroughly competent. Slowly I get her mood. We are heading home, home. Sad to leave friends, but in seven weeks, maybe six, possibly five ... No, must not tempt fate, in seven weeks the *St Elizabeth* will be sailing triumphantly into Weymouth. Or lie wrecked somewhere. But it's no good. Not even my Scottish caution lasts long in such perfect sailing conditions. Seagulls dip and soar astern, till we sail out beyond their invisible boundary; the sea sparkles and gurgles with delight at the sight of such a jolly ship, and she just cavorts with joy. I take out the reef and we hasten forward anew. It is such a wonderful sail, and to think that it is all mine alone to enjoy. Mine because I wanted it, mine because the other poor, blind, ignorant, narrow-minded earth-bound fools would not take the chance. And to think that I offered it to them, offered it! Why, if they only knew, they would have come clamouring, begging, insisting. It was worth the frightful moments, the contriving and striving, the hitch-hiking and the doubting, the sweat and, yes, I admit it, the near breakdown of the very grim times; it was worth all that and more for that superb sail the first day.

As the last of the islands came abeam, I reached down on to the chart-table and grabbed the log and line. A lifeline was already tied round my waist, so after lashing the tiller I crawled aft to the end of the counter to fit the log in position. Sailing downwind as we were, the boat would not keep on course for long with the tiller lashed, so I had to make two journeys out to the extreme stern to get the log working, jumping back into the cockpit in time to prevent the boat swinging far off course. And my course was 140 degrees magnetic, which is not at all in the direction of the English Channel, but would take me well clear of Sable Island. My original plan to visit this lonely place had been made before I had looked into the pilot book. This tome had discouraged me, saying that there is no anchorage, an extensive variety of dangers, and little to see. What finally persuaded me to keep well clear was a chart in the Chester Seacraft office, showing the island with all the numerous wrecks in its vicinity marked. Having decided not to go there, the next thing was to ensure that I did not find myself there accidentally. The island lay in the path of anyone wishing to sail from Chester to the English Channel, so I decided to go south of it because this would make the best use of the ocean currents and minimise the danger of meeting ice. As I expected to meet fog, and hoped to get plenty of sleep at night when the boat might wander somewhat, I planned to keep well south of Sable Island.

Two Canadian fishing schooners passed. These boats were the traditional shape, which is more yacht-like than that of any commercial craft in the world, with rounded bow and neat counter, something like the *St Elizabeth*. Unhappily, it is usual nowadays for these craft to have a reduced rig and an engine. One or two other ships passed in the distance.

As usual at the beginning of a voyage I was seasick, but to my inexpressible relief, not painfully. This cursed malady has never incapacitated me; but I have been afflicted so often, that I can steer a fairly straight course with my feet for minutes on end, while lying over the side feeding the fishes. It is often a very painful disease, but the suffering can be reduced by eating immediately after each bout. This makes the next spasm (which is inevitable with me) much easier.

On this occasion I nibbled my life-boat biscuits and decided that they were pleasantly palatable, and a big improvement on the old-fashioned kind. I was doing 'acceptability tests' on them for the Canadian government, and my conclusion was: Most acceptable.

By 9 p.m. (2100 hours Atlantic standard time, which I was using at that moment) it was getting dark, I was well off shore, clear of the coastal shipping route, the log said 24 miles and I was pleasantly tired. Leaving the jib up, I lowered the mainsail, left the tiller to swing free, had a light meal, and turned in. A white all-round light shone brightly, hanging on the backstay, where I could see it without leaving my bunk. In a few minutes I was fast asleep, while the boat sailed peacefully on, doing about 3 knots sometimes a little north, sometimes a little south of the course, but never far off, as I checked every 2 hours. During the night I continued feeling squeamish, so my tours of inspection were very brief. The alarm clock would wake me, I would wriggle out of the sleeping bag, thrust my feet into my low rubber boots, and slide back the hatch. The sight that met my gaze as my head was poked through the hatchway was perfect, just the ocean-cruiser's dream. The sky was bright with stars, the moon threw glittering silver on the sea, nothing in the way of shipping or land was in sight, and a fair wind pushed us onwards 3 miles every hour. After a quick glance round the horizon, at the compass, then aloft, I would retreat below, slam the hatch, reset the alarm, and so back to my bunk. How cosy it was in the cabin. Once I sat for a moment savouring the delights of the game; then scrawled a note in the log, and back to the bunk and sleep.

There is, of course, some danger of being run down by another ship at night. This risk is real enough; some friends of mine very nearly lost their ship and possibly their lives after a tanker holed them, as they lay slatting and motionless in a calm. They saw the ship coming but could neither move clear nor attract the attention of the ship's company. The tanker did not stop, and the nearest dry land was several hundred miles away; they made it more by good luck than anything. Whereas I do not voluntarily amplify the risks of ocean cruising, I do not believe in pondering on them too much. They are not wholly avoidable, which is just as well, for without danger there is no sport. By keeping clear of the main shipping lanes, by reasonable vigilance, and with a big white all-round light, I hoped to avoid trouble. If the *St Elizabeth* had herself run into another ship, I have no doubt we should have done very little damage, for I sailed slowly at night, and anything we were likely to meet would be too thick-skinned to hole easily. I did consider steering at night and sleeping all day, but this is such a dull business, and so much increases the discomforts that I decided against it quite firmly. As the trip was to be a holiday, I considered then, and still do, that the risks were justified.

In the morning of the first day off-shore I noticed the rigging was not tight enough, so went from turn-buckle to turn-buckle (also known in different parts of the world as rigging or bottle screws), undoing the safety wires, tightening them, and refastening the wire. This took some time as the ship was dancing about a little and I particularly wished to avoid losing tools overboard. Once the daytime rig of full sail was set the *St Elizabeth* was lively and occasionally took a splash aboard. I sat at the helm with oilskins over three layers of wool clothing, for it was not warm, even with a beam wind and blue, cloudless sky. I had not been steering long when I felt damp about the seat and learnt a horrible truth: my oilskin trousers were not waterproof. I had purchased them with some reluctance, for they did not seem much good to me, but were the only kind available. The salesman assured me that 'all fishermen use them.' 'Well!' I said, 'don't they complain? Look, this seam is bad, this button will not go through its hole, nor this one. And they are too short in the leg.'

'That is the biggest size.'

'Exactly. Yet I'm not tall. What do bigger men do?'

To this question there was apparently no answer, and I had to take what I could get.

An oilskin that leaks the second day it is worn is a tragedy, an insult and a calamity. I ruefully looked forward to seven weeks with a damp tail. It is just because there are no shops at sea that every item has to be as near perfection as possible.

In the evening I interrupted my reading long enough to ship the lower weather-board, for the spray was beginning to fly around. One of my cardinal ocean-cruising precepts is: Keep the boat dry inside. This can be surprisingly hard and always meant shipping the weather-boards early. These boards drop into slides in the doorway to the cabin. This day I read at the helm from after lunch onwards; and thereafter, whenever the weather was reasonable, and could be relied on not to soak my book to pulp before I reached the last page, I always read at the helm. The books I had were paperbacks. Though I have a great respect for books, I have never been able to keep the sea from ruining them when aboard a yacht, and so never take any afloat that are not expendable. This is true of so many things. Flashlights, cutlery, even clothing do not last long once they are carried aboard. It is not only the hard life but also the salt atmosphere and the frequent damping followed by haphazard drying.

Steering and reading together is not difficult. The tiller pulls gently all the time with a constant pressure so long as the course and the wind remain unaltered. The angle of heel, the feel of the wind, and the noise of the ship as it passes through the water are all indications of progress. If one of these changes, the helmsman will notice almost certainly, and usually several change when the boat gets a little off course. After a very few days' practice most people can steer a straight course for hours on end through chapter after chapter. The eye soon learns to glance at the compass before beginning a new paragraph. The compass position favoured reading, for I used to sit with it by my knee, about 12 inches from the book when on the usual starboard tack. On the other tack it was almost as good.

All that day we ran fast, with the boom well forward. I used to lash it in place with a fore-guy to prevent gybes. By evening the log showed 126 miles since starting, and morale was rising all the time, though I continued to feel squeamish. I turned in and slept like a hog or log till it was time for the first inspection of conditions. Putting my head through the hatch I saw nothing amiss, on the contrary it was a most beautiful night, almost worth sitting up for, but my warm bunk was too inviting, so I scribbled in the log: 'Moonlight, bright clear night, damn-all in sight', and turned in again. The alarm clock failed to call me regularly; it may have failed to ring, or I may have slept through it. Certainly the rest was a tonic. I rose late in the morning, in spite of the fact that I had gone to bed just after dusk. This was mighty luxurious. With no crew, I had no need to set an example, no one to relieve at the tiller, no one to please but myself. It was rather hard to get up in the morning; in fact, the only problem I never solved on the trip was how to overcome the lure of the bunk when the sun was already well up. When I did get up on the third morning, I found the jib was beginning to chafe, so before breakfast I put a canvas bandage on it. This was the only chafing gear fitted or needed on the whole trip. The main reason that none of the usual chafing gear was needed was that the whole boat was so simple, so stark. It is all very fine to fit lazy-jacks, double topping lifts, intermediate runners and a plethora of gear, but the disadvantages begin to outweigh the advantages. The weight aloft decreases the stability, the windage cuts down the speed, the maintenance is a waste of time. The boat looked just as if she had been for a day sail at the end of the crossing, partly because she had no ugly baggy-wrinkles. The sails did not suffer because they were not over-worked and because they were either lowered or lashed rigid with a forward boom guy and tight sheets when they showed a tendency to flap about in a calm. Admittedly 2,600 miles is not a very long journey. Nevertheless I never needed to use the sail needle once, and arrived without a loose seam or even a tiny hole.

The third day was remarkable because it was the last chance I had to dry clothes for many a day. I hung the trousers out that had got wet the previous day through those damned oilskins (may Allah bring curses upon their manufacturer and his spawn, even to the seventh generation).

I continued to sight ships occasionally, but always far away. It was a black freighter with a black funnel and white superstructure far over on the port beam this day. The wind was light and variable and the sky gradually got cloudier all day. The log notes: 'Holding down food – I think and hope'. This was the first time on the voyage that porpoises appeared. Many times after this they gambolled alongside, often so close I could have leant over and touched them as they rose to the surface. More than once, when sailing in a fairly heavy sea, I saw them swimming in the advancing face of the waves and level with, or even above, my head. They looked as if they were in an aquarium. It was just a trifle uncanny. After all, one mistake, one trip of the tail, and they might have landed in the cockpit with me. This would have been most uncomfortable, for these beasts fight like wild-cats. I once fought with one for several minutes, trying to haul it aboard. That was on another yacht. It lashed about with its tail and we became worried lest it should smash in a plank.

As the day advanced there were the first signs of fog, away to the S.E. The wind died to force 1, and the boat sailed slower and slower, just gently moving foreward, silent, peaceful, serene. After the evening meal I started the vitamin tablets. There were twenty-five of each sort, so I planned to have them spasmodically for the first few days, then regularly till they ran out. Between them they contained Vitamins A to D, liver concentrate, and a number of other things with high-sounding names, including Pyridoxine (B6) and d-Calcium Pantothenate, about which the chemist had this to say on the packet: 'The significance of these vitamins in human nutrition is not yet established.' What complete witchcraft! They should have put in some of the dried, powdered toenail from the dexter foot of an emaciated male lizard; after all it might have had beneficial results. I must admit that something, perhaps these pills, kept me in very good health throughout. Two people who crossed the same water in a small boat a few years before me, arrived in the United Kingdom with loose teeth and other indications of scurvy, which is due to vitamin deficiency.

The third day was tinged with worry about the signs of deteriorating weather conditions. On the other hand it was pleasant to have done with seasickness, from which I expected to be free till the next time I went afloat after a stay ashore. By nightfall it was very calm, and as the wind was from the S.E. I left all sail up and turned in, just a mite anxious about what the weather had in store. Sure enough I had to get up at midnight to tuck the first reef in the mainsail, and at the same time the jib was hauled amidships, which had the effect of steadying the ship and keeping her on course.

Back in my bunk, I lay for a few minutes awake. Was this the beginning of the first gale? The log showed less than 200 miles and the wind was on shore. A prolonged gale might drive me back on to the rocks of Nova Scotia. The ship had hardly settled down, or the crew. I did not doubt that we could put up a fight, but ... well, a few more days' grace would have made life easier. I like to be 400 miles off-shore if a gale strikes; with this distance there is real room to let the boat heave to in comfort, drifting and sliding back to ride the blows of the waves. Then I fell asleep. The boat sailed on through the night, a tiny speck of life on the cold sea, a sea that was beginning to fret; the waves became more insistent every minute, slapping against the hull at first, then smacking more sharply. Suddenly they became imperious. The yacht began to fight back. The noise woke me. It was almost two o'clock. The boat was more lively than when I had fallen asleep. I lay for a few minutes, hoping that the wind would not increase further. It was noisy in the cabin now, and the wind sang urgently in the rigging.

In the comfort of my bunk I weighed the pros and cons. If I did not reef I should stay awake and perhaps make good progress, but if I cut down the sail further I would get a good night's rest, at the expense of a few miles. Besides, there was every indication the wind meant business and I should have to reef anyway. Out of the snug sleeping bag, I sat on the settee, bracing one foot against the settee opposite. Enough light came in through the companion way and ports to see my oilskins, lying ready to hand. Trousers first, a quick wriggle, one strap, then, where the hell's the other? Twisted, dammit. Hitch them up a bit, and button it on. Now the boots, nice and easy these, just loose enough to kick off easily if I fall overboard, not too sloppy for nipping about the deck; now an extra sweater, the old blue one that has sailed – how far? Must be over 30,000 miles, and it looks like it. A scarf to stop water trickling down the neck. Now the oily coat. It feels clammy, but there's no time to bother about this, as I grab the sou'wester, cram it over my head and secure it, and climb on deck.

Here is a bit of an anti-climax. The conditions are not all that bad. More lively than when I went below, but rather pleasant. For a moment I consider staying on deck and steering for a while, then reject the idea and start reefing. This is easy with such a tiny mainsail. The rope lifeline is fastened round the waist, then I go forward to the mast. The main halyard is on the cleat on the fore side of the mast. Free it, and hook it under the cleat; then aft again, paying out the halyard. By the end of the boom I ease the halyard and jerk the boom into the crutch, holding it in place by tightening the main sheet. At this stage of the voyage the topping lift was never used; in fact, it was not even made fast to the boom end. Back to the mast again, the sail is lowered enough to tie down the reef cringle with the line that is kept permanently in place. Then aft to the leech cringle. Here too the reefing pennant is all ready. Holding on with one hand, I haul it down with the other, round its special cleat, and back through the thimble, round the cleat again, to the eye a third time, then thrice round the boom and end in a nice easy clove-hitch, which will not jam, and which just uses up the last of the pennant; the whole job will stand a gale. After easing the main sheet I work forward along the boom tying the reef points, putting them between the sail and boom (instead of under the boom) as this is kinder to the sail. Back at the mast, the main halyard is sweated up, but not extremely hard because the halyard will soon get wetter and shrink which will tighten the sail up. In the cockpit again, a critical eye looks over the complete job and finds no fault. The ship is very comfortable now, sailing effortlessly along, so back to the bunk for me. Untie the lifeline first, and coil it ready for the next time, putting the coil in exactly the same place, where it can be found in the dark. Back in the cabin the oilskins are peeled off and laid ready. A glance at the watch shows the whole operation has taken 16 minutes. Later on in the voyage this time is halved and nearly halved again.

As I pull the sleeping bag up, and arrange the duffle coat over me, I muse about the excellence of the boom gallows. It makes reefing so safe and easy in a seaway. The boom is rigid, and makes a reliable hand hold. This gallows is the only piece of varnished mahogany on the ship, and was a present from the yard.

Chapter Ten

The voyage was beginning to change in a subtle way. The course was now 90 degrees magnetic, roughly in the direction of the English Channel. I knew I was well south of Sable Island, and confirmed this with a good noon sight. The threatened bad weather never developed; instead, the sail was unreefed and fine cruising ensued. Morale, which is the most important factor of an ocean cruise, began to creep up and up. This is a thing which has long interested me and I made a number of enquiries about it. Doctors and others assure me there is no known method of measuring morale, which is unfortunate. I tried to devise a morale-meter, and in the end decided that a simple hair comb might work. I had noticed that crews comb their hair when they are cheerful, but as the cold and wet, the wild motion and uncomfortable meals sap the enthusiasm, morale drops and the comb falls out of use. I thought that by putting a comb handy, in a canvas loop over the chart-table with the spare pencils and rubbers, I would just have to note how often I used it, and hence have a crude gauge of my own morale. This was not very satisfactory. I tended to comb my hair morning and evening only, more or less regardless of conditions, often doing so while waiting for a stew to heat, just to pass the time.

On the other hand I did keep a log of morale studiously throughout the trip. There was a blank column in the log, which I labelled 'M', and I recorded my morale as a percentage. Taking between 70 per cent and 75 per cent as the mean, weekday, middle-of-the-morning average, good-weather, illness-free, cheerful condition, I noted as dispassionately as possible my own morale as I thought it was at the time. In practice I never recorded below 40 per cent, which was just after seeing the last of the *Cheerio*, nor above 89 per cent. The very act of writing down my own mental state was a steadying and desirable influence. A rocketing enthusiasm is risky, it may plummet down too easily and sharply, and a low feeling is to be avoided for a dozen reasons. By writing in the log my impartial feelings about the state of the voyage and myself, as expressed in cold figures, the whole matter was put in the correct perspective. For any long journey, such as an exploration, a major mountain climb, or scientific voyage, I would keep this morale log and have other people on the trip do so too, of their own morale and other people's. I believe such a record has both interest and value.

While steering on the fourth day I noticed that the tiller was vibrating, though we were only travelling quite slowly. It is not rare for the tiller to vibrate when a boat travels really fast, but at low speeds this was the first experience I have had. It only occurred at a certain precise speed, apparently. This is just one of those things that give a boat character. The *St Elizabeth* and I were beginning to know each other.

In the evening, when I started to light the primus, I discovered a serious loss. The methylated spirits bottle had fallen over, and most of the contents had leaked away through the plugged hole in the cap. This hole was made so that I could pour the meths at a controlled rate into the cup of the primus. After this I was careful with the meths. There were only three bottles in all, and though it is possible to light the primus without spirits, it is dirty and dangerous. Another disappointment was the deadness of the radio. The first day or three I was too seasick to want to spend long fiddling with the dials, but when I tried now it gave no sign of life. It was an ordinary domestic medium-wave portable set. While travelling from Vancouver by goods train its case had got broken, so it was put into a semi-watertight wooden box, specially made to hold the spare batteries and aerial extension which hooked on to the rigging. I had consulted the Canadian Broadcasting Corporation about reception off-shore. They said that, given good conditions, I might pick up signals 500 miles off. If I could do this both sides, that would leave only 1,600 miles in the middle when reception was impossible. In practice nothing was audible 250 miles off-shore, even at night when conditions are best.

All this time I had been on the starboard tack. Now the wind went round to the west. I gybed, and we sailed along in light winds. About 8.30 a.m., fog began to appear and for many days it was always about. My course was the great circle route, once I was sure of clearing Sable Island, and this took me quite close to Newfoundland and into an area which has an average of forty-five days per hundred foggy, during July. I knew this from studying my pilot charts. These are issued monthly by the United States Hydrographic office, and they may be described as 'a child's guide to ocean-cruising'. With these it is virtually impossible to go wrong, as far as routing is concerned. They tell you, for each month of the year, just what to expect in the way of fog, winds (force and direction), calms, gales and ice. They show the position of weather-ships, which remain almost stationary far out at sea, sending back to land reports on weather conditions. These charts give the histories of hurricanes, magnetic variation, ocean currents (both direction and speed), and they indicate the best routes between major ports for different types of vessel, including sailing ships. Finally, in spite of the fact that they have 'Price 30 cents' on them, they were given to me free by the US consulate at Halifax, and not because I was rushing about in a very small boat, for they knew nothing about that. These charts also have at the top, prominently, NOT TO BE USED FOR NAVIGATIONAL PURPOSES. However, I turned a blind eye to this and used them in conjunction with plotting-sheets to keep track of my position. Naturally they are no use for coastal work, and I had charts of the shore at both ends, besides a book containing plans of all the English and French Channel ports.

The fog was not worrying because it was expected and hence a few precautions had been taken. It used to be said that fog is a yacht's worst enemy, because the average yacht sails in coastal waters, where shipping is heavy and the chance of being run down correspondingly great. Add to this two facts, that yacht fog-horns are usually inadequate, and that when there is fog there is often little wind, so that a sailing yacht cannot get out of the way of trouble. Nowadays I believe that a yacht is safer in a fog than during a clear night, for almost every ship will be using radar in a fog. This statement requires a good deal of qualifying. During the night a yacht will, we hope, have her navigation lights on, but these are usually dim glow-worms, often blanketed by the sails, and too near the water to be really effective. She is not easy to see from the height of a big ship's bridge. In bad weather ships' radar sets will not indicate the presence of a yacht because the waves are higher than the hull. However, the sea is usually, though certainly not always, calm during foggy conditions, and hence a yacht will show up on the radar screen. On the *St Elizabeth* I had a fog-horn of the Admiralty pattern, as fitted on naval picket boats and similar small craft. It makes a short sharp barking noise, by pulling a handle, which is better than the tiring kind that have to be blown like a trumpet.

The mast of the yacht was coated with aluminium paint with the idea of making a good radar reflector. Nobody seemed to know much about the effect this would have, and it was not until I reached England that I got an authoritative opinion. My informant was cautious and said in effect: 'Nobody knows much because nobody has experimented much.' He also said that it would make little difference if the yacht were made of steel or other metal, and that though a metal mast would be better than a wooden one, the improvement would be small. 'Furthermore,' he went on, 'the use of metallised paint on the mast would in my opinion provide little guarantee of any certainty of detection. A yacht with her sails up may provide considerably better signals than one with her sails down operating on an auxiliary (engine); [the words in brackets are mine]. This effect may be small if the sails are dry, but quite appreciable if the sails are wet (as they soon would be in fog). The hauling of metal objects up to the mast is again likely to have very little effect unless these are of considerable size or specially designed to yield a strong echo.' (I had asked whether it was worth putting a saucepan or two up the mast, and had put some faith in the lantern I put up each night, which is of course metal.)

What interested me was the time factor. If a ship's officer only looked at the radar screen every 10 minutes, and it takes another minute for him to see that something is in the way, and another for his helm order to take effect (for freighters cannot dodge and turn like a yacht), then in all that time the ship may have moved quite 2 miles, since it might well be doing 10 knots, relying on the radar to keep it clear of trouble in the fog. 2 miles. My authority says this: 'It is difficult to quote precise figures because so much will depend on the type of radar, its height above sea level, the state and type of sea and the details of the yacht. But I would expect that with a modern high-performance radar mounted at a height of about 60 feet, then a yacht of 30 feet to 60 feet would be detected in calm weather at a range of between 3 and 5 miles. If, however, there is a wave height in excess of, say, about 4 feet, it is quite possible that such a yacht would escape detection completely.' This was the voice of one of the leading manufacturers of radar sets. There is an almost infallible method of making a yacht detectable, and that is by hoisting a special radar reflector, reported to show a yacht up at a range of 7 or 8 miles if the reflector is 30 feet up. However, none of these reflectors were in use in Nova Scotia at the time, nor available.

Ignorance is bliss, and besides there was little I could do about the matter. I hoped that my customary luck in fog would hold, for boats I have sailed in have always been heaven-guided in murky weather. Once, we crept into Le Havre without any frights after sailing through thick fog from the middle of the Channel, and another time we worked our way down the Thames Estuary and up the River Crouch almost completely blindfold in a sluicing tide of unknown and varying speed and direction. Clearly I have a skilled guardian angel.

This good fortune and my conviction at the time that I was bound to be visible on all radar screens made me almost welcome the fog. It was an indication that I was making progress. It would slow down shipping and make them study their radar screens, day and night. Besides, sailing in fog is a wonderful, almost ghostly experience. Every noise is deadened. A tingling hush is the feeling it gives. The yacht seems tense, moving forward like some serene being, with just an occasional lapping of the water at the bows. I used to sit at the helm, every so often looking up from my book to glance about me. A blank wall rose all round, often less than 200 yards away. I was in a tight little island, a warm, snug, mobile home. I knew (approximately) where I was, and the compass showed me where I was going. The wind was gentle, but never entirely died away. It was all so peaceful, so secure. I was faintly astonished to find myself revelling in the solitude and the certainty that I would find my way through this maze to England alone. It was not till a few days after the fog had passed that I had a qualm about the compass. Had I corrected for variation the wrong way? Yes! No! Damn and blast! I worked it out from first principles and found I was right all the time. Just to make sure I consulted a textbook. Horror of horrors! I was wrong. Then I must be halfway to Greenland, or would it be South Africa? But how did my sextant sights come out right? They showed I was progressing correctly. I re-read the textbook, it certainly was confusing. It gave some rules for correcting variation. Then I realised I had used the wrong rule. Everything was all right, but I was deeply worried for a moment. This is one disadvantage of being single-handed. There is no one to consult or reassure. This was the only navigational alarm on the voyage, and quite enough too.

From the fifth to the fifteenth day it was foggy, though only for three days was it completely blinding. One day, while cooking breakfast, I heard a ship's siren in the distance. Quickly I went on deck with the fog-horn, which was stowed in a special place, clear of other gear, right beside the port bunk. A couple of seconds after that siren, mine answered. For the next 10 minutes it got nearer. The fog baffled the sound waves. It was impossible to gauge the exact position of the ship; sometimes it seemed well ahead, the next time it sounded on the beam. She was using an air-horn, so I thought she might be diesel-driven. As I could not hear her engines, I considered that she was not close. Gradually her siren sounded farther astern, then stopped. She was past, so I went back to my breakfast, leaving the horn in the cockpit.

The next day I heard faintly, and as from very far, another ship, and later an aircraft. The day after that a ship passed quite near. She had a three-cylinder diesel, and I smell their eggs frying as they passed close to windward, but never saw them, and could not get them to answer my fog-horn. It was a little uncanny knowing that another worldlet was so near, with human beings like myself, who liked a fried breakfast, who could talk and listen; I was sorry they did not pass within sight. I felt like a talk now that I had not spoken a word for thirteen days. This was one of the very rare times that I missed conversation. I did not notice the absence of wireless, but did crave a good newspaper with my breakfast; not one of those rubbishy sheets the North Americans have to tolerate, but a serious, well-informed, intelligently written paper.

About this time a sad loss occurred. I had bought a double saucepan; the only pan I had on board, in fact. It was easily stowable, and I had planned to put porridge in the top and an egg in the bottom, thus cooking all my breakfast on one flame, using the water that cooked the egg for the washing up. It was the sort of economical arrangement that delights my Scottish heart. The pan was of aluminium, which corrodes in sea water, but heretofore such pans have always lasted at least one season. On this trip the lower pan lasted only a few days before two minute holes made it useless for cooking. Thereafter I used the lower part of the pan for priming the bilge pump and bailing the cockpit when the water came aboard too fast for the cockpit drain. The top part of the pan lasted well, and I used an enamel teapot for boiling vegetables in, which is a very sound scheme, for the vegetables are drained by pouring the water out of the spout. My plates were a great success; they were pliable plastic boxes, roughly cubic in shape with lids. They held food in the wildest weather when any ordinary plate would have spilt the food long before it could be eaten. Being shaped as they were, they did not roll, and stowed easily. The beauty of the pliable plastic is that it is completely unbreakable and stands much abuse. The lid was the final stroke of genius as it kept the food hot, and on the rare occasions when I ate on deck it kept the spray out of the food, besides making the plates almost spill-proof if I wanted to put my food down in the middle of a meal. There were also mugs like the plates, of the same material, also fitted with air-tight lids. These mugs do not give a taste to their contents, as I discovered by obvious tests. On board there were twenty-four cans of beer, which were a present from a brewer. I decided to keep them for raising the morale in emergencies. However, morale never needed boosting, and day after day the beer remained canned, while the skipper stayed sober. Eventually one can was drunk, just to make sure that the beer was not going bad, and the remaining cans got involved in a celebration party on arrival. Tobacco was not taken aboard the *St Elizabeth*, because back in 1945 when I bought my first boat, I gave up smoking, preferring to buy a new sail on the savings of three months' non-smoking, rather than burn the money.

The fog sometimes gave way to rain; and on several occasions there was a torrential downpour. These rainstorms were exceedingly heavy, far worse than I have ever encountered in temperate climates before. They reminded me of the outrageous deluges I had met in the middle Pacific. Sometimes the rain was accompanied by hard wind. Then I would sit at the helm, huddled up with my back to the blast, sou'-wester pulled well down, while the rain streamed over the deck and the boat charged along. Visibility was reduced to a few yards, the sea was lashed and flattened by the torrent and the uproar prevented me from hearing ships' sirens. To complete the misery, these outbursts were unpleasantly chilling. They convinced me that I was right to be so cautious in the matter of sail area. I usually carried one more reef than I should do if coastal cruising, plus an extra reef at night. In actual practice the sail area at night was even more modest than I wished, for if the wind was in its usual position on the quarter, I had to lower the mainsail to remain on course. As a general rule I tried to keep the boat going as fast as possible, remaining approximately on course, as if at the beginning of an ocean race. As I approached the Scilly Isles, I steered an accurate course which occasionally meant loss of speed. The *St Elizabeth* was theoretically capable of doing about 7¼ knots or 175 miles in a 24-hour day. To do this she would need a strong quartering breeze and would have to be sailed continuously throughout that time. In practice she was sailed between 11 and 15 hours daily and had a large proportion of light winds. Besides this, I started out tired and determined to arrive with an undamaged and seaworthy ship. As this was her maiden voyage, she was largely unknown, so that she was very rarely driven hard. Once in a while I hung on half an hour after reefing conditions were reached, just to see how she liked it. On the whole, though, I took the usual excitements of ocean cruising as they came, and did not try to add to them by racing.

When it rained or was so foggy that my glasses misted up, I could not read. Sometimes I beguiled the time by pondering on the various emergencies that might arise. These accidents often strike rather suddenly so that even the most experienced and phlegmatic helmsman suffers a moment's heart-moving panic before setting matters right again. So I thought that if every detail was planned and memorised I might save the vital second or two. First there was the problem of ice. One of my reasons for cutting down sail area, and therefore speed, at night was that I did not wish to ram a berg hard. If the keel hit, or the stem, there was a very good chance that no serious damage would be done. If the *St Elizabeth* crashed her planking against some ice, there was a reasonable chance that the holing would not be severe; in fact, if the ice-flow was small, or brittle, the planks might remain intact. The only damage, in that case, would be to the skipper's mental equilibrium, which would receive an enormous blow. If the ship were punctured, the first job would be to stuff any available clothing or bedding into the hole. Next, some of the spare timber would have to be nailed over the outside of the hull, if possible, or inside if not. There were nails, waterproof compound and canvas for this. The big emergency bilge pump, a centrifugal rotary affair beneath the companion steps, would have to be put in action after the patching of the hole was attended to. The crux of this operation is to plug the hole first, then work the pump if necessary, and not the other way round. During the day I expected to be able to see the ice before hitting it, though the fog made this doubtful at times. To have sailed south round the limit of the ice-ridden area would have put several hundred miles on to the journey.

On the whole, ice seemed a comparatively minor problem. What seriously exercised my planning ability was the prospect of a broken arm. There is a good chance of breaking a bone on a small yacht, what with the constant lively motion of the ship, the wet slippery decks, the hindrance of many clothes and oilskins, and at night the dark. A broken leg would be troublesome, but one can put on a splint and crawl about. But a broken arm, that is another

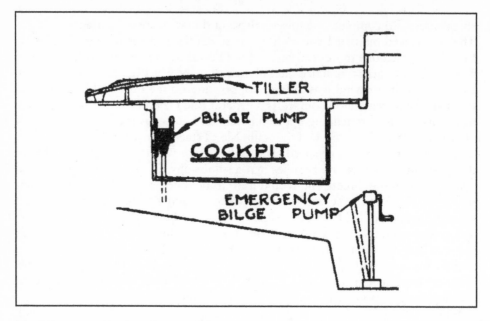

Two bilge-pumps, both easily accessible.

matter. On the *St Elizabeth* it seemed that the best thing would be to sit on the cook-and-navigator's seat and lay the arm on the galley bench or chart-table, according to which arm was damaged. Here at hand were pieces of timber for splints, also rags, handkerchiefs and scarves for padding and binding the affair together. Dopey with drugs, and working quickly, a satisfactory repair job might be complete before the pain became too acute. To handle the ship with one arm in a sling, some ingenuity would be needed, but the difficulties are not insuperable. I once cruised 1,700 very pleasant miles with a one-armed man, who cooked (very adequately too, even in rough going), steered, hauled on sheets and halyards, using feet, teeth and profanity to help his one hand.

Another excitement that had to be considered was dismasting. This is quite common in racing dinghies, though few carry it to the extent of one owner I used to crew for. On his boat it was not a question of whether, but when, we would be dismasted. However, out at sea things are very different. Even if there are other boats or ships near at hand, there is little they can do. They could not tow the yacht to port unless land was very near; no freighter captain would slow down to 7 knots just to pull a small boat to safety, and to tow a boat like the *St Elizabeth* faster would wreck her. Nor would it be much use asking a skipper to use one of his derricks to hoist a jury mast unless the sea was quite unusually calm. No, the only outside help that would be useful in a case of dismasting would be from a fishing boat or naval craft, or another yacht, though it would be extraordinary to meet the latter far out at sea. This means that the mess has to be cleared, and jury rig set up, by the crew. As soon as the spar crashes down, the boat stops, and if there is any sea, as one would expect in a case of dismasting, the planking may be battered in by the mast, so the first thing to do is cut the mast free. This is one reason why ocean cruisers carry axes, traditionally, though I have never seen a case recorded of one being used. Anyway, the *St Elizabeth* had an axe, kept greased, sharp and ready to hand; it was also used as a hammer and mallet. Once the mast has been discouraged from holing the ship, the sails, rigging, and, if possible, the spar have to be recovered. This would be very hard work single-handed. Almost certainly the sails would get torn, and the crew too, perhaps. When the weather has moderated, the deck is padded with spare timber and the boom lashed to the stump of the spar, if this is still protruding a few feet above the deck. If not, the stump is pulled out of the mast step and the boom put there instead. Then the mainsail is hoisted, triple reefed on the boom track, which is the same as the mast track, and the storm jib set; and on we sail. This sounds easy; in practice it would probably be fiendishly difficult. Getting the boom up on end would require a lot of skill. Ropes, guys, and tackles would have to be rigged, and two or three tightened simultaneously. Just at the critical moment an extra big wave would throw the yacht's bow up wildly and the whole contrivance would crash down, making a hole in the deck. I can just visualise it, and a horrible vision it is.

But the worst problem of all is falling overboard, or getting knocked unconscious and into the sea at the same time. The wire life-rail round the ship is a good hand-hold and works well most of the time. However, a single wire is no guarantee, it is easy to slip underneath, or tip over the top. Many times when working on deck, I tied a good rope round my waist; but it is quite possible that this line would have dragged me along through the water, while I tried in vain to get back aboard. Admittedly in a serious situation it is surprising what can be done; nevertheless it would take a great deal of strength to pull the body up a rope and over the weather, or high, side of the ship, as she careered along fast. Fortunately one would almost certainly fall over the leeward side, so that getting aboard would not be too hard. I kept my life-line as short as possible, but it had to reach to the extreme bow. Very frequently, when a job had to be done on the fore deck, I left the tiller, hurried forward, completed the operation, and got back to the tiller before the boat had a chance to sheer up into the wind. If I had fallen in on such an occasion the boat would soon have stopped and remained roughly head to wind, waiting for me. Undoubtedly the danger of being clouted by the swinging boom was the thing to guard against. With the tiller lashed, or free but with the sails balanced so that the boat sailed on a straight course, it would be rather disturbing to come to the surface after being flung in, just in time to see the boat disappear into the cold fog.

One evening as I sat at the helm for a few minutes after the evening meal, before turning in, I saw a ghastly thing ahead. It was dusk and very foggy, so that the apparition was close when it was first seen. The gloom of evening, and the fact that I had been isolated in the fog for so long, made a perfect setting for a ghost story. As I pulled the tiller over to avoid hitting this narrow, black, wobbling horror, my mind selected and rejected explanations at a high rate. First I thought it was a spar buoy, which the Canadians use frequently. Then I realised that we were much too far away from Newfoundland (the nearest land) for that. A lobster pot buoy, perhaps? The water was flowing past it, piling up at the base, like a strong tide. For a moment I imagined that the *St Elizabeth* had gone wildly astray in the fog. Perhaps the coast was just behind that bank of fog ahead. We must be close inshore if the tide runs so fast. With great relief I realised the real explanation. It was the dorsal fin of a basking shark. The water was not flowing past, it was moving itself, with a little bow wave. Actually, of course, I knew all along it was not a ghost. They are white, not black. I brought the yacht back on course and looked closely at the fin. It showed about 2 feet out of the water and flopped from side to side, as if it were made of cartilage and could hardly support its own weight. As it passed abeam I saw it was triangular-shaped above the surface and about 2 feet along the base. The shark's tail occasionally broke the surface, but how far behind the fin was hard to say, perhaps 20 feet. These sharks go up to 40 feet in length (the *St Elizabeth* is 30½ feet) and up to 8,000 lbs in weight (the yacht's weight is about 6,500 lbs in deep sea cruising trim). It was an interesting moment when the fish turned and followed us for a few yards, before swimming off into the foggy darkness. Everyone says these beasts are harmless. I have repeatedly discussed them with people who claim to know. But when I ask how often they have tickled a shark's tonsils, or made other experiments to ensure that basking sharks are really friendly, I always get equivocal answers. It seems to me that the person who discovers the real truth might not come back to spread the news.

Apart from seeing porpoises almost daily, the only other big creatures I saw were some whales. Here again the experts are full of confidence. They point out that a whale has quite a small mouth, that it eats plankton and tiny crustaceans by drinking in seawater, and straining the food from it, spitting out the unwanted liquid. All very convincing, but what about those numerous old marine prints showing an enraged whale swiping a boat into matchwood, with a flick of the tail? 'The whale is angry,' say the experts. 'see how the men have infuriated it by jabbing harpoons into its tender skin?' I remain doubtful. Suppose a harmless whale is snoozing just below the surface and the *St Elizabeth* collides with it? The whale might start lashing out first and seek explanations afterwards. Or it might be the mating season, and so many beasts have belligerent habits when the fever is upon them. The whales I saw were disappointing. They were merely big, instead of enormous, and they refused to approach close enough for a good photograph, or to raise a tail clear of the surface. They just rolled and snorted, blew little wisps of spray in the air, made old-gentlemanly noises, and passed on. It was too calm to chase them in the hope of getting a good picture.

Chapter Eleven

Almost all the way across I had an escort of birds. Their type changed from time to time, indicating the progress of the boat across the ocean. One little black, pigeon-like fellow arrived out of the fog, flew round in a weak manner, and landed on deck. He was very unsteady on his feet, so I fed a few crumbs of bread to him. Later he seemed to perk up and flew away strongly. He circled, once, twice, dipped in salute, and disappeared into the fog again. When the weather cleared the fulmars came. They look strong and independent. They glide and glide, till I wondered how they could float on the air for such long periods. They reminded me of the albatross in the Pacific, except that these, though superb gliders, are hopeless at landing and taking off, whereas the fulmar is a good all-rounder and somehow seems to suit the North Atlantic; they seem tougher for a harder climate.

By the time the last of the fog melted, I was conditioned and ready for a gale. Instinctively a hand slid along the rail when I walked forward. The course steered was accurate, regardless of how interesting I found the book I was reading. Meals might take a few minutes longer if the motion was severe, but there was now no doubt that a substantial meal would materialise, even if the boat pranced about in a way that seemed calculated to unbalance both the cook and the stove. The log extracts on the fifteenth day are typical of this period. The first morning entry is: 'Set all plain sail to cutter'. This meant the storm jib was set on the inner forestay, as an extra sail to get the best out of the light wind, which is logged at N.W.2, later rising to force 3, and in the afternoon to 4. Morale is 75 per cent in the morning, rising to 77 per cent in the afternoon. This daily rise is usual. The nadir is usually around 3 or 4 a.m. and the zenith just after the evening meal. The limits of the morale scale are scarcely attainable. At 1 per cent one would be sharpening the sheath-knife in preparation for suicide, while the passage from the sixth to the seventh heaven is denoted by 99 per cent.

Further log extracts for the fifteenth day read: 'Bread still fresh – wax wrappers help – slicing no disadvantage' (to the freshness, that is, as it is a great advantage for handling); and later, 'Weather conditions pretty damned good'. At 1400 hours (2 p.m.), '6 knots – real speed – sea good for fast running'; and then: 'Fog cleared – sky low cloudy – greasy, bit worrying'. The next day raw weather gave further signs that it had unpleasantness in store. The log becomes more laconic, and on the seventeenth day it is positively terse. Morale drops below 55 per cent and the wind rises to force 6. Then the only trouble of the whole voyage occurs.

The main shrouds are more important on the *St Elizabeth* than on many boats, for there are no topmast shrouds or intermediates. It was therefore most disconcerting to see the lee main shroud suddenly swing free and flick its shackle into the sea as we bowled along, double reefed, but with the full jib, in a short lumpy sea.

I lashed the tiller and nipped forward to tie the shroud down with a piece of line, then quickly back to the tiller before the boat could get off course. If she had swung round on to the other tack the mast would have snapped off immediately.

The temporary lashing would prevent the shroud getting fouled or winding round the other rigging but the damage had yet to be repaired. I sat at the helm pondering. For the moment all was well. I could not go about on the other tack, but there was no danger on the present course. The cause of the trouble was obvious. All the shackles up the mast were carefully wired up, so that there was no chance of their coming undone accidentally. This is good, normal practice; what is not usually done, and I confess I have never done, is to wire up the shackles at the bottom of the rigging, on deck. Here everything is near at hand, close under the eye, where it can be frequently inspected. Every fortnight or so I usually go round tightening up whatever seems slack. But on the *St Elizabeth* the rigging was new, and had stretched a little. This made the lee shrouds slack enough to shake as the boat plunged along. The main shrouds were the slackest because they were the longest. The constant movement of the lee shroud unwound the shackle pin, and set the shroud free. That was the cause; the cure had to be worked out.

There was plenty of time. All afternoon we sailed on; I hoped that the wind and sea might go down in the evening as they had frequently done before. It continued to blow force 6, so well before dark I got all the sails down, being very careful to keep the wind on the starboard side where the intact shroud was. Then I discovered another trouble. The main shrouds pass over the crosstrees. At this point some people put a heavy lashing covered with a big spherical pad, which is intended to prevent the sail chafing. It is my observation that this projection from the crosstree has the reverse effect. It pushes into the sail, stretching it locally and making a bagginess. So instead I lashed the shroud with a light piece of line into the Y at the end of the crosstree. This lashing had chafed through on the sail, and the rigging was flapping about freely. My problem was to coax the wire back into its tiny slot in the crosstree end, 13 feet above the deck and of course well out of reach, then quickly shackle it back in place, and tighten the rigging-screw before the wire could escape from the slot.

The wind and sea were no help. I tied the crook of the boathook to the shroud, and slid the crook up to crosstree level, after slacking off the rigging-screw. With much awkward overhead manoeuvring, the shroud was coaxed into place. To do this I held the bottom of the boathook; the top had to be kept under perfect control, and placed so that the wire entered the narrow slot. It was like writing

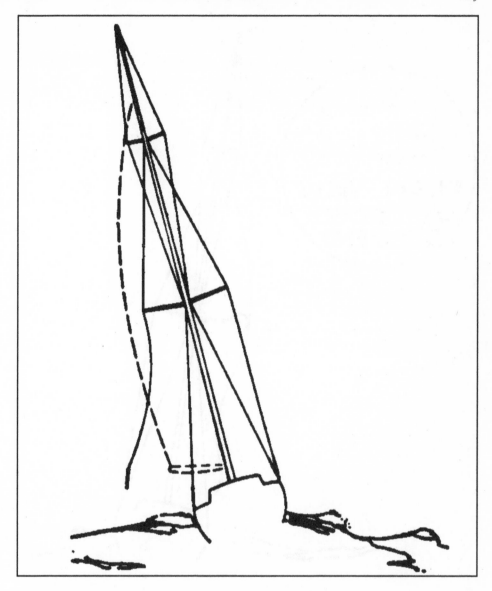

on the ceiling with a 12-foot pen. Eventually the wire was lodged home, and shackled back at the bottom. But before it was tight it got out of the slot again. The second time I left it shackled at the bottom, struggled with the boathook till the wire was in place, and quick as lightning put a tension on the wire with one hand, while tightening the rigging-screw with the other. Fine. The rigging was set up nice and tight now. I looked aloft to ensure that nothing else was wrong. It was, seriously so. The weather shroud was off its crosstree. This was a shock. I saw the mast give some sickening jolts. The lashing on the end of the crosstree had chafed through on the weather side too, and when the lee shroud was off, it made the weather one slack enough to come free too. Rather desperately I

PLAN VIEW
OF CROSS-
TREE END

repeated the repair procedure on the weather side, but before I could succeed, the lee one escaped again. The mast was now unsupported in an athwartships direction except for the lower shrouds.

The mast and my heart moved in an unconventional way. The sea flung the ship about in a manner well calculated to make repairs difficult. After several attempts I got the weather shroud in place, but had to keep a pull on it sideways to prevent it shaking free when the mast whipped sideways and slackened it. The lee shroud was maddeningly uncooperative. I have no idea how long it took, or how many times I nearly succeeded, before at last both shrouds were cradled in their slots and tightened down. Surveying the repairs, I found that one jib halyard and one

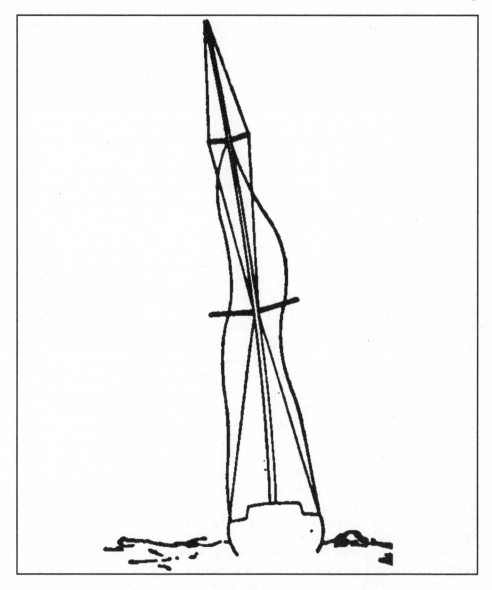

of the emergency runners had got themselves the wrong side of the crosstrees. It was only possible to free them by going up the mast, which I did there and then. Sitting on the crosstrees, the view was magnificent. Waves stretched out to each horizon, long rows of marching hills. The boat looked tiny below. It was not comfortable aloft, being flung about as the boat rolled and pitched, so I sorted out the rigging and slid back to the deck. Down in the cabin it was peaceful and restful after the hectic trouble. For some time it had seemed almost certain that the mast would break. Later there was the exertion of climbing the mast, and clinging on once aloft. All this made me unusually ready for the evening meal, which was a feast of thanksgiving and celebration.

With the rigging well tightened and that crisis over, I thought we were ready for the gale which I suspected was approaching. The boat carried no barometer, because though it might have given an indication of bad weather, one barometer alone is seldom of much use. A whole lot of observations, made over a wide area, and correlated into a weather map, are needed to give a proper forecast. Besides it was no use knowing bad weather was around, for the *St Elizabeth* was too small and therefore too slow to escape. She had to take the weather as it came. Gloomy predictions would merely depress the owner, without serving a useful purpose.

The eighteenth day out was foul. With the wind ahead of the beam the boat crashed along under double reefed main and storm jib. It rained a lot. My supply of dry clothing was being depleted. There were several reserves still available, but I began to wish for a chance to dry out. When ocean-cruising, it pays to change clothes when they are wet rather than soiled, at least in cold latitudes. I believe the biggest boon that could be given to ocean-cruisers is a device for drying clothes and bedding efficiently. On the nineteenth day the weather calmed and I tried drying some clothes on deck, but the wind died right away. Not for long, though. After lunch it came from the west. Soon I was reducing sail. One reef, then the second. Then the working jib was lowered, fighting and flapping as if it wanted to stay up and brave the rising gale. By evening I was glad to lower the mainsail and let the boat run off under the storm jib.

She rode more easily then, allowing me to cook in comparative comfort. How wonderful a hot meal is after 13 hours at the helm, especially when reading has been impossible. Afterwards I snuggled into my sleeping bag, which was made out of one of the traditional Nova Scotian quilts, sewn up, and soon fell asleep. At 2300 hours (11 p.m.) I woke up, put my head out of the hatch and was met by a blast of wind. The sea was high and crashing all round. I gazed on this tumbling mess for a minute, then I ducked below. Thanking the Almighty that it was night so that I was not sailing, I wrote 'Gale' in the log and returned to the comfort of my bunk. It probably was not a full gale, but the wildly swinging lamp hanging from the rigging lit up a circle of chaotic water, and the wind howled in the rigging; it was late at night and it certainly was windy, so that at the time I thought it was a gale.

Honesty now makes me admit it might have been only force 7. Next morning at 0600 hours I poked my head through the hatch. The sea was a mass of big noisy waves rushing about with complete disregard for anyone who wanted a pleasant day's sailing. The wind blew force 7 from the west, and the boat pottered along under the baby jib, making useful progress, though heading too much to the north. I considered the conditions for a moment, then started to write the log. First the date. The date! It was my birthday. That decided the next move. I celebrated with an extra half-hour in bed. For just such an occasion as this I had a book which a shipmate on a previous cruise had recommended; it was *Tales of the South Pacific* by Michener. My sense of the appropriate was tickled. It seemed just the book for the North Atlantic. Wedged in the berth, I was soon lost in this book. Occasionally a wave broke with a sibilant cataclysm of tumbling foam. It was none of my worry. The boat was built for these conditions. She rode well, the decks seldom took on water. She was tight, a fine little ship. If only the wind would go north a few degrees, we would be on course. Should I have an extra good breakfast? An extra egg, perhaps. This certainly is just the book for these conditions. Good job it is daylight, no chance of being run down. Radar would never pick up the little *St Elizabeth* in this muck.

Then, startlingly close, a ship's siren sounds. I scramble from the sleeping bag, and thrust open the hatch. There she is. A freighter, about 10,000 tons, just a few waves behind me. I raise my arm towards her and duck below again. In a second I have my oilskin trousers on, and am up on deck. Out with the sheath-knife, and two quick slashes free my notice board, which is kept ready for such an occasion as this. Sitting on the cabin top I hold the board up, first on the side showing 'YACHT St ELIZABETH' till I judge they have had time to read it, then I turn it round to show 'REPORT TO LLOYD'S'. After a few seconds I turn the board to the first side, then back to the reverse side a second time. The freighter hoots, a deep booming note, to acknowledge. I wave, feeling wildly cheerful. The figures on the bridge and along the rail wave back. The freighter is the *Southland*, obviously American, though I see no ensign. She plunges and pitches, with a long, almost lazy motion, in contrast to the skittish way the *St Elizabeth* dances about. It is cold on deck. I return below, standing with my head out of the companionway. She looks massive, and somehow invulnerable, though the sea is not giving her any rest. Another blast from the siren, more waving, she increases speed and is soon gone.

Down below I start to cook breakfast, thinking of home, allowing for the difference in clock times, they should hear about me by tea-time, perhaps even lunch-time. The wireless operator will be tapping it out now, and 1,500 miles away, someone will be scrawling down 'Sighted yacht *St Elizabeth* 49 degrees N., 36 degrees 15 minutes W. Requests report to Lloyd's.' It was a perfect birthday present. I had seen no ship for fifteen days, and the last one I had heard in the fog was seven days before. At home they would plot my position on a chart. I hoped they would note I was halfway across, clear of the ice area, and getting clear of possible hurricanes. They knew enough about sailing not to worry that the nearest land was 800 miles away, and to windward. The *St Elizabeth* was probably safer where she was than in the confined waters of the English Channel. I hoped someone would give the fatted calf an extra big feed, as a result of this news of the prodigal son.

After breakfast I set the big jib, leaving the small one up, and sailed the boat along exultantly, and slightly over-canvased. The blinding, lashing rain, arriving in fierce squalls, was not nearly enough to damp enthusiasm. The sea sent big growling waves in to attack us, but what did the *St Elizabeth* care? She flung her dainty stern in the air and rode along, disdainful of the monsters that tried to overwhelm her. It was a slashing, dashing sail. The whole boat and crew thrilled and pulsated. This was what she had been built for. This was what made the sport. No regrets now about being single-handed, that fact just made it all the better. I was a conqueror, and this was the moment of triumph. Blow, you bloody wind, higher you waves, we don't care (provided the wind does not go round to the East)! There was a tiny regret. If only some of my former regular crew were here. Jerry, who could mend anything, any time, in any weather and always carried a copy of the *Bab Ballads* on our cruises. Barry, whose joy it was to wake the forenoon watch and announce that breakfast was served, as indeed it was, most elaborately with four courses. My sister, diminutive but a ship driver with an uncanny knack of gently coaxing a boat to windward faster than anyone else could. Or my mother, who took up sailing at an age when plenty of people retire, in a converted 6-metre, a fast, wet boat that was often in such a hurry it would almost jump the wave troughs and then crash through the crests, so that green water cascaded along the deck. And dozens of others who would have loved that sail. If only the Stevens family could see the yacht now as she tore along, the sea piling up in a frothy bow wave, the decks wet and glistening, the rigging bow-string taut, the sails bellied out, reaching forward in lovely curves. The boat rolled, the sea sometimes came aboard, but not in heavy dollops.

By nightfall the wind had eased to force 5.

Chapter Twelve

Wet, windy conditions prevailed for some days. I did not like to get the log-book, or indeed anything in the cabin, wet. This meant that the log was written up less frequently, because, though it had a plastic cloth cover, when I sat with it on my knee in the cockpit as soon as it was opened the pages got drips of rain and spray on them. At this time instead of logging frequently I wrote it morning, midday and evening, and when anything outstanding happened. Being well out at sea, wind changes were not frequent, though I had noticed during the early part of the trip that the wind tended to rise to a maximum around the middle of the afternoon and die away towards evening. Previously I had thought this a phenomenon found only in coastal regions, where it is quite usual.

Little incidents occurred daily. The last of the eggs were eaten. The clock was set on an hour. The first bosun-bird was seen, and the next day the first tern. The yacht nearly ran over a small shark, which just cleared our bow with a wriggle and a waggle of its tail. The porpoises were in daily attendance, sometimes in dozens, often leaping right out of the sea, and almost always one or two came so close I could have reached outboard and touched them.

Every day I tried the bilge pump and usually got half a bucket of water out. The damp weather made me hungrier. Meals, especially the evening one, became bigger. Water consumption remained extraordinarily low. I kept a log record of it, noting the number of cans used daily, and the number remaining. Seldom were more than three used, usually it was two, and on some days only one. There was plenty of liquid in the tins of food, the fruit in particular being packed in syrup. Possibly I absorbed moisture through the pores. It was originally decided to fill the water cans two-thirds full, to allow for expansion. However, when the job was done, they were filled nearly to the top. This meant that the cans were under pressure. When punctured with the opener, a fine jet sprayed out, so a technique was developed to avoid hosing the cabin. A subtle upward jab, holding the can over the sink or saucepan, caught the escaping liquid. The water remained fresh and palatable right to the end of the voyage, and long after, though it became a little flat, which is hardly surprising, about eight weeks after it was canned. It was ordinary Halifax tap water. A reliable source stated that it contained 'a slight excess chlorine'; so that it ought to have been free of germs. The canning was done without special precautions, by people who were expert canners, but had never previously tinned water. They worked in the usual highly sanitary conditions of a food-testing laboratory and their product was faultless.

This method of carrying water has many advantages. The cans stow low, and can be put anywhere and everywhere, thus keeping the weight in the best place. The accidental puncturing of one or even two cans is not a serious loss, whereas a leak in a big tank could be very embarrassing to an ocean wanderer. It is easy to keep a check on consumption with individual cans. Admittedly not everyone is able to find several good friends who are prepared to go to the trouble of filling 400 1-lb size cans and sealing them. These good people also presented me with a toilet roll, a sensible and useful gift as one would expect from scientists. Another gift I prized consisted of two enormous candles, presented by a dentist, who made them from wax his profession use to make casts. Candles are excellent for a small boat. Neglected in the bottom of some damp locker for months on end beneath a heap of gear, they come up smiling every time, lighting with the first match. Smell-less, indestructible, reliable, they are the quintessence of what all small boat gear should be like.

After dying away to light, pleasant airs, the weather again looked foreboding. It was clear that a depression had passed across the Atlantic and another was now following. On the twenty-sixth day the sky was grey and overcast, with flushed, unhealthy yellow streaks on the horizon. The log says 'Put in one reef,' and an hour later 'Put in second reef.' This was a quick, easy job now, familiar as breathing. Later on the log laments 'Rain', and towards evening, 'Rain, Rain.' This meant no reading, no wonder the log is irritable. Next day the rain was forgotten because there was every indication of an approaching gale. Under jib only we ran off before heavy breaking seas. The log is terse, I was too busy steering; it says 'Damn near gale' at 1100 hours. 'Inevitable porpoise,' at 1300 hours (1 p.m.). The writing is getting ragged, this should probably read 'porpoises.'

2 hours later, 'Pooped three times, b****** oilskins – wet to skin.' This was the first time waves had come aboard over the stern when running. Each time it was an awkward breaking sea, approaching diagonally. With a heavy roar, a mass of water poured over the deck, and tumbled into the cockpit, to slop back and forward till it drained away. The cabin was kept tight shut, so no water went below. These waves were annoying. Big, vociferous bullies, they seemed intent on overwhelming the ship. They had a horrible habit of giving a vicious hiss, like a serpent before striking, followed by a silent pause with a background noise of distant breaking seas, and then, with a thunderous bellow, the wave would shatter the peace and rumble aboard.

The use of swear words in the log book is a useful and enlightening way of abbreviating. Everyone will have their own scale; that it will vary from person to person is a disadvantage. On this occasion I was manifestly very annoyed by the inefficiency of the oilskins, which leaked in several places.

That night I lay a'hull. The wind was down a little, but still strong. The following morning the seas were bigger, and they increased all day. By 1400 hours I estimated the wind as force 7. The boat was running fast under reefed jib only; she was easy to handle, and drier than the day before, probably because the seas were more regular. By 1700 hours the waves were really big. Astern, the ocean was like a big hill, acres in extent, stretching up and away. The horizon was only briefly and intermittently visible. The wind was extremely strong, definitely force 8, and possibly higher in the gusts. The whole scene astern was rather grim, with great masses of grey water, streaked with foam, always higher than the boat, and apparently about to descend on her. It was heartening to see the way she always managed to rise over these monsters. Sometimes it seemed as if she could not do it, but at the crucial moment the buoyancy swung her up. The wind showed no sign of abating, rather it seemed to be on the increase, so I decided to down sail and lie a'hull. I looked astern for a lull, but none came for several minutes. Steering was a bit hectic now, it was important to keep the stern to the sea. I was particularly anxious to get the jib on deck without letting it flap too much, because it might shake itself to rags, besides endangering the crew with the flailing canvas and sheets. Choosing a longer, smoother wave than usual I let go the tiller, scrambled forward, flung the halyard off its cleat while watching the sail and, before the boat could turn beam to wind and sea, snatched at the sail to drag it down. It refused to move. Jammed aloft, I thought, working my way back to the tiller, which I wrenched over; the boat was back on course in a second. Steering by feel, I gazed aloft, trying to see what was caught. Nothing looked wrong. I looked at the foot of the mast. Here was the explanation. In the rush I had not freed the correct jib halyard. The spare was in use, I had uncleated the other. This is easier to do on the *St Elizabeth* than most boats, for every halyard end is permanently made fast so that none can accidentally run aloft. The main advantages of this arrangement are the big safety factor, the speed and ease with which sails can be hoisted or lowered, and the fact that the halyard can be quickly freed in the dark, or without looking.

A second time I went forward and soon had the sail down. Kneeling on it I passed a lashing round it, down to the bow cleat, round the sail again, to the lifeline stanchion; another lashing completed the stowage. Even heavy seas sweeping the foredeck should not tear the sail free. Crouched up in the bow I was glad that the boat had plenty of sheer. The deck was sometimes a bare inch or two clear of the sea, but very seldom did it come aboard. The boat lay comfortably enough, heeled away from the wind, rising and falling in great sweeping arcs, calm in the loud affray.

After a glance round to make sure everything was satisfactory I went below. As I slammed the hatch closed I noticed a strong chemical smell. 'The methylated bottle is broken,' was my first thought. This would have been serious. I had taken much trouble over stowing the two remaining bottles because they were so precious. If one was smashed it might mean no hot meals for a period, besides the damage to my self-confidence. After all, if one cannot learn to stow a bottle or two it is better to stay ashore and take up tiddlywinks. But the second sniff reassured me. It was not the meths; in fact, there were the two bottles, smugly glinting, quite safe. Then I saw the fire extinguisher lying on the cabin sole. I picked it up and smelt it. A big whiff of carbon tetrachloride tickled the nasal membranes. That was it. I put the extinguisher back in its socket. We must have rolled prodigiously to throw it out. It was the press-button type. As it banged about the cabin it must have knocked the button frequently, for the smell was powerful. I sat down on the settee and tried to remember if 'carbon tet' was poisonous, while pulling off my oilskins and sea boots. All the chemistry I ever knew left my brain. I looked at the label of the extinguisher. The instructions concluded ... 'keep away from the fumes'. The fumes of the fire or the extinguisher? My heart started banging and I could feel the blood pounding and pumping, just as if I was being gassed in a dentist's chair. I had a vision of the *St Elizabeth* being found drifting with an undamaged corpse aboard. A second *Marie Celeste*, almost. To clear the gas I opened the hatch a little, expecting a wave to pour down into the cabin at any moment. The next problem was how to get the gas away. Was it heavier than air? Would it lie in the bottom of the boat? I recalled that 'carbon tet' was used for cleaning clothes, so it could not be very dangerous, one never heard of dry cleaners dying on the job. I had a vague recollection that a bottle of the stuff would evaporate. Therefore surely it must be lighter than air? I cooked the evening meal in a gradually clearing atmosphere, then shut the hatch. Lying in my bunk later, I could detect no smell, so decided I would not die in my sleep, and promptly fell asleep.

During the night the boat jumped about wildly. Every so often a sea broke against the ship with a reverberating crash. I woke infrequently, noted that the light still burnt in the rigging, and fell asleep again. It was quiet and peaceful below compared with the uproar on deck. In the morning I spent no more time on deck than it took to extinguish the light; the weather was immoderate. After a breakfast that was not easy to prepare, I returned to my bunk and book. All day I read in comfort, leaving the struggle to the ship and her namesake. The only unpleasant incident of the gale was the loss of the Oxo and tea. The former was in a bottle, which was unused. It tipped over, and the cap came unscrewed during the night. Half the galley was coated with Oxo, which was in turn covered with tea; quite how the tea escaped remains a mystery. This mess was confined to one end of the galley. The rest of the ship was dry and warm, except below the ventilator, which let in some water. On the whole it was a good gale. It showed that the boat could take rough weather, it gave the owner a rest which he truthfully did not need, and it did no damage, except for the loss of most of the Oxo and some of the tea.

By evening it was calmer. Suddenly a ship's whistle sounded. It was nine days since the last ship, so in a very short time I had dragged on my oilskins and was up on deck. Out came the baby sheath-knife, which is really a light, stainless-steel-bladed kitchen type of knife, with a rosewood handle. It is easy to keep razor-edged, and does not mind constant wettings. It lives in a specially made leather sheath with a small chromium adjustable spanner for undoing shackles, and a pencil. The whole affair is quite small and flat, so that I have slept without discomfort with the sheath belted on. This ship was another American freighter of about 10,000 tons, the *American Manufacturer*. As I slashed the lashing and held up the notice board, it occurred to me that the board was just the right size, as big as I could hold aloft in a gale. The ship whistled to indicate that it had seen and understood the message, then circled once round, gave a final hoot of farewell, and steamed away. Next morning Lloyd's reported to anyone interested that the yacht *St Elizabeth* had reached 50 degrees 23 minutes N. 24 degrees 15 minutes W.

Several weeks later I corresponded with Captain R. O. Patterson of the *American Manufacturer*. A keen yachtsman himself, he was delighted with the whole incident. He confirmed that the wind had been gale force, and in reply to my question about the appearance of the *St Elizabeth* he wrote: 'There is no doubt that you have a seaworthy craft. Not only was it surprisingly steady with scarcely any roll, it appeared quite dry on deck.' In another paragraph; 'Perhaps something which impressed me most favourably was your obvious preparation in having a placard handy and printed in letters big enough to see from a good distance'; and a number of other kind remarks. So this encounter pleased everybody. It confirmed my idea that 3 feet 6 inches by 1 foot 9 inches is a good size for a board, and that it is best to keep it handy on deck. Mine lay flat on the cabin top so that low-flying aircraft might see it. Captain Patterson also said: 'My main feeling when I saw you poke your head out of the hatch was this: "I'd sure as hell like to be with him."' It is my experience that the celebrated American generosity is as much in evidence afloat as ashore. Skippers of other nationalities do not always go out of their way, and spend quite a long time, ensuring that the ocean-going tiddlers they meet need no help.

Next morning, conditions were almost perfect. With a gentle N.W. breeze I was sailing along peacefully, thinking that this was the sort of weather every owner visualises when he buys a boat. I was replete after a good breakfast, and had just hung out some wet clothes to dry, when I saw a ship head, coming towards me. After a few minutes it looked as if she would not pass very close, so I altered course to intercept her. Rapidly she came up, a big black hull. More than a mile away she turned towards me, so I returned to my original course. She grew bigger and bigger, till her towering bow was just abeam, and I read *Georgic* (28,000 tons, 712 feet long and she looked every bit of it from below). I sat in the cockpit, steering with one hand and holding the notice board up with the other. As her bridge came abeam I yelled: 'Can you give me my longitude?' A figure hurried into the wheel-house, then back out on to the bridge wing and bellowed through a megaphone: '083 degrees true 500 miles to Blah-blur.' The *Georgic* was rapidly passing astern, and I thought they might not have seen or understood my notice board, so I shouted: 'Report to Lloyd's All Well. Yacht *St Elizabeth*, Halifax, Nova Scotia to Weymouth, England.' I said Halifax because that is a well-known port whereas Chester is not. These were the first words I had spoken for thirty days, but the vocal chords did not seem unduly weakened. There appeared to be half a million passengers, in serried ranks, lining the rail on deck above deck. In a very short time she was past, and sinking over the horizon aft.

Now the problem was to plot my position on the chart. I had not been worried about latitude, which I could get any day the sun was clear of the clouds at noon. Longitude was different. I had to rely on my watch to get this accurately, and the watch gained 43 seconds in 24 hours, but not always exactly that amount. I have caught it sulking in damp weather (though it is genuinely waterproof) and once it repented and galloped away at 45 seconds' gain in a day.

I had whipped the pencil out of my sheath and scrawled '083 degrees T 500m from …?' on the painted deck. The question was: what double-syllable word had the officer of the watch used? Obviously it was some point of departure. The Lizard? No. Coming out of the English Channel, the last sight of land is the Bishop Rock. Three syllables. But then 'Bishop' might sound like a single syllable. I plotted a position 500 miles at 083 degrees true bearing from the Bishop Rock. It put me far south of the position I had worked out from my last celestial observation. Ushant is another point of departure, and a two-syllable word, but this is farther south than the Bishop Rock. It was perplexing, but the weather was clear and at noon I got a latitude sight with my sextant. This confirmed my earlier idea. I was 50 degrees 18 minutes N. I marked this on the chart, crossed it with my dead reckoning longitude and drew a line through it at 83 degrees to the true north. The line went straight through the Fastnet, and this was the two-syllable word. Of course: how obvious now. I had assumed that the *Georgic* had sailed from Southampton. Dredged from a recess of my memory I brought out a half-forgotten fact about the *Georgic*. Surely she operated from Liverpool? The jigsaw fitted neatly together. My position was now certain.

Reviewing the previous day's gale as the *St Elizabeth* slipped along, I remembered that I had not tried the sea-anchor. Conditions were never serious enough to warrant the use of the sea-anchor, and the only damage was the loss of half a bottle of Oxo, a quarter of a pound of tea and an undetermined quantity of fire extinguisher fluid. The ship looked just the same as the day of the first trial. While I was examining her to make sure all was well, an aircraft passed over, just in sight. The log records: 'Place getting crowded,' but for the next two days I saw no more ships or aircraft. The weather was bleak and the wind went ahead, so that on the thirty-second night I could not make any useful progress to the east. The seas were short, sharp, snappy lumps and the wind rose to force 5. For the first time the *St Elizabeth* seemed unhappy. A variety of sail arrangements, with different tiller settings, failed to get satisfactory results. In the end I left her under bare pole, and was glad I did so, for the wind and sea conspired together and behaved badly. Before midnight I wrote in the log: 'Hellish squally – thank God I'm below and no sail set'.

Next morning the wind was round to the N.W. but no lighter, so I piled on sail to make up for lost time. A ship appeared in the distance, then the sun came out, in the afternoon I saw a bird like a puffin which I took as the first sign of approaching land. The waves changed in character, indicating the beginning of the continental shelf. Little things like this were a useful check on my navigation. The sextant was a reliable one, though archaic, but I still could not get any reception on the radio, so still had no check on my watch. I had therefore very little faith in my longitude signs, but this was not disturbing. What I planned to do was to get on to the same latitude as the Bishop Rock and sail due east. This light would be visible 20 miles away at night, in good weather, and if visibility closed in I could sail well south of it in clear water.

It would have been possible to sail across the Atlantic without any instruments at all. Sailing into the sun in the morning and away from it in the evening, the continents of Europe or Africa would eventually be reached. Admittedly the sun is modest some days, hiding behind clouds, but its approximate position is usually discernible. The coast of Europe is well lit, and has few outlying dangers. Rockall is a notable exception. So if all else failed, I could have sailed until land came in sight, coasted along till I found an inlet or sheltered bay, anchored, swum ashore and asked where I was. Even with only my light list I could have coasted at night until I had identified several lighthouses or lightships. This crude method would almost certainly waste a lot of time. The landfall might be Cape St Vincent or Iona. I preferred to use log and compass, sextant and chart, navigation books and tables, wireless and chronometer watch as well as my own observations.

Even so, my position was often marked as somewhere in a circle of 30 miles radius. For five days the fog was so thick I never saw the sun and horizon together, during which time I was in a current that ran approximately 9 miles a day. As the speed and direction of the current varied, both with wind and with my progress, and the log is not accurate at low speeds, it was inevitable that the yacht's position became doubtful. When the weather cleared, the sea was rough enough to make sextant work difficult. I would sit in the cockpit with the tiller lashed, or steer with a knee. As the sun appears from behind the cloud, up goes the sextant. My glasses are misty with spray. They are dried and the sextant given a wipe, then it is held up again. The sail gets in the way, so the boat is turned off course. At last the sun is visible, and I wait for the boat to ride to a wave crest. Just when the crucial moment is imminent, the sun retires behind a cloud. 10 minutes later the rain is lashing down, or a mist blurs the horizon. However, for the navigator the west–east crossing of the North Atlantic is not difficult, because the foggy area only has one danger, Sable Island, and though the landfall is a lee shore, the English Channel is like a wide funnel, so that with only a sextant and book of declination tables it would be possible to aim at the middle of the gap between France and England, then edge northwards and approach the coast diagonally. The only trouble is that the Cherbourg peninsula juts out inconveniently. On the *St Elizabeth* I had to consider several different approaches to the landfall just in case the chronometer watch misbehaved and the radio gave no reception, or none in time. The ocean current on the European side is 2 or 3 miles a day almost due east, so that was not much trouble. The pilot chart predicted less than 5 per cent days of fog and 2 per cent days of gale for August. These figures are based on observations of previous Augusts in the area, and are therefore an indication of the average weather throughout the month, not the certain conditions on an individual day. Given average weather I would have no trouble making a landfall.

Reviewing the navigation instruments, I decided that the two compasses were utterly reliable, but the boat might wander a little while I slept, also the course indicated on the compass did not allow for leeway. This varies from boat to boat, and with different conditions of wind and sea. As the *St Elizabeth* was new, her leeway was something I had to learn about. My charts, almanac, light lists and navigational tables were all accurate and up to date, but the log could not be relied upon. At night the boat's speed tended to drop, perhaps to half a knot, which the instrument would either not record, or do so inaccurately. The sextant, like every other instrument, depends to some degree on the person using it. As night after night the radio remained silent I became more convinced that the prudent course would be to sail in on a latitude, and this I did.

On the thirty-fourth day another ship was seen in the distance, and thereafter ships became more and more numerous. In fact the thirty-fifth day was crowded. Two French tunny-fish boats were seen. One altered course to pass close astern of me. She was a picture of massive reliability. Beamy and full bowed, she looked lively, though no doubt the *St Elizabeth* was waltzing about just as much. Later a third of these craft came to inspect me, and see what a small yacht was doing so far from land, and heading east. A tanker was sighted, and just before I turned in a well-lit ship passed quite close. All this was exciting in itself, besides confirming that I was on a shipping lane. The dilemma now was whether to drive on hard or go cautiously on the principle that there's many a slip 'twixt cup and lip. In practice I found that reefing was put off fully half an hour longer, and my reading became more spasmodic. The sails were trimmed often and carefully. Little ocean-racing tricks crept in. The jib luff was kept tighter, stores were put lower; I nearly threw overboard unwanted tins of water, for only one quarter of the original supply had been used, but decided against this thus rashly tempting fate. One way or another the boat was hurried on.

Chapter Thirteen

The sea became daily more crowded. I had a new and very fine pair of glasses and a second similar pair with green-tinted lenses which were a great asset in bright sunshine. It is incredibly hard to keep the spray off the lenses, but by using a large sou'wester with a big brim, and by discarding one pair of glasses when it was hopelessly fogged up, and by using a pair of skiing goggles, I kept excellent vision most of the time. Once salt spray has dried on the lenses it is necessary to wash them, dry-wiping alone will not clear them. I was able to pick out ships long before they were hull up on the horizon, for the weather was clear. It was diverting and useful to try and place the builder, owner and type of each craft, and thus try to guess her last and next port, in order to confirm my position and course.

On the thirty-seventh day out I thought I saw the liner *United States* far astern, but bow on and heading on the same course as the *St Elizabeth*. The colouring and proportions looked right when she first came in sight, and the New York to Southampton run would converge with my track. As the ship got closer I saw she was a freighter and a sister ship to the *American Manufacturer*, She came nearer and nearer, but kept down to leeward of me so as not to take the wind from the *St Elizabeth*. When she was so close I could have thrown a biscuit on board I got an answering wave to my hail. 'Report me Lloyd's please. Yacht *St Elizabeth*.' The men on the bridge had to look far down to see my notice board, and as they did not sound their siren I feared they might have missed it. The *American Scout* had not slowed down, and she soon passed ahead. Suddenly the *St Elizabeth* seemed to swing off course. A quick glance at the compass showed we were still heading due east, whereupon I realised that watching the freighter so closely, as she circled across my bow, had given me the illusion that it was I who had altered direction. This was all right, but still a trifle worrying, because it was obvious this ship was coming back for a second look. There was a force 6 beam wind and choppy sea, so that the yacht danced about. The freighter had passed very close the first time, though carefully and to leeward. I decided to steer a meticulous course and leave the manoeuvring to her. As she turned in a big arc I had plenty of time to examine her. She was trim, but what a funnel! I should like to meet the draughtsman who designed that. Why that shape? Now if I had done it ... Surely it was not aerodynamic?

The ship was obviously well kept. She slowed down. With accelerated heart I watched her bow creep up till it looked so close I thought I could swat a fly on it. She slowed down to 5 or 6 knots, which was my own speed. Keeping just astern of me, so that I was not bothered by wind eddies, her skipper held that freighter superbly. A ship like this is not designed to steer quickly like a warship or yacht, and at low speeds they are extra difficult to handle. Add a beam wind, a half-empty hold, so that the ship presents a great wall of wind-resistance, and you have a very tricky situation. Keeping the *St Elizabeth* precisely on course, I was painfully aware that if anyone made a mistake there would be trouble, possibly a sinking, perhaps a slicing of a body by the freighter's propeller. I remembered a certain incident when I was crewing a yacht in the Pacific. We smashed against the side of a freighter just like this one, in just such an encounter. No one was hurt, though the damage took four people 24 hours to repair. On that occasion there was plenty of time to stop the propeller, which was done. No one lost his presence of mind, and when our skipper suggested that the freighter should start her engine in order to get clear of the yacht no one heard, which was fortunate as we were practically on top of the propeller. It was one-third out of the water, a clean, gleaming bronze and very hygienic mincing-machine. On the present occasion I need not have worried. Captain Archie Horka of the *American Scout* is an old square-rig sailing-ship man with a soft spot in his heart for all sailing craft. Keeping beautiful control on his ship he shouted down: 'What name?'

I held up the notice board and yelled: '*St Elizabeth*. Please report me to Lloyd's.'

'Yes, we got that. What's your name?'

'Nicolson.'

'What's that?'

'Nicolson. N-I-C-O-L-S-O-N.'

'Ok,' someone else bellowed down.

Then came the question I most feared:

'Are you alone?' What could I say? I had to answer, but no one in England, particularly my family, knew I was single-handed, and I did not want anyone to worry on my account; especially as the whole trip had been so easy, so utterly painless. As I was nearly home and they would get a message there that all was well, I roared:

'Yes, single-handed. Halifax, Nova Scotia to Weymouth, England.'

'When did you leave?' The conversation continued at the top of our voices, above the noise of wind and sea.

'July 16th. How far Bishop Rock?' This question I put most reluctantly. It is not seamanlike, I think, to sail around asking the way, like a helpless motorist, but it is also unseamanlike to neglect obvious precautions. The wireless still remained mute, so it was a sensible thing to get a position check.

'170 miles due east true.' Then they gave me the weather forecast. I had to take off my sou'wester to hear as they were shouting into the wind, using megaphones. They dipped their ensign and I replied; with a final shout, 'Good man. You're doing a fine job,' Captain Horka edged his ship gradually away, so as to avoid disturbing the *St Elizabeth* with wash or back-wind currents. It was a masterly display of seamanship, besides a great kindness. Some weeks later I had a salty letter from Captain Horka which included: 'I know what it is to have a hungry gut and a wet behind'. This was a reference to his sailing-ship days. In my case the 'hungry gut' was quite absent; in fact, I was very well fed; but the second part of the quotation was all too true.

As the *American Scout* steamed away, doing 3 miles to my 1, her wireless operator tapped out the fact that she had passed me, gave my position and added various details. Lloyd's message to my family ran as follows:

American Scout reports sighting yacht St Elizabeth 170 miles due east Bishop Rock. Reefer down ('Reefer' has been queried; the word should perhaps read 'sail'.) No flag on yacht. Owner Nicolson sailing single-handed – left Halifax Nova Scotia July 16 – reports all well. Signed the Master.

This mistake over the word 'reefer' is interesting. The word should read 'reefed'. In morse code R is dot-dash-dot, while D is dash-dot-dot; the two are not dissimilar so that a mistake is easily made, but it is extraordinary that Lloyd's should not have realised this and shows how completely sailing ships have been driven from commerce by steam and motor ships. Probably the signal staff knew nothing about reefing as indeed few merchant seamen do today, yet during the crossing on the *St Elizabeth* the word 'reefed' (or 'unreefed') occurs thirty-nine times in the log.

The cat was out of the bag too. I could never have explained in that bellowed conversation to Captain Horka that I did not want my single-handedness noised abroad. What I did not know until much later was that my noncommittal letters had not been convincing, and my mother had air-mailed a letter offering to fly across and sail home in the yacht. This letter arrived in Nova Scotia after I had left. As I make it a practice to mail my last and penultimate letters by slow mail, my mother did not know of the departure until I was several hundred miles on my way. This makes the period of waiting much shorter. Ocean cruising is much harder for those who stay at home than for the people who have all the fun.

The *American Scout* raised morale to 89 per cent, the highest recorded, and the boat was driven harder. More and more ships were seen, till it was unusual for 2 hours to pass without sighting one. I passed close to a trio of rusty, grimy, smoky, pitching French trawlers; more tunny-boats with their long poles out either side like antennae, which never seemed to catch anything; and more freighters. The wind gradually died away, but the sailing was pleasant and I was cheerful with many thoughts. The trip had been so simple. If other people learnt how satisfactory trans-Atlantic sailing is there would soon be hundreds of voyages yearly. So many boats would cross that by joining them together it would be possible to walk across. But then who the hell wants to walk when you can sail?

There was a tightness inside me. Once I would have been content to crash ashore, stagger up the beach and shake the first person I met by the hand. Now I wanted a faultless landfall, followed by an impeccable cruise up Channel, and a neat manoeuvre up to the moorings. Though I always hoped to sail straight to Weymouth the original plan had been to put in to Falmouth, which is the first easy port, or Plymouth, which is not much farther and which I know. It makes a great difference whether or not a port is familiar to the skipper if it has to be entered under difficult conditions, such as at night, with heavy rainfall, high wind and rough sea. Tucked well away in my mind had been the proviso that, if all went very well, I would sail right along the coast to Weymouth, which is the port nearest to my home. Now I was quite certain that wild sea-horses would not stop me till we reached Weymouth. I was well rested, pleasantly overfed, the boat showed not even a tiny sign of fatigue or wear and tear, except the boom gallows, which got cracked when the mainsheet fouled them once during a gybe, and the chafe on the jib sheets.

She romped along in a good breeze with the sun joining the party occasionally, and the owner at the helm effervescing with delight. Even after thirty-eight days and nights of continuous sailing it was easy to revel in the progress, the sparkle of salt spray, the crash and hiss of the bow tearing a passage through the waves. Porpoises came to gambol, curving and leaping, rolling and diving. They knew the thrill of slashing fast through deep water; taut and vibrating, they escorted the *St Elizabeth* homewards. If the wind eased a little, the reefs were taken out, in quick practised movements now, in an operation measured in seconds, not minutes.

The boat heels a little more, the water flowing past hisses louder, the spray flies and splashes hard, pebbly, more determined, flashing in the sunlight more often. Then I would fling the book into the cabin, brace my feet on the cockpit seat opposite and let the yacht drive. Sitting on an inflated life-jacket, four fingers gently caressing the tiller, with a packet of biscuits handy, and four layers of clothing on beneath my oilies, I knew life and joy. There is no need to give an excuse for single-handed sailing. It has been called eccentric, mad, dangerous, psychologically unsound and a dozen other derogatory names. It may be all this and more, but heaven and the lone sailor only know the special thrill of an empty horizon and a God-given sail in a fine boat.

I confess part of my happiness was due to the success of the small experiments incorporated in the boat. She had remained warm and dry inside, which so many ocean cruisers most certainly do not. The light but scientific rigging, without the customary and archaic masses of antichafing gear, was faultless, once I had wired up all the shackles, including those at deck level. The diet never bored me, in spite of the fact that it was much cheaper and simpler than I have previously read about (with the one exception; he was a nameless but true pioneer who lived entirely on dates, for a fortnight's cruise, and claimed to have enjoyed every minute of the time; incidentally he lost no weight) and despite the important fact that there was only one cook, for two cooks make the same rations, even tinned fodder, taste different. The galley and the chart-table were both luxurious. I had not run out of dry clothes, there was three-quarters of the water and half the food left, including some luxuries, and still a few unread books. None of the emergency gear had been used except a shackle which replaced the one which unscrewed and dropped overboard. The reserve jib halyard was exercised occasionally instead of the first one, to check it. The notch and hole drilled through the rudder remained filled with putty; these were to be used if the tiller broke or the rudder-head sheared, when I would have rigged steering lines over each side of the boat through the notch or hole. Only the radio failed to live up to hopes, and before the trip was over its successor was designed on a scrap of paper. It is significant that the radio is the one branch of ocean cruising I have least studied. The radio had been repaired before leaving, and fitted into a special damp-proof case.

This was one of the things Reuben and I did not do on the boat. Sails and some of the metal work were the other two.

On the thirty-eighth day, well after dark, I connected the radio aerial to the rigging, switched on and tuned to the BBC just as the announcer said: 'And that is the end of broadcasting on the Home Service for tonight'. Turning to another part of the dial, the wireless picked up music from Spain for me, till that station closed down for the night. More fiddling with the knob and I heard: 'You have been listening to a concert of Italian church music. That ends our broadcasting on the third programme of the BBC, goodnight everybody. Goodnight.' However much commercialism adulterates radio broadcasting in the United States, it is pleasant to have several stations transmitting all night. My radio was now silent. All Western European stations slept, so I followed suit, after a few minutes studying the new chart I had laid out that morning: the English Channel Chart, western section.

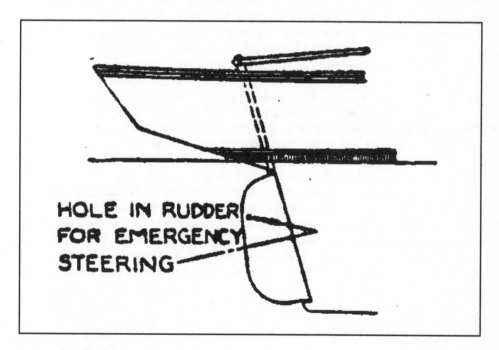

In case the tiller broke.

Chapter Fourteen

During the night I kept the boat sailing slowly and was frequently up, staring ahead into the starry darkness. It was just possible, if the log underregistered, if the current was running harder than the chart suggested, if the night was clear, that the Bishop Rock light might show its loom, just before dawn particularly. A lighthouse range is given on the chart, but the pale, sweeping, pencil-thin beam of light is sometimes visible beyond that range. Nothing was seen.

The morning was recorded in the log as 'Fine, sunny, no sea, slight swell. Full sail. Wind W.2.' This was when I most wanted a nylon headsail; a big fairy-light genoa would have made a big increase to my speed. Sailing conditions were perfect, though, and I was not discontented. I tinkered with the radio while steering with an elbow. It had not woken up in the morning. A loose connection was traced and mended. Still it remained mute. The reserve batteries were fitted. This produced results. Evidently the salty damp atmosphere had discharged one of the batteries before it could do an hour's work. Clearly wireless sets, like everything else in small boats, need to be hermetically sealed and capable of total immersion; in truth a really good set would work as well under water as above. All morning I listened in. Fishing boats were all round, and about midday I saw one stationary and almost dead ahead. Most of them were French, including this one, which was from Douarnenez. It was crowded with typical Breton fishermen in blue cotton trousers and jackets, patched neatly and faded to different shades. Each man wore a black beret. Feeling almost guilty and like a novice I shouted to them as the St Elizabeth passed close astern: 'Ou est Bishop Rock?' They pointed to the south-east and I thought someone shouted: '15 miles'. This was curious. I thought the rock was due east. But they had a radio-direction-finder, as I saw by its big loop on the wheelhouse. Looking to the south-east I saw a haze over a limited area. That is the Scilly Isles, I thought, wondering how I was so far to the north. A brief check over the previous 24 hours' navigation showed no error. Those fishermen ought to know. I was doubtful now, and properly ashamed of myself for asking the way. To atone, I decided to have faith in my own navigation. Just before the one o'clock news I left the helm, gathered all the materials for lunch and returned on deck. The news filled me with curiosity. For over five weeks I had had no word of the world, but it had not changed noticeably. The news ended and I glanced ahead. Ah, there it was. Land, just where it ought to be, in the form of three brown and green hill tops. I left the helm and climbed on to the cabin top for a better view. No doubt about it. Nice to notice, too, that the skipper shows no sign of disgusting exuberance. He has made enough landfalls now to have a little faith. He displays a commendable nonchalance. His entry in the log is a trifle dramatic, but one may perhaps allow this, since he has not before done more than a 30-mile voyage single-handed. I wrote: '1315 LAND – thank God and *St Elizabeth*. Dead ahead – well done navigator.'

10 minutes later a powerful wave of reaction swept over me. Done it! DONE IT! We're across! Home! Only another 200 miles to Friarmayne, and a bed with sheets, meals at a table with a cloth on. In my own little tub, too. She floated all the way, the right way up. In a nauseating show of cheerfulness I pounded my feet on the cockpit floor, felt tight in the throat, and started a sentimental musing about a happy return after two years' wandering. I excuse myself by pointing out that approximately fifteen Frenchmen and a radio-direction-finder were wrong, my antediluvian sextant and I were right.

An hour later the islands were much bigger, and getting more distinct every minute. Gannets flew around, fishing spasmodically. I was welcomed by the RAF, who skimmed low overhead in a four-engined aircraft. The pilot's helmeted head was visible in every detail. They took little notice of me, for which I was thankful. Just as I thought, no one at the home base had lost their head or got unnecessarily anxious; this aircraft was not part of a search party. The departure point and base are important to any ocean cruiser. They should know the proposed route, probable date of arrival, what will be done in the obvious emergencies such as: if dismasted, head for the Azores, or Newfoundland, according to the position of accident. Same procedure for serious sickness. Then any search can be narrowed down, from the last report of the yacht to the next likely port. The home and starting bases should be occupied by experienced yachtsmen, preferably people who have sailed with the skipper, so that they can make intelligent decisions. Ocean cruising is a great game, but serious. No one is justified in setting out in a foolhardy way, because it is not fair on those at the shore bases, or on those who have to work a search. Seeking a tiny boat at sea is a hard, monotonous task. But a search should be started once the elapsed time of the journey is complete without the yacht's arrival. The Navy and Air Force are maintained by the taxpayer and are to defend and protect those people. They may moan if they get called out in foul weather but it is their job, and excellent training for hostilities. If the maiden voyage of the *St Elizabeth* has seemed easy, that is because it was backed by a great deal of good luck. While it is true that anyone with a little experience, say, seven seasons' cruising in the English Channel, or along the North American Atlantic coast, together with a trifle of intelligence, pertinent study of the best books, lots of thrust and all available enthusiasm, can cross the oceans between the Arctic and Antarctic circles, nevertheless it is best to remember that some have not come back. The sea is no respecter of crazy notions, unseamanlike ships or men.

As the islands came closer I studied the charts. These were not sufficiently detailed for me to sail between the islands, so I regretfully turned slightly north and skirted them. They looked so pleasant, colourful and quiet; by the time they were abeam I had planned a cruise among them for the following year. The radio sang merrily and I looked forward to a pleasant night's sailing with its company, whereupon it fell silent. Nothing would coax it to life; it had burnt out a vital part and I had no spares for it; it was almost the only item of equipment on board without them. As night fell I cooked a meal, standing in the companionway steering. The sea was calm, and the ship's motion not noticeable.

After dark I sat at the helm, watching and identifying the lights as they appeared. The luminous compass glowed dimly. Towards two in the morning I began to feel drowsy. The channel shipping had been active all night, but now I was between the coastal lane and the ships heading for the open Atlantic. The wind died to a zephyr. I gybed and later gybed back again. The breeze got more and more fickle. The *St Elizabeth* crept past the Wolf Rock lighthouse and into an area of clear water S.W. of the Lizard. I lashed the tiller, collected an inflated life-jacket and a kapok one for cushions, and curled up in the bottom of the cockpit. Every few minutes I woke up, sat up, saw nothing approaching, nor was the yacht getting near land, so I dozed off again. This fitful sleep in the open lasted less than 30 minutes, but was refreshing. The long, comfortable nights in a warm dry bunk all the way across had stored up sleep, so that I was not tired when the day came. Just before dawn, several fishing boats came out of Falmouth. They were the traditional type of Falmouth Quay punt which used to take pilots aboard ships in the days of commercial sail. With the false dawn breaking behind them they were a picturesque sight, a compensation for the disturbed night, though I was not yet reconciled to coastal cruising after the comfort of having no land within 300 miles. These boats seemed to be dancing about a lot in the short seas, and I realised that the *St Elizabeth* was probably just as restless, but was myself too acclimatised to notice.

After breakfast I sat in the warm sun, reading and steering. A coaster passed very close, a beautiful thing, designed by a master, built by craftsmen and kept perfectly. She was a lovely ship, as delightful as a pretty girl in a new evening dress. She made me long to get back to the drawing-board. The mate on the bridge waved, and to complete the perfect picture she flew the Red Ensign. She was just the sort of sight I wanted as a welcome home.

The weather continued perfect, sunny and windy, but with the breeze now on the quarter. Another perfect day's sailing followed. With the English countryside sliding by, fast progress and a lively boat, it was so perfect I felt a tinge of regret that my home port was round the next two headlands. In the late afternoon Start Point was abeam. I did consider sailing close enough to signal with my sign-board, but decided against it, hoping to be home before a message could get through. Glancing astern I saw a ship about 2 miles away with a heavy list. Seen from dead ahead she looked dangerous and uncomfortable. She soon overtook me, a white-painted Panamanian; she looked like the converted steam yachts used in the banana trade around Central America. As she passed, the officer of the watch waved and I replied. The channel shipping was all very friendly, till I got a rude awakening half an hour later. A patch of oil-befouled water appeared dead ahead. The *St Elizabeth* was sailed round it, though it was unavoidable at one point. A mile beyond was another filthy oil slick. These patches were in long streaks, dead in the wake of the ship that had just passed, and there was strong evidence that she had pumped the oil overboard. This is absolutely illegal, a disgusting habit which spoils beaches, decimates sea birds, dirties ships and causes endless trouble. It is comparable to throwing sewage into a street. Boiling with rage I scrawled down a note of the time, position and name and course of the ship. The excitement of getting ashore put the matter out of my mind for a few days, and by the time the matter was followed up nothing could be done. The evidence was only circumstantial, anyway. Even if I had collected a sample of the oil and sea water, I was single-handed, so that it was not a water-tight case. Later two freighters, contemporaries of the Ark, overtook me. Loaded with timber, they wallowed along. With a fair breeze they could only just get past the *St Elizabeth*, because she was sailing near her maximum speed.

That night I sailed continuously. There was a lot of shipping about and no chance for much of a nap. Due to the restful nature of the crossing I did not feel tired, which was surprising and satisfying. Formerly I have had a desperate battle to stay awake during the hours of darkness for one night, let alone two. During daylight the eyelids do not weigh crushingly, but at night it is a torture trying to stay awake besides navigating and handling the ship. It is so easy and so desirable to let go the helm, heave-to, and flop down in the bottom of the cockpit for an hour or two. And in shipping lanes, so dangerous.

With the strong breeze of the previous day, I expected Portland Race to be in a ferocious mood. The Race is a restless body of water, south of Portland Bill. Technically it is a submerged weir, the continuation of the rocky promontory below the sea. As the tide flows over this miniature submerged mountain range it sets up waves that are unpredictable and vicious, making life dangerous for craft as big as destroyers. The Race has been described as the greatest danger to yachts in the Channel. The confused water extends 6 miles south of the Bill in bad weather. There are innumerable tales of damage and destruction told about it, so the *St Elizabeth* kept 6 miles off the headland, till the four flashes of the lighthouse were abeam.

As the yacht swung northwards on the last lap, the wind laid her over till the water gurgled and splashed along the lee deck. I thrust the helm down, let go the jib sheet with one hand and hauled in the weather one with the other. The boat lay comfortably hove-to. Going forward to the foot of the mast, I checked the shipping in the immediate vicinity. A collection of lights that looked like a coaster was passing ahead. Nothing else was near enough to be of interest. The night was pitch black. Feeling for the topping-lift, I set it up tight, then eased the main halyard till I could feel the metal ring of the reef cringle was down to the boom. The reefing pendant, a rather hard, easily recognisable cotton line, was ready at hand. All easy this, after so much practice. Leaning comfortably against the mast, my fingers tied and tucked the rope, knowing what to do without thinking. Then aft, with one hand sliding along the lifeline. No point in falling overboard now, even if there are only 6 miles to swim ashore. At the end of the boom the manilla pendant is lying waiting. It is hauled tight, fingers seek the cleat, make the pendant fast with one, two, and a third turn for certainty, then round the sail and boom, back to the cleat, and it will hold in a hurricane. I go forward again, standing on the cabin top, resting against the boom, feeling, finding and tying the reef points. A satisfying job, now that practice makes it swift. Back at the mast the halyard is bowsed up, by holding it with one hand, pausing to wait for the roll of the ship, then throwing the whole weight of the body against it. When the halyard is hard up, the topping-lift is eased, and in 3 seconds more the jib is pulling and the boat surges forward. Three-quarters of an hour later the wind has eased, the *St Elizabeth* has lost her urgency, and I take the reef out, this time lashing the helm, and not losing speed during the operation.

Through the black night we sail, an owner happy in the knowledge of his ship, and the ship responsive, eager, thrusting, willing. The Shambles lightship is dead ahead, our next turning point. The wind eases more, progress slows from the slashing fight with spray lashing, and wet foaming water pouring along the lee side deck; now the boat glides, effortlessly, the most graceful and animate of man's creations. By the time the lightship is abeam the wind is a breath. The lightship not only has the big revolving lantern on the thick central mast but the whole deck is lit by lesser lights. One of the crew wanders aft, and waves as the *St Elizabeth* slips past within a biscuit-toss.

The dawn comes slowly. For the first time it is not ahead, but well over on the starboard side. The course takes us more and more into the wind. I wish I had a poet on board. They are too fond of raving about the dawn. No doubt they see it from the comfort of a well-covered bed, in a warm room. If only I could get them afloat they would change their tune. Dawn is cold, damp, sleepy and hungry. When racing, it is at dawn that other ships come in sight. Always the smaller ones are in front, or worse perhaps, no one is in sight. Then anxiety gnaws at every brain. Has the course been wrong all night? Have the others tacked to the south to anticipate some change of wind? When cruising, dawn is the time when the boat looks most bedraggled. The cups lie unwashed in the sink, left there after the snack at the change of watch 4 hours earlier. The sails are hanging far too slackly, or have tightened too much and stretched ruinously. Men's chins are rough and stubbly, neither romantically bearded nor trimly smooth. Girls' hair hangs dejectedly, damp, dispirited. This dawn was slightly different. These were the Dorset hills ahead. With a small piece of artillery I could lob a shell on to the immaculate lawn of Friarmayne to wake the household. If only I had done the trip 130 years earlier I could at least have roused the citizens of Weymouth with a noisy salute, loosing off a charge or two from the serried rank of guns in the waist of my frigate. Instead, I beat slowing into Weymouth Bay, ghosting through the water, leaving scarcely a ripple behind.

Bulbous dark grey clouds lay around the skies, the wreck of an Olympian pillow-fight. The wind kept changing direction, and I tacked frequently. There was nothing to do on the ship. She had been tidied. She looked unaltered, as if the Atlantic were no wider than the Channel; she had that indefinable 'je ne sais quoi' of a happy ship.

At last the twin breakwaters of the harbour were reached. Doing short tacks, the *St Elizabeth* worked her way slowly up harbour. At the bend the foul tide and flukiness of the wind made progress difficult. The harbour is so narrow, and the buildings around so high, that the yacht's sails scarcely felt the wind. After five or six tacks in the same place a motor launch came by. I waved a rope's end, the conventional signal to ask for a tow. The launch came alongside; the yachtsman in it said:

'We're only going to the steps.'

'That's fine. I only want a plug past this windless spot.'

'Where are you from?' A pleasant moment this, I confess. I paused to think back before answering.

'From Nova Scotia.'

'What? Today? Alone? In this boat?' Incredulously.

Certainly the boat did not look weather-beaten, nor the owner. I never felt fitter, better fed, more rested.

A hundred yards on, they cast off the tow and the *St Elizabeth* felt the faint airs that ruffled the water. I selected a berth alongside a gaff cutter; it looked a trifle awkward to reach, and though I had sailed 2,576 miles according to the log when I took it in at the harbour mouth, I had had no practice at bringing this boat alongside. It was now nine o'clock and plenty of people were about, but no one was in sight on board the cutter. I shouted to it, and a tousled head and pyjama-clad figure emerged from the cabin.

'Will you take my line, please?'

'What's that? Oh, sure.'

The *St Elizabeth* bore away, gathered a little speed, luffed till the sail shook, slid forward, gently losing speed. Leaving the helm, I went forward with a warp. It was new and stiff. It was heaved across the closing gap of water, caught, and made fast. Back at the helm, I turned my ship parallel to the cutter at the latest possible moment and made a stern warp fast; then I lowered the sails.

The *St Elizabeth* had brought me home.

Technicalities

The *St Elizabeth* is a conventional wood yacht, 30 feet 6 inches long and 7 feet 11 inches broad. She has an over-hanging bow and counter stern, and at the start of her trans-Atlantic trip she had a waterline length of 22 feet and draft of 4 feet 9 inches. As stores and water were consumed these two dimensions diminished slightly, not that they have much significance in a seaway, because the constant motion, the unceasing arrival and departure of the waves means that the boat is continually varying her actual draft and waterline length.

The rig was sloop with an inner forestay, which rig some people call 'slutter', others bastard cutter, and still others say is cutter, plain and simple. The offer of a complete schooner rig and all its gear was turned down because for yachts of this size the rig gives poor all-round performance. Presumably the reason why small fishing-boats use, or used, schooner rig in Canadian waters is that it is convenient to handle when working nets or lines.

Sail area was theoretically 285 square feet. In practice the sails never stretched to their designed size, due, I believe, to the over-cautiousness of the sailmaker, who was rather shocked that anyone should wish to meander across the Atlantic in a boat the size of the *St Elizabeth*. He made the sails undersize, doubtless thinking he was contributing to my safety. Unfortunately this made the boat a trifle slow in light airs, even with the 45-square-foot storm jib set as an extra sail. Much against my better judgement I did not have the sails mildew-proofed, and they very soon showed the black specks of this fungus. The cost of the protection was more than I could afford.

I own that my worries about the shape of the stern were unfounded. Gerald Stevens did a good job when he designed the yacht. Running before the growing gale, the *St Elizabeth* performed just the way we hoped and prayed.

The boat was built of pine planking on timbers of oak, which were steamed and bent into the boat while hot, this being the usual method of framing craft of this size and type at the time when she was built (1954). Pine, spruce and oak were used throughout, as well as plywood, all this timber being Canadian.

The standing rigging consists of one lower aft shroud each side and one lower inner forestay to balance these two. The main shrouds pass over crosstrees and reach to the jumpers. Jumper shrouds are balanced by a permanent backstay, and finally there is the jib-stay. Reserve runners are carried but seldom used.

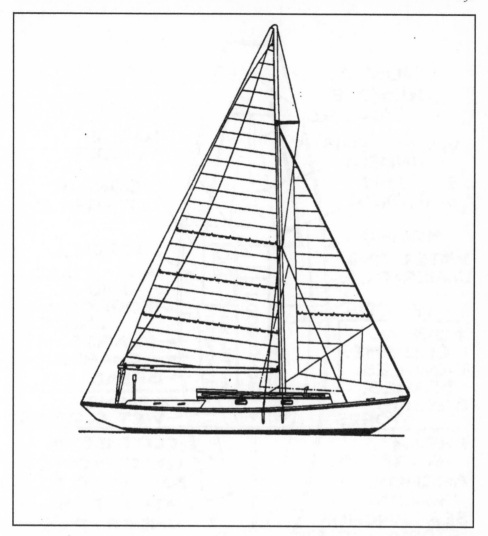

Sail Plan.

The running rigging includes a wire main halyard with two-part rope purchase and downhaul. The two jib halyards are similar. The topping-lift is of rope, and doubles as a spare main halyard. The main sheet is three-part, single-ended, and this gives more than enough power. The jib sheets are led straight from clew, through the fairlead to the cleat. They have no purchase.

The whole boat is very simple, and gadget-free. She was built in about one-third the time it normally takes to build a yacht of the same size, because of this. For instance the toilet was a portable bucket, with a plywood seat. The hull was not even painted internally before the crossing, because I thought I was going into battle against an ocean. Naturally the tendency was to ensure that the weapon was sharp rather than decorated.

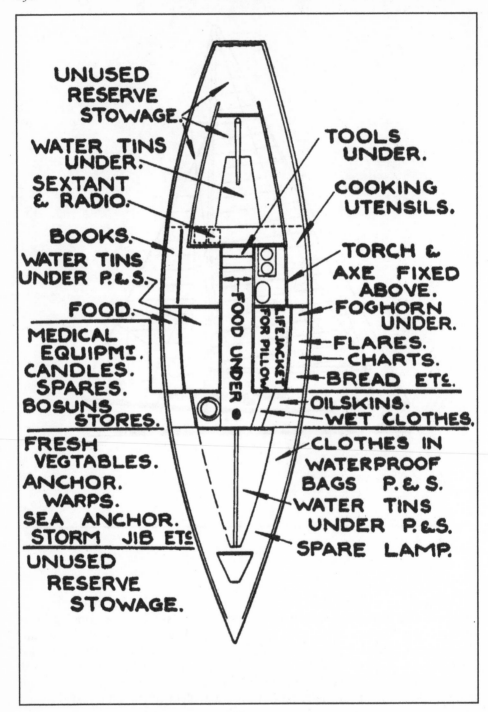

UNUSED
RESERVE
STOWAGE.

WATER TINS
UNDER.

SEXTANT
& RADIO.

BOOKS.
WATER TINS
UNDER P.&S.

FOOD.

MEDICAL
EQUIPMT.
CANDLES.
SPARES.
BOSUNS
STORES.

FRESH
VEGTABLES.
ANCHOR.
WARPS.
SEA ANCHOR.
STORM JIB ETC.
UNUSED
RESERVE
STOWAGE.

TOOLS
UNDER.

COOKING
UTENSILS.

TORCH &
AXE FIXED
ABOVE.
FOGHORN
UNDER.
FLARES.
CHARTS.
BREAD ETC.
OILSKINS.
WET CLOTHES.

CLOTHES IN
WATERPROOF
BAGS P.&S.
WATER TINS
UNDER P.&S.
SPARE LAMP.

FOOD UNDER

LIFEJACKET FOR PILLOW

Stowage Plan (P. & S. = Port and Startboard).

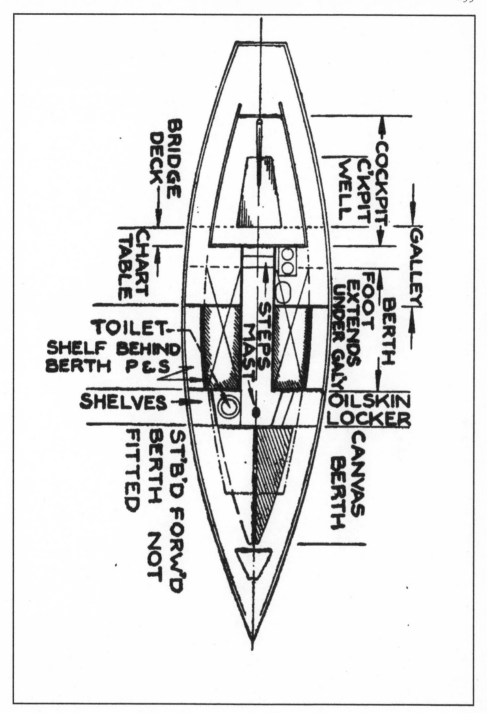

Accommodation Layout (P. & S. = Port and Starboard).

Building
the *St Mary*
1963

Chapter One

I am minding my own business. This is a good thing as we are doing about 105 mph. The speedometer on the dashboard says 112 mph, but one and all know these are lying dials. We roar down the empty road, the dark green Triumph car and I, going nearly flat out on a cold, clear winter's Sunday.

The rest of the world has just struggled out of bed, collected the Sunday newspapers, and carpet-slipper shuffled to the fireside to await the start of the day's televiewing. So the road which stretches ahead is completely deserted. On our left the Clyde glints dully. I dearly want to glance at the river, to see if there is any interesting shipping. But at this velocity the road has to be watched the whole time. Apart, that is, from a snatched glimpse of the oil-pressure gauge. Once before under conditions like this, I drove a similar Triumph engine to destruction by batting flat-out too long. The oil department just could not cope and after a wonderful run, a bearing went home and we had to limp along at sixty till we came to a garage where dreadful things were diagnosed.

Right now, I cannot afford to burn out a cigarette lighter, let alone a car's engine. For we are building a yacht and every farthing goes towards the boat. As proof of this, the Triumph thunders along making rather more noise than a potent Grand Prix car. This is due to a large hole in the silencer and it is, of course, much more important to spend money on sails than a silencer. Naturally the police take notice of my progress, in fact such is the noise that everyone for seven parishes around knows of our coming and sighs with relief at our going. However, to quieten the worst suspicions of the police, I have worked out a technique when driving past a constable who looks efficient. I approach at my normal gait, which is not exactly lethargic, and as we get abreast I shove down the clutch and let the engine note die down to a mere warble, like forty howitzers popping off about a quarter of a mile away. Thus we coast for a hundred yards before letting the engine get to work again. And as our boat takes up all my spare time, there has been no car washing for months, so no policeman can read the number plate, unless he is prepared to get very close indeed. Which is, of course, rather difficult as I keep going at the briskest pace.

However, when Dumbarton comes along it is necessary to slow right down, for here the scenery is always enlivened by a drunk and a pretty girl. It's a different beer-basher and a new girl each time, and the extraordinary thing is that regardless of the day or time, there is always one of each. Naturally, I have to navigate with extreme care to avoid bumping the drunk, and this makes for exciting driving, for some of them are clearly determined to sit on the bonnet of the car. It's all a tiny bit frustrating as of course it's my fault if we impinge, and I have to drive all over the country, with other traffic likewise dodging the obstruction so that we have a thrilling time. But this leaves no time to appraise the pretty girls. Even if I have passed one drunk there may be another waiting to lurch away from holding up the lamp-post to tack giddily my way. So I drive through Dumbarton as righteously as a monk, and hardly ever have a chance to size up the local talent.

No wonder the green Triumph crescendoes up till the rev counter needle swallows itself round the dial, once we leave this town and enter the zig-zag road to Helensburgh. Now it's truly interesting motoring, being just a series of corners laid on end, with much of the route lined by walls. So there is no room for error, no handy verges to slide onto if the accelerator pedal pushes too hard. With a cacophony of outrageous roars, we sing along, up and down the gears, glad to have the road to ourselves, going as fast as safe to get to the boat just as soon as possible.

Down a back street of Helensburgh, at an old garage turned boatyard, the Triumph stops. In a flurry of overalls, tools and pieces of wood, I'm out of the car and into the shed to see how much the boat has progressed since I last saw her. There she lies, like a languorous, curvaceous girl. The rich mahogany is as breath-taking as sunburnt skin. The very shape of the boat has that suggestive promise of exciting things to come. The hull feels smooth, yet delicate. No wonder most people prefer wood boats to metal or fibreglass ones. The wood is reminiscent of … of. … well, it's hard to explain. But if you just gently touch a girl's cheek, you learn the same sort of magic.

So I run my hand over the hull for the thousandth time and say:

'She's coming on George', and George, who understands these things says, 'Come and stand over on the pile of timber, you can see her better from there.' So we go and look, for 5 minutes which we cannot afford to spare. But we do, because there's solid satisfaction in just drinking in the shape, and talking over how we can best enhance it.

George is the most important person in this story. He is a shipwright, but no ordinary one. I first found out that he can work faster, harder and longer than anyone else, when he was involved in building two motor-cruisers to my design.

A new firm called 'Arden Yachts Ltd' run by Donald Crocket and John McNiven owned these boats and charters them out through the summer, this being the basis of the firm when it started.

In the autumn of 1960, I was trying to find someone to build the hull of a yacht for me, when Donald came to dinner. Conversation ranged back and forth, from boats to masts to engines to sails, as it will with people who are sailing-mad, and a great range of subjects were covered, all about yachts. Long after dinner was finished I said:

'It's very hard to find anyone interested in building a hull. All the yards expect plenty of work this winter and do not want to take on just a hull.'

'Why do you only want a hull?' Donald asked.

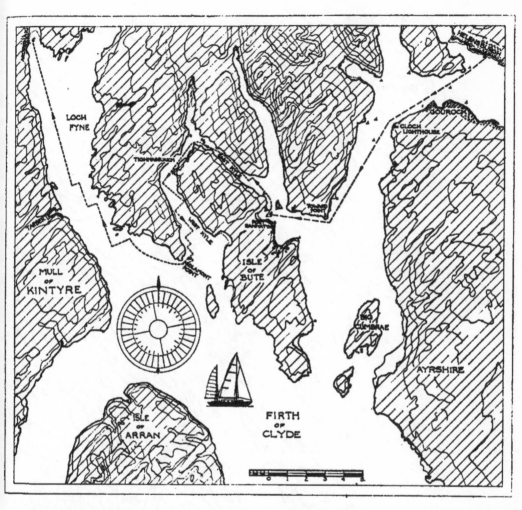

The maiden voyage and the first race of the *St Mary*. Immediately after launching she sailed through the night to the start of the race at Port Bannatyne. The first half of the race finished at Ardrishaig, which is at the entrance to the Crinan Canal.

The second half of the race was from Crinan to Tobermory. The homeward cruise from
Tobermory via Sunart to Crinan and Port Bannatyne is also shown on this chart.

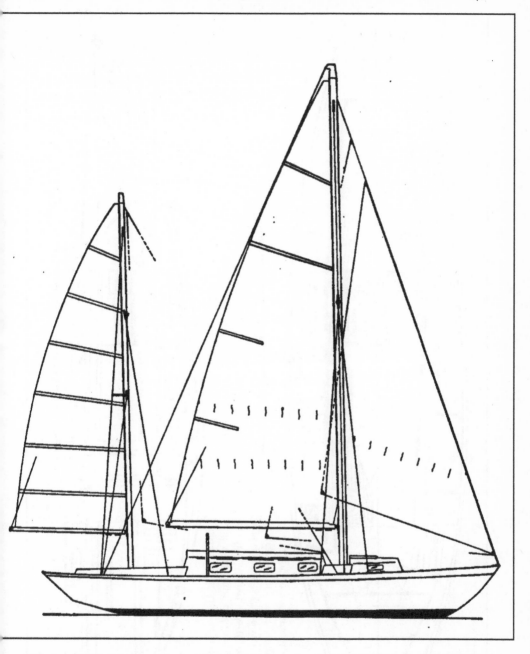

This is what the *St Mary* looked like during her second season, when she had the new mainsail. It has long battens at the top. For the technically minded: the working jib can be set as a mizzen staysail; note the reef points on the jib; a pushpit and pulpit with lifelines all round have been omitted for clarity.

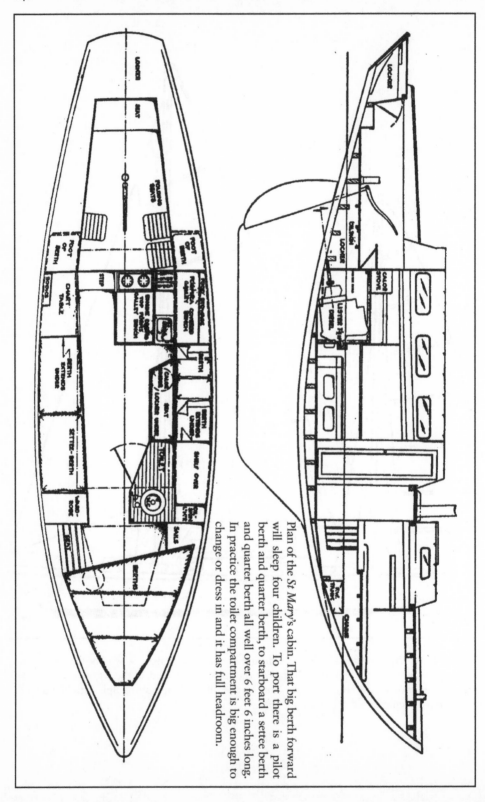

Plan of the *St Mary's* cabin. That big berth forward will sleep four children. To port there is a pilot berth and quarter berth, to starboard a settee berth and quarter berth all well over 6 feet 6 inches long. In practice the toilet compartment is big enough to change or dress in and it has full headroom.

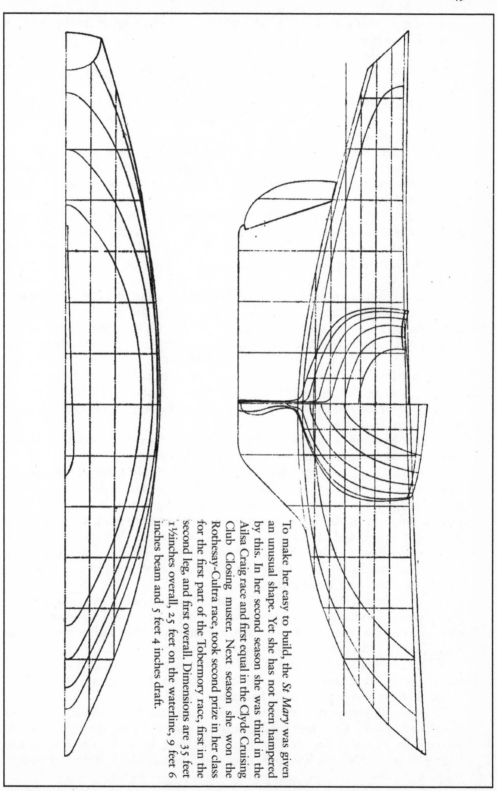

To make her easy to build, the *St Mary* was given an unusual shape. Yet she has not been hampered by this. In her second season she was third in the Ailsa Craig race and first equal in the Clyde Cruising Club Closing muster. Next season she won the Rothesay-Cultra race, took second prize in her class for the first part of the Tobermory race, first in the second leg, and first overall. Dimensions are 35 feet 1½inches overall, 25 feet on the waterline, 9 feet 6 inches beam and 5 feet 4 inches draft.

'We plan to do most of the remaining work ourselves, apart from putting in the engine, stepping the masts and so on.'

'How big is this boat?'

'Come and look at the plans,' and I rolled out one drawing after another, till Donald said:

'We'll build your boat.'

'How can you? You need power tools, and more than one man. You need a fair amount of space too.'

'That's easy. We are moving from our temporary shed to a big one in Helensburgh. We can get an apprentice to help George, and we are planning to get wood-working machinery anyhow. This is just what we want, something to get the firm going.'

Donald has more drive than four ordinary mortals. Two or three days later, timber orders were out, machinery was selected, between us we drew up a contract (which is essential even between friends) and snatching a day from his work Donald hurtled south with George in their little van to pick up a band-saw.

To this day no one quite knows how the band-saw got into the van. The saw is definitely bigger than the van, and no two men could possibly lift the saw. Yet those two humped the massive great casting with its heavy electric motor into the truck and roared back to Glasgow, travelling through the night to work next day. This set the pace for the whole operation.

The speed the boat was built at was murderous. It had to be, to finish for the summer, with our small labour force and limited facilities. The keel was laid late in November, and right away we met a snag. George found a dud patch in the oak stem timber.

All boat-building is a series of loosely linked crises, but we found that at times ours were upon us in droves, from all directions.

The original idea was to build the stem and keel all in one, of mahogany planks, glued together in layers. This is called laminating, and it has a number of advantages. For a start, each plank is fairly light, which is a help when there is only a man and a boy to carry it. A keel or stem made of solid oak is downright heavy, and about as handy as a dead giraffe. Another thing, each plank or laminate is fairly thin, say ½ inch thick. So there is no chance of a fault in the wood going undetected. For these and other reasons I designed the yacht's stem and keel laminated.

However, right at the start I said: 'We want to make building as easy as possible for everyone. As this is Arden Yachts' first sailing boat we will make any minor alterations to the plan as we go, to suit available material, and to make things easier for everyone, especially George, who has the brunt of the work.'

When he first studied the plans I told George that if he would rather use solid timber for the back-bone, and not laminates, he was to go ahead. Naturally he chose the type of construction he had used most.

We were all pretty impressed when the stem and keel arrived, rough cut from the saw-mill. Each part looked just too massive, too gigantic to go into a boat only 35½ feet overall. The reason was that this was to be a fin-keeled boat. This meant the hull was to be built first, like a canoe, and the iron keel to give stability and sailing ability was to be bolted on later. As the iron fin-keel weighs over 3 tons, the wood supporting it has to be strong. But it's amazing how intimidating a piece of rough-hewn oak, 14 inches wide and over 4 inches thick, looks when cooped up in a small boatyard shed. After all the sweating and labour on this great baulk, it was rotten luck to find it had to be discarded for a fresh piece, all due to a small internal defect. A laminated stem and keel would never have had this trouble.

This new boat was only slightly longer on the waterline and overall than our last one. Yet to see the back-bone in the raw it looked as if there had been some gigantic error in the plans. Admittedly the previous boat was a light and delicate thing. She was the joy of our hearts, a curvaceous beauty, so safe and dry, so much of us and with us. I built her with the help of one shipwright in Nova Scotia and sailed her home, so that we had been her first and only owners. Our characters and personalities were stamped on her, and hers on us. We sold her to pay for the new one. This was tantamount to selling a favourite daughter in a slave market. It was a grievous blow to part with her, and she felt that way too. She ran aground with the new owner aboard within an hour of his taking possession. She did this right in front of as many people as possible, off Greenock, and got her name in the papers. As Morag, my wife, said:

'We should keep her really. If we have to part with her, then the only proper way would be in Viking style. She should only leave us as a funeral pyre, drifting off down tide, blazing from end to end.'

We had been in and out of all sorts of hair-raising situations with the *St Elizabeth* and she always got us out unscathed.

There was that time three of us sailed the *St Elizabeth* from Shoreham to Dover. We left the lock after a long delay which prevented us getting a weather forecast. It was a grim one, with gales threatened all round the coast. We were only a few miles on our way before the wind freshened from dead astern and we started to roll somewhat. This was too much for Tony, who was thoroughly seasick. He retired to a bunk and took very little further interest in proceedings till we hurtled into Dover hours later.

As time went by the wind got truly vicious, and piled up a roistering sea. We were safe enough but it was a bit hectic. I reefed the mainsail and jib, then took the latter in, before going below to make sandwiches. Peter was at the helm and I said:

'You can do what you like with this boat, under this snug rig. But don't gybe in this weight of wind.'

When the first sandwich was ready I handed it up through the hatch. Peter leant forward to take it, a sea caught the yacht's stern at the same moment, and WHAM! We'd gybed, Chinese style. The mainsail, which had seen a few thousand miles' service, just could not take it. A tear went from leach to luff, where the sail caught the cross-trees.

Hanging on with determination I clambered forward to sort out the mess, while Peter kept the boat going off downwind. Her speed was still impressive, even under semi-bare poles. Clawing down the sail was not easy, as it wanted to whistle off downwind at about 40 knots. I coaxed it as best I could, but the upper part, above the tear, caught in the jumper stays, where they came into the mast. No amount of tugging from below was going to free them. It would only make the tear worse, and I meant to save that sail for many miles' more work, once it had been repaired. So there was nothing for it but to shin up the mast and sort out the mess up there. This was no fun, and it was more than average relief to be back on the semi-solid wildly swooping deck.

We set the trisail and reefed jib and still made fast time. The wind was beginning to mean business, especially when it hardened up at dusk. Normally the wind dies at that hour. By darkness we were pretty worried and were off Folkestone with about 6 miles to go. A few miles down channel two of a crew of three of another yacht were being drowned, though we only found this out later. But it was definitely that sort of night.

I decided that we should have the engine going to enter harbour, and in case anything went wrong, we made plans to foam off into the North Sea and heave-to clear of the shipping lanes. I reckoned we had no more than a fifty-fifty chance of getting into Dover, and was more than somewhat worried about being flung against the outer harbour walls.

Now there is a well-known trouble with all yachts' engines, which is 'Water down the exhaust pipe.' All boats have a tendency to this malaise, and it is perfectly devastating. No engine will go once the disease strikes and the cure is usually costly. It is a well-known illness, and the accepted way to prevent it is to put a sea-cock (a big tap, in shoregoing language) at the outer end of the exhaust pipe. Then no water can get down the pipe even when the waves leap high up the ship's side. Of course the sea-cock has to be turned on to start the engine. And this is where much trouble accrues. For in the interval between turning on the cock and getting the engine going, one or even three waves can easily plunge down the exhaust pipe and fill the cylinders. Naturally this can only happen in bad weather, but of course that is just when the engine is likely to be most urgently needed. On the *St Elizabeth* we knew all about this problem, and instead of a sea-cock we had a plain wooden bung. This was kept thrust up the exhaust outlet till the last second, and so we never had engine failure at critical moments. For that matter we never had engine failure, but that is another story, or set of them.

On this occasion we did a bit of carefully prepared teamwork. I went below and made sure the little Lister engine had fuel and lub oil, set the fuel pump to the starting position, decompressed the single cylinder, and put on the starting handle. Peter grasped the tiller in one hand, and leant over ready to whip out the exhaust bung at the vital moment. As the cylinder was decompressed I was able to swing the engine with the bung in. Round and round I wound the handle till:

'NOW. PETER. BUNG OUT!' I yelled above the gale, and his reply came back:

'OK. It's free,' and at that moment I flicked the compression lever over, and as usual the baby Lister thumped into life. Which was a very reassuring sound.

We now turned to another problem. There are two entrances to Dover harbour. The western one is blocked by a sunken obstruction, a wartime legacy. This makes it very dangerous to pass through, unless the skipper has sound local knowledge. I had seen plenty of locally owned motor-boats pass that way, but had never done the passage myself. Also I had seen wires stretched across the entrance on some occasions. To blunder into one of those wires in the dark would have been very interesting. It would almost certainly have whipped the mast out of the boat. So we were faced with the eastern entrance. This is used by a great many packet-boats at all hours of the day and night. The correct procedure, before entering, is to heave-to outside, well clear and await the signal to go in. Fine in theory, ruddy well impossible in practice. We were quite incapable of stopping. It was now raining with a viciousness that rivalled the wind. We could never expect to signal a request to enter, then proceed in a gentlemanly manner through the gap in the harbour walls.

In the end I decided on the bold course. This was an easy decision, as there was no alternative, apart from heaving-to for maybe a week somewhere off the Dutch coast, or maybe around Denmark, while the weather eased off. We whirled towards the harbour entrance, the boat leaping with wild abandon as we got near the great stone walls which threw back rebound waves of great size and impossible shapes. The boat fought. We prayed.

She came beam onto the wind and I opened the engine throttle to full. Even under the tiny trisail we were hove down till the gunwales were under water, with the wind roaring out through the gap in the massive walls. Somehow we struggled into the outer harbour, but it was so dark, and the sea even in here so bad that Peter refused to believe we were in harbour. For a sickening moment we slithered sideways towards the eastern breakwater, where the sea was dashing with a nice line in demented fury, waiting to pound the boat and crew into matches and mince-meat. Then we seemed to find just enough power from the sails and engine and eased our way up against the gale, away from the wall.

After an exciting 10 minutes, we entered the inner harbour and tried to tie up alongside for the night. It was quite a party. None of us got much sleep, but we did better than most of the other yachts huddled there. On one boat a girl broke a finger, someone else had an arm severely wrenched, various masts were strained, topsides torn, in fact it was a real boat-builders' benefit night, with enough damage distributed throughout the fleet to keep a dozen shipwrights doing repairs for days ahead. Somehow we came through it all without more fuss than a bit of lost sleep.

Chapter Two

Naturally most heart-snatching moments occur in breezy weather. There was the occasion which we later called the 'Hatfield Roofs Squall' because the short sharp gale that dusted us also lifted off a whole row of roofs from some new houses in Hatfield. The newspapers made a great song and dance about it. We can confirm that they were not exaggerating, for once. It was indeed draughty.

It occurred in November. Most other yachts were laid up, but Morag and I went for a weekend cruise from Burnham-on-Crouch to the Blackwater and back, with a young married couple. On the Sunday, when we got up in the morning, we felt that maybe other owners had a certain basic wisdom, in that they were laid up. It was just a mite chilly. However we had a fine sail towards the Swin Spitway and the sun shone, so that we realised we were right after all, it was far too early to lay up. The boat behaved perfectly, the sky was clear, the sun gilded the sea, and the fresh wind flushed our cheeks.

It was when we were well on our way home that we noticed signs of excitement to windward. As we sailed up the River Crouch, a thin black cloud came towards us from the Kent shore. It looked like a heavy charcoal chalk mark, drawn by a giant hand across the sky. I'd seen nothing like it in Europe, and only in the Pacific once or twice. When it was fairly near us we saw a second, very similar.

We were in a very difficult position. To windward was a sandbank stretching miles behind us, and ahead till it met the low Essex shore. To leeward another hidden sandbank likewise lay in wait for any ship unlucky enough to blunder onto it. The channel between was about a quarter of a mile wide, and hardly marked at all. At least the buoys were there, but far too far apart, and not specifically on one or other side of the channel. Indeed it's no exaggeration to say that the buoyage into Burnham River is so bad that at least one cruiser goes aground every summer weekend, and plenty remain in the river almost permanently because of the navigational difficulties outside.

Before the squall hit us we got the mainsail well reefed down. With a lash and roaring hiss of rain mixed with wind, the cloud came overhead. The boat went over as if she had been swiped by a massive fist right in the middle of the mainsail. I scrambled forward along the wildly sloping side-deck, wondering if it would not be more sense to climb outside the life-line and walk along the topsides. They seemed more nearly horizontal than the deck. At the tiller Ron nursed the boat along as best he could. The two girls put their faces down below the cockpit coaming to try and get some protection. The wind seemed to throw razors at us till all exposed flesh was stinging raw.

By great good fortune we were abreast one of the buoys when the squall struck, and I determined to stick near this seamark till visibility improved. With the rain slashing down we could not see more than 50 yards, and had no wish to wander about till we thumped into a sandbank. Steering a compass course or sounding under those conditions would have called for more than skill.

The boat made it clear she wanted to either roar off at a high speed, or lay over and wallow. Ron was an experienced dinghy sailor, and he somehow managed to keep a balance between these two inconvenient extremes.

But every time the boat started to move away from our one link with geography we had to tack. The tide was running hard so that we were constantly being swept away into the murk. The one bright feature was that the waves were small. With the sand so close to windward, the sea could not get up.

If we missed stays and failed to tack we would sag off to leeward, onto the sandbank. If anything broke, if we made the smallest mistake, if anything went just a tiny bit awry, that sandbank lay in wait. Under any normal conditions one would just fight off to windward away from it. And this was just what we could not do, with no sea-room in any direction.

At last the rain eased. I could almost see again as the water stopped pouring down the inside and the front of my glasses. The girls emerged from their cocoons, the wind went down from hurricane to mere strong gale. We set off up river, watching the sky to windward very carefully. Other squalls came, but they were fleabites compared with their leader. Once safely between the river banks I went below.

The cabin was as neat as ever. Nothing had shifted from its stowage position. There was no more than the usual slop of water in the bilge. As usual the crew were a damn-sight more frightened than the boat.

Naturally most of the testing times come when the wind howls wild fandangoes in the rigging, but there are other emergencies too. There was that night off Berwick-on-Tweed.

Morag and I were moving from Essex to Glasgow to live. Naturally, we went by boat. We wanted to sail into Berwick-on-Tweed, and arrived off that harbour late one dark night. We had come in from seaward, having been out of sight of land for 36 hours. As we closed the coast we could see the town lights, which seemed to confirm our navigation, but we could not see the flash of the lighthouse on the breakwater. As this light has a range of 12 miles we were more than somewhat mystified. It is on a harbour wall, linked to the mainland, so it was unthinkable that the light would be out. The town lights showed we were much closer than 12 miles from the shore, so I drew the only possible conclusion: the north flowing tide must have been stronger than I thought, we must be off the next town to the north, Eyemouth. There are no towns for many miles to the south.

So we turned south, as we were determined to go into Berwick. I plotted a course to take us from off Eyemouth to get us opposite Berwick at dawn. It was glassy calm so we were under power. After a time I noticed the shore lights disappear, then the night seemed to get solidly, densely dark. Fog was shutting in all round. Morag went back to her bunk, and I stood at the tiller. Time passed. No stars shone through the almost tangible blackness. It was long past midnight, and I'd had little sleep the night before, in fact not much for a week.

Then, with clear certainty, I knew something was wrong. Desperately I tried to see, but there was moisture on my glasses. I snatched them off, but that made no difference. The thump of the engine prevented me hearing anything. I could not tell what the danger was, or where it was coming from. There were no controls from the engine to the helm, so I had to dive into the cabin to stop the engine. As its last beat died away I was back in the cockpit, with Morag, both of us straining to hear we knew not what. There was no need to strain, the sound came all too loud. Just ahead of the bow we heard the thunder of surf on rocks and the crying of wheeling gulls. We were right in, almost ashore, and to judge by the booming, pounding waves it was a wicked place to get caught.

In a bound I was below, whirling the starting handle. Heaven bless Listers and all their employees. As ever the engine chugged into forceful life at the first swing. Back at the helm, I wrenched the tiller over and headed due east, off into the safety of the deep North Sea. That doubly damned light off Berwick HAD been out. It was Berwick we saw in the first place. Our navigation had been spot on. Due to the faulty lighthouse, we had been rushing into the Holy Island shore.

What saved us? I think it was the boat. She started to heave and pitch just that fraction more, as we got into the shallow water. We knew each other well enough for that faint extra motion to be familiar to me. She knew we were heading for bad trouble, and in her own quiet efficient way she told me.

She had a remarkable ability of wiggling out of difficult situations, like a wild Welsh pony I used to ride which was too small to jump anything bigger than a sizeable molehill. So he used to scramble up, over and through, or round hedges, ditches, walls, fences, barricades, fallen trees, mountain sides, bogs, and any other obstruction to forward progress.

The *St Elizabeth* showed this sort of pertinacity one very windy weekend in December. As usual we seemed to be having a fine time cruising when almost everyone else was laid up ashore. There were three of us aboard, and we left Poole going like a rocket, downwind towards the Solent. We were well reefed down, and the boat was a delight to sail. I sat at the helm thinking how pleasantly warm it was, considering Christmas was only three weeks away. Andrew sat in the cockpit getting steadily sicker and sicker. He had never been sailing before, and by the colour of his face this would be positively the very last time.

Down below Martin was brewing up and making sandwiches as we foamed and rolled across Poole Bay. Poor Andrew looked so sorry for himself, I thought a little psychology might help him. If I could get him to take an interest in his surroundings perhaps he would snap out of his seasick stupor. So, from me with nauseating brightness:

'We're just getting over the Dolphin Bank.'

'Uh-huh.'

'Of course, it's not shallow on the bank. It's a submerged bank. Favourite place of fishermen.'

'Uh.'

'The only way we can notice we are on it is by watching the waves. They will get steeper over the bank.' (This was a highly inappropriate remark as Andrew obviously reckoned they were already too steep.)

'Uhhhhh.'

Not to be put off, I went on even more cheerfully:

'Oh! Look! There's one wave much higher than the rest, right astern.' Whereupon with a wild wet splosh the aforesaid wave reared up over our counter and came down on top of us. It swept sideways into the cockpit and left by the 'side door', taking Andrew with it. He grabbed the guard-rail wire (to this day I cannot fathom whether he went over the top or underneath it), I grabbed him and we both yelled to Martin.

Now we used to cruise the sensible way, with the dinghy on the cabin top, not towed astern. However this meant that the hatch would only slide open two thirds of its full travel. Martin was wearing three, or maybe four, sweaters under his oilskin, and he's no undersized person. So as he tried to fling himself out of the cabin to help us he jammed in the hatchway.

The situation just hung, suspended in time. Andrew clung, literally for his life to the thin wire life-line, being dragged through the water. I clung to Andrew with tortured fingers, holding the tiller with the other hand, trying to keep the boat going in the required direction. Martin wrestled to free himself.

I thought that if I rounded up into the wind the boat's acceleration might be too much for our hold, and Andrew would be wrenched free. So I just kept the boat going downwind. Martin only stuck for a tenth of a minute, or maybe a fifth. In that eternity the boat moved gently. She'd made it clear that we should have been wearing personal life-lines. We needed no further lesson, and she did not want to make the rescue impossibly hard.

Martin heaved himself on deck. One of his muscular hands seized Andrew by the collar and with a beautiful heave, Andrew swept up on deck. Poor wretched Andrew, he just sat in a collapsed heap, weak with sickness and exertion, shivering with the mid-winter cold and reaction.

'Get all those clothes off,' I tried to snap him out of it, 'take off everything and wrap yourself in the blankets. They're warm and dry. You can have my spare clothes, but first get warm.' Martin and I had to give a lot of help, getting the sodden clothes off. We tumbled the poor fellow into a bunk and there he stayed, through two or three crises, till a moment more hectic than average dragged him out again.

All the way up the Solent the boat went, after going through the Needles Channel without taking a drop of water on the deck. For a time the weather eased, though it still blew very smartly from the west. We decided to go into Portsmouth because it looked too threatening astern to continue sailing up the Channel comfortably.

As we rounded up for the approach to the harbour, black clouds came over very low. The wind hardened intensely, and the tide was flowing out against us. At this time we had no engine in the boat, and it looked as if we were in for a real battle to get in through the entrance.

We tried to nurse the boat at the helm, tried to keep her footing fast, without reaching off to leeward, tried to keep her pointing high into the wind. But the odds were too great. She just could not make progress against combined wind and tide. It was no place to anchor and wait for the tide to change, and after some agonising moments, when it looked as if we would be flung on the shore to leeward, I decided to run off to Bembridge. Here the wind would push us into the harbour, and by the time we got there the tide would be running slower.

To keep our speed within reason, I went forward to take in the jib. Having cast off the halliard I grabbed the flogging canvas. It lashed me across the face and tore my glasses off, though I always wore a lashing to keep them on. As the glasses flashed overboard to sink in about 6 fathoms, I saw all too clearly that we were now in a moderate mess. I knew the way into Bembridge, but not at all well. Martin was very unsure of the entrance. There was no chart of it aboard, and before the accident I had planned to go in using all the cunning I could. For instance, the way the waves break gives a clear indication of shallow water. Also though the buoys into Bembridge were, at that time, a law unto themselves, and not in accordance with international practice, I reckoned if we stuck close to them we would have enough water under the keel, even on the wrong side of the buoys.

As we approached Martin tried to explain the layout, and I peered vainly shorewards. I could see where the land ended and the sea began, but could not pick out a single buoy. Apart from the short-sightedness there was a naked feeling, as my eyes, used to being protected from the wind by their own private windscreens, felt the chill blast on them most keenly. After jilling about briefly, we decided that we would have to chance it. To windward another lot of vicious squalls were bearing down.

We sailed in on what we thought was the right bearing. The water was obviously shallowing, but neither of us knew which way to turn. Soon enough we thudded aground. Poor Andrew had not been warned of this likely contingency, and he reckoned that the end of the world had come.

There was so much surplus wind around, I decided we might make good use of some of it. As the boat bumped and floated, only to bump again, I brought her round beam onto the blast. We hove in on the main sheet, heeling the boat over as much as possible. This reduced her draught a lot. She slithered forward, still bumping a few times more, then we were in deep water and the rest was easy. Well, fairly easy.

It was clear that we wanted our best ground tackle to hold us in the harbour. As the boat was fresh from her maiden voyage across the Atlantic at this time, she had no chain pipe through the deck. Such a pipe would have been no use for the trans-Atlantic voyage, it would have been nothing more than an inlet for unwanted water. So as we came into the harbour we had to man-handle the chain up from below, through the main companion hatch, and onto the foredeck. One person had to steer, and so we had to bellow at poor Andrew to lend a hand.

This he did with difficulty, as he was still racked by seasickness. Next the reserve anchor, a massive piece of ironmongery, had to be hauled out of the fore-peak and lumped onto the foredeck. We selected a good berth, rounded up, and dropped anchor. This, we thought, was fine. Here we are, with masses of land between us and the source of this outrageous wind. We should lie here snugly. The sea in the harbour was windswept but not rough.

But the wind had other ideas. Without a pause the boat dragged straight off downwind. All our cable and the really heavy anchor were no use at all. The boat paused once or twice in mid-skid, but it was obvious that unless something radical was done, and that soon, we would be aground, and on a lee shore.

So Martin and I launched the dinghy. Into it we put all the warps that we could find, together with spare halliards, sheets, the lot. Then I rowed off up wind, battling against the gale, till I got to the beach on the windward side of the harbour. Here I tied our heaviest warp, and to it our second best, and so on. Then into the dinghy and back to the *St Elizabeth*. Martin and I took a firm grasp of the rope leading to the shore and HEAVED. Andrew was by now tottering about, so he came to help. Inch by inch we dragged the boat forward till she was in the middle of the fairway. None of us had the energy to pull her further. Our only trouble now was that we had our warp stretched halfway across the harbour, and anyone coming in or out after dark might run into it.

So we went below and fried up a great meal of sausages, before going ashore. Andrew would eat nothing. No doubt his stomach had been working so hard in reverse, the very thought of going into ahead gear was repugnant. Martin and I ate with that disgusting heartiness of people who have spent the whole day in the fresh, very fresh, air, and have laboured hard. We swooped through our own share and Andrew's too. Then we put Andrew ashore, whence he went home, and as far as I know he has never since set foot near anything that might under the remotest chance even try to float.

Martin and I tramped round the village trying to find out if there were any other maniacs afloat at this time of year. Of course none were. Only the pilot launch was likely to be afloat during the hours of darkness and we warned the crew.

All this may sound as if we were fooling around in what was only a capful of wind. But it truly was draughty. That same set of squalls hurtled on up Channel and sank the South Goodwin light-vessel, drowning all her crew. Only a visitor aboard, a bird-watcher, was saved. The loss of a light-vessel was almost unprecedented.

This and various other experiences helped to formulate in my mind the type of boat we wanted to succeed the *St Elizabeth*.

Chapter Three

If only a yacht was designed for one purpose, how relatively easy it would be. But in practice the designer's mind has to work like this:

Now we MUST have a fast boat. That means something long and narrow and deep. Of course she MUST be roomy, with lots of space inside, headroom, plenty of lockers and so on. That means to hell with narrowness, a wide beam is essential. Also she must be within the owner's financial means. He cannot afford a big boat, so she cannot be long. Also he wants to cruise in her, and this calls for a moderate draught, so that she can get in and out of little creeks and anchorages. So she simply cannot be deep.

Then of course she MUST have a big sail area, otherwise she will be dreary to sail in light winds. However as the owner will (particularly in our case) often be handling the boat alone, she must have a modest sail plan. For efficiency and economy she MUST be a sloop. Only the owner would not be able to handle either the big mainsail or the large jib without help, so she'll have to be a ketch, yawl or schooner.

When it comes to designing the cockpit the obvious thing is to have a long, narrow, shallow well. This will be very safe in wild weather, have lots of room beneath it for storage, the engine, maybe part of the galley and so on. However this sort of cockpit is no use for a family, who want a deep roomy well, so as to have protection from the weather, and safety, so that the children cannot fall out or get washed out. Or the adults too, for that matter.

As for the engine, a light, cheap petrol engine will give the boat the best performance under sail, and should suit us in so far as first cost is concerned. It will not take up much room, and as it weighs little, it will not require much effort to lift aboard when building. But for a number of first-class reasons we rejected a light, cheap petrol engine in favour of a heavy diesel.

And so it goes on. Every item and aspect of the boat is a compromise. Basically, we wanted a cruiser which I could handle by myself under any conditions of wind, weather and awkward situation. It had to be extremely inexpensive. As my sister and brother-in-law were to be part-owners and builders, it had to have enough room for them and their five children. As their children were very young, the boat had to have the ability to get into harbour each night, even against a foul tide and head wind.

Also young children do not like to sit still for hours on end. So the boat must contain space for playing. In the end we went to town here, so that the cockpit forms an outdoor play-pen, and the saloon an indoor one. Then at night, adults want to sit around a bottle and yarn, while the kids are asleep, so there must be a separate dormitory and day-cabin. The adults have to be able to sleep off a heavy lunch, when lazing on moorings while the children are playing, so it is no good having only children's berths in the dormitory. Besides, children grow up, so short, child-length berths are no use anyway. Especially when it comes to selling the yacht.

Most important of all, any boat of mine is a floating testbed. Even my battered conscience would not allow me to try out some of my wild schemes on friends' boats. Nor would the friends.

As for performance, naturally we hoped the boat would be able to get out of her own way, but she was not designed for racing. Of course the boat would be raced, but we were happy to rely on the handicapper and favourable wind shifts. Much more important, the boat should be a good-tempered cruiser. She must sail herself on several different courses relative to the wind. She must do this without recourse to expensive or complex gadgets. In the event, we succeeded here beyond our wildest dreams, and achieved self-steering beyond anything anyone we have met has ever encountered.

Above all we wanted comfort, so that the children would not be put off yachting. When they reached their teens they would no doubt be happy to withstand hardships in order to sail long distances, or to win races. But at this stage the great thing was to avoid putting them off the sport for life. Besides this, we had done enough sailing ourselves to realise that the sea would make things rugged enough, and the clever thing is to set out with the intention of being comfortable. It breeds efficiency, quite apart from the fact that sailing is not intended for purging the soul.

Having decided what the boat had to do, there was the problem of her type. She could be light displacement or heavy. She might follow the overwhelmingly strong trend found in the south of England that dictates that all cruisers shall be like ocean racers. She could be on the lines of an ocean cruiser, all ruggedness and safety factors. She might lean towards the American type, thoroughly beamy with a centreboard and acres of canvas.

In the end she was just ... herself. She is moderately heavy in displacement because this is the easiest and cheapest type to build. The craze for light-displacement yachts made sense, but it was virtually killed because few people could afford the high initial cost of the true lightweight yacht. To be successful a light yacht requires a very high standard of construction, with every piece of timber delicately shaped and pared away till nothing remains but a highly stressed and exactly proportioned piece of engineering in wood.

As I knew that I would have to do a lot of the work myself, and would be very pressed for time, I had to have a boat that would not be oversensitive to weight. If I was making a bunk front for instance and found that I only had available a piece of half-inch ply, then that must serve. When building a light-displacement boat it is essential not to make do with what is to hand, but to go out and buy the lightest material that can be relied upon to stand the strain. For a bunk front, a piece of quarter-inch ply will often be correct, which is of course only half the weight of the half-inch ply.

As the boat's home waters were to be the Clyde it was essential that she should suit the winds and seas thereabouts. Being so far north the winds tend to be cold, and are therefore denser than further south. This means that for a given wind-speed the pressure on the sails is greater. More important, the gaps between the high hills and mountains send down vicious gusts. So a boat that could stand up to a blast was essential.

This does not mean a boat with tiny sails. One like this would be helpless when in the lee of a hill. Between the strong gusts, and regularly when the weather is fine, the wind strength on the Clyde is light. So a stiff boat with a moderately big area of canvas was essential.

When it came to overall length, I decided that we would increase slightly on the *St Elizabeth*. In practice she was delightful to handle alone under all conditions, during the day or darkness, come calm, gale or torrential rain. So we decided on a waterline length of 25 feet, and an overall length of 35 feet 6 inches.

The beam is 9 feet 6 inches. This gives a lot of room below, but it is too much for fast sailing to windward in a rough sea. Never mind. Only clots go to windward when cruising. The draught is 5 feet, which is moderate, but more would have been difficult to build into the boat. Also it does mean that there are few harbours that we cannot enter or leave at any time.

So far there is nothing unconventional. However, when we come to the hull form we are plunged into controversy. We finally built a fin-keeled yacht. That is to say the hull was first built, like a large canoe, and the ballast keel, or fin, added later. By this means we hoped to save both time and expense. We knew we would sacrifice performance and perhaps a little comfort, but we hoped the former would not be marked, and by cunning we sought to circumvent the latter.

It is this way. A normal sailing yacht has a deep bilge, with the ballast keel tacked on below. When water gets into the hull it runs down into this bilge, and is eventually pumped out. The bilge water should, at least in theory, stay down well below the cabin regardless of the boat's behaviour. In practice there are those hectic occasions, when the sea fairly flings the boat about and the bilge-water slops away up the side of the boat. It wets the bedding, soaks clothes, ruins bread or cakes left unprotected in galley lockers and generally causes chaos. But this happens so seldom that no one worries much.

Now a fin-keeler has no deep bilge. The floorboards are only a few inches above the bottom of the bilge, so that even a few gallons of water inside the boat will soon make its presence felt. As the boat heels, the water creeps up the boat's side. Bedding left against the inside of the planking is soon sodden. The settee cushions soak up water like sponges. Clothing in lockers that run out to the ship's side blots up more water. Misery runs rampant through the boat.

We knew all about this trouble before we started and got round it by fitting thin sheets of ply inside the yacht's frames. This means that when she has a lot of water in her, she heels, as she heels, the water runs up the ship's side but it cannot do any damage as the ply keeps bedding, clothing and everything else away from the water. Also we fitted a really effective self-priming pump right in front of the helmsman. So whenever he has a moment he can give it a pull or three and this way keep the interior of the boat as dry as a drunk's throat on a Scottish Sabbath.

When we came to decide on the rig we did not hesitate. A ketch was the obvious answer. First, because this meant two small masts and a couple of short booms. As the former had to be made in our garden, and the latter in our hall, we were obviously limited by the space available. Also the completed spars had to be carried halfway across Dumbartonshire. When we started work on these long structures we had no idea how they would be carried to the boat, but we knew damn well that the shorter the spars, the easier the problem.

Also short spars mean small, and therefore easily handled, sails. Of course they likewise mean relatively inefficient sails, because a boat with two big sails goes faster than one having three or four smaller ones, assuming the total areas are the same. But we did not plan to go very fast anywhere, and we had one or two ideas to improve the sails' efficiency. For a start we used aluminium for the masts, so that they could be thinner and lighter than wooden ones. Also we put full length battens on the mizzen sail, so as to make it work better. The only reason many cruisers do not use these long battens is that they are very heavily penalised by the Royal Ocean Racing Club Rule for handicapping yachts. Why this should be is a mystery. Full length battens are a thoroughly seamanlike idea. They prevent a sail flapping, so lengthening its life and making it safe in a gale. Many a sail with the traditional short battens has flogged itself to tatters in seconds in bad weather. A fully battened sail cannot flog, so it does not shake itself to death.

Another great advantage of the ketch rig is that it is variable. As a result the boat can be made to sail herself. When one person is doing all the handling this is a great asset. He can leave the helm unattended to cook or navigate, to don oilskins, or peel off sweaters if the sun burns down, write the log, or amuse the children. It so happened we succeeded here beyond our wildest dreams. In the past I had got many boats to reach (at right angles to the wind) or beat (into the wind) without anyone at the helm. But without special gear no boat, to our knowledge, will run downwind. Within a few weeks of launching, Morag and I were alone aboard. I wanted to potter about the boat doing odd jobs. Morag wanted to sleep. Our course was downwind. Not expecting any success, I lowered the mizzen and left up only the main and jib. The wind was about force 3. I let go the tiller and the boat went straight on.

After a few minutes a packet-boat hurried past, leaving behind a lot of lumpety waves. I fully expected the *St Mary* to lurch off course, surge all over the place, then turn into the wind and stop. She did no such thing. As if on rails, she sailed straight on. It was thoroughly and utterly satisfying. After 3 miles, and in spite of the wash from other craft, as well as a little sea thrown up by shoal water, the *St Mary* was still going straight as a die. It's for occasions like this that naval architects live. There's nothing quite so wonderful as achieving infinitely more than one dares to hope for. She did not even need the tiller lashed.

When designing the boat, above all I wanted a yacht to be proud of. A boat that would invite voyaging. One that would laugh at rough weather, a fighting boat, a boat that might throw up acres of spray, might roll, would perhaps slam and crash her way along, but would never falter, never break down, never lie helpless when a screaming squall lashed us. And she had to do this when being handled by one person only.

Knowing my own limitations, which include under-average height, weight and strength, knowing just how suddenly dangerous a situation can be if the only person on deck gets hurt, or makes a mistake, I decided that we needed a fool-proof, gale-proof, reliable boat.

This was very hard to reconcile with another requirement. I wanted to try out a couple of dozen ideas. These included amateur-made aluminium masts, hollow booms with the topping lifts and reefing gear inside, an aluminium cabin top, a cockpit without fixed seats, a double berth right forward, wooden topmasts for the halliard sheaves, an engine accessible from the top and both sides as well as the forward end, a fully battened cruising sail, very light springy battens for bunk bottoms to give extra comfort, a patent type of window-edge seal much used in vehicles which I suspected might not stand up to hard-weather seagoing conditions, a molybdenum-disulphide-impregnated nylon rudder strap which I hoped would never wear out itself or the rudder, halliard winches with self-lubricating ferrobestos drums, and so on and on and on.

Added to all this there were fifteen years' cruising experiences to be packed into this boat. All the time I was drawing the plans my memory served up little cameos ...

'Remember that time,' it would say, 'that you and Elizabeth made a record passage from Ouistreham to Portsmouth? At least it would have been a record, for the dear old *Finetta* sailed flat out all night till you got off the Nab Tower. Then it got too damn squally and it took you an hour and a half to reef.' *Finetta* was a converted 6-metre, with the original enormous mainsail, far too big for swift reefing in the grim hours before dawn, using old-fashioned gear.

Or the occasion you took out a farmer and his wife in their misbegotten old tub. The boat had a bad reputation, which no one thought of mentioning. She carried weather helm, would not obey, was cramped, ugly, a thorough bitch. By a stroke of luck she carried away a shroud, and instead of mending it and carrying on, it was made the excuse to pack up and go home. Quite right too, that boat would kill her crew given half an opportunity.

A boat which taught me more than most was Mike Pruett's *Black Soo*. She was fast, almost immorally so. She had a speedometer calibrated up to 20 knots. Sailing through the tail of Portland Race with a power of wind astern, we whipped that speedo up to 18 knots, time and time again. Then the skipper took the helm, spat on his hands metaphorically, and really sailed. In no time he got her properly travelling, roaring in a fantastic plane, with the bow wave flung crosstrees high; the speedo surged up and up, then dropped as we fell into a hollow. There was a whoop from the skipper:

'Here's a big wave,' and we were OFF. The speedo needle whammed round to the end-stop at 20 knots and fell back broken. The owner was a wonderful ship-driver. In the 1957 Fastnet, going to windward against half a gale through the Needles Channel witnesses from other boats said they gave up praying for themselves to spare a thought for us. Describing it later someone wrote ... 'the triumph of mind over matter' for she was little more than an overgrown plywood dinghy and she was just HAMMERED. We put into Weymouth with the mast-step snapped clean through. I went round tightening the rigging screws, for the mast had dropped a couple of inches. In fact it was impossible to tighten the rigging properly, as the rigging screws could not take in all the slack of the shrouds. The mast had dropped too far. We set out again after a sleep to try and batter round the Fastnet Rock. As usual I was sick and sick and sick again, but by the time we were off Cornwall that was over. The cook wondered why I wolfed my food, not understanding what it's like to work hard day after day and keep no food down. We cleared Land's End and it was my watch below. I went forward to sleep, it was drier there. After a time the boat started to pound. She came right clear of the water forward and thudded down. Then up to the next crest and CRASH into the trough. Lying curled up on a heap of sail bags I found myself airborne in every crest. Too exhausted to crawl aft, I stayed there and tried to mentally redesign the boat to ride easier under these conditions. It kept my mind off some of the cracks I'd noticed in the structure. At the midnight forecast more gales were promised, and the skipper decided we could not stand more risks, so we retired. It was the right thing to do, but a bitter blow after taking all that punishment. No boat I've ever sailed in gave more thrills or went so fast. But then one paid and paid and paid again for the fun.

Black Soo is a hard chine, very light-displacement boat. Experience in her made me admire the type but realise that they have their limitations. On the other hand a single wonderful race in the conventional ocean racer *Pym* showed up other lessons just as important, and this time not so relentlessly driven home.

Again I was sick before anyone else, and one of the last to stop being sick. But on this spacious, light airy yacht, with full headroom everywhere, it was easy to be seasick and still carry on. Well, fairly easy. Also though her sails are much larger than *Black Soo*'s her foredeck is wider, longer, well wired in, and easier to work on. Besides this she kept up a good average speed, though she did not take off on those wild wonderful breathless planing surges that just went on and on, pure high velocity speed boating under sail.

Another thrilling offshore race, in the American *Carina II*, brought home once more the advantages of comfort at sea. Again it was a question of keeping up a high average speed rather than a spectacular speed on one point of sailing. This yacht was superbly fitted out. She had just about everything and in triplicate. She even carried double sheets so that if one broke the other was right on the job. It's also a help when sheeting in hard, though I never saw the tough, experienced crew use the two sheets at once. Because the galley was thoughtfully laid out, everyone ate magnificently. Even me, between the usual bouts of seasickness. On this ship once again I learned that if everything is properly arranged then even a seasick man can and will do his share of work at the right time, without wasting time, and without mistakes.

Back over the previous fifteen years, there were cruises and races in a useful variety of boats. In one, a midget, we slept on the floorboards. Also she leaked. One night before turning in I was brewing up a milk drink. In the sea-way I spilt the primus so that milk and paraffin went into the bilge. We slept like logs that night and woke in the morning to find that the water had leaked in to the level of the floorboards. My face was partially immersed in a mixture of sea-water, paraffin and milk.

Then there was the wild *Red Angel*. She had no engine and to get back to work on Monday morning we drove her through the night, Sunday after Sunday. As a result, we were exhausted every Monday. And Tuesday, Wednesday and often Thursday for that matter. I was apprenticed at the time, and had to be at work by 7.30 a.m. so we often got virtually no sleep by arriving on the mooring around dawn on Monday mornings. Once I remember sailing up the complex Poole main channel and falling asleep between each buoy. My head, cradled on the dew-soaked side-deck, would raise itself wearily, glance at the next buoy, pull the tiller round till we faced it, then slump down again. Somehow we held our course without grounding, though it must have been a hectic time for guardian angels.

As I mulled over the design of the *St Mary*, all these cheerful and grim times influenced every line. The time we had to cram two in each saloon settee berth on the *Rosalind*, hove-to all through 50 hours of gale, with the deck forward leaking so badly that the forward berths were untenable, the way the ex-6-metre *Finetta* used to drive right through the wave-tops, without going over them, so that green deep water tumbled along the decks and torrented into the vast open cockpit faster than we could pump it back where it belonged; her enormous mainsail which scared the living daylights out of everyone within 4 miles around every time a squall hit us; the half-decker *Silver Wave*'s inability to stand on her feet in heavy weather, she made life awkward as she needed constant bailing after I'd botched up her frightful damage received in the first gale of the season. I was determined not to miss a day's sailing and too hard-up to get anyone else to put the trouble right competently. If she was not bailed constantly she sank, if she was, the absence of crew's weight to windward made her roll slowly but relentlessly over.

Our boats, friends' boats, rivals' old barges, good ones, lousy ones, fast ones, slow and dreadfully tedious boats, power, sail, oars, over-canvassed, under powered, beauties, bitches, death-traps and stodgily safe-as-church boxes, ply crates, cans, alloy machines, for racing, cruising, or built for just plain boozing, they all taught something. And each one contributed to the final design of the *St Mary*.

Chapter Four

Once the hull was started down at Helensburgh, I worked there every Saturday and Sunday. At first Morag was with me, but boat building, both amateur and professional, has an infinite variety of occupational hazards.

One evening Morag announced she was going to have a baby. Of course I was delighted. However, it made hay of our neatly worked-out plans and schedules as far as the boat was concerned. On the other hand it suddenly made the boat vastly more satisfactory. The design was largely influenced by the fact that my sister had four children who would want to use the boat. What suited them would be right for our own offspring too.

In passing it must be noted that boat building is quite unlike any other occupation. Consider just this aspect of the *St Mary*. We had no sooner started building her than we find our first baby on the way. Within a few weeks my sister announces that her fifth will be due in the autumn. George, the shipwright, gets presented with one within a few months of starting work on the boat. The painter, Walt, likewise has an increase in the family. So does John, one of the firm's partners. Out of the blue, Don, the other partner finds his wife knitting wee bootees after a lapse of about nine years. Then the owner of another boat in the same shed wandered too near the *St Mary* and the following spring he was given another cot-full by his wife.

One has to contend with this sort of thing apart from more sedentary hazards like delays in the delivery of material, equipment lost on the railway, and power tools which break down. One ghastly afternoon I cut a piece of timber on the bandsaw. Having finished with the tool I turned off its motor, and walked away. Behind me there was a crash, and turning back I saw that the blade had snapped. George put a new blade in the saw, with me standing by trying to help. Later I cut another bit of timber. Exactly the same thing happened. Two blades within an hour, and there was only one left. If that broke the whole job would be held up.

Then there was the 'stopping' between the planks. Each plank does not fit tight up against its neighbour, except on the extreme inner side. On the outside the planks have a long groove between each adjacent pair. Into this groove caulking cotton is hammered. The groove is not entirely filled with the cotton, on top goes the stopping. Now there are dozens of different types of stopping. Some are secret mixtures. Some are plain glaziers' putty. Some work well. Others crack or drop out. Some will not take a coat of paint. Still others stain paint, while some are complex chemicals which have to be mixed before insertion. None are perfect, and we decided to try a new one made by a reputable firm. It was a ghastly failure. It was not supposed to go hard and dry, but to retain just a little softness so that it would ease and stretch just minutely, as the timber of the planks swelled out or shrunk. This they would do according to the air temperature, or much more importantly, according to the amount of moisture in the timber.

Our fancy stopping did just what it was supposed to avoid at all costs. It went hard as cement. It cracked away from the planks. It refused to smooth off, nor would it retreat back into the seam when the seam opened a fraction. This was one of the experiments that did not come off.

Another hazard was the weather. It could not have been worse, alternating between dry warm windy spells and prolonged rain. The dry intervals sucked all the moisture out of the timber as we built, so that we had constantly to guard against cracking. I slobbered linseed oil on the oak of the backbone but this only checked the trouble, and did not cure it completely. Also it was just one more extra job, and right from the start we were constantly battling to try and keep up to schedule. The frequent rain was a setback in another way. Our garden sprouted weeds, the lawn and hedge grew and grew. As we had moved into the house only eighteen months before and found the garden in good order, we strove intermittently but desperately to keep the place at least neat, and not let the jungle encroach too far.

The net result was one long, and at times completely exhausting, battle with time. After spending Saturday morning in the office I would dash home as early as my conscience would allow, snatch lunch, thunder at full throttle down to Helensburgh, work through the afternoon, hurtle back home to a meal, then to the typewriter or drawing board. Sunday was the same, without the morning hours in the office, but instead with an occasional tilt at the garden or other domestic matter.

Every evening saw the typewriter hammering its heart out, for there were dozens of letters to write, apart from the occasional magazine article which I tried to squeeze into the schedule. So many items had to be ordered, and each order meant getting estimates from different firms. Some firms would not reply till prodded. Others quoted but did not state whether delivery cost was extra, which could make all the difference. On plenty of occasions manufacturers did not have just what I wanted, so we wrote to and fro discussing the virtues of alternatives. A yacht is a mass of bits and pieces, being at once a home, a ship, and a racing machine. Added to this a break-down cannot be put right by anyone but those on board. So there must be complete reliability to avoid breakdowns, coupled with spares and equipment to make the craft self-contained.

So letters poured out to makers of masts, echo sounders, carpets, sails, nails, ropes, shackles, sinks, aluminium sheeting, iron castings, stoves, cushions, and so on, at great length. To add to the complications, 1960/61 turned out to be a boom year for yacht chandlers and their ilk. They had more orders than they could handle. Some were evidently overwhelmed, and delays in replying to letters were only exceeded by delays in sending material.

One upholstery firm sent in a quotation three months after the order had been placed with a more business-like concern, which in turn was a month after the specification first went out for quotation. As I was too busy to visit timber yards to select wood, we had to accept whatever they sent in answer to our orders. When they sent a dud piece of mahogany it happened to be, inevitably, a vital plank that we were desperately waiting for.

To add to our problems, Arden Yachts was not like a long-established yard. There was no large reserve of fastenings, no stores full of items discarded from other craft, or bought but not used. There had not even been enough time to build up stocks of common-place spares, screws or off-cuts of timber. We tried to foresee every need, tried to predict, down to the last tiny nut, just what would be wanted. But this is virtually impossible, especially when time is short, when the boat is unusual, when so many situations could not be foreseen. Boat building is not only a series of loosely-linked crises, it is also a succession of snags.

The basic job of building a boat is quite simple. A backbone is made by bolting together long lengths of timber. These have to be shaped and then recessed or 'rabbeted' to take the ends of the planks. This backbone is erected, and this gives the first impression of the final size of the yacht. Next the moulds, sometimes called 'shadow sections' are put up. These are frames of rough timber, spaced every 3 or 4 feet from the bow to the stern. When they are up it is possible to gauge the final shape of the craft, though to do this effectively requires a good few years experience. Next stringers are nailed longitudinally, so that at this stage anyone with half an eye can see what the final hull-form will be.

Now comes one of the exciting jobs, the timbering. The *St Mary* was built with no solid frames cut to shape. All her frames were put in a steam box, batches at a time. When they were heated right through, they were taken out, one by one, and quickly bent in place. The hot steam makes the thin laths of oak, 1 inch thick and 1¼ inch wide, bend like stiff rubber. Provided the frame is forced into place before it can cool, it takes relatively little effort to force it into a sweeping curve round the yacht's hull from keel to gunwale (as the upper edge of the hull is called). In many boatyards, four or five men do this work on a boat like ours. We planned to do it one weekend when there was a group of us available. But that human dynamo George could not wait for the weekend. With one completely inexperienced apprentice he tackled the job with his usual whirlwind energy. It took him less time than it takes many yachtyards with a full team of shipwrights. I was sorry to miss the excitement, but it was a most thrilling moment to arrive one Saturday afternoon to find the boat already had the first few planks on. The frames nestled in place as if they had been there for weeks.

Planking comes next and this is a long job. No plank is parallel sided, nor is it straight. The first one, which goes on at the bottom, must fit along the keel. Its upper edge tapers towards each end. Skill and artistry are needed to get the correct taper, and there is virtually no science involved in this stage of boatbuilding. The second plank up must lie exactly along the first, so the second plank has its lower edge shaped to conform to the first plank. The upper edge tapers, again the builder's skill and experience tell him how much the plank must taper.

This vital tapering of each plank comes about this way. The girth, or distance round the tummy of the boat, is not the same all along. At the bow she is narrow, and likewise at the stern. However, amidships the boat has a goodly bulk. Now on each side of the boat there are some twenty-five or so planks. The same number of planks is found at the bow, amidships and stern. As the girth is much greater amidships, naturally the planks have to be wider here. So far so complicated. But life is much more awkward than this simple theoretical explanation. For a start the garboard plank, that is the very lowest, and maybe one or two above the garboard, do not always extend right from bow to stern. The builder knows this, and knowing it, he has to allow for it. He has to ensure not only that the planks fit the boat exactly, but also the planks must sweep in a fair and attractive curve. It is here that the good boat builder excels. Each of his planks is a delightful shape, it is somehow just right. A second-rate builder finishes up with one or maybe half a dozen planks that look distorted. Until his boat is painted, and often even then, his hull looks twisted, ugly, contrived. Sometimes, in boatyards where there are enough men to have one squad working one side of the boat, and another gang planking the opposite side, the two sides of the boat will look a different shape. In fact they may be identical, and after painting be satisfactory, but before painting the distorted planking on one side may give the highly disconcerting impression that the two sides of the vessel are different.

Once the planking is complete the beam shelves go in. These are long pieces, like deep thick planks, extending the whole distance from bow to stern inside the boat at the top edge. As their name implies, the beams lie on them. However, it is no use just dumping the ends of the beams on the shelves. Even screwing them down is insufficient. Each beam end has to be dove-tailed into the shelf, as well as screwed.

The reason for this is that a boat is not like a house, or even a car. It does not sit still, ever. Nor is it subjected to simple vibration or bumps, such as affect road vehicles. A boat is HAMMERED. She is shaken, POUNDED, thrown about, BATTERED by waves, she judders and shudders when a fierce wind makes the sails flap like demented demon ghosts. Sailing hard to windward puts ferocious distorting strains on a yacht that try to twist her. Indeed, some lightly built yachts do actually writhe and visibly alter shape as they sail up and over wave crests, to plunge into the moving, yawning hollow beyond. The stress on a yacht driving relentlessly to windward is cruel because it is a jerking, reversing, highly variable force.

The motive power, which is the wind, acts high up the mast. The bulk of the yacht is far below the point where the wind's pressure acts on the sails. And several feet below the surface is the massive force of the ballast keel which tries all the time to wrench the hull upright. No wonder some yachts leak even when brand new. It's not surprising that after several hundred miles of intensive sailing against the breeze even well-built yachts creak and grind, sometimes crack planks and frames, tear structure and fittings, and sometimes even come home slightly but noticeably altered in shape.

Admittedly these are extreme cases, but it is essential to build a yacht bearing in mind all the time that the sea and the weather are quite without friends and never give favours. They find out weaknesses far more effectively than any human being. I often think, when surveying a yacht on shore, that to do my job properly I ought to launch the boat off, and thrash her to windward for a couple of hundred miles in half a gale. During that time I would learn whether the boat was well built in the first place and still well maintained. The only snag to this ingenious scheme is that a dud boat would neatly drown me in the course of proving her poor condition.

So all through the course of building the *St Mary* we regularly put in that extra screw, made things just a fraction stronger than pure science would dictate, and whenever there was a tiny doubt that a part was perfectly capable of its job we reinforced it. As a result, when a brutal squall howls out of the darkness on a black gale-torn night we have confidence that at least the boat will hold together, even if our nerves don't.

Chapter Five

One of the big factors in ensuring the stiffness and rigidity of the new yacht was her decking. This is of plywood, laid on in big pieces. Not only is this entirely leak-proof, it also makes it well-nigh impossible for the boat to wrack, at least in a horizontal plane. The old method of decking was to lay long narrow strips of timber, teak for the wealthy, pine for the poor, fore and aft on the beams. The trouble with this method is that the deck planks move fractionally, one against the other. This movement is very slight indeed. But even a brand new well-constructed boat suffers this movement of one deck plank against its neighbour. As there would be about fifty deck planks across the yacht, the tiny movement between adjacent planks is multiplied by fifty. This amounts to a sizeable distortion, and leaks are one of the consequences.

On top of the ply we glued plastic sheeting called Trakmark. This looks like canvas with a skin of polythene on the top surface, the polythene having a small diamond pattern. However, I will not describe Trakmark in this way, as the makers are bound to write and tell me it is nothing of the sort. Suffice to say that we chose a light grey colour for our Trakmark and prayed for fine weather.

Why? You ask. Well, Arden Yachts were far too busy building boats to fiddle on with mending leaks in the roof. So when it rained very hard, which was a frequent occurrence throughout our saga, we suffered drips all over the boat. Some drips were of the proportions of a mountain burn, and of course it is essential to glue Trakmark down to a perfectly dry deck.

For the gluing we assembled a goodly crowd, but George was not among them, as he was busy on another job. With precise care we cut our Trakmark to fit the boat's deck, leaving a small margin all round to be trimmed off later. By taking care we were able to cut the cloth so that there were very few joins. But this meant that each piece was large. In fact almost the whole boat, apart from the stern, was covered with two pieces of Trakmark, one to port, one to starboard.

These great long lengths of material were lifted off the boat, and laid, upside down, on the floor of the building shed. The next ploy was to smear the whole of the plywood deck, and then the underside of the Trakmark, with adhesive. This latter is a super sticky substance, rubbery, tacky, tenacious, gluesome and goosome, the very devil to handle. We had no sooner started spreading it on the Trakmark than a clumsy boy decided to carry buckets of water to and fro, for some obscure reason. Every time he lurched past us he slopped water everywhere. Then a dog thought it would be fun to investigate. Added to this the shed was, every weekend, thick with children. Apart from the boatyard partners' many children, all the owners of boats laid up in the shed seemed to be well endowed by nature. They all wanted to look and got too close. Naturally a brisk wind sprang up to blow shaving all over the half-dried glue as well.

Our next problem was to lift the length of Trakmark, some 32 feet long, turn it over without touching anything, carry it to the boat, lift it up to the height of the deck, say 10 feet off the ground and lay it exactly in place, since it could not be misplaced by a fraction of an inch. Once that Trakmark is down it's there to stay, one cannot have second thoughts and lift it up to restick it inwards or outwards just a hair. This operation makes such minor skirmishes as the Normandy landings, the building of the Forth Bridge, or the Exodus from Egypt pale into insignificance. The sheer organisation, coordination, cooperation, skill, timing, forethought, engineering, planning and other allied skills which went into that job cannot be described. Suffice to say that those that lived to see the first piece of Trakmark laid (and I had no time to count the casualties as they fell off the scaffolding round the boat or got trodden under foot) will forever say, as they bare their scarred arms, 'I was there that day ...' and then they will launch off into the saga, to the intense boredom of their grandchildren.

Consider some of the difficulties. If the sticky substance touched ANYTHING, it stayed there. Clothes, dogs, children, flesh or hair, nothing was immune. How was this great glue-encrusted Chinese dragon to be held without the fingers becoming inextricably held in the relentless glue-grip? We found out the hard way. At the height of the crisis, George came to help with his apprentice, Jim. This event is roughly comparable to Blücher's arrival at the crisis of the battle of Waterloo. I don't recall what appropriate phrase Wellington unleashed but he can have been no more relieved than I, as I gasped out:

'Get hold of the bloody thing there George, and don't let it touch a blind thing. No JIM! HERE, for the love of Neptune ...' and so on, in a completely unprintable vein. Crisis piled on crisis. While spreading the glue Morag was affected by the fumes, for it is a most volatile substance. Still reeling from this gas attack she was gamely battling along with the rest of us when her rubber gloves became inextricably glued up. All this of course perched aloft in the narrow plank supported on the trestles round the boat.

By super-human effort we got the forward end of the Trakmark in place, but as we worked our way aft, sticking it down foot by foot it became obvious that we had misjudged. The strip of material was at a tiny angle to the centre line and when we reached the aft end we would be adrift. With desperate energy we pulled the Trakmark off the deck. It cannot be done but it was. The two glued surfaces fought grimly to hold together but somehow we wrenched them apart. With pounding hearts and straining muscles the Trakmark was relaid along the correct line.

We stood back to survey the battlefield. We had definitely won. There, down the length of the deck stretched the smooth dove-grey expanse of almost wrinkleless Trakmark. With rollers we eased the last few lumps, caused by air-bubbles in the glue, out at the edge of the Trakmark. So far so good, apart from the fact that we were obviously doing the job the wrong way.

In most well-conducted battles the troops are allowed a rest between the fiercer spells of fighting. Boat building against the calendar allows no such relaxation. At once we tackled the other side of the deck. Only this time the tactics were different. George was in on the second half from the ground floor and he made this point:

'It's much easier if you spread the glue on the bottom of the Trakmark and let it get thoroughly dry. Then roll the Trakmark into a sausage, lift it onto the deck and unroll it in place.'

This sounded to me a lot of tripe. Attractive tripe, admittedly, but I found it hard to believe that if the Trakmark were rolled up like a Swiss roll, the glue being the jam, that it would ever unroll. It sounded fantastic that the top wearing surface of the Trakmark would not stick to the glue. I reckoned that glue would stick to a rainbow. I said something to this effect. George displayed patience:

'The secret is to let the glue dry. The glue on deck must be nearly dry too. The two glue surfaces will stick very well even though virtually dry. Here! Let's try.'

So we did, and it all went as George said, which was a lot simpler than the first round, if rather duller. Till the end. We had almost finished, when we found that up forward the Trakmark was not lying correctly. Hell and Brass buttons! We grabbed at the edge of the covering before it could stick fast and eased it up, then relaid it, but in the excitement a tear appeared. George was straining the Trakmark into place and I was just behind him. I saw the tear, and tried to stop it. Before I could do anything the rent was 6 inches across.

Everyone was very pleasant about it:

'It will never show.'

'You can only see it if you know where to look.'

'Look, lets put a drop more glue under it. Then with a couple of tacks it will stay down fine.'

But I was in no mood to be consoled. We had so damn nearly won. It's thoroughly satisfactory to do a good job well, and to get within seconds of finishing and have that tragedy flung at us was frustrating. For a few minutes I thought about it, then had a good idea; later we fitted a wide mahogany king plank over the central join in the Trakmark and by virtue of its width it covers the tear.

Chapter Six

Building a boat is like digging a hole in the road. Everyone reckons that they personally could:
1. Do it better.
2. Do it quicker.
3. Do it neater.
4. Do it with less noise.
5. And less fuss.

They also feel it is essential to tell everyone on the job how it should be done, how they saw it done back in 1926, how it is done in Eastern Patagonia, how old McSwithers did it, and just how wrong it is now being done.

Fortunately I've met this situation before, more than once. I have one or two fairly effective counter-attacks, which includes such comments as:

'Oh, that old-fashioned method. That went out before the war.'

'Most interesting, but this boat is for a different purpose.'

'You don't say? But then it wouldn't do for racing (or cruising, or under power, or any other damn thing, preferably something I was sure the other fellow knew nothing about).'

Most effective of all, and one ploy which I used more than once was:

'That's most interesting. Do show me how. Here's all the tools you need.' And after watching for a minute or two I'd go on with another job, leaving the erstwise hinderer now a helper.

Another counter-attack which went off well was on a party which poured aboard uninvited, including a woman in a fur coat. 'Careful how you go,' I said brightly, 'or our wet varnish will be spoilt by having fur all over it.'

On the other hand we genuinely did want a great deal of help to get the boat finished in time for the sailing season. With that merciless callousness which all boats breed in their owners I went round my friends and lured them down to help in their own sphere. One came to do the electrical wiring of the engine. Another, most knowledgeable in all things concerning aluminium, spent a whole day painting. I was able to get unlimited valuable advice from him about the cabin top and masts, while he laid the paint on and I worked alongside. He even brought his wife down to paint too. By nightfall I could see she would never again complain that housework is hard work. Casual acquaintances, friends, students, my partner, his son, no one escaped the net. Anyone rash enough to mention within my hearing that he was interested in boats, or did a bit of work about the house, was roped in.

My mother came to spend a week with us. Most of it was used in working on the boat. She took up yachting when we got our first cruiser, a converted 6-metre. This high velocity thoroughbred was very, very hard work to sail aboard. As a cruiser it was wildly exciting, but wickedly uncomfortable. There was no headroom, no water tank, just a big heavy steel can, only a primus to cook on, the berths were often damp and sometimes sodden, the deck leaked, both hatches let in more water than a large bath-tap. The pump was a killer to operate and it frequently needed energetic use, in a moderate breeze the sailing angle was such that comfort sitting or standing was impossible. But how we loved that boat. She was the fastest piece of wood for miles around. She would shift in only a gentle zephyr and in a brisk breeze she was a whirlwind. However she was no boat for a mother of a nineteen-year-old boy newly taken up sailing. In spite of this my mother came with us weekend after weekend, hauling sheets, cooking, keeping us awake as we fell asleep over the helm late on Sunday night after trying to go too far between Friday night and Monday morning.

On one occasion we were racing from Poole to Yarmouth. It was a beat and blowing hell's delight. As usual we had too much sail up because we did not know any better. When we got to the Needles Channel the seas were fearsome. But the boat cared for nothing, she just shot along, leaping the troughs and hurling herself through the crests. As a result the water ran deep, solid green along the deck and cascaded into the big open cockpit. A young friend, knowing precious little about sailing like myself was the only other crew apart from my mother. He and I took turns to steer and pump. But the pump would not keep pace with the inflow, and the water got deeper and deeper in the cabin. My mother looked at all this and decided some action was required. So she stood at the forward end of the cockpit, facing aft to act as a human breakwater. This way she stopped a lot of water getting into the cockpit, though many of the waves broke over her shoulders. At first I was decidedly worried, but I brightened up when my mother said: 'I like being with you, then I know you're all right.'

In those days we really knew very little about sailing indeed. For instance we thought that it would be a good idea if my mother wore a naval duffle-coat rather than oilskins, as we imagined it would keep her warmer, and be more comfortable. As a result she was soon wearing a completely sodden mass of wool. In fact when we got into harbour and she took it off, it was so saturated it was too heavy for her to lift.

Throughout the whole *St Mary* project we were very dependent on our many helpers. A yacht this size built professionally takes something like 4,000 to 5,000 man-hours to complete. Naturally I could not manage all those hours myself, even if I spent every waking hour on the job. As I had to do a week's work, keep a garden roughly in order, write articles, finish a book, paint our kitchen and do other incidental work about the house which became essential, there was a limited time available for boat building. Of course George and his apprentice did a vast amount of work, but on the whole job I spent more man hours than either of them, quite apart from drawing the plans and doing the secretarial side of the job.

In some ways we saved a lot of time on the building by cutting out complicated ideas, simplifying where we could, and inventing easier, quicker methods of doing things. But against this the amateurs on the job naturally took longer than a professional would. Also there were the experimental ideas incorporated in the boat, such as the rather elaborate hollow booms, which took up a lot of time. Nothing actually beat us, but there were some worrying moments, when I wondered if I was not being too ingenious.

Drawing the plans took a great deal more time than it usually does for a yacht of this size because almost nothing was standard. Normally fittings like the gooseneck, which join the boom to the mast, are bought from a yacht chandler. Our metal fittings were first drawn out, then studied to see how they could be made simpler from the fabrication point of view, then redrawn where necessary and finally sent off to my brother-in-law for making.

Even things like the stanchions to carry the lifelines round the deck were specially drawn out. And if there is one job that no one can really speed up, it is drawing plans. Added to this, the stream of correspondence which any boat generates is colossal.

A yacht is at once a sporting vehicle, a home and a ship. She has all the attributes of these things, and each is complex in itself. Thus for a home one needs a kitchen with all its gear and gadgets, sleeping accommodation, complete with mattresses and bedding, as well as somewhere to stow clothes, somewhere to put the bedding during the day, and so on. Every piece of gear has to be made or purchased. And before it is made the various materials all have to be ordered and bought.

Fortunately the yachting industry is one of the friendliest there is. Plenty of manufacturers went to great lengths to make sure we got just what we wanted, and in time. But we had to fight to persuade others to sell us their products. A case in point was the plastic water-can. When it was obvious that we would not have time to install a water tank in the boat, complete with its piping and pump in the galley, we decided to make do, for a season or two, with a plastic 2-gallon water jerrican. I went to a yacht chandler which advertises many products, including 2-gallon plastic jerricans. I was actually buying other gear, and when I reached the end of my list I was asked if there was anything else I wanted.

'Yes,' I replied, 'I need a 2-gallon plastic jerrican.' They were very apologetic, but they had none. I turned to go, but just then someone rushed up with just what I wanted. It was dusty and everyone was apologetic about this, explaining that the can had been lying under a heap of other gear. Then someone said:

'You'll need more than one jerrican on a boat like yours. Let me fetch another for you.'

'No thank you, we plan to keep a few ordinary bottles full of water. With this container that should be ample.'

'Oh, but you MUST have two cans. Here, wait a minute and I'll go and get another.' And before I could stop him he was off to fetch it. A few minutes later he came back, breathless and apologetic:

'I'm so sorry. But we haven't got any more in stock.' 'That's all right,' I told him, 'as I don't want a second,' and I turned to go. I was just starting the car outside the chandler's when one of their assistants rushed out:

'It's all right. We've found a big pile of plastic jerricans lying under a bench which no one knew anything about'.

'Thank you very much, but I honestly don't want any more. One is quite sufficient,' and I quickly drove off before the farce could reach another climax.

In contrast was Gordon Hindmarsh. A few years ago he bought an old boat called *Wayward Lass*. She was in a desperate condition but he worked on her with that intense single-mindness that grips small-boat owners. He transformed her from a scarcely floating wreck into a smart yacht, complete with tiddly teak rail all round. The teak was from a ship which was broken up, and it make me covetous. I asked Gordon to get me some teak, if he could, from a ship-breaker's.

Two days later he reappeared at our office with two fine teak doors, thick and heavy. At that time our office was very high up, with no lifts, and I had to carry the doors up an infinity of stairs. However, by this time I was beginning to get fit with the hard work at the weekends and most evenings. My precious teak cluttered up the office for several days, then I brought the car in, and had to lug what felt like twenty hundredweights of teak down all the stairs and half a mile to the only place in Glasgow where I had been able to find a parking space.

Next I discovered that a sports car is not designed to carry doors. However the long-suffering vehicle somehow managed to take the load, and for once we went home at a reasonable speed.

I made the rudder from one of these doors because teak is the finest wood for the job. As it is also one of the most expensive, using second-hand timber was a worthwhile economy.

First I had to cut the rudder to shape. A door is naturally door-shaped, that is rectangular. What I wanted was a D-shaped piece of timber. So I drew out on the door the required shape and started to cut away the surplus timber. Now that door was made of several slabs of wood, held together with steel rods driven edgewise through the door. Naturally wood-cutting tools cannot be used on steel, and steel-cutting tools are deadly slow used on wood, or anything else for that matter. My plan was to cut the timber with a saw till it nearly reached the first steel bar, then hacksaw through the steel bar, then on again with the wood saw.

I started, but it was grimly slow work, and as usual I was in no mood to brook delays.

'George, how in Hades can this job be speeded up? Any ideas?'

'Why not mark out in chalk where the steel bars run through the timber. Then we'll cut the wood right up to the steel with the bandsaw, and all you'll have to do is cut the steel bars through.'

'That's fine in theory. But if anything goes wrong we'll ruin a bandsaw blade, maybe lop off a hand or two, in fact the whole thing sounds wickedly dangerous.'

'No. Nothing to it.'

Full of foreboding I chalked the exact location of the hidden steel bars in the wood. We heaved the weighty teak onto the mechanical bandsaw bench, and George started the motor. When the menacing hissing throb reached a steady

high hum, showing that the saw was going full pelt, George pushed the timber
at the saw. The blade bit through the wood, and in no time it was within half
an inch of the concealed steel. Very carefully, for a mistake now could mean a
frightful injury, George pulled the timber back, cut again, back and once more
the saw carved its relentless way into the tough teak. As we had to cut out
sections of wood between the steel bars it meant turning the door as the saw
cut. If the door was turned too fast the saw blade would not be able to follow
and would snap. All in all it was a thoroughly tense session, but it reduced the
job from a day's slogging to half an hour's nerve-stretching. I've never really
loved high-speed wood-working machines since my apprenticeship. That was
just before the war finished and we had to use what timber we could get.
One batch was studded with shrapnel. The vicious little splinters of steel lay
hidden in the wood so that no one could tell they were there. A saw-miller
would be working away on a piece of apparently harmless timber and the
next thing he knew there would be a loud sharp bang as something broke off
the tool and shot it across the shed, clean through the asbestos wall and on
across the boatyard. No one ever actually stopped one of those flying pieces
of steel, which was just as well, because we should then have had to waste a
lot of time making a coffin.

After the rudder was cut to shape it was carefully faired away so that it
would cause no drag as it slipped effortlessly through the water. Then I put it
aside till it would be needed, weeks later. Likewise the bunk fronts were made
and varnished and stored till they were wanted.

As soon as the hull was finished I started putting the furnishings in the
forward cabin. This was laid out in an unusual way, with most of the available
space taken up by a big shelf right across the ship. This shelf is covered by
mattress cushions and forms a multiple berth, with room for four children.
There is a seat by it, because the berth is too high to sit on comfortably when
undressing, and because a seat is handy for clothes overnight. Opposite is a
small slatted container, known as the play-pen because it looks like a miniature
one. This is the sail locker. The idea of making it with a battened front is to
allow the maximum circulation of air, so that damp sails can easily dry out.
Also of course one wants to save timber and weight wherever possible when
building a yacht.

Under the berth is a rack with a hole cut in it which exactly fits round the
spare calor gas cylinder. Beneath the seat is a fiddle, so that no space is wasted
and every spare corner can be used for stowage. All this sounds simple enough,
but it's surprising how long this work can take, especially when each piece of
mahogany is carefully planed on all sides, then all the edges are smoothed off,
the corners are rounded so that in a rough sea no one will jag themselves. Every
piece must be screwed home well and truly so that if someone should lurch
against it as the boat heaves over a wave nothing will come adrift. Finally the
whole, including the interior surface of the hull, is four times coated with lovely
smooth, syrupy yacht varnish. This last was Morag's speciality, and if someone
made a tiny scratch on the varnish, even if it was only on the first coat, they
were told in no uncertain terms that GOOD boat builders, people who KNEW
their job, would never do a thing like that.

Of course with a bunch of amateurs it was to be expected that all did not go according to plan. But it did. Maybe we worked our guardian angels over-hard, maybe we took just enough trouble, maybe George had enough skill and to spare to cope with every emergency. Whatever the cause, there was no wasted timber, no one spilt paint, or dropped a sharp chisel on pristine furniture. Somehow things on the boat nearly always went as planned. Part of the reason for this was the genuine shipyard atmosphere, for which George was largely responsible. For instance the traditional shipyard jokes would be heard:

'Don't come down this ladder, I've taken it away,' from someone borrowing a ladder, and quick as lightening from inside the *St Mary*'s hull would come back:

'Well put it back. I'm halfway down.'

Then if anyone was painting too delicately someone would say:

'The boat will start laughing any moment now.'

'Laughing?'

'Yes, laughing because you're tickling it with that paint brush. SLAP it on. Work the paint into the wood. The boat can't bite back.'

Also at any time of the day someone would be sure to be saying to one of the many children who played around the boats:

'Come away from that circular saw. Here, take that brush and sweep up the shavings.'

'Do I get six pence for an ice-lolly if I sweep up?'

'If you do it well.' 10 minutes later, after a flurry of energy which fills the whole shed with dust and shavings:

'I've done it. Can I have my sixpence?'

'Here, take this half crown. Go and get ices for all of us.'

'I couldn't carry all that number.'

'Well take your little sister and brother too. Go on. Scram.' Everyone who owned one of the other boats laid up in the shed seemed to have a quiverful. There were so many children about, often playing around the woodworking machinery, I sometimes wondered if they were like little worms, when one got cut in half the result was two of the little devils.

Chapter Seven

The *Nellie Marie* was a fine motor cruiser. I had the job of delivering her from Bangor, in North Wales, to the East Coast. From the moment I stepped aboard I admired her fine construction and sensible planning. However, the voyage turned out to be a farce. We had thirty-one engine breakdowns before I gave up logging them and concentrated on keeping at least one of the two heaps of machinery churning over. On one occasion both engines died when we were up tide of Skokholm Island, off Milford Haven. Fortunately I had given the island a good berth, because the tide was fast-flowing and directly towards the rocks. We tried all we knew to get the engines going, then one of the crew thought we should get on the radio-telephone and yell for help. I pointed out that we would be well and truly wrecked long before anyone could get out to us, for as usual on these occasions the horizon was empty of ships. We got as far as preparing the dinghy for abandoning ship, and looked out the life-jackets. Just in time we managed to coax one of the misbegotten lumps of iron-ware to start thumping again.

That voyage, with others, convinced me that no boat is any good unless her power plant is satisfactory. There was the beautiful brand new sloop I took from Burnham to Bridlington. Off Lowestoft it blew a series of shrieking squalls dead on shore, and likewise straight into the harbour mouth. I'd never been into the harbour before, but the chart suggested that it was cramped inside. As seems usual on these occasions we were short-handed, the tide was foul, the seas shaped like paving stones stuck on edge, it was raining and a black, dark night. My plan was to take sail off outside the harbour and go in under power, as this was both the seamanlike and the safest course. If we blinded in with any sail up there might not be room to round up and drag the sails off her without bashing holes in something ... maybe ourselves. And she was brand new, the owner had never seen her complete, so I was on my best behaviour, and not given to trying anything exciting.

That was the plan. What happened was that I started the engine well before we got to Lowestoft, to make sure all was well. It ran for a few minutes then stopped. I got it going again, but it stopped after another 10 minutes. Once more I did battle, and again we had a few minutes run out of it. And so it went on. When I should have been conning the yacht through the inshore passage, which were new waters to me, I was busy trying to get that brand new engine, a famous and much advertised make, to run without faltering for just half an hour.

In the end we had to enter harbour under sail, which we did at a high rate of knots. We rounded up like a rocket in a tight orbit, all the sails went mad as they flapped and cracked and resisted our efforts to get them down. The yacht refused to lie still and charged towards the hardest, roughest, dirtiest harbour wall for seven parishes around. Just in time we got the boat to turn parallel to the wall, and the only damage was a scraped pulpit. This drove home what I already knew perfectly well. An engine must be reliable above all else.

Not everyone agrees with this. Owners of racing boats prefer very light engines because they do not retard the boat when she's under sail. Owners who are hard up think that they can save money by putting in cheap heaps of machinery, and the inevitable result is that the first time there is a flap the engine won't go. The resulting damage costs more than a good engine, and even if there is an insurance company to bear the brunt, the owner loses his no-claim bonus and probably a lot of sailing time while the boat is repaired.

A friend of mine firmly avows that his engine is better than mine because his is so easy to repair.

'Why,' he says 'more than once I've stripped down, cleaned out, and replaced my carburettor all within 15 minutes while off a lee shore.'

To which I reply, truthfully: 'My engine never breaks down. I've no idea how long it takes to repair.' This was referring to our one-cylinder Lister. That little motor got us out of every sort of over-interesting situation, so that we looked upon it with great affection. It is the same basic model that is used for all sorts of industrial purposes, including driving concrete mixers. So when someone tried to be rude about our engine, and called it the concrete mixer, we took up the insult and turned it into a compliment.

Typical of the way it went was a trip three of us made from Poole to Burnham one November. It was a fine run, not especially cold, and it made us realise once again how wise we were not to lay up in the middle of the autumn when most other people did. It was dead calm for the last part of the trip, and we motored right across the Thames Estuary. Long before we reached Burham it was clear that we would not have enough fuel to get us right to the moorings. I poured the last of the fuel from the reserve can into the engine's fuel tank, poured the paraffin from the primus stove into the engine's tank, emptied our paraffin lantern into the engine's tank, added a dash of lubricating oil, and screwed the cap back on. One of the crew watched this in some surprise and asked:

'How long will the engine run on that cocktail?'

'Running slowly we can do 30 miles to the gallon. With luck we may get within a couple of miles of Burnham before running dry. The trouble is the tide will turn against us just as we run out of juice.'

We motored on across the glassy still winter sea, cutting corners over the edges of sandbanks where we could. The tide helped us up the River Crouch and eventually the moorings came in sight, with a few yachts still afloat. We kept in the middle of the river to get the best of the favourable tide. With less than half a mile to go, we saw the boats begin to swing as the tide started to slacken before turning against us. I steered for the nearest mooring. One of the others went forward and unlashed the boat-hook. As he did so the engine faltered, picked up, then died as the fuel ran out. At the bow the man with the boat-hook reached out as far as he could. The *St Elizabeth* slid imperceptibly to a stop, just close enough for us to catch the first mooring buoy.

This sort of thing made me favour a Lister air-cooled diesel for the new boat. Apart from the fact that our 'concrete-mixer' always started, it was very easy to install, and cheap both to run and to buy. Unlike most marine engines, the fuel tank is fitted on the engine. This saves buying a separate fuel tank, together with its piping and connections. It also saves fitting the tank, complete with straps round, a filler through the deck, an air pipe, and so on.

Also most marine engines are water-cooled. This means they have to have a sea-cock fitted to the ship, to let the seawater flow to the engine. After the water has circulated round and done its job cooling the machinery it flows back to the sea, via another pipe and another sea-cock on the ship's side. Now all this piping and these sea-cocks do not grow on trees. They cost the earth and have to be sought out, bought, found to be too big, or to have the wrong thread for the engine connection, taken back, changed, invoiced, tagged with a delivery note, then eventually they get down to the boat where they must be fitted, complete with a wooden pad, bolts must be found the right diameter and length, complete with nuts and washers. No wonder it is easier to fit an air-cooled engine.

Of course there is a penalty to pay for the facility of air-cooling, namely extra noise. However, I personally don't mind a noisy auxiliary. It is an encouragement to turn the thing off, get up the sails, and use the boat properly. A motor cruiser calls for a different approach. Here the noise is less acceptable, and it is necessary to put sound-proofing round the engine. But on a motor yacht sound-proofing is essential anyway, if the boat has any pretensions to quality and comfort.

Another mild disadvantage of the Lister two-cylinder engine I decided to fit is that it is a bit more bulky and heavy than a petrol engine of comparable horse-power. But as these same petrol engines have been known to refuse to start, even when brand new, even when carefully installed by competent mechanics, I can see no good reason for fitting them. Their great trouble is that they must have electricity to go. Wherever there is salt water there is a damp atmosphere, dampness soon seeps into the electrical parts and wiring, and even without actually getting the engine wet it can lose the vital spark through shorting. And like it or not, even the best designed and maintained yacht tends to have a great deal of moisture on everything aboard fairly frequently.

On most yachts a bulky engine is inconvenient, but on the *St Mary* it threatened to be disastrous. I wanted the engine to be installed so that it would be really accessible. Then in the unheard-of contingency of a break-down it would be easy to repair. Also the infrequent maintenance which this reliable machinery needs would be simpler if the motor could be approached from the top, both sides and both ends. After wrestling with this design problem for a number of hours, I achieved all I set out to do. Most yacht engines are tucked away, like troglodytes down some dark dank hole, so that neither a normal human being, nor even a yachtsman, can get at them. Ours is accessible on all sides and from the top too.

From all this it might be inferred that all my savings have been used buying R. A. Lister & Co. shares. In fact I have no holding in the company, it's just that I cannot see the point of soaking up a lot of experience and then not using it. My eyes were opened some years ago when I wanted a Lister service man to look at the engine in a hurry. I rang the factory in Dursley, Gloucestershire, from Poole, where the boat was lying. The service manager said that there was an engineer in Southampton, and he would get him to Poole as soon as possible. Within 90 minutes of laying down the phone I went down to the boat, and there was the service mechanic, at work. He must have driven like the wind to cover the distance, get down to the boatyard, which like all its kind is at the end of a rutted tortuous lane, parked, changed into overalls, got out his tools, found the right boat ... Heavens, how did he do it? He genuinely was in Southampton when he got the phone call, too.

Almost every item of gear arrived late, but not the engine. It stood in the shed, looking rather daunting:

'Donald, how the devil are we going to get that mass of iron-ware into the boat? The roof will never carry the load, so we can't sling it up.' I asked.

'Don't you worry about that,' was Donald's typical reply. Sure enough, one weekend when I arrived at the shed, there was the engine, half in half out of the boat. I took one horrified look, my mind grappling with the best way to get someone out from under a dropped engine, where the nearest ambulance could be called for, the likely breaking limit of a 12-inch by 2-inch plank and sundry associated problems:

'Can I help, Donald?' I wanted to know.

'No. Everything under control. Just don't come too close.' So I went and cut out bunk fronts and studiously looked the other way. However, a little extra muscle-power seldom comes amiss on these occasions, and besides I was missing the fun.

So I joined in the fray. Little by little, using levers and planks, the engine was eased onto the side-deck. Next it was slid across, very gently, then down into the gaping hull. It was left suspended above its final resting place, so that we could work round and under it. As we hammered and chiselled beneath this brooding bulk of metalware we were, at first, all too aware of it. If the supporting chains and wires parted it would be mince-meat and sawdust and precious little else left to put into the coffin. But after a time we grew too familiar with the risk, and would stand up in a hurry (we were always in a tearing rush), to crash our heads against the engine's projecting parts.

The actual installation of the engine is basically simple. To save time we omitted, for the first season, all remote controls. As a result, once launched, when the engine has to be put in gear, revved up, or otherwise given instructions, it is necessary to dive below into the cabin, lift up the engine casing lid, and pull the gear-lever or whatever needed operating. While this is less than convenient, it saves us a lot of building time, and of course it sharpens up the standard of seamanship aboard.

The only additions to the basic engine which we had to put in were the propeller shaft, with its stern-tube and propeller, as well as the exhaust. Our propeller is a very cunning device. It has two blades which are hinged so as to fold shut when the yacht is sailing. As a result they have very little resistance to the flow of water and don't slow us down. When the engine is started and the gear-lever pulled ahead, the propeller shaft whirls round. This turns the propeller, of course, and the centrifugal force throws the propeller blades out, where they grip the water and start thrusting the boat along. So far there is nothing special about the arrangement, which is similar to that used on boats for well-nigh fifty years.

However, our folding propeller can also work going astern. Up to now any simple type of folding propeller always folded itself if you tried to drive it backwards. Only special, rather elaborate, folding propellers, with blades which twisted by a fairly complicated mechanism could drive ahead and astern, apart that is from the solid type of propeller, which suffers from the serious disadvantage that it slows a boat down a great deal when she is under sail.

Our fancy propeller has first to be put into gear ahead before it can drive astern. Also it throws the boat off to starboard when going astern, and in practice does call for some skill in operation. However, it is a big advance over the *St Elizabeth*, which had no gear or clutch. With her, whenever the engine started the boat at once moved forward. The only way to stop her was to stop the engine. And of course she then drifted on a fair distance, this depending on how fast she was going before the engine was stopped. So it was essential to be very alert and cut the engine off well before a standstill was required. Otherwise the boat would clobber smartly into whatever barred progress.

Once when coming through the Forth–Clyde canal we were short-handed. Apart from Morag and me there was only a friend aboard. At some of the bridges there was no lock-keeper to raise the two halves of the lifting spans. So we had to work out a complex system to get through. It is not easy to get near the canal bank without running aground, but we repeatedly succeeded in putting someone ashore at every untended bridge. He would raise one half of the bridge, and where possible we would sail through, taking care not to catch the shrouds on the unraised half of the bridge. But it was difficult and risky. After wasting a lot of time, Morag suggested that as she was not muscular enough to wind up half a bridge, using the primitive handgear, she should stay aboard and we two men each take one bank. When we had raised the two bridge halves she would steer the yacht through, then stop the engine. That would give us time to close the bridge, both get onto the same bank, and run along to rejoin the yacht.

We opened the bridge, the engine was started and the boat steered neatly through the gap. As soon as the obstruction was passed Morag left the helm to stop the boat, which could only be done by stopping the engine. This in turn needed a visit to the cabin, as we had a perfectly watertight cockpit which meant that the controls could not successfully be led to the helmsman. Morag turned off the fuel pump and let it go. However, it is spring-loaded and when she let it go it flicked back to the operating position and the engine at once picked up, for it was nothing if not a willing goer. Of course the boat at once gained speed. This happened before Morag had returned to the helm, so she went back to the engine and held the fuel pump control firmly in the off position. This stopped the engine but it all took time, and the canal meanwhile bent round a corner. Of course the boat went straight. It met the grass bank at a firm 4 knots and the rounded bow drove up in fine style, so that the whole effect was of a hunter taking a fence. The *St Elizabeth* slid back into the canal without so much as a scratch on the paintwork, but then she always was a sensible boat; she'd chosen a nice soft grassy bank.

On the new boat we thought that a reverse gear would be worth having, though plenty of people do without one, traversing canals and coming up to crowded tide-ridden moorings without one.

We also decided on a very simple exhaust system. On the *St Elizabeth* we had followed recommended practice and had a flexible exhaust pipe. The trouble with this type of piping is that it corrodes. Ours was no exception, but it chose a bad time to let us down, when we wanted to sail the length of the east coast from Burnham to Edinburgh. At first we thought the engine was just fuming. Then we noticed it was more than stuffy in the cabin. Eventually even I had to admit that the cabin was untenable with the engine running. Close inspection showed that the continuously salt-laden moist atmosphere aboard had eroded the flexible exhaust pipe till it was badly split. This was difficult to patch at sea, and of course we found the trouble when off a rather inhospitable lee shore, while we were trying to make Lowestoft before the tide turned against us.

We made a repair, but the pipe failed again later. As it was only a season and a half old, and the previous pipe had failed just as quickly, we decided the new boat must not have this source of trouble. The idea behind the flexible pipe is that it absorbs the vibrations of the engine. But I argued that if the exhaust was fitted with two gentle right-angle bends, and provided there was a fairly long piece of straight pipe between, then the two bends and the straight would absorb all the vibrations the engine was likely to produce.

Getting the piping for the boat was incredibly difficult. If I had wanted 30 tons of piping, I would have been welcomed by a dozen different firms. If lead piping or plumbers' material would have served, I could have had all the help I needed from a dozen house-plumbers. But no one was interested in my tiny little job. Not at any price. After a time I gave up trying to do the job economically and struggled to get it complete regardless of cost.

There was one firm of ship-pipe specialists who managed to pull out all the stops when it came to being frustrating. They were quite hopeless at getting a job done, but they certainly have worked out a wonderful method leading potential customers astray. I telephoned them:

'Is that the Super-pipebashing Company?'

'Yes, this is Mr Snuggelip, the ship-piping manager.'

'Can you do a small job for me in a hurry?'

'Oh, yes. Very keen to get work, things are very quiet for us. It's hard to find anything in our line these days, especially for the ship department.'

'I'm afraid this is a very small job indeed. All I want is the piping for a small boat's exhaust. She's only 35 feet long, with an 8 horse-power engine. There is less than 12 feet of piping.'

'That's all right. We're very keen to take on anything. Just let us know what you want.'

'Can you let me have various lengths of piping, cut and threaded, also some bends, threaded both ends?'

'Yes, yes. Anything like that. It's right up our street. We can even send men to the boatyard to fit the pipes ...' And so on in that vein. After a few minutes I began to think that they really wanted to do some work for me. It certainly sounded that way. Now the job was so simple that I described to them over the phone exactly what I wanted. Two weeks went past. Then a third started to waste away. Other jobs were started, rushed through and finished. Booms, upholstery, plans of the cabin top, anchor chocks, a dozen assorted parts were made, ordered, improved, designed, the deluge never stopped. But there was no sign of my piping. I telephoned the firm again. Alas, I cannot report the conversation, it would sound too fantastic to be creditable. No one had done a thing about my piping and everyone from the managing director down to the office-boy (and I was passed from one to the next on the phone) took care to tell me he knew nothing about the job, and couldn't help me. At last someone changed tacks, and said that they were very sorry, and they would do all they could to help me. Of Mr. Snuggelip there was no mention. So once again I explained exactly what I wanted, and offered to visit the firm next day to collect those parts which were most urgent. The voice on the other end of the telephone said that this would be quite unnecessary and added that he would send a messenger to my office with the parts. This sounded like service, and my morale was fool enough to take a small bound upwards.

Of course I should have done the whole thing on an official level, with letters requesting quotations, reminders three weeks later that I had not had the pleasure of a reply from them, a further courteous request two weeks later for at least an approximate quotation, and so on. But I'm naïve enough to think that a customer should be given prompt, efficient service. It seems to me that a firm should not ask its customers to damn near grovel before they get attention. After dealing, or rather trying to deal with a dozen or so firms around Glasgow in certain trades which had been bleating pretty loud about shortage of orders, I came to a well-confirmed conclusion. Those people had only themselves to blame, they did not deserve any sort of prosperity. Excuse this outburst, but I never did get any piping from the firm who claimed to be short of work. In the end I bought some parts from a wholesaler, one of the rather rare type who does not first ask if you are in the 'trade', then ask for bank references, then refuse to deal over the counter, then insist on a confirmation order, then state bluntly that the goods cannot possibly be delivered before next Friday, then complain about the smallness of the order, and so on. Bless this particular company. They handed me a comprehensive catalogue, left me in peace to find what I wanted, took me to the store, showed me alternatives, helped me choose the best parts for the job, were happy to take cash, had change on the spot, didn't complain because I arrived around lunch-time, wrapped up the rather grubby awkward parts so that my suit didn't get soiled, and told me to come back if I needed anything more. You see, there's more to building a boat than bashing in nails.

The wiring for the engine starter motor was another battle. Again the job was very, very simple. All that was needed was a few feet of wire with special terminals soldered on the ends. If I had had a soldering set I would have done the job myself. I drew out a plan, such a simple plan, of the wiring. With it I trailed from one so-called electrical engineer to another. Some of them behaved as if they could not read the plan. Most, in spite of their boast in neon lights over the works, were not electrical engineers at all, merely stockists of electrical household gadgets. And if one of the 20,000 or 30,000 electric toasters which they sold annually had given a minute spasm of trouble they would have been helplessly incapable of repairing it. In the end a garage mechanic took one glance at my plan, asked a few pertinent questions and promised to have the job complete in 3 hours. Which he duly did.

Chapter Eight

If the *St Mary* sank tomorrow, which heaven forbid, she would not have lived in vain. For she proved beyond doubt that the 'super-long-wire method' of making masts is a success.

It was this way: I decided that I would make the two masts for the boat at home. They would occupy the winter evenings, and making them would be vastly cheaper than buying them. In fact, one of the many reasons we decided on the ketch rig was because the two short masts would be no great trouble, stretched across the garden, whereas one enormous one might protrude into the road and cause embarrassment to those tall passers-by who belted their heads on it. Likewise the problem of moving a couple of moderate masts from the city to Helensburgh was a mild worry. Moving a really long mast would have been an expensive and complex undertaking.

However, when I came to look into the technical problems involved in making a pair of masts I got several frights. First I would need a spar bench, or its equivalent. This is a long, very long, straight, perfectly straight, carpenters' bench. In practice a series of rigid trestles are often used as they cost less. But it still needs a lot of timber to fabricate and when I had finished the masts I would end up with a garden cluttered with a lot of superfluous trestles. Also being outside in the winter would make accurate and delicate work difficult. There are warmer cities than Glasgow. Then again, the lining up of the spar-bench calls for a lot of precise work. And of course a bench out in the open would tend to warp and change shape with the weather. Then how was I to get the glue to dry in the cold? Also the number of hours' work involved, with my limited power tools, was going to call for a lot of late-night work. The neighbours might object to the noise if it went on after 3 a.m. Also there was the problem of lighting. In the end it looked as if I would be driven to buying masts.

However, even that was no answer. There was no one in Helensburgh to make the masts, the nearest boatyard being about 20 miles away. If, to save money, I only ordered the bare spars, and put all the fittings on myself, then the masts would have to be moved from the boatyard where they were made to our house. Then after I had put on the fittings, varnished the masts repeatedly till they were well water-proofed and protected, and generally got them ready, the wretched spars would have to be moved once more by road to Helensburgh.

All this trundling about would almost certainly have damaged wood masts, for they are made of that softest of woods, spruce. Also road transport may be cheap, but it still costs money.

There was one other possible solution: alloy masts. These are much lighter than wooden ones. However, they are also much more costly. Against this they require no maintenance, so that in the long run they cost less.

Needless to say, there is one gigantic snag. Or there was. It used to be impossible for an amateur to buy a bare alloy tube and put on the fittings himself. In other words he was forced to buy the complete mast with all the bits and pieces riveted on by an alloy spar manufacturer. The difference in price between the bare aluminium alloy tube and the assembled mast is considerable, so I argued that if I could devise some method of fixing the fittings to a bare alloy tube, and thus complete the mast myself, I would have triumphed.

There is no difficulty in explaining the problem I had to tackle. It's just this: To fasten the rigging to the mast it is necessary to have metal straps and bands on the mast. These straps and bands can be riveted on, using a special tool and an unusual type of rivet. Or welding can be used. However, it very seldom is because even an expert finds it very difficult. It is impossible to bolt fittings onto a spar because the latter are narrow tubes. My biggest was only 6¼ inches by 4¾ inches. Obviously no one could crawl up inside and put the nuts on the bolts. Nor could anyone reach up inside the masts to put the bolts through from the inside, so that the nuts could be put on outside. The masts are over 30 feet from truck to foot. The problem called for some simple stroke of ingenuity, and I knew that only constant thought would find the answer. At least I hoped there WAS an answer.

One day I thought I had it. All I had to do was to put the fittings on the sides of the mast, and bolt right through. The bolt would go in one side of the mast and come out the other. The strips of metal to which the wire rigging is attached, called tangs, would all be bolted on in pairs, one port, one starboard. However, there were some serious snags. Tightening the bolts would pinch the mast. Also all the bolts would have to be in a straight line vertically up the mast. This is bad engineering as it makes the mast weak and might cause a failure. Worse still, some of the fittings had to be on the front of the mast. There is no way of putting these on satisfactorily since the fore and aft bolts could not be used as the mast track would be in the way. I could have put on fittings wrapping round the mast, with bolts athwartships but rigging coming off the fore side. But at best this would have been heavy, crude-looking and inefficient.

After covering many pages with diagrams and notes, after looking through innumerable books and magazines, I suddenly hit on one of those fantastically simple ideas which completely solve the apparently insoluble. I was so tickled I at once named it the 'Nicolson super-long-wire method'. It's probably as old as the hills, but I can find no published reference to it anywhere and until I find that someone else has sired a similar infant, this is my pride and joy.

To understand the 'super-long-wire method' watch me fit the first tang to my main mast. The tang is a piece of steel flat bar, 10 inches long and 1 inch wide, by 5/16 inch thick. It is drilled to take five bolts. I lay the tang on the mast exactly in place and hold it firmly. Then I take my electric drill, and using the

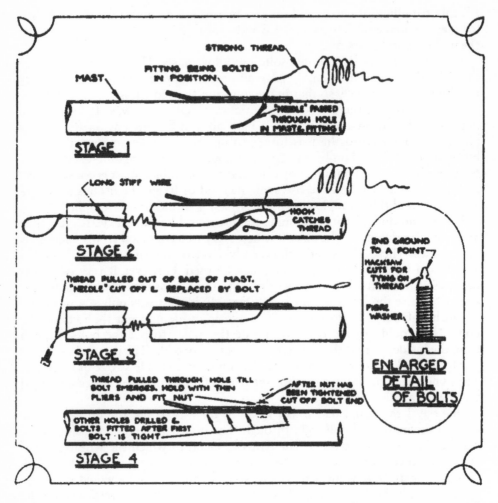

This is how the 'Long-wire method' for making alloy spars works. It requires no special tools, no skill and is most inexpensive. Having sailed through rough seas on the *St Mary* with two masts built by this method, and used it on other yachts, I'm satisfied it is reliable if properly applied.

Before starting a supply of bolts must be prepared. A simple grinding machine or a carborundum stone on an electric drill is best for putting the points on the bolts, but a file can be used. The two saw cuts on the nose of the bolt are to hold the thread. Some purists will prefer to drill a hole instead of using the saw cuts.

To hold the fitting in place just lash it round the mast tightly. Once the first bolt is fitted it will hold the fitting firmly. Each fitting must be carefully designed, with ample bolts and a good safety factor to take the full stresses, which can be fierce in a gale.

It is best to use a nylon or terylene thread, or tough sail makers' thread. For the long-wire itself, use the thickest wire that can be bent conveniently. Wire 1/8 inch thick works well. The 'needle' must not be longer than the smallest inside diameter of the mast minus 1 inch.

tang to guide me, I drill a hole where the top bolt is to go into the mast. Now I take the tang off the mast, and with the electric drill I slightly enlarge the hole. Now comes a critical moment, the first of several. I have previously made a long, thick 'needle' out of a piece of heavy brass wire. The 'needle' has a hole at one end, and tied to this hole is a long length of very stout thread such as sailmakers use. I pass the needle into the mast through the hole I've made. It will not go (this was our first setback). The needle is too long and will not drop right through the hole. I withdraw it and wonder if I should cut the needle shorter. I decide to bend the needle instead, so that it is crescent shaped. Again I push the needle through the hole and it drops into the inside of the mast. Now I go to the head of the mast and push down the length of the spar a great long piece of stiff wire with a hook in the end, the 'super-long-wire' itself. When the hook has passed the point where the needle and its thread have dropped inside the mast I turn the super-long-wire round and round. This should, and nearly always does, at once catch the thread. I pull the 's-l-wire' out. The hook on its end has tangled with the thread and the brass needle. Wonderful! We are halfway home. I cut the needle off the thread and attach a special bolt to the thread. This bolt is an ordinary galvanised one which has received special treatment in this way: first, I ground the end to a point. Then I flattened the point a little, and finally I drilled a little hole in the point. Through this I can tie my long thread to the nose of the bolt. This is done with care, as we are now reaching the climax. I rush back to the middle of the mast where we have the first hole drilled. Down the hole disappears the long thread. I pull the thread very gingerly. It comes easily, which is a damn sight more than my breath does. I pull and pull till suddenly with the easiest click in the world the bolt appears, point uppermost in the hole. Now all I have to do is to hold the bolt in place, put the tang on it, and put the nut on.

This calls for delicate handling, otherwise I shall drop the bolt inside the mast. I manage without much difficulty by holding the bolt close up to the mast with a pair of tin snips. These act like thin-ended pliers. The tang and the nut go on with no trouble at all. Now taking a pair of pliers I hold the extreme nose of the bolt to prevent the bolt turning and apply a spanner to the nut. In a second the nut is hard tight. It's WORKED! No one who has not been through that sort of gamble can know the deep solid satisfaction of pulling off a long shot.

It was a fair-sized gamble because I had to buy a mast before I could try out the idea. If the 'super-long-wire method' had failed, I would have been landed with two uncompleted masts lying in the garden and would probably have been forced to send them back to the suppliers to be completed with all the fittings. I was lucky to get the bare tubes from the leading people in the metal mast making game, Ian Proctor Metal Masts Ltd. They joined two lengths of tubing together to make a spar long enough for my mainmast. The join is so perfect it is virtually undetectable.

Of course there were some heart-snatching moments during the development of the 'super-long-wire method'. For a start I did not think of the long wire. I had worked out the rest of the procedure well enough. My idea was to push the brass needle inside the mast, then lift one end of the mast high up, so that the needle would slide down to the end. I tried this. It was a complete failure. A friend, Sandy Baillie, who lives nearby, came to my rescue. Together we tied a rope to one end of the mast. I went upstairs to the spare bedroom, flung up the window and caught the loose end of the rope thrown to me from the garden below. With Sandy steering the spar I hauled one end up to the window level. It was a horridly hazardous game as the mast tried to sway about. Right below me was another window and the mast was obviously determined to plunge its butt through the glass. When at last I got the end up to the window, the needle was still reluctant to slide down inside. We got the first bolt in, but it was obvious that we could not, except as a last resort, heave the spar halfway up the side of the house for every single bolt. There were, in the two masts, well over a hundred bolts.

That's when I thought of the 'super-long-wire', and for a time all our troubles in that sphere were at an end. For a time. One night I was working with Morag on the mizzen mast when the 's-l-wire' broke inside the mast. This was a frightful set-back. I had no more wire, and even if I had I could not see how I was going to get the broken part out of the mast. It just could not be left inside. It was late in the evening. I was tired and on top of a few other troubles this brought on a few pretty bleak thoughts.

Without pausing to think, for long, I said to Morag:

'Stand on the end of the mast. I'm going to lift up the other end. That way I'll push it up till it's vertically on end. Then the broken wire will drop out.'

Morag duly took up her position, putting as much weight as she could on the heel of the mast. With wild energy I started to lift the other end of the mast, thinking that the only way to get it right on end was to run it up. I'd only got the mast up to about 45 degrees before Morag was catapulted off.

'For heaven's sake,' I said, 'can't you stand firmly on the blasted thing.' This was quite uncalled for. Sailing wives put up with enough without being asked to perform circus-wise.

'Here, let's try again.' Morag took station on the end of the mast. I picked up the opposite end and started to lift. I got it over my head, up at a good angle, and started walking towards Morag. Too fast. The next thing I knew Morag shot off into a flower-bed, the mast zoomed upwards under my thrust and we dodged as it toppled back to the ground. I was horrified.

'Are you all right, darling? Gosh, I'm sorry, I didn't know that was going to happen,' and having made sure she was unhurt I rushed over to the spar. One end had dug itself into the flower-bed and was plugged with moist earth but there was no other damage. Nor was the wire extracted.

By this time it was almost dark. I was roaming about like a caged beast trying to think of some way of getting my lost wire out of the mast, fretting and worrying instead of sitting down and puzzling it out quietly. Morag said:

'Why not push the rest of the wire up the mast and hook the broken part out.'

'Don't be silly. How could that possibly work?'

'Go on, try it.' So I took the wire we still had, made a hook in the end, pushed it up as far as I could reach, turned it round and round and round, and withdrew it. The broken length was neatly caught on the end.

On another occasion the brass needle jammed inside one of the masts. I pulled the twine harder and harder in a vain attempt to get it out, and eventually the thread broke. By thrusting a long length of wood up inside the mast I managed, after a bit of a struggle, to loosen the needle. Then we had the business of going up to the spare bedroom window, throwing a rope's end out, tying it to the mast, hauling the mast up and up, steering it past the window below, hanging wildly out of the window to keep the butt of the mast from damaging itself by scraping up the wall, till we were puffing like grampuses but the mast was within grasping distance. Then it had to be still further hoisted till at last it tilted steeply enough to make the needle slide out.

Apart from these minor setbacks the 'super-long-wire method' was a wonderful success. In fact I was so pleased with it I did not at first notice its outstanding disadvantage. This was the slowness of the job. I would plug away all evening, and by the time I came to chop the excess length off the couple of dozen bolts I had fixed in it would be getting dark. It took a very short time to work out that the current rate of production was going to be disastrous. We would not have the masts ready when the rest of the boat was complete. I could not waste weekends working at home, they were reserved for the sole dedication of twisting in as many screws as possible into the hull, painting as many square feet of planking, cutting and fitting as much furniture as the fleeting moments would allow.

Chapter Nine

Turning from the masts to the rest of the boat, I worked out that the whole job was not going to be finished in time for a reasonable amount of sailing in the 1961 season. And weekly there was increasing evidence of our first-born. So I was constantly reminded that this season we would not be able to go on sailing almost till Christmas. Furthermore if we were to race, and to go off for a week's cruise in the untried boat, we would need a crew. The obvious course was to find a couple of keen people who would help finish the boat and also crew for us. A notice on the Glasgow University Sailing Club notice board brought five replies.

This is how we met the two Alans. They turned out to be the sort of crew that every owner dreams about. They worked till all hours on the boat, they came week-end after weekend, as well as innumerable evenings, they tackled anything from painting to victualling, they picked up boat building techniques in a couple of minutes, they saw the virtue of the 'super-long-wire method' and worked it with added improvements and speeded up the whole process. One of their special virtues is that they are both science undergraduates with strong practical talents, so that they could apply their science to our innumerable problems. If they had any defects I only discovered one; that both should be called Alan was a mite confusing. We shortened Alan Livingstone to Alan-L, and Alan Haimes to Alan-H.

There was also an engineering graduate, Malcolm Smith who, like the two Alans, helped us with the later stages of the construction of the boat.

Long before these fellows came on the scene, in fact well back in the winter, the two booms were started. As we were building a ketch we had two short booms to complete instead of one long one. This was just as well, because our hall is of limited length, in fact it was just, but only just, possible to ease the completed main boom out through the front door. The builders of our house had foolishly not foreseen the need to be able to manoeuvre long spars in and out of the house and had put the front door at right angles to the length of the hall.

Each boom was built up like a long thin box. By making them hollow we achieved a light, strong structure, which used the minimum amount of wood. Inside the boom we can carry some of the rigging. For instance each topping lift, which supports the after end of the boom when the sail is lowered, runs along inside the boom. It is fixed at the top of the mast, comes down to the outer end of the boom, round a nylon sheave (pulley wheel in shore language) and inside the boom to where it emerges and is fastened to a cleat. The more usual method of carrying the topping lift along outside the boom has one serious disadvantage: the lift can droop down and when the boom swings across the loop of the topping lift, may decapitate someone, or nearly so.

Also inside the boom is a tackle which can either be used to haul the clew (the outer bottom corner) of the sail taut, or it can be used for reefing. Each boom had therefore to be rather carefully put together. Apart from the end plugs of wood, there were six long, thin pieces making up each boom. These parts were glued and screwed together, and before I got a 'pump' screw-driver, I ended each evening with wrist limp and hand blistered. After one of the booms was finished I decided to have a birthday, and to give myself a present. This was the 'pump' or Yankee screwdriver, a miraculous tool and a wonderful time saver. Now instead of laboriously turning and turning and twisting each little screw right in its full length, I just put the tip of the new screw-driver on the screw head and SHOVED hard. The blade of the driver would spin with satisfying speed and in a second, literally, the screw would be driven right home.

When the first boom was finished I picked it up to try its weight. It seemed like thistle-down. This was just what I'd hoped, as I still had vivid memories of the gear aboard the only other ketch I'd owned, the *Maken*. Her gear was so heavy that reefing was too often a battle, with excess weight and unhandiness the enemy. The sheer weight of the gear nearly caused us to sail ashore on Alcatraz Island in San Francisco Bay, and made reefing a 20-minute job even in good conditions because we had to lash everything down with such complex stout tackles.

When the booms were finished, I turned my attention to the mastheads. The two tubes I bought for masts were perfectly straight, parallel sided for their whole length. The suppliers offered to taper the spars. Their method of doing this is to cut out a long wedge from the front of the mast, at the top, close the sides up and weld the gap closed. The advantages of this are a slight saving in weight and windage aloft and a better looking spar. But of course this extra work costs money. Besides, our headsails are carried from very near the masthead, so that we needed strength high up. For this reason I decided to have untapered spars. But to give the boat a good, and I hoped distinctive, appearance I decided to have short tapered wooden topmasts. Each was designed to plug into the top of its respective mast.

There was some trouble getting the right quality of clear-grained smooth spruce, free from knots. Each masthead was made up of a great number of parts, glued together and shaped in a rather complex way. These mastheads would have cost a fortune made in a boatyard, but because I had only to buy the wood, and could devote as much time as I could spare from other jobs, I decided that it would be well worth going for the elaborate design in order to work in all the features I wanted. The mizzen head, by far the smallest and least complex, was made from eight pieces of wood, each a different shape, each glued to its several neighbours, and the whole strengthened with long screws.

First the basic masthead was made, rather crudely shaped initially. Then the bottom was pared away till it plugged into the alloy tube. This had to be a precise fit, and took an age. Next the topmast was tapered away both at the sides and the front. After this the centre part was hollowed away, and the masthead sheave fitted. This is of nylon, as it is wonderfully light and self-lubricating. I needed two pieces of thin brass sheet to put on either side of the sheave. Without this brass, the wire halliard which hoists up the mizzen sail would ride off the sheave and jam between the wood and the sheave.

Now surely there can be nothing simpler than a couple of pieces of brass sheet. For preference I wanted brass as thin as a visiting card, but was prepared to take what I could get. What I could get! The trouble I had getting that brass, I might have been looking for a 4-inch-square diamond. After innumerable telephone calls, miles of walking from store to engineer's shop to scrap yard to hardware merchant I began to wonder if there was a government regulation against making thin brass sheet. After all, there are some pretty lunatic decrees. For instance the standard government-approved pattern of life-jacket in use for years used to be a killer because it was easy to put on backwards. And if it was worn back to front it naturally killed off the wearer by pushing his face into the water.

After hunting high and low I was telling Sandy Baillie my troubles one morning when he suggested a visit to a metal merchant less than 5 minutes' walk from my office. And there, of course, was brass sheet by the mile. A whole basement stuffed with the stuff, in every thickness and size met my gaze as I tottered unbelievingly into this store. This typified the whole of the manufacture of the mastheads. There were the special long thin bolts needed. I thought they were in my workshop, so set about looking for them. After weeks of high pressure work the room was rather chaotic. Morag made occasional sorties to try and keep the confusion within bounds, but of course though this organised things a little, and cleared the floor of the mountains of shavings, it did tend to move things around and so make it hard to remember where anything had been left. The workshop was designed as a maid's bedroom fifty years ago, adjacent to the kitchen, and is only 5 feet wide by 11 feet long, so that to say it was crammed full shades the truth. I just knew those bolts were there. Or were they? Had they been used on one of the innumerable jobs done on the previous boat, or the one before that? In the end I decided to use a length of brass rod lying handy in one corner. It took a deal of cutting, considering it was brass. When I came to examine the cut I found the rod was a curious fabrication of steel covered with thin brass sheeting. This sort of setback is the kind of thing that takes up so much time. By now the boat dominated our lives. I wished I could neglect the office, the garden, my writing and concentrate solely on the *St Mary*.

Our house reflected this. Morag commandeered one spare bedroom for the coming baby's gear, but I was ahead of her everywhere else. The drawing room had the air of a drawing office, with a steadily growing pile of plans, drawing-board, instruments, ink, paper, prints, notes, a basically simple filing cabinet which on close inspection is seen to be a series of cardboard boxes. In the hall the carpet is rolled back, and has been that way for weeks. Instead there is a layer of newspapers to keep the floor free from varnish when we work on the booms. The kitchen is a transit store. Sails arrive, are unpacked, admired, examined, pushed back into bags and stowed away wherever we can find space. The dining room takes the overflow from the drawing office, I mean drawing room. On the table is the typewriter, a heap of quotations, another of bills, a third of catalogues and a fourth, technical literature. The only reason these are not all muddled up is that occasionally we have to eat off the table, so Morag patiently sorts out the latest batch of mail, classifies each item and puts it on the correct pile. The garage is fortunately bigger than the car needs. All the surplus space between car and walls is filled with anchors, warps, fenders, boat-hook, and spare timber. The only evidence of the major construction project in our bedroom is heaps of books on rigging, sailmaking, designs, yachting magazines and library books. The garden, quite apart from its neglected air, only has the dinghy and masts to clutter it up. Poor garden, it did take a beating. But I did try. I weeded all right, but I found out that whoever invented the saying 'A job well done doesn't need re-doing' has never tried weeding.

I also lost my admiration for those Olympic-style athletes who boast they can run a mile in 4 minutes. That's really nothing. Try covering the same distance in short rushes, pushing a lawnmower. In fact if anyone wants to brighten up that dreary quarrelsome festival, the Olympic Games, they should insist that the running events are enlivened by each man pushing a lawnmower.

As a background to the work, which was almost always thoroughly satisfying and great fun, there was the maddening frustration caused by the sailmakers. A ketch needs three basic sails, main, mizzen and headsail. We started off with a terrific asset in the mainsail. This was a scarcely used cotton mainsail, presented by Hugh McLelland, the owner of the *Periwinkle*, when he changed over to terylene sails. We had this sail cut to fit our mast and boom by a very famous firm of sailmakers. I asked one of their technical directors if he would have the sail recut incorporating the longest battens he could expect us to carry with advantage. Perhaps this was an unfair request, anyway he came back with the reply that normal length battens, which are quite short, are the best for all-round cruising and the occasional race. I accepted his advice, but the first season's experience with our mizzen convinces me that I should have asked for long battens, extending right to the mast, at least at the top of the sail.

The mizzen is indeed my pride and joy, and it comes close behind the 'super-long-wire method' in the technical satisfaction I get whenever I look at it working just the way I hoped it would. I went to one of the leading specialists in Britain for fully-battened sails. Up to 1960, fully-battened sails were used almost exclusively on catamarans and a very few dinghy classes. Actually it is in cruisers that I foresaw this type of sail offered special advantages. Yet virtually no one was using full-battened sails on boats more than 18 feet overall. Part of the reason was that racing rules and handicapping regulations, notably of the Royal Ocean Racing Club and Cruising Club of America, very heavily penalise fully battened sails. This seems to me to be the height of bad biasing.

We discovered that our fully battened mizzen sail did far more work per square foot of area than the old-fashioned pattern mainsail. In fact there were occasions when the mizzen seemed to be pulling harder than the mainsail almost twice its size. As the season progressed, I began to think that fully battened sails on large craft was only common sense and wondered about adding full-length batten pockets to the mainsail. This can be done, but it is liable to look a patched-up job.

Our mizzen sail caused endless worry because it was delivered so late. The sailmakers never acknowledged the order for it, so I had to phone them to make sure the order had arrived. It had, and they promised the sail in good time. Before it was due I telephoned to make sure it would be on time. They promised it would. When it was late I telephoned again, wrote, telephoned. The cost of the sail looked like being doubled, to the immense profit of the GPO. When eventually it did arrive, it lacked an important feature.

During the initial discussions with the director of the sailmakers who was their technical specialist, I asked how we would be able to tell if the sail was stalled. It would never flap at the leading edge, like a normal sail, to indicate it needed sheeting in. The director came up with the bright idea that the sail should have light nylon threads sewn through it all over, or at least at the leading edge, and when these were all straight aft, it would show that the sail was working. When the threads blew all over the place it would mean the sail was stalled. The sail arrived without the promised threads.

The two headsails were ordered from Jeckells of Wroxham, Norfolk, who put in a keen quotation. We could have cruised with a jib only, but for racing there would have been little fun without a genoa. Normally one would fit a cruiser with a storm jib too but we compromised and had a row of reef points put in the working jib. With this we could reduce sail area without much effort. I'd tried this idea out on the *St Elizabeth* in all kinds of weather, and it seemed a sensible economy.

Jeckells also put a big black circle at the tack of the headsails, at my request. This makes it easy to find the right corner first when the sail is jumbled in its bag. I asked for this mark without knowing that Jeckells sew onto the head and tack of all their headsails little name labels. But all labels feel alike in the dark, so though I think their idea is excellent, I like mine better for a cruiser.

Chapter Ten

I was very lucky when it came to making the standing rigging. This rigging consists of long lengths of wire to hold up the masts, and it has loops or 'eyes' at each end to join it to the spars and the boat. To make these 'eyes' one normally splices the wire, and this is a fairly easy job, but as bloody as a small battle. The reason for this is that rigging wire is made up of stiff, intractable wire threads. These have to be tucked and twisted and coaxed in under and over each other. Few amateurs tackle this job. It's hard on city-soft hands. Even professionals draw blood often enough. However, it's one job I pride myself in. When I bought my second boat she had no rigging and I had very little money. The boatyard where I was apprenticed had a fine rigger, a man of enormous strength, experience, ingenuity and common sense. When I asked him to teach me to splice he just pointed to a little handbook, pointed to his workbench and its tools and said:

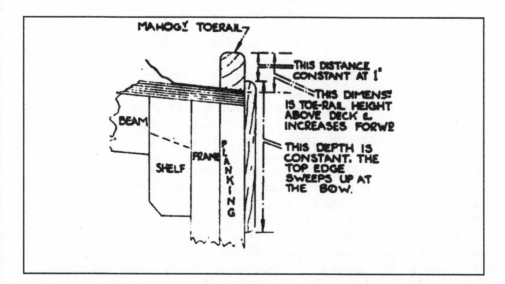

This is how the deck-edge was made. By varying the height of the toerail the yacht was given the appearance of a sweeping shear, though in practice her deck was flattish.

'It's all there. You teach yourself and you'll learn fast. Nor'll you ever forget.' Since that day I've always rigged my own boats, and to-date, touching wood firmly, my splices have never 'pulled out'. This is, of course, the big danger. An imperfectly wrought splice lets go without warning and the mast comes down.

I wanted to tuck all the splices on the new boat, but by the end of May it was obvious we were going to be so far behind I should have to get professional help. This was doubly disadvantageous as it meant drawing a rigging plan, whereas doing the job myself I could work from a few sketches on the back of an envelope. Now it so happens that splicing, which is an ancient art going back before Drake's day, is being superseded by a new idea called Talurit splicing. Basically this consists of making a splice by looping the wire round and holding the loop closed with a short length of metal tube cramped very tight round the wire. Crushing the short length of pipe round the wire requires a special hydraulic vice. This is not a small cheap tool, but I knew a firm of riggers like J. G. Clarence of Weir Street, Glasgow, would have one. I also knew that using a Talurit machine would save me a great deal of time and trouble, so I telephoned them, asking to hire the machine and one of their apprentices for an afternoon.

Like so many other aspects of the *St Mary*, the rigging is a mixture of simple inexpensive traditional work and a leavening of new ideas. Since I was doing half the rigging work myself, all I needed was a few cryptic notes. With these I drove to Clarence's works, in a side street of one of the oldest parts of Glasgow. It is almost Dickensian in aspect, not exactly clean and in strong contrast to the rather clinical feeling of modern factories. However, it has a grand character of its own. The rigging loft is full of coils of wire, long benches worn almost through in places with constant hard usage. There is a tang of the preserving oil used on wire, and of tar, though there is very little soft cordage here, almost all the modern riggers work being on wire.

As usual I was in a tearing hurry when I got to Clarence's. They gave me the services of a fourth year apprentice, and in seconds we were uncoiling the first roll of wire. The boy was a winner. He pitched into the work, and when I said I wanted the whole gang of rigging finished that afternoon we fairly flew through the job. For 20 minutes. Then I found we were out of thimbles, those little metal rings which fit inside the splices to protect the wire from wear. Major flap! We searched every bin, box, drawer, cupboard, rubbish bin (for discarded thimbles) tool-bag, everywhere. Hell's bells! No thimbles anywhere. There was nothing for it but to go and buy some. So out in the car and tyres scream on every corner to a ship chandler's. More hell's bells! There's no one in the appropriate department. Everyone is very sorry. Joe shouldn't be long. He's probably just gone to get some tea. No one knows where the thimbles are kept. There's no manager about. No one offers to help or even to look for Joe. I fret and fume and think of the running rigging unmade, bunk cushion patterns to make, toerail waiting for planing off, cockpit coamings unmade, apart from work piling up in the office. At last Joe comes back. No apologies, I'm only the customer, he'll get paid on Friday night. With boiling blood pressure I try to hurry him on. He does not know how much the thimbles cost. I tell him, thrust change into his hand and am out of the door, with car engine roaring up and tyres screaming in a high velocity take-off before Joe can count the change. I'm past caring if it's right.

Back at the riggers' the boy has been going fast enough to please even my impatience. With flying fingers we whip through splice after splice. In between grunts, swearing, and 'Here, hold this end. 22 feet 4 inches. Right. Cut here. Fine. You slice that one while I measure off the next,' we discuss boats. My helper, in filthy overalls, with grimy fingers, looks the sort who might take part in any of the rougher tougher sports. He turns out to be a flyfishing enthusiast. Slightly extraordinary. He tells me he's a fourth year apprentice. Also rather surprising. Does it really take more than four years to learn to be a rigger? There must be more to it than meets the eye. Certainly he's doing a good job on my precious wires, as I know by keeping a very close watch on everything that he does, while measuring, cutting and coiling myself.

The riggers' shed has one remarkable feature, a large hole in the floor, down which two men are loading a lorry which is on the ground floor a good many feet below. I ask:

'Anyone ever fall down that hole? It's in a dark corner, and has no guard-rails round it. Looks dangerous.'

'Och aye. I've fallen down it twice.'

'Twice! It's a long drop. Hurt yourself much?'

'A bit,' which might mean anything.

Knocking-off time comes, and I ask if the apprentice will see the job through. He will. Bless him. We finish in a flurry of coiling up each carefully labelled wire, pile the load into the back of the car, checking each item, and I'm off to the tune of more tyre-torturing. Back in the office there is a string of telephone messages. Never mind, another hurdle is behind.

If building a yacht consisted solely of shipwrighting, plumbing, rigging and kindred work it would not be complex. It's the planning, ordering, checking, reminding suppliers, and so on that takes up a disproportionate amount of time and complicates the whole project. We were very keen to have the boat in the water in time for the big Clyde race of the year, round Ailsa Craig. However long before that date, June 3, it was clear we would not be ready. The keel, like virtually every other component, was late. It was a particularly difficult and unusual shape to cast, so we selected a firm in Glasgow with very good facilities for doing elaborate work. Their massive foundry with all manner of machinery was known to me, and I had long discussions with various members of their technical staff. They were all most helpful, and I re-drew the keel plan to suit them, complete with numerous dimensions, which they also asked for. They were also to make the pattern, which in itself was a fairly elaborate job.

Twice during the time the pattern was being made I trekked across the concrete forest which is Glasgow to have further consultations with the firm's foundry management. A few days' silence followed. A friend who works for the firm telephoned: 'We're casting your keel tomorrow, Ian. Do you want to come and take photos as you said some weeks ago?'

'Blast and damn. Yes I most certainly do. But I can't get away from the office. I've got to do some work in between building the boat.' And so I missed one of the exciting parts of the game.

Getting the keel across Glasgow and out to Helensburgh called for thought. It weighs over 3 tons and it has no hooks, rings, or knobs on it. This makes it almost impossible to handle. It cannot be lifted by crane without a cat's cradle of elaborate slings, and even then there would be a good chance it would slip out. In shape it is shaped like a tall, very thin wine glass turned upside down, when viewed from the front. From the side it resembles nothing, though technically it might be described as an inverted truncated triangle with hollowed base.

By great good fortune I had become friendly with Jim McKelvie some months before this time. He has a big fleet of lorries of every sort. I telephoned him:

'Can I hire a lorry to move my keel to Helensburgh?' and I described the load.

'Yes, that's easy. You need a low-loader. A big one; a true low-loader is far longer and bigger and more expensive than you need. We have what we call cable carriers. They're used to carry coiled electric cables, and each of these trucks has its own winch. It's far handier for you, and unloading will be much easier than a normal high lorry. There are heavy baulks on the truck, and you can slide the keel down these, pulling it off with the winch.'

And so it was arranged. I telephoned the keel casters to confirm that all would be ready for the next day, as arranged. They were very sorry, the keel had been cast but was not ready for dispatch. It would be, though in ten days. TEN DAYS. I nearly blew every fuse in the Glasgow telephone system. They were most apologetic. I was apoplectic because this was already late June and we were working a schedule planned to the nearest hour. Without the keel we were snookered, unable to make useful progress except in minor matters. No amount of persuasion could bring forward the delivery date, so we had to accept another setback.

Boat building is largely a matter of dove-tailing together many components. In our case we had to get the masts, booms and dinghy from our house in Glasgow down to the hull in Helensburgh, and we planned to do this on the same lorry that carried the keel. Alan Livingstone took the day off to help. The two of us collected the usual bags of tools, and twenty different items like coils of rope, rags, string and so on 'as they might come in handy'. We also packed a lunch, and at last the lorry arrived with the keel on. The casting looked enormous, and already its weight had gouged the timber as it lay on the bed of the lorry.

Jim McKelvie had sent a most willing lorry driver and he helped us load the masts and booms on top of the keel. They had to be very carefully handled, because they are so easily bruised and dented. Each one had to be lashed down with padding all round, for even the vibration could scratch a spar and ruin hours of careful work. Finally we tied a rag on the end of the over-hanging load, piled into the lorry's cab and rumbled off towards Helensburgh.

There the fun began. We backed the truck as far into the shed as we could, lashed a wire sling round the keel after the spars were taken off, took the wire from the lorry's winch away up the shed, round a block and back to the keel. The lorry driver took one winch handle and took up the strain. I grabbed the other handle and heaved with all my guts. The wire went twanging taut, but the keel did not move. We leant on the winch handles till they bent. I saw the wire quiver with tension and realised that there was a serious danger.

'Stand well back,' I let out, 'if that wire breaks it means mince-meat,' but the people around, George, his apprentice, Alan-L and two or three others, weren't here to watch. One ran for grease. Two others grabbed wooden beams. In a flash the great wood baulks supporting the dead iron weight of the keel were made slippery with tallow. A second time the driver and I took the strain, till the wire stretched humming tight. Again I tried to persuade the others to keep clear, for a breaking wire is a killer. But they just gathered round the more and HEAVED. The keel gave a convulsive lurch. That got part of it onto the greased area. Next time the two crow-bars levered in concert with our force on the winch the keel moved again. And again. In no time we had it down to the end of the lorry. Now it had to be tipped over onto sloping baulks to get it off the lorry and onto the massive steel trolley which Arden Yachts had fabricated.

We were not sure whether the keel would slither wildly down the slope off the lorry, or need help. So we took the wire off the pulling end of the keel, and put it on the other end. The idea was that if the keel took charge and wanted to rush down the baulks out of control, we would, we hoped, be able to check its progress by slowly unwinding the winch. But in practice the bitter iron was just too plain heavy. It lay on the baulks and bit into the timber.

By now it was raining. Working in the slippery conditions doubled the risk. Of course by this stage not only was there mud and hazards due to the rain, but the tallow had found its way onto everyone's shoes. Thence it transferred its slimy affections to every horizontal surface for five counties around. So we had to be ten times as careful, otherwise we would find ourselves slipping under the iron. Also there was a risk that the keel would lurch sideways off the two sloping baulks and crash onto the ground, impinging on toes as it did so. We wanted to grease the sloping baulks, but dared not, and in the end just levered and shoved, sweated and heaved, and suddenly found we were there. Another hurdle behind.

The next job was obviously an easy one. All we had to do was to haul the trolley up the shed, which was not too steeply sloped, swivel the trolley round half a turn, run it in close to the boat, jack up the keel, slide the trolley out, and there we were, ready to start putting the keel on. Like hell!

A trolley robust enough to carry over 3 tons of iron is not exactly a child's wheelbarrow. We got the blasted thing up the shed easily enough, by simply bending on a tackle, putting all the ready and willing man-power on the end and pulling plain hard.

Unfortunately the trolley proved a trifle hard to manoeuvre. Obviously its wheels were very rugged jobs, since each was capable of carrying around 2 tons. But they could not swivel, so the only way to turn the trolley was to lever it round. As it weighed about a ton, combined with the keel it made a refractory and recalcitrant burden. We broke wooden levers like matches. There were other boats in the shed which occupied just the corners we wanted to use. The load was so great that if a wheel dropped into a slight gutter in the concrete floor it took fantastic labour to lever it out again. A pad of wood put under a wheel to ease it over a gutter was crushed to splintered pulp by the shattering load. Lunch-time came and went unnoticed.

The other Alan came to help. We bent on more tackles and pulled, reversed the pull, eased the trolley backwards and forwards, till little by little it was turned round. At last the keel was as near to the boat as we could get it and we worked it off the trolley. Late in the afternoon we knocked off for a quick bite. This consisted of standing round and between mouthfuls saying:

'Must jack the boat up absolutely level.'

'Got to raise it a good height before the keel will slide in.'

'It's going to be a bit dangerous. With the boat high up how'll we prevent her falling over?'

'Here, have one of these sandwiches. Oh, I expect we'll think of something clever when the time comes.'

'Pity the roof's not stout enough to support the boat.'

'Roof's altogether too light. We can't even rely on it to keep the boat upright by ropes taken to the rafters.'

'You know it is going to be hard to keep the whole boat upright, and high enough to slide the keel under.'

'How many blocks of timber do you think we'll need?'

'About three times as many as we've got.'

'Can we borrow some? What about the wood-yard next door?' and we all trooped off, still eating, to see what could be borrowed.

I once read a description of a team of motor-racing mechanics. It was said of them they worked so hard, and so relentlessly that they had not had a proper tea-break in thirteen years. The same could certainly be applied to the people who helped to build the *St Mary*.

We selected some massive logs to act as supports for the boat, but then found that the timber, which was second-hand, was too soft. It might let us down under load. Instead we decided to start raising the boat, supporting her with the blocks available. First we jacked up one end, and slipped thin pieces of wood under the keel. Then the other end was pumped up. Without the two hydraulic lorry jacks the work would have been cruel, as it was it was just slow and demanded constant extreme care. Only George was a professional amongst us, and even he was more used to moving smaller boats with rather more elaborate tackle. A slip could mean a shocking wound.

As we lifted the boat up higher and higher our troubles multiplied. She had to be raised till she was at least 5 feet 3 inches above the ground. At this height her topsides would tower up into the eaves, and the props supporting either side of her would be wickedly long, and correspondingly rickety. Doggedly we plugged away: In jack, pump the handle, up she goes half an inch. Put in a piece of wood, lower jack. Push the side props in. Same again at the other end of the boat. Every so often the boat gave an interesting lurch to remind us that she was not to be trifled with.

After a great deal of work, we began to realise we were heading for trouble in large doses. We just did not have sufficient blocks of wood and pit props to support the boat high enough to slide the keel under her. And even if we had, she would be perched so high she would be wildly dangerous. Already she was swaying on her supporting towers of wood baulks.

A possible alternative was to dig the ground away under her, and lower the keel into the hole to bolt it on. There were two disadvantages to this. Firstly the floor was concrete. Not that a concrete floor would have stopped the men round the boat at this stage. A 5-foot layer of concrete would have been disposed of with rather less fuss and waste of time than the average person digs a potato patch. However, once we were down through the concrete we would still have to get the keel into the hole. Again this was not too much of a problem. But getting the joined keel and boat up out of a deepish hole was rather more than we felt we could tackle, without a great expenditure of time.

It so happened that when I built the previous boat, the *St Elizabeth*, we had a similar situation. On that occasion the boat was smaller and lighter. Also it was in a bigger boatyard. So we gathered every man in the yard round the boat and picked her up bodily, by hand, laid her on her side, and the rest was relatively easy. One of the reviewers of my first book, *Sea-Saint*, took a sceptical view of this method of putting on keels, and stated that in his opinion it was not the sort of thing anyone else was likely to copy. Which shows how far adrift you can be, because it was clearly the only way out for us on the *St Mary*.

We were not numerous enough to pick the boat up bodily, so we now canted her over by a mixture of science, art, heavy breathing and tense muscles. Also used were heavy hammers, wedges, guys, tackles, invective, plain cunning, and those invaluable lorry jacks.

We first built a bed of wooden baulks on the port side. Then we forced the starboard side up. Blocks (or as the landsman will insist on saying, pulleys) were fixed to the shed wall and the boat pulled over on her side. By hammering in wedges, she was rolled over till she lay at about 45 degrees. Then we drove wedges in all round, and put long poles fixed firmly in place against her so that she would not roll back on an even keel, or roll right over on her side. By this time it was very late and we tottered home somewhat played out.

Chapter Eleven

Next day Alan-L and I were the only ones available and we tackled the keel together. We had to move it across the concrete floor, then lift it up at 45 degrees till it lay nuzzling against the yacht's underside. It had to be exactly in line, at precisely the right angle, and so firmly held that anyone could walk about on top, or work underneath.

First, we greased the timber baulks on which the keel lay. Then we laid the jacks on their side behind the keel. By pumping away on the jacks we forced the dead weight to slide towards the boat. Good progress was 8 feet an hour.

When the keel was right under the boat we jacked the iron upwards, little by little. However, at this stage we found that the iron was slippery with tallow, and as we forced it upwards into position it slid down the slight incline of the boatyard floor. This seemed unavoidable, though we tried all sorts of dodges to hold the keel up the very mildly sloping floor. The trouble was that there was nothing on the keel to which anything could be tied or lashed.

Eventually we had to jack the keel up the hill further than we wanted it, then as we forced it up against the boat, it slid down till it aligned itself just where it was wanted. Of course it was not correctly in position the first or the third time, but in the end we won. Part of the trouble was that the supports, the levers, our shoes, everything, inevitably got covered in the tallow, which had to be used liberally under the keel to induce it to slide. So we worked with the ever present risk that someone or something might slip. We only took the minimum risks, but there were times when I thought it would have been good sense to have the ambulance actually waiting outside with its engine running, facing the hospital, with rear doors open and a hot water bottle under the blankets on the stretcher.

Because of the thoroughly irregular shape of the keel, it was incredibly difficult to hold it in place once we had got it there. No part of the underside was even roughly horizontal, so that supports underneath just would not stay in place. Then when we got the keel firmly resting on a bed of blocks we found it refused to stay hard up against the hull. We would lever and jack up the aft end, only to find the forward end had moved an inch away. Attempt after attempt was made to fix the heel of the keel while we forced the toe upwards. Much of the trouble stemmed from the sheer mass of the iron. Being 12 feet long and so heavy, it was possessed of a gigantic inertia.

At last we decided that the keel was as near as dammit, and knocked off after another exhausting day, to totter home in my case to tackle a few last minute plans, check the list of rope needed for sheets and halliards, write out a further list of jobs to be done in the immediate future, and so, thankfully to bed.

The keel was so resistant that it took nearly three days from the time it arrived to the moment when we drilled the first bolt hole. Our plan now was to put in a few bolts, and with these draw the keel up snugly to the boat. This worked wonderfully and from then on our struggle with the keel was fairly easy.

It might be suggested that the obvious thing to do is to get the keel first, and build the boat on top of it. This is the usual procedure, but we could not do this as the shed where the boat was built was too low. One night before the keel arrived the hull of the *St Mary* was moved out of the shed where she was built into the yard, then into the adjacent shed where other yachts had been laid up all winter.

This move was done by Donald, John, George, Bill Osborne who owned one of the yachts laid up and other volunteers. I had to go home and leave them around 7.30 in the evening when they were just STARTING the job. By midnight the *St Mary* was out of the shed and halfway across the road outside.

To move her she had to be put on the same trolley which we later used to shift the keel. This job took an hour or two. Then the firm's retired farm tractor hauled the trolley and its load out of the shed and started to move it into the other shed. This sounds straight forward, but in practice it called for hours of patient work, backing and filling, easing the load round corners, edging it forward, working it round pillars and other obstructions and lining the trolley up with the narrow entrance of the shed.

I never did find out what time they finished the job. It must have been well on in the early hours of the morning. And of course the tractor was not exactly a silent operator. Its outrageous bellow rent the still night of Helensburgh for hours, yet the good people all around never once protested. In fact a kindly retired couple living in a cottage beside the yard took us all under their wing and supported the whole venture. When we were tired they would call:

'Come and put your kettle on our stove,' and the old man would wander into the shed with an encouraging word.

Another job that had to be done before the keel could be attached to the boat was spreading the sealing compound on the top flange of the keel, so that water would not leak into the boat through the keel bolt holes. This glue is the stickiest, treacliest, tackiest muck it has ever been the genius of mankind to devise. It had to go on before the keel was finally worked into place, and during those last hours of labour the goo transferred a good proportion of itself onto everything in sight.

Drilling the holes for the keel bolts would have been a grim labour but for the massive electric drill we had. This cut its way through the oak, taking something like 10 or 20 minutes for each hole. It was no good just thrusting the drill up through the iron flange and hoping that all would be well. One person held the drill while a second lined it up most carefully. Then the electric switch would be pressed and the drill starts to rotate with a loud shrill whine. At first it quickly bites into the timber. The man lining up shouts above the shriek of the motor:

'More towards you. Whoa. Not so much. Right. There!' The man gripping the tool hauls upwards with all his might, pushing the drill into the wood. He is helped by someone else who crouches under the machine and just shoves dumbly and continuously. Every few minutes the drill is withdrawn from the hole to let the shavings clear, to cool the electric motor, and possibly for a brief consultation. Inside another man waits for the drill to appear, shouting every so often:

'I can feel the drill coming through,' as he puts his hand gingerly on the wood where the drill will appear. Below a voice says: 'Right. Up again. Should be another 3 inches,' then from above:

'Well done, you've come through exactly where you should,' or sometimes: 'Not so good, you're an inch too far aft.'

This part of the building called for a lot of cooperation. We had to make sure the people working the drill didn't make a large hole through the fellow inside the boat. He had to be told where to expect the drill to appear. Then if one hole was not exactly on line, the drill had to be tilted accordingly so that the next hole was made more accurately. And the man inside had to be kept supplied with nuts, every sort of spanner to get into awkward corners, and ample washers as well as grease, a torch for dark corners and so on.

Down below, the gang working the drill had an assistant who greased each bolt to help it slide in easier. George hammered the bolts in, for a bad shot might bend a bolt or dent the planking. And it's not easy to wham a hammer really hard working upwards, at an angle, when you cannot stand near the job because the keel is in the way.

While all this was going on Alan-H worked on the rigging. We laid the masts out with the crosstrees fitted, and very, very carefully measured the length that each piece of wire should be, remembering to deduct the length of the rigging screw and its shackle at the bottom. Each measurement had to be checked and re-checked, as otherwise the whole complex, precisely timed launching programme would be ruined and the boat delayed.

At home, little jobs continued night after night. A pair of stout boxes were made for the batteries. Each was lined with wax. When I crossed the Atlantic in the *St Elizabeth* I had been given the father and mother of all candles, made by a dentist out of dental wax. We melted this down and poured the liquid wax into boxes, turning and twisting them so that the wax covered all the inside. This was a precaution against acid spilling out of the batteries.

I cut and whipped the ends of ropes, and tried out another idea which none of us had ever met before. This is tapered halliards, and it works as follows:

The main part of the halliard is of flexible wire. This is shackled to the sail, and leads up, over the sheave and down to the hauling part. The hauling part is of rope, as no one can pull on wire, especially thin wire with bare hands. So far everything is as usual. However instead of using 1 inch or 1½ inch circumference rope for the hauling part, as normal, we used a short length of 1½ inch circumference rope next to the wire, spliced to a light rope for the rest of the length. The reasoning behind this is obvious when you think about it. For the major part of the operation of hauling up a sail there is very little load indeed. Only for the last few feet is there any weight, and it's the last few inches when on the winch, or when bousing up that really count. So very light rope is adequate for hauling up the sail almost the whole way, and it's only sense to use the lightest rope possible for that part of the job. It saves cost, weight and space. The short length of stout rope takes care of the stress and strain of getting the sail really tight up. Of course this idea involves a bit of extra work, but we consider it well worth it, especially when all sails are up and we only have small coils of rope nesting at the foot of the mast.

At this stage too there was a great gathering together of gear for the boat. Compass, fenders, warps, pencils, lifejackets, torches, flares all have to be given a quick examination. We decide that the flares will last another year, but we really must set them off next bonfire night. Some fenders need re-canvassing but there's no time for that till the boat's afloat. Nor is there going to be time to make a bookcase, or a special shelf for the radio, but I know that if I don't make a rack for the pencils then they will end up in the bilge the first time we are out in a bit of a gale.

Once the keel was bolted on, we had to stand the yacht up on her feet again. This was relatively easy, after the battle to lay her down and heave the keel under her. We simply put a jack under each end, pumped away gingerly, blocks were lugged in, wedges driven home, jacks withdrawn and repositioned. Then the whole procedure starts all over again. We had to be careful the boat did not come upright and at once topple over the other way. Then she had a tendency to tip aft or forward, according to how the mood and her current set of supporting blocks and props biased her. We were now dealing with a dead weight of well over 6 tons so any error would be firmly and devastatingly punished.

Once upright the boat looked absolutely and utterly terrific. She had a sense of purpose, a defiant, brave determination which was a good augury for her behaviour in rugged weather, and a reward for the hours of backbreaking labour.

My mother came from the south coast to stay at the end of June when the boat should have been ready to launch. Like everyone else, she at once pitched in and worked to get more of the jobs done which were still outstanding. At one time she was painting one side, Morag the other, one of the Alans worked on the rigging, the other wielded a paintbrush, while I worked on the rudder. Then three college girls, friends of the Alans, turned up and we found three more paint brushes. The *St Mary* seemed to have an insatiable appetite for paint. Five coats on the keel, six on the topsides, three of varnish everywhere inside was the aim, but in some places there was not time for all this. When the cabin tops arrived they were gleaming aluminium. They had to be treated with a de-greasing liquid, washed, painted with an etching solution, then a priming coat, next, an undercoat of cream-coloured paint, another of the same, and finally the enamel. All this was done on the outside, then repeated on the inside. And there are two cabin tops. All of which represents solid hours of plying the paintbrush.

We all knocked off for the naming one afternoon. If my mother could not launch the yacht, then at least she could name her ready for the immersion. We rigged up a staging at the bow, and hung a bottle from two light lines, one on either side of the stem. My mother climbed onto the rather wobbly platform and grasped the bottle. Cameras and cines hattered and buzzed.

304 The Ian Nicolson Trilogy

'I name this ship *Saint Mary*,' my mother said, loud and clear the way it should be, 'may God bless her, those who built her, and those who sail in her.' and with that she threw the bottle down against the stem. Bonk! But nothing more. We had put so much decoration round the bottle to protect everyone from flying splinters that the bottle was too well padded. My mother had another try, and on the third go CRASH, and the foaming liquid ran down the topsides. We all had a drink, but before I could refill half the glasses Alan-H was back on the job. The two Alans were to crew for us on the Tobermory Race. This was due to start in fourteen days' time and we were all utterly and completely determined to be there, regardless of the weather, setbacks, disasters, plagues, other peoples' strikes, piracy and barratry, wars and rumours of wars, pestilence and privation. After the naming we all went back to our tasks with renewed vigour, in some cases with a full glass close by.

One job at least was easy, and that was painting the cabin tops. These were like big aluminium boxes, with top, sides, ends, but no bottom. We could not fit them till the boat was outside the shed, as the doorway was too low. So the cabin tops lay on the ground and we painted them outside, turned them over and painted them inside. The only trouble was we had to wait for each coat of paint to dry before applying the next. We got over this partly by working down at the yard in the evenings instead of at home.

My drawings of the cabin tops had been sent to my brother-in-law, who supervised the construction. He made a superb job of them, though like all craftsmen he was by no means satisfied with the results, and mutters darkly about them:

'Next time we'll ...' and here follow a string of technicalities. Basically they are made of thin aluminium sheeting with stiffeners across inside in the form of beams. The sides are also stiffened, and brackets join the side stiffeners to the beams. In practice we were so keen to make a strong job we overdid it, and the cabin tops are relatively speaking one of the toughest parts of the whole boat. Heavy crews can clump about on them without fear that they will suddenly disappear, boots first, through the cabin top. The sides are fitted with large windows held with a cunning form of rubber strip called Claytonright, which seals the windows watertightly and makes them so well bonded to the aluminium that the windows contribute to the strength of the whole structure.

One of our great worries was that in a rain storm the alloy would rattle and reverberate so that life aboard would be intolerable. It so happened that within a few weeks of launching we were caught out in a thunder storm that was as ferocious as anyone in Scotland had ever met. I have never seen rain fall like it did that night, except once or twice in the Pacific where the weather tends to ultra extremes. Suffice to say that the rain came down so fast that our well-sloped decks were deep with water, it just could not clear fast enough. Visibility was down to a few feet, and a bucket left out in the open was filled within a very few minutes. We found this out by trying the experiment. Under these conditions any cabin top would be expected to be as noisy as a tank rattling over cobbles. Ours was just normal. It was quite easy to converse below, the drumming was by no means thunderous.

The great advantage of an aluminium cabin top is its lightness. When our two arrived George and his new apprentice, Ted, between them lifted both cabin tops off the high lorry onto the ground. The big cabin top is 11 feet long, 5 feet wide, over 1½ feet high, and has eight big glass windows. Glass is heavy stuff, and added to this the stout steel main sheet horse with the main boom gallows were all riveted onto the cabin top. If the cabin top had been of conventional wood it would have been twice as heavy, at least.

One mistake I made, but it proved a fine fault on the right side. Because the *St Elizabeth* had been built initially for sailing across the Atlantic, she had a low, safe cabin top. There was thus little risk that a big sea, crashing aboard, would wipe it clean off the deck, leaving a gaping hole into which the next wave would pour. Of course we had to pay for this safety factor with poor headroom in the cabin. So when I was designing the *St Mary* we agreed that as offshore sailing was unlikely to be our lot for some time, we would have plenty of headroom. Also ample height below decks does more than anything else to make a boat pleasant to live aboard. It gives a light, airy sensation, makes the cabin seem bigger than it is, and generally adds to the enjoyment of a cruise.

So we gave the *St Mary* 6 feet 2 inches clear headroom under the beams on the drawing board. Later, the beams were changed but the profile of the cabin top was not. When building we put floorboards a little lower than originally designed, and the net result is that a tall man wearing a top hat can wander unscathed through our saloon ... almost.

The novel way of making the cabin top worked well. It took only an afternoon to fit the light alloy 'lid'. This sketch shows how it was done.

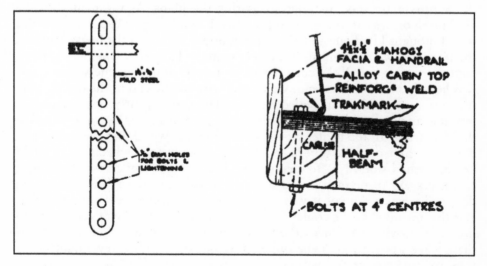

To save weight the chainplates were drilled with lightening holes. These same holes were correctly sized to take fastening bolts, hence the chainplates could be made without templates with the certain knowledge that there would be holes clear of the plank edges to take bolts.

Chapter Twelve

To get the cabin tops on we had to move the boat outside the shed, but she could not lie in the open yard for long as she would impede the traffic of lorries from the other firms round about. Added to this the Tobermory race started on Saturday 15 July, and we were now at Sunday 9 July. So the whole building programme was tuned up to a crescendo.

First, we had to load the almost complete boat onto the special heavy-duty low trailer. To do this the trailer was taken apart and reassembled underneath the boat. This was child's play, as the various components only weighed about 3 hundred-weight each and we were by this time able to throw this type of load about as if it were match-sticks. However, I made a serious error. When asked where the centre of gravity of the boat was, I pointed to the approximate spot, without consulting the plans. As the plan with the vital mark on was at home, 20 miles away, I could give no exact answer, but we all thought I had guessed about right. So we soon had the boat sitting on the trailer, as we thought in the correct manner. However, when we came to haul the trailer out of the shed it was all too obvious that the whole affair was heavily biased to one end. We fixed a wire to one end of the trailer, took the wire to a tackle, and pulled heartily. The trailer gently tipped and dug into the concrete. We wedged it up and put planks under the corners so that the steel frame of the trailer would slide along the wood. But the trailer just dug in. It had purposely been made very short, as the wheels on it could not be turned sideways. To change the direction the trailer was heading it was necessary to pivot it round by main force, since there was no steering device. To make it pivot it was essential to have the wheels close together and this meant that the trailer could all too easily tip endways. There were little corner wheels to check the trailer and prevent it tipping endways, but these wheels proved too light and we tore one off within a few minutes. 6½ tons are not to be trifled with.

There was no alternative but to halt the whole job and go back three moves. We put massive blocks of wood under the boat, wedged her up till the weight was on the blocks and no longer bearing on the trailer, dismantled the trailer, moved it a few inches, and reassembled it. Now the wedges were eased out, the boat's weight taken on jacks set high, the wood blocks were removed and the hydraulic jacks cautiously lowered by bleeding them most carefully. This brought the boat once again onto the trailer.

Our next job was to hitch the trailer to the old farm tractor. From now on all conversation had to be carried out at a quiet shout, except when near the tractor, where a lung-bursting bellow was needed to make anything clear. Donald was away on holiday (and how we missed his flair for overcoming impossible situations), so John mounted the tractor and backed it up to the trailer. Because the boat extended far beyond the trailer, the tractor could not be brought right up to the trailer. This had been thought of, and long steel bars were ready to join the tractor to the trailer. When all was hitched up John very gingerly let in the clutch and the train edged forward. We were about eight in number and everyone had a vital job. Some stood close to the trailer to see it did not put one of its wheels into a rut. Some stood by the tractor to help John and relay messages to him. Some stood back to ensure the boat did not touch anything as she inched forward. All prayed.

I tried to take a calm detached view and foresee trouble. As the boat moved she seemed to have far too much freedom. She seemed to lurch and roll horrendously, and I yelled to those close under the boat to stand back in case she fell over. One of our troubles was that the shed sloped quickly down to the doorway, so the trailer tended to move far too fast downhill. The tractor was quite unable to stop this as the towing bars just bent, in spite of their ample size.

So we hitched a tackle onto the back of the trailer, and made the other end fast to a pillar. As the trailer moved forward we let the tackle out, but it took some skill to do this at just the right speed. Once or twice the trailer went forward with sickening lurches before the tackle came taut and held the rampaging load.

The door to the shed was wide enough to get the boat out by a bare 6 inches. This was luxury compared with the opposite side of the shed. When Donald and his gang had moved the boat out of that part they had a TOTAL of ½ an inch to spare. With only ¼ inch either side, and working in the dark outside, intermittently blinded by the lights inside the shed, they had had a frantic time edging the boat out. However, she had then only weighed a bit over 3 tons.

Little by little, we got our load through the doorway till we came to the widest part of the boat. Everything seemed all right, but we were all watching the narrowing gap between the topsides of the boat and the steel doorpost. Someone gave the signal for the tractor to pull ahead, the trailer gave a dreadful lurch as one of its wheels sank into a soft patch of ground and the boat thumped against the doorpost. Yells and shouts! Curses and rushing forward, with planks, wedges, crowbars, we all plunged into the fray. The actual damage was very slight, but it taught us that everyone had to stick to his job and not worry about crises arising all round. We jacked the trailer up, put planks under its sunken wheel, and gently edged a piece of wood between the boat and the steel doorpost.

Once more the tractor eased forward, and at last the boat was out in the open. In between sweating on this and that, sending someone to buy pies for snatched lunch, lugging planks out for the trailer to run on, and hasty consultations with John above the thundering roar of the tractor, I could not help thinking how fine the boat looked.

Our next problem was to get the cabin tops onto the boat. She was high off the ground, and we had to be careful not to break the cabin top windows or ruin the paintwork. Two long planks were laid against the side of the boat. The main cabin top was held on edge against these planks by one gang, while another crowd scrambled gingerly aboard. It was important not to clump about on the boat, or to have too many people on her, or to collect all on one side or at one end, otherwise she might have toppled over, in spite of her temporary shores.

Now with a heave the lads below pushed upwards and those above pulled and the cabin top flew up and into position. The little cabin top forward was child's play after this. Our next job was to bore holes all round the deck, at 3-inch intervals, to match up with the holes we had bored in the bottom flange of the aluminium cabin top. We used a punch and heavy hammer, bashing a small marking hole in the wood deck through the holes in the aluminium. Then we lifted off the cabin top, and put it a few inches to one side. Now with electric drills we went round the deck drilling downwards through the carline. At this juncture it started to rain, so the electric tools became liberal with their source of power and we found ourselves getting electric-shocks. As usual the Alans were working flat out. One would hammer the bolts in, the other spin on the nuts, and a girlfriend tightened the nuts. Outside I put the cockpit coamings in place, while George and Ted fitted stanchions and pulpits. These could not have been put on before, because like the cabin tops they were too high to let the boat out of the shed.

By Monday evening it was clear that we were not going to be ready to move the boat down to the water's edge that night, but we consoled ourselves that we still had a day or two in hand. Tuesday I had to do some work in the office but Tuesday evening saw us round the boat in force once more. We loaded the masts onto the deck, also the booms, and some of the gear.

Everything had to be well lashed down, with padding round the spars, wedges driven hard in under the supports holding the boat up, and over all tight lashings to keep the boat on the cradle. As evening drew on the drizzle came down once more. At long last someone grasped the starter handle on the tractor, wound it, wound again, again, and with its special throaty roar it started. John climbed into the lofty seat and ever so gently let in the clutch. The caravan moved forward. Already two of us were out on the street to hold up any traffic that might happen on the scene.

Once out on the road we got going at a good walking pace for it was over 2 miles to the concrete ramp where we would launch. After a short distance we came to a HALT sign at a major road. Several of us had gone ahead to stop the traffic in our favour, but no one had warned John that it was essential to keep rolling once in motion. He brought the tractor and trailer up to a gentle halt, but to us standing round it looked anything but gentle. We watched horrified as the boat lurched forward, swayed back, and let a wedge drop out. Yells from all sides:

'Keep GOING. John, for heaven's sake don't stop for ANY DAMN THING.'

'Hell's buckets, you should see the boat wiggle!'

'Just keep moving regardless. If you meet forty coaches trundle through the middle of them!'

'We'll stop all the traffic, you just keep on going till we arrive!' And so on fortissimo above the mighty roar of the tractor.

So John once more eased the tractor and its load smoothly forward and away we went. In a few yards we passed two policemen and my heart rushed mouthwards. We had no number plate on the trailer, I suddenly realised. I wasn't sure if the tractor was licensed for the road, whether John had a licence. We had no lights, we were holding traffic up without authority, we intended to stop for nothing, certainly not for HALT signs. But the policemen took an intelligent view of the situation. Traffic was very light, most Helensburgh people had more sense than to leave their mid-summer firesides that chilly wet summer's evening. Several local yachtsmen who had followed our progress nail by nail, plank by plank, were there to see the climax and lend a hand.

By now it was getting dusk, and we had twisted and turned through the town, trying to keep on the smoothest roads till we were down on the main road running along the shore. One of the party ran off to a telephone booth to ring home, apologise for being 3 hours late for dinner, and explain that he would be in soon, not long after, well … maybe … well it shouldn't be long after midnight by the time he got home. Someone else went to phone home to say he would be a bit late but confidently expected to be in time for breakfast next morning. A couple of others, George included, had not eaten for hours, so went to buy some pies to eat on the way. Morag and someone else went to get our car, to drive ahead with all lights full on, since the tractor had none. Another of the party went to get his car. And so it happened that I found myself padding along behind the boat alone. The rain came down with that steady Scottish drizzle that would dampen anyone's ardour except the owner of a brand new about-to-be-launched boat. I was wearing bright yellow oilskins, and thinking that they would show up well in the gloaming, so that we would be visible to anyone driving up from behind. Curious, I thought, but I could have sworn that the two wheels on each side of the trailer were exactly in line. On the right side the back wheel was well outside the forward one. Then, OH NEPTUNE! My rather tired brain saw all too clearly that A WHEEL WAS COMING OFF!

Just to be sure I darted to the left side and made sure. Yes, on that side both wheels were exactly in line, one behind the other.

'STOP! JOHN! STOP! FOR HEAVEN'S SAKE. THE WHEEL'S COMING OFF.' And to John's everlasting credit he did not just stamp on the brake as anyone might have done, for my shout was such as could be heard, and its urgency understood, three counties away. With the utmost delicacy, the tractor was stopped. The boat teetered, its blocks and supports creaked, and the crisis was over. I got down on my knees to look closer. The wheel was right off the axle except for a quarter of an inch. Only the tight fit of the wheel on the axle prevented it dropping off and then, most likely, the jolt as the cradle dropped down on the ground would bring the whole boat crashing down onto the road, with me beneath.

We had been going along near the crown of the road, as there was a heavy camber, and we had wanted to keep the trailer as upright as possible. So when we stopped we were well away from the side of the road. Up to this moment there had been virtually no traffic, but now cars arrived in ones and threes from both directions. And still the only two on the job were John and me. Some of the others were coming along, still collecting suppers from wherever they could find restaurants open. George was locking up the shed, Morag was still collecting our car. So John stayed by the boat, directing traffic, while I trudged back to get help and tools.

With a jack we carefully took the weight of the trailer off the wounded wheel. Using a large heavy hammer we belted the wheel back in place and put a new pin through the end of the axle to replace the one which had disappeared. By now it was nearly dark, but we had our car and a friend's van too, parked behind the trailer with lights ablaze. Cars came zooming in out of the gloaming, their tyres swishing so that I prayed none would arrive too fast and not be able to pull round the obstruction in time. We had a well-organised traffic control, and the gang on the repairs worked with furious energy, but as every pair of car lights bore down on us I couldn't help wondering if it was a police car, and whether they would take kindly to our activities. Every few minutes I thought of a couple more laws we were breaking. The trailer had no brakes, its load was more than the statutory 7 feet 6 inches wide. We had not informed the police that we were taking an outsize load along the highway, and so on and on.

When at last the trailer was repaired, we set out with Morag driving our car in front, and the friend's van astern, all lights showing up to all in the vicinity what was going on. John drove carefully away, but Morag in the car in front was not used to the saloon we now had and stalled. So John had the choice. Should he keep moving as instructed and crunch over Ian's car, which might annoy Ian more than somewhat, or should he risk stopping the tractor again, with consequent risk to the boat. Just when the decision became imminent, Morag got the car going again.

By now the whole crowd were back around the *St Mary*, some munching pies, some watching the wheels on the trailer, others directing traffic past the caravan, everyone suddenly in a very cheerful frame of mind. We'd met every possible hold-up and overcome them, surely nothing could possibly stop us now. We still had to watch the cradle on the trailer, as the wedges worked loose, especially when the trailer rocked horridly over a manhole cover in the road. So we devised an advance lookout to warn John well in advance of manholes so that he could steer off well before them and avoid them. For of course if he saw one just a few feet ahead he could not avoid it, sharp turns being out of the question.

All in all we reckoned that the tractor train crossing the Antarctic had nothing on our tractor train. After all there are no highway laws, or other road-users, in the Antarctic. All went well till we came to a down-slope, and we found that the trailer was tending to over-run the tractor. There was nothing for it but to speed up the tractor to keep ahead, but this meant that the wheel axles might get hot, and the bearing seize. We had no alternative but to take the risk, and so at last we came to the turning off the main road. This was on a bend, and we had to swing the whole juggernaut out onto the wrong side of the road before it could turn down the narrow private road. So once more we posted patrols to stop the traffic both ways, with a group in each direction detailed off to apologise to the drivers for the delay and explain that we would not be long blocking Her Majesty's highway.

The private road was so narrow we had trouble keeping the trailer wheels on it. Also it was now dark so that we tended to be blinded by the car lights. As a result we were all so careful making sure disaster did not overtake us by letting one of the trailer wheels drop onto the soft soggy verge that we let the trailer get itself in a tricky position against a protruding concrete block. The tractor made so much noise that it was quite impossible to tell John what to do. Someone would spot that the trailer needed edging further right.

'GO RIGHT A FRACTION,' he yells.

'RIGHT A BIT JOHN,' yells the relayer walking by John.

'WAS'AT? CAN'T HEAR.' John bellows back.

By this time one trailer wheel is half off the concrete and the fellow in charge of that side has visions of the whole works toppling on top of him. So his next shout raises the sky some inches.

'RIGHT. TAKE THE B****** THING RIGHT,' and John, realising that things are touchy gets the steering wheel hard over and averts catastrophe. But the man on the left side then finds the trailer is edging fast over his way, and he sets up a counter-shout.

When the trailer was stopped, it was touching the concrete block which was immoveable, being the corner of a building. By this time we would willingly have lifted any building out of the way with our bare hands, but this building did not belong to us, and we were indebted to its owner, so we set about moving the trailer back. Now a really enthusiastic bunch of thoroughly determined people can move mountains, but that is far easier than a trailer weighing a ton, with a 6-ton load. It was out of the question to manhandle the trailer clear, so we unhitched the tractor, reversed it, and put it on the back of the trailer to haul it clear, edging one pair of wheels along the concrete with breathless care. If those wheels had slipped or rolled off the edge of the concrete all the previous months of work would have been wasted. For though the drop off the hard road was only a few inches, the result must have been a capsized trailer and load.

It was now well past midnight, but at last the *St Mary* was within sight of the sea, and only a few yards from the concrete ramp which would carry her to real birth. We piled our tools into our car, crammed ourselves in on top of each other, and drove wearily home. I drove round Glasgow dropping one off here, one there, for all public transport had long since stopped. Fortunately we had, some weeks before this, decided that the Triumph was no good for boat building. All it would carry at one load, we found, was a couple of pre-fabricated parts of the galley, an anchor, two warps, four tins of paint, two settee cushions, a sail, a gang of rigging and set of rigging screws, my tools, spare timber, and a bottle of turps. This left no room for Morag. So we found an old Jaguar, which proved its worth that night, as we drove home breaking another highway law by carrying considerably more people in the vehicle than the manufacturers intended.

Chapter Thirteen

Next day, Morag and I felt very reluctant to get up. However, it was essential to get the masts stepped, and as soon as possible, for we wanted to launch on the midday tide. So with the Alans I drove down to the boat, and we tried to decide how to get the masts up. Originally we planned to put the trailer under a steel girder high up, and lift each mast from above, then lower it in place. On the spot this looked rather hard, if not well-nigh impossible.

We were working out the details of a scheme which was going to be plain risky and shockingly hard work (and by now we felt we were competent judges of what hard work could be) when an angel came to help us. Admittedly he didn't look like the popular image of an angel, he had a gruff voice, but he obviously was an angel because right away he wrought a miracle. He caused a certain machine to pick up each of our masts in turn and lower them in place. More than this I cannot and will not say, because this angel might get into trouble if I did.

Not even our angel could prevent one or two heart-snatching moments. For instance we got the main mast up, and found that ALL the rigging was the wrong length. After all the trouble Alan-H and I had taken, after the checks and counter-checks, it was a bitter pill to find we had boobed thoroughly. Rather wearily, for by now the pace was beginning to tell, I climbed down off the boat, to collect some shackles so as to lengthen the short rigging. And when I turned to look at the boat, it was all obvious. We had carefully put the mast upright. But the boat was canted over slightly to one side, to list her against the supports which were only on one side of the trailer. So of course the mast should have been lined up with the boat, not put perfectly upright. Saved again. The rigging proved to be exactly the right length.

But it did prove how tired I was getting, not to spot a thing like this earlier. Another thing I noticed about this time was that I kept cutting my hands when using tools. I don't claim to be skilful with chisels, screwdrivers and planes, but since those far off days when I caused chaos at the age of five, by taking all the screws out of all the lavatory door fittings, I've seldom been for long without shipwright's tools in hand. So I've learned a certain aptitude, but fatigue was undermining this.

By midday it was obvious we were going to miss high water, for there were hundreds of tiny details still to be worked out. One or two vital shackles did not fit perfectly, some of the rigging screws were tight, one of the shrouds got the wrong side of a crosstree. This was serious, as we dared not scramble up the mast, it might have toppled the boat over. But we could not launch without rectifying this matter. We tried hooking it down with a long boat-hook; we tried throwing a light weight over the crosstree with a line tied to the end, but were beaten by the strong wind. We tried almost every trick in the book.

Then George climbed up a narrow precarious steel lattice-work right out to the end. He leant far out, grabbed the wire and pulled it up and over. It was a brave thing to do, for the steel-work was slippery with grease and by now the wind was strong enough to blow him off his perch.

It had been flat calm when we first got down to the boat. But the wind soon got up and swung round almost dead on shore. By launching time it was obviously impossible to put the boat afloat that day. This was Wednesday, three days to the race.

I went back to the office, but cannot pretend to have worked to much advantage. I kept wondering if the boat was all right. By now it was blowing nearly gale force and the boat was in a most exposed place. A really strong gust, dead on the beam, with all her rigging and two masts, might tip her over.

Next day, we were down early in the morning. Again it had been calm enough in Glasgow, but by the time it was high tide the wind was vicious, whipping on-shore and carrying spray with it. No launching on Thursday. We worked on the cockpit coaming, put gear aboard, checked the rigging, wandered around like caged beasts. Someone was fool enough to suggest we were too late to make the race. I flared into a blazing anger, but was too tired to keep it, and anyway it was not an intentionally unkind remark. But the pace was beginning to tell. At home Morag had been going flat out on the domestic side. In one room were piles of sleeping bags, in another clothes. Here were our oilskins, plus a spare set, hard weather gear and rubber boots. In the kitchen boxes of tins, of fresh food, first-aid gear, spare blankets, a couple of bottles of sunshine, and two more of fruit juice, a spare primus in case the calor gave out, meths for it, and paraffin, and primus prickers, and matches. The piles grew and Morag's share of work was immense. We not only had to commission the boat but at once set out on our annual holiday. And anything forgotten could not be bought on the way.

On Friday I was determined to launch unless it was blowing very hard dead on shore. I reckoned that with an off-shore gale, if we timed things right, we could pull the boat down the slipway and into deep water so fast, with the wind's help, that she would not have time to hump and bash herself and the trailer. All Thursday I haunted the radio, listening to every forecast, and in between studied every weather map available.

In the event I worried unnecessarily. It was a lovely day, sunny with a gentle breeze. By midday all was set and we waited for the Arden Yachts cruiser to motor round to the slipway, to be ready to haul the *St Mary* off.

The tractor was hitched on to the trailer and we pulled it near the top of the ramp. After unhitching, the tractor was put on the back of the trailer, to hold it back. By now there was a good crowd. We pulled the chocks from under the trailer wheels and eased it down the slope. The weight tried to take the whole affair fast, and we had to be ready with blocks to stop a run-away. Under the tractor we had a long wire led to a post, to check the trailer if the tractor could not hold the trailer and the wheel chocks did not work.

As the trailer touched the water I hopped into a dinghy and rowed out to the anchored motor cruiser, collecting a rope from the *St Mary*'s stern on the way. Aboard the cruiser I found that she had not been anchored in line with the slipway, and that if I hauled on the rope it would tend to pull the *St Mary* off her cradle sideways, instead of pulling both boat and cradle into deep water. There was not a moment to lose. With feverish haste, I scrambled forward and hauled up the cruiser's anchor chain. Once up, I dumped the anchor on deck and flew aft to grab the wheel. There was a bit of wind, and I had to be very careful not to get the rope to the *St Mary* caught round the cruiser's propeller. Fortunately Ted was in the cruiser's cockpit. He handled the rope in a masterly fashion, which was lucky for me as this was his first time afloat in this sort of situation. I worked the cruiser astern, got the helm hard over, came ahead, let the wind take her bow round, and within a minute we were dead in line with the slipway.

'Take a turn of the rope round that bollard, Ted,' I yelled above the rumble of the cruiser's engine. As he did so I jammed the gear lever ahead, opened the throttle to full to take the cruiser offshore into deep water, slowed her down as the rope came taut, then gave her full throttle at what I thought was just the right moment to haul the *St Mary* off the cradle and into deep water. If this sounds tricky ... it was.

But Neptune recognises that there are times when he might as well cooperate because the mere men above him mean to succeed. The *St Mary* floated off without a wiggle of protest, and we hauled her clear of the shallows. We still had her fast by the stern, and it took some manoeuvring to get her warp attached to the bow. Meanwhile, John on the tractor had trouble. He had driven his vehicle into the water to push the trailer down far enough to float the yacht off. When he wanted to reverse and haul the trailer back on dry land a wave splashed up and drowned the magneto. So we had to jill around while a lorry hauled the tractor on to land.

We towed the *St Mary* back to Helensburgh, but all was not well aboard. Like all planked wooden boats she is dependent to some extent on the wood swelling to tighten the seams between the planks, and so exclude the water. So we were not at first worried when we found she was making some water. However it was coming in too fast. George whipped up the floorboards and found that the trouble stemmed from one seam.

'It looks as if all that shaking on the trailer has started a seam. One plank must have taken a lot of the load, and the leak is just where we put the wedges in.'

Normally we might have let the leak plim up, but with the race now less than 24 hours away there was no time to spare. We towed the boat back to Helensburgh pier, slipped the tow and beached the *St Mary* alongside the pier. As the tide fell she settled on the ground, and George was soon over the side in a dinghy. When the water left her he caulked the offending seam, while above we loaded gear, rove off the rigging and tried to stow everything in its correct place.

It was now long after three o'clock, and I had promised Morag I would collect her at one o'clock. The delay at the launching and now this grounding and caulking had set my schedule badly awry, but I tumbled into the Jaguar and set off for home at its best speed. Morag knew enough about boats to know that launchings can be dangerous. The transformation from an inert shape to a living thing, man's nearest approach to the divine creation, is like any other birth, not conducted without serious risk. So she was going to be worried, I knew. But the Jag was not the Triumph. She seemed positively sluggish as I tried to wrench the rev counter round to near the red line and keep it flickering back and forth near that line as I whipped from gear to gear. This is not so hard in a Triumph, but the Jag's gearbox just does not like that sort of thing. It seemed an age before at last I could flick in overdrive and concentrate on the coming corner. As late as I dared I snicked the overdrive out, thumped the brake, revved the engine mightily, jammed in third and hurtled into the corner. It felt like a block of flats going berserk after the taut tyre-shrieking dead-upright tail-waggly cornering of the Triumph. I felt faintly sick and decided that next time braking a little earlier might be better. It wasn't. Then on the third corner I realised that in fact the Jag wasn't worried one iota, it was me that was flapping. So I set out to cover the ground as swiftly as possible consistent with the usual nightmare through Dumbarton.

At home the gear lay in neat piles, all ready for loading into the car and we were back in Helensburgh with no more than a brief pause for a meal that might be called lunch or tea. From now on it was just a question of whether the months of planning and preparation were perfect, or whether some vital item had been forgotten. If I had not remembered to bring spare shackles, if one of the sails did not fit, if one of the booms had been made a fraction too short, or the bilge pump suction was too short, if the main sheet would not fit its blocks, if … if …if.

However, things were now going our way with a swing. As evening drew on, a small but increasing crowd of friends and local yachtsmen came down the pier to where the *St Mary* lay, with the tide creeping up to refloat her. First someone from the crowd offered to bend on the mainsail. Someone else clambered aboard to help. Below Morag and one of the Alans were stowing food. The other Alan and I were fitting the long battens into the mizzen, and setting that sail. Another yachtsman climbed aboard and started reeving off the sheets, another came to help and was soon lashing down the dinghy. Darkness fell and the *St Mary* floated. By the lights on the pier we worked on, while some went away for a meal and came back.

Below decks Morag and her helpers had transformed the bare cabin into a delightful home, with bunks made up, food arranged in the galley, pots and crockery cleaned and stowed, spare gear tucked away, clothes stowed, shoregoing jackets on hangers in their locker, oilskins and seaboots in their special locker, even the midnight snackery of sweets was in its place, for it was obvious we would be sailing through the night to get to the starting line.

All this time the wind had been dying from light to faint, and it was now barely a zephyr. Our friends climbed back on to the pier and untied our warps. John was back on the job after a flying visit home to grab a meal. He tied a rope to our bow, and took the other end to his dinghy, to tow us clear of the pier and point our bows to the open sea.

It was well past 11, and full dark, but a clear fine night. Almost at once the *St Mary* felt a tiny air and responded. We threw off the towing line, with a shout of thanks to John and then one of the nicest things of the whole adventure happened, the crowd on the shore cheered. We cheered back from the yacht and glided off into the night, towards the starting line.

Chapter Fourteen

As soon as I realised that the boat was a honey under sail, perfect to handle, responsive and easy to coax, I handed over the helm to Alan-H. He took over and sailed the boat right through the night, non-stop, without relief. This was quite a feat. He had never sailed a cruiser before, had been working flat out the whole day, and for days before, with snatched meals, often insufficient sleep. Now while I worked to get the boat tuned for racing I had no need to worry about our progress towards Port Bannatyne some 12 miles away, where the race was due to start in 6 hours' time.

Soon after midnight the wind died right away. We dared not delay, since we had to average at least 2 knots if we were to be at the starting-line in time to make a good start. There had been no time to line up the engine properly. This cannot be done until the boat is afloat, since wooden craft change shape slightly when launched. Ideally, we would have spent a few hours carefully lifting one end of the engine a minute amount, fitting thin slivers of metal under the engine feet till the engine coupling and propeller shaft were perfectly aligned. Now we wanted to use the engine and had to risk running it without this very important preliminary. We might easily damage the propeller shaft and the tube through which it passed to the propeller. Also of course the engine had never yet been run, and might refuse to start.

Morag and Alan-L were by this time trying to get a little sleep. I had to wake them to warn them the engine was about to start, since it might make a frightening amount of noise. Full of worry I set the controls, swung the starting handle, flicked over the compression lever, and at once the Lister burst into life. Keeping it running dead slow, I put it in gear and we slid forward through the water, with a merry gurgling chuckle of water at the bow.

Three times that night when the wind left us we resorted to the engine, and each time it started at once, with what was to prove its unfailing reliability. In between starting the engine and stopping it, I went round the deck making sure all gear was lashed down, pumped the bilge, looked under the floorboards to check for leaks, felt the stern bearing to make sure it was not over-heating, checked the racing instructions, chocked off the tins in the galley that rattled, helped Alan-H navigate, trimmed the sails to get the best out of the faint breeze, and once or twice just stood and revelled in the beauty that was our *St Mary*.

As dawn came up we crept up to Toward lighthouse, and rounded the headland to see Port Bannatyne in the distance. The others rolled stiffly out of their bunks and we had the first meal aboard, a gigantic breakfast. By the time the dishes were being washed we could see plenty of yachts leaving moorings, running up sails, and motoring clear of the bay. With 10 minutes to go before the first gun, we sailed up to the line. We'd done it; after nine months' relentless driving, driving, driving, we were in time, with 10 minutes to spare.

The race for me was such a climax it would not have mattered if the boat had sunk after the first 3 miles, she would not have been born in vain.

From a cloudless sky the early morning sun blazed down, one of the finest days of a consistently wet summer. On the *St Mary* we all felt 8 feet tall, on top of the world, ready to take on all comers, the larger the better. Certainly we were up against stiff opposition. The total fleet of some sixty boats was divided into two classes. Though we were one of the smallest of the big class, and the only small one with a ketch rig, our handicap put us well up the list. So to do any good we had to come in well up the fleet. As we were quite unready for racing this was obviously expecting miracles, but we had one asset. While almost the whole fleet was manned by people just out of warm bunks and feeling early-morningish, we felt on top of our form.

It was obvious at the jilling round for the start that some crews and especially some helmsmen were feeling the effect of the early hour. Many boats made little attempt to assess the best end of the starting line, or to try different approaches. With the very light wind I decided to stay as close to the line as I could and told the crew:

'We'll make as few tacks as possible, as we're all new to the boat. But we must not get more than 100 yards from the line, this light wind may die right away. The port end is favourable, and it's a reaching port tack start. Stand by, we'll gybe now.'

Then the boat was spun, and how she whipped round, as swift and light as a polopony. We nipped under someone's stern, waved to an acquaintance, and sailed back toward the line.

'We'll aim high up on the windward end of the line. It doesn't look as if it will be crowded. The only gamble is that the hills may take the wind that end, and leave a cats-paw at the leeward end of the line.' So we tacked and gybed, never moving far from our chosen spot. Alan-H went up onto the foredeck to hand the genoa round every time we tacked, and to keep an eye open for boats in our way, for there were plenty now, all like us jousting for the best position.

Alan-H had my watch and was calling the minutes to the start: '8 minutes to go.'

'Right. After we've passed that sloop we'll tack again. Stand-by. Ready. Lee-oh. Here, take the helm a moment while I give Alan a hand with the sheet.' This showed up our outstanding weakness. With no sheet winches, we could not get our headsails tight in. Another strong man aboard would have been a big asset. While on all the other yachts' crews could pump their headsails into an efficient sheeting position, we had to sweat them in. Even under ideal conditions, working very fast to get the headsail in tight before it filled with wind, we were under a big disadvantage.

'7 minutes to go,' from Alan-H, 'there's a big sloop coming up astern.'

'Right, thanks. It's him to keep clear. Morag, just check once more below that everything's wedged in position.'

The sloop luffed and we got a close view of some of the opposition, close enough to have stepped aboard. They did not seem to be going past us at a great rate. Fine set of sails, not a crinkle in them. I looked at ours for the ninety-seventh time since we had got into the starting-line area. The fully battened mizzen was almost perfect, setting like a beautiful wing, its special creaseless cream-coloured terylene taut and efficient. The terylene genoa looked good too, though not sheeted just right. But the cotton mainsail was setting far too full. With no halliard winches (something else that had not arrived in time, though we could scarcely have found time to fit them if they had) we could not hoist the sail up bar taut. Also the very light wind was not enough to press the heavyish cotton sail into a perfect curve.

'6 minutes to go,' from Alan-H.

'See if you two lads can get the main halliard tighter.' I luff the boat into the wind and hold her there, gently coming to a standstill as the sails flap lazily. The two Alans scramble back to their position.

'5 minutes-BANG-to go.' The crash of the gun interrupts Alan-H. Now we hug the weather end of the line, seeking to keep to windward of the other boats, only a few thank heaven, that want the same piece of water. Some of the yachts are still getting up sail and hastening off the moorings, but they are mostly the smaller class which starts after us.

'4 minutes to go.' The tension is getting fierce. We throw off sweaters, tack and gybe, the gear all working perfectly, nothing jamming, and now the wind is so light that we do not need sheet winches to get our headsails in tight enough.

'3 minutes to go.' We all feel dry-mouthed. I want eyes on every side of my head, to watch the other boats.

'There's just time to run off from the line once more, whip round and go for it. Ready about. Lee-ho.'

For a moment the sheet of the genoa catches:

'Free the sheet! Alan-L! Weather side!'

'Right. It's clear.' The boat is now pointing away from the line. I head her for a gap between two boats moving towards the line, guessing they will be there too early. One turns, we slip in behind her.

'2 minutes to go.'

'Right. Gybing. Just watch the main sheet.' The booms thump across, and we are going for the line.

'Give me every quarter minute now, Alan-H.'

'One and a half to go.'

'Ease the genny sheet a fraction.' This to make the sail set fuller and draw better in light airs.

'One and a quarter to go.' My heart's thumping wildly now, we look like making a really super start, and well to windward. A quick glance shows only one boat threatens our weather, and she's astern.

'1 minute to go.'

'Give me every 10 seconds from now.' I bear away just a fraction to get the boat going full tilt, though this is only 2 knots in these conditions.

'50 seconds to go.'

'Ease the main just a fraction. No. That's worse. Put it back as before.'

'40 seconds to go.'

There's not another boat ahead of us except one well down to leeward.

'30 seconds to go.'

We are going to be a few seconds late I think, but not much. Many yachts are already 5 minutes behind us in these light airs, giving themselves that much handicap.

'20 seconds to go.' I suddenly realise that besides making a good start we are holding place with the other boats in our locality. There are plenty of boats near which have to give us time. It looks as if the beamy floating nursery we've built ourselves is at least as swift as some of the so-called cruiser-racers.

'10 seconds to go.' By now the tension aboard is at a dry-mouthed, heart-thundering breathlessness. The others are concentrating on the commodore's yacht, watching for the gun, except for frequent glances at the watch by Alan-H. I just keep my mind on getting the boat to go as fast as she will in the light airs, 'time', says Alan-H and almost at once the gun cracks out away down to leeward.

'Well done everyone,' I say, feeling like a million pounds plus a 10 per cent bonus. 'We've made a good start, we're going as fast as most people, which is a ruddy miracle, and if the race only ended a mile ahead we would win easily on handicap. Now let's concentrate on getting the best out of her. Try easing the genny sheet again ...' and so we settle down to do our damndest.

Of course after our trumpet-blowing period the anticlimax sets in. The faint breeze fills in enough to give the other yachts some speed, and the bigger ones, as well as the small fast ones, start to catch us up. For an exciting time there are about five of us slanting in to the Bute shore in close company. We sail along, exchanging a little banter, each boat almost near enough to jump on. Under these conditions it's wonderful to find the *St Mary* will dodge and turn so well, and while there is a very real risk of collision, at least we can keep out of the way as well as anyone.

In this tight bunch I see that the danger is we may get blanketted by boats to windward, so I tussle and wriggle and keep our wind clear. This pays, because though some eleven or more boats get ahead of us, most are close to another boat and plenty are getting a confused dirty wind. A few minutes later the breeze again goes down to just a knot, and then we really triumph. Slowly but relentlessly we start to sail through the fleet. From around thirteenth to eighth, then past two more appreciably bigger boats. Now we're fifth, then fourth, till there is only an 8-metre cruiser-racer and *Leezie Lindsay* ahead of us. The former is a bigger, much more race-bred type than the *St Mary*. She should, under any and all conditions, do at least 3 knots to our 2. *Leezie Lindsay* is no more than our size, but a sloop, tuned, just a year old, and to keep within shouting distance of her exceeds our wildest dreams. We heard later that on some of the other boats there were some low soft solemn words when they saw us ghost away ahead, eating out yard by yard till many fast, well-sailed boats were thoroughly thrust astern.

While this blissful state of affairs could not last, it was enough to make the past months' solid, relentless, sometimes tedious work all well worthwhile. Gone was any idea of tiredness; we adjusted sheets, plotted and planned and tried every trick in all the books to keep our commanding position. When the wind made a more determined effort, the rest of the fleet soon came up and our position went back to twelfth again. However, the excitement was by no means over. We were now sailing up the Kyle, with the lofty hills of Bute on our port hand, to starboard the almost mountainous shore of Argyll, green and every other colour in the morning sun. The wind slanted in from the port bow, so to get over near the Bute shore meant taking an unfavourable tack. Many yachts did this, working on the assumption that it always had paid in the past to stick close to Bute when beating up the Kyle. But I argued that it is bad tactics to take the unfavourable tack, the slant which is furthest away from the direct line to the destination. As this was only my second season on the Clyde, I had little past personal experience to guide me.

So we watched almost the whole fleet, or at least that part of it which led, (for there were dozens of boats far, far astern), take the Bute shore. At this stage the sun was getting high, and though still early morning, it became hot. This seemed to kill the wind. The sea was like a glass floor, unrippled, solid-looking. Not a boat stirred, all sails hung lifeless, slack, exhausted-looking. We searched and scanned in every direction, watched our light cotton tell-tales for the first wisp of wind; it might come up astern and call for a quick trimming of sheets to get every advantage.

Chapter Fifteen

When the wind did come it was a faint ruffling on the water, clearly defined, a long patch, quite narrow, and it tantalisingly avoided every single boat in the fleet ... save one ... the *St Mary*. It was no more than an angel breathing, but it took hold of our sails; they stretched just a tiny fraction. We glided so slowly, so imperceptibly, forward that our rivals could not at first notice we were stealing ahead. Once more we worked our way up to the head of the fleet. I steered with desperate concentration, determined to keep within that small area of scratched water, the only place for miles, as far as our eyes could scan, that had any wind. The mainland shore was slanting out towards our track, we began to get worried about running aground, but foot by foot we gained over the others till at last we dare not stand on longer and had to tack off the shore, and so lost our private zephyr.

Every boat now lay virtually motionless, though occasionally one or other might get a slight urge forward from some tantalising breath. We could do absolutely nothing to hasten our progress and so relaxed, took photos and kept an intense lookout all round. I feared that the wind might come up astern, bringing with it all the laggards. After a long wait this happened. We noticed spinnakers blossoming far astern, and boat after boat was clearly getting a useful breeze while we lay helplessly becalmed.

We had to watch while yachts we had left virtually out of sight astern caught us up. When the wind at last reached us we pushed our booms out and started sailing once more, but we no longer had a commanding lead. Indeed at this stage we made poor progress while yacht after yacht sailed by. The night without sleep began to tell, we found we were thoroughly tired and it was an effort to work the yacht.

Though we had a spinnaker aboard, we had not had time to rig the spinnaker boom lift. This meant that we could not set our spinnaker, and for 10 minutes we sat discussing how we might get the sail up without a boom lift. The others were naturally restless to see our advantage slip away. I was too, but I felt whacked, tired from the concentration piled on top of the pressure of the past weeks.

'It's simply a question of nipping up the mast to fix a block up there,' I pointed out, feeling listless and not inclined to rush up two steps, let alone our mast, which was small and smooth and far from easy to shin up.

'We're dropping back fast,' one of the Alans pointed out, quietly, just a little disappointed.

'Can't you rig the spinnaker without a lift?' he asked. I said: 'We've no idea how it sets even, it's a second-hand spinnaker I bought from a friend. I'm not sure it's even going to be much good when it is up, it's rather small for the boat.'

'It's certainly sad to see all these laggards come up so effortlessly.' For 10 minutes we sat and suffered while our position in the fleet worsened. At last I could stand it no longer.

'Alan-L, take the helm, I'm going up the mast. Alan-H come up forward with me and pass this light rope up, clear of the rigging as I climb up.'

In an instant we were organised, and I was struggling up the mast, a rope tied to my belt. I fixed a temporary spinnaker boom lift over the inner end of a crosstree, and thankfully slid down onto the deck. The sail was scrambled out of its bag, shackled on, and up it went. We were back in the hunt.

At this juncture boats were grouped in bunches, each boat taking the wind from the one ahead. We lay well back in the second phalanx, and with those all round us entered the narrows by the Burnt Isles. The first group of boats, the fastest of the fleet, had got through the limited channel between the islands and the mainland before the tide strengthened against them, and with enough wind to carry them past the well-sheltered places.

When we arrived the tide was running quite fast, while the wind had once again got tired. We found the *St Mary* able to hold her own as well as the next boat, and better than some, but it was a trying time. For long periods we stood still, our speed through the water being exactly matched by the adverse tide. No one dared approach the shore too closely to get out of the tidal flow, for fear of going aground. It was all too easy to slip out of what little wind there was, into the shadow of the overhanging hills, and be set back relentlessly towards the rocks. This sort of creeping battle of wits, with the other boats close all round, and our own boat so much an untried craft, had its own excitement. But it was mainly frustration, for we knew that the faster yachts were by now clear of the sheltered zone and must be gaining miles, literally, on us.

And so it was. When at last we slipped free of the clutches of the wind-shadowed narrows we glided round the bend and there we saw several yachts far far ahead, and going like Hades. However, we ourselves had left behind many, still held firm by the protecting rocky hills which prevented the wind from wafting them onwards. We were now in close company with a big ketch, and to our delight managed to keep up with her for some time, though admittedly this other vessel has the reputation for being slower than a one-legged tortoise going uphill to a funeral against the wind. They were naturally interested in the new yacht which was hanging on to them and shouted:

'What yacht's that?'

'The *St Mary*.'

'The *Sea Fairey*?'

'No. *St Mary*.'

'Oh. Is she new?'

'Yes, newer than tomorrow. In fact she's far from finished. We're still working on her,' and one of us waved a screwdriver that was lying in the cockpit.

'Not finished? Well she can certainly go.'

'We only launched 18 hours ago. We've no cabin door. In fact there isn't a door or drawer in the whole boat. No sheet winches either. Just a hull sandwiched between a keel and some sails,' which was a most unkind way to refer to our lovely boatlet.

It was true she had no cabin door, nor a toilet, just a bucket with a simple wooden seat, nor was there a door on the toilet compartment, just a curtain which we had not yet had time to rig up permanently. Nor was there stowage for the cups and plates. We just wedged them securely in a spare bunk. However, Morag had laid it down firmly that no boat could possibly go racing round the Western Isles without proper galley stowage. So in the hectic moments between putting on the vital parts of the boat I had grabbed a bit of teak, whipped it into shape, planed it all over, and screwed it onto the galley bench, to form a high fence, or fiddle as a yachtsman would say. Behind this we stacked our jam, cereal, salt, ready-to-use tins of soup and corned beef and so on. However much the boat heeled, everything stayed put. And when I think of some of the elaborate galley stowage plans I've worked on, plans which have taken two skilled shipwrights a couple of weeks' work to translate into the solid ...

Our course was now round the top end of Bute. We sailed as close to the land as we dared without actually denting the rocks. With baby 3 months away, Morag had to take things easily during the race, just cooking, grabbing the tiller when the rest of us were handling the sheets, washing up, keeping an eye on yachts astern to let the helmsman concentrate on the job in hand, restowing gear after the two Alans had been through the cabin in a hurricane of a hurry to get another sail out, and so on. At this stage the wind varied a lot and we had to tack often. With some weight in the wind, not much but enough to make our genoa really fill and pull, there was only one way we could sheet in properly.

It went something like this:

'Ready about! Ready Morag? Right, here's the helm,' and I would pass the tiller to her. Alan-H would uncleat the weather sheet while on the foredeck Alan-L would gather the sail forward, and pull it clear of the mast. Timing it carefully, I'd haul in the lee sheet like fury, keeping well forward so that Alan-H could get round behind me and put his weight on the sheet with mine. By that time Alan-L would have nipped down the lee side deck and grabbed the sheet ahead of me, then:

'Right. NOW ... And again. Right. Got it ...' (puffs and panting follow after this) and we all settled back till the next time. All for the want of a pair of sheet winches. But we were going, and not slowly.

Down the West Kyle it was a long and short tack. We had hoped to be able to lay the buoy in one close fetch, and to this end, sheeted in as hard as we could. Which was not hard at all. Here our lack of winches made a serious difference. However, we were not alone with this problem, and we decided to exert a little cunning. As the leaders made for the buoy, we watched carefully to see if any overstood. Several did, and I was fairly sure that though the wind was now true where we were sailing, at the headland it was freeing a little every so often.

So though it meant a lot of extra work, we made shorter tacks as we came to Ardlamont Point. Some other crews in the area were now having lunch, and as so often happened their attention wandered just enough to let us catch up one boat and overtake two more by cutting tight round the buoy.

Out in Loch Fyne we were faced with a long and short tacking match again. The wind was by no means constant and as the afternoon wore on it died right away. The race instructions said that the race would finish at 6 p.m., regardless of the position of all boats in the fleet. This rather harsh ruling was to allow the fleet to lock into, and pass through, the Crinan canal. The second part of the race was from Crinan to Tobermory the next day, and almost every boat in the first leg of the race was to go on for the second. This meant a great strain on the locking facilities.

So as we tacked and tacked again, trying to gain a few yards all the time from the fickle wind, we kept looking at our watches. Eventually it was obvious that we could not possibly make the finishing line by 6 p.m. Indeed, by four o'clock many yachts all round us had given up and motored away. By five o'clock we were almost the only boat not under power on the glassy sea. It looked as if one other yacht had no engine and we were discussing whether to go and give him a tow, when he picked up a shaft of wind and made the line ahead of us. But like the vast majority of the fleet, all the boats in our area including ourselves were quite unable to make the six o'clock deadline.

The end of the race and the entrance to the Crinan canal at Ardrishaig were the scene of some activity after the quiet of the closing stages of the race. We motored slowly up, nursing our engine. As soon as possible, we dropped anchor and I got the front off the engine box. While the others tidied ship and cooked a meal I realigned the engine. We did not have any metal shims (as the slivers of metal put under the engine feet are called) but some scraps of bronze served well enough. Using Heath Robinson methods we realigned the engine as best we could, though there were one or two occasions when the lack of tools and equipment nearly beat us.

Chapter Sixteen

As we had anchored well clear, and were 'new boys' in this race, almost every other yacht was in the canal before us. At long last, around 11 p.m. we entered the lock and finally tied up in the basin. There seemed to be a fair amount of partying going on all round, but after 40 hours of what felt like hard, non-stop work we flopped into our berths and slept deeply. 6 hours later we were up and working our way through the canal.

By great good fortune we were in company with John Kyle and his 5-tonner *Nattee*. He knew the ropes, and had had a reliable engine installed many years before. Ours was reliable enough, but it still needed final aligning. Also none of the controls had been led to the helm (no time, the usual complaint). So at every stop, which meant every lock, I had to handle the machinery below decks while the others brought the yacht into the lock. We worked out a good system, with one Alan at each end of the boat, Morag at the helm, and the slightly over-worked guardian angels hovering overhead.

As we came into the lock I would shove the engine out of gear in good time. Coasting along, we would glide into the lock. Aft Alan-H throws the stern warp up to the lock-keeper (on the shore) who grabs it and drops the loop in the end over the mooring hook. This brings us up with a slight jolt, but Alan-H knows the trick of taking some of the snatch out of the stopping. Forward, Alan-L has the bow warp ashore and it's soon made fast, then tightened in twanging taut. This is important, because as the water is let into the lock there is a tendency for the yachts to surge about like enraged lions in a cage. The only way to check this, and save a lot of damage, is to tighten in all the time on the bow warp.

At first we were a bit short of man-power, but my partner, the designer Alfred Mylne II, and his son arrived on the bank of the canal before we had been through three locks. They came aboard and after that it was easy. They knew everyone all along the canal-side, could warn us before we came to sharp corners, and as a result we spent a wonderful, relaxed morning. As we motored through the lovely countryside, eating breakfast, then later coffeeing, we hadn't a care in the world. Apart from the engine line-up. This was still giving trouble and the stern bearing, where the propeller shaft passes out of the yacht, kept getting hot. I put a dish-cloth over it and kept it saturated, which cooled the bearing effectively.

Before long it was clear that we were going to be pressed to arrive at Crinan in time to start in the second half of the race. This was at 2 p.m. So we ran our engine a little harder, worked more quickly through the locks, and tried to calculate how many more miles, what the average speed was, wondered whether we should put up sail to speed us on … it became a race between the races.

There was a third yacht locking through with us. They had not worked out a good procedure, and at the last lock I thought they were drunk. However, apparently they always behaved like that. We could see all the other boats milling round at the start. To us as strangers there seemed to be precious little room in Loch Crinan with Black Rock all too prominent in the middle, and heavens knows how many yachts charging round in the remaining space. Some were getting up sail and going dead to windward using engine to keep them into it. Others were beating energetically back and forth, others lay almost hove-to, while one or two others were 'casing the joint', making trial starts.

All this we saw as we worked into the last lock. Even before the lock gates closed behind us, the 10-minute gun crashed out. We were going to have to work very fast to get to the line in time.

'Alan-H, quick. Tiers off the mainsail. Alan-L, give me a hand with the mizzen. Morag, square away everything below. We'll be going to windward. Stow everything movable in the bunks if there's no time for a neat job.'

And we jumped to it. I decided to sail straight out of the lock and ran the mizzen up while the water was still dropping. To hell with the consequences. We were going to be in at the start or know the reason why. It seemed like a month before at last the water was down to sea level. Every few seconds, in between hauling on halliards, clearing away sheets and taking in all but the last two vital fenders, we snatched a glance at the watch. The rules state that every yacht must be clear of moorings before the 5-minute gun. We had to have our lines on board before that gun, yet if the gates were not open we dare not let go of our hold to the lock-side. Also we would be disqualified if we used the engine after the 5-minute gun.

At long last the water no longer flowed out of the lock. We yelled blue murder till someone threw our lines down to us. There were still 15 seconds to go, but we were held fast in the lock. Its high walls kept the wind from getting at our sails. In desperate haste I dived below yelling:

'Alan-L. Whip the bung out of the exhaust.' In a second the starting handle was on, whirled round, compression levers over, and bless it, the Lister as ever started at once. Without giving it a chance to settle down, I jammed the gear lever ahead and the throttle wide open. The propeller foamed round, bit solid water and we slid out of the lock. At once I cut the engine. As its note died away the 5-minute gun thundered. Done it, with a second to spare.

Now to try and settle down. The mainsail was set dreadfully, which was hardly surprising. We luffed into the wind to try and tighten it, but without winch or tackle it was almost impossible. Both the Alans and I sweated at the job while Morag nursed the boat and dodged her through the other competitors. We had no time to make a trial run over the starting line.

And with so many boats in such a small area, the wind was chopped into a mass of flukes and flaws.

After our thrilling start the day before we made a very poor effort this time. We were still coming up to the line when the gun went. There was one boat astern of us at least, but my quick glance round made it all too clear that not many more had done worse. The line was so compressed, with shoal ground so close behind the line, the rocky shore to port and the islet of Black Rock to starboard that it was impossible to make a really bad start, there just was not room to get away from the line.

We settled down to a stern chase: 'A bottle of beer each for every boat we pass.' I promised. We stood on slightly further than most of the fleet on the first tack, to cut the labour of going about. As we came about we saw we were already ahead of one boat. On the second turn we were three bottles up each, but 10 minutes later down to two again.

This part of the race I found as hazardous, navigationally, as anything I've ever tackled. We dived between Craignish Point and the rocky lump of Garraeasar, while the tide gripped us between its watery jaws and swirled us sideways, the rudder giving no alteration to the course. This passage, the Dorus More, is most disconcerting for the new-comer. There is a shortage of prominent objects to give an accurate bearing, and the combined effects of wind and tide, coupled with the narrowness of the gap, make precise navigation almost impossible. We were so well back in the fleet we could afford to follow the others, but that's no way to win races. I wanted to cut the corners, chop big lumps off them.

Clear of Correasar we bore away on a close reach, past silent, frowning Scarba, whereon not a beast nor bird moved. It was here that we overhauled the mighty *Sea Wolf*. One of the biggest of the fleet, naturally when she had a bit of trouble it was man-sized. Somehow her weather sheet caught as she tacked, and this set her well back while the trouble was cleared. With the tide whirling us over the ground at a superb speed we foamed past Lunga and *Sea Wolf* repassed us, a magnificent sight, clouds of canvas and a crew so numerous as to look like a crowd on deck. She looked such a fine sight, doing 3 knots to our 2, and it was such a tiny thing that put her out of the race later. A runner lever caught a girl a vicious smack in the face, so *Sea Wolf* had to give up and put into harbour. One of *St Mary*'s many assets was that she had no runners, and in consequence no levers.

Ahead lay Fladda lighthouse guarding one side of the passage, and the light on Dubh Sgeir on the other side. Though these two lights are about 700 yards apart, it looks less, since they are not exactly opposite. Coming up from southwards for the first time, as we were, it looks wholly disconcerting. In the grip of the relentless tide we swirled past the rocks, apparently close enough to throw a biscuit ashore. To Morag and me, used to the sandy flats of the Essex coast, where it's usual to be 2 and sometimes 4 miles from dry land even when in very shallow water, this rock-dodging was more than somewhat hair-raising.

According to the chart, which tends to be scientifically exact, the tide here runs at 7 knots. When it's remembered that this is appreciably faster than the *St Mary*'s top speed under power, and is a speed she will not often reach under sail, it's easy to realise how we felt. I would put the helm over to ease away from an outcropping rock, and for seconds we would swirl onwards, apparently skidding, before the boat would turn towards the middle of the channel.

A few weeks after this, a friend of mine came through this pass in his rather ancient converted fishing boat. Right in the narrowest part his engine failed. With desperate haste the crew got the anchor over. As it plunged down, it dragged the chain roaring and rattling after it. It was no flea-weight anchor, and it took a firm hold of the sea-bed. With a frightful wrench the boat snatched at it, snubbing viciously, so much so that her structure could not stand the strain, and distorted. The whole yacht careered round in a half circle, the chain pulling her over sideways. Then with another jarring jolt she brought up, all standing … and broke the chain.

The crew were now in real danger, but they jumped to it, and got out the second anchor. There was no more chain aboard, so they bent on the best warp. This time they let the anchor go more carefully, and the boat was pointing into the tide. She brought up without too much of a snatch and rode safely, while the engine was repaired.

All this happened some weeks after the race, otherwise I would have been even more worried about diving through such a gap in the grip of the tide. As it was we were thankful to see the vista open up, and then thrilled to see that the yachts ahead had run into a calm patch. All of us set about spotting the flat patches.

'Everyone out to port is becalmed.'

'That suits us, this wind is setting us off to starboard.'

'We're gaining on all the leaders.'

'Yes, but we're slowing ourselves. There's *Kotick* coming up from behind, and that looks like a Scottish Island Class boat. With her big sail area, she'll creep up in no time if the wind gets much lighter.'

'What about some sandwiches?'

'Good idea. We only need two in the cockpit now, to watch for flat patches and see we don't sail into them.'

'It's very calm to port and starboard.'

'Aye, but not bad ahead.' So we trimmed our sails and slipped gently along, passing several boats which had stood over by the shore of Mull. For a time we managed to keep going, till at last it was dead calm all round.

In our area there were four or five yachts, all trying to catch a breath of wind. The swell threw us about, till one of the Alans began to feel queasy. He went to lie down while we tried to squeeze a few yards' headway out of the non-existent breeze.

All through the late afternoon we lay between Mull and the mainland, while the tide gave us a few miles' progress. Then a series of clouds started to move away over to port. We spotted a whisp of white, smoke-like cloud waft along the mountainous Mull coastline, and tried to edge over that way. But with no wind we could not move. It was infuriating to be stuck, knowing where the wind would come from, knowing that several boats had not seen it and were allowing themselves to drift off to starboard.

Those clouds got darker, moved faster, but still we lay, rolling, slatting, flopping about, but not moving forward. We could see exactly what would happen. Several of the leaders had closed the Mull shore, using a faint coastal zephyr. They would catch the strong true breeze and be well on their way before we would feel it. Our only consolation was that several boats were far off on the mainland shore, and we would have the advantage over them.

Just as we guessed, the wind came in from the west and then north-west. But not for us. It filled the sails of the group away to our left, and we saw them heel and go. Feeling madly frustrated, we saw one or two of the smaller ones lie well over. A rail-down breeze, a close reach at first, while we lay still becalmed, 2 miles away. I've never known a strong breeze take so long to move that distance. By the time it came I was consumed with impatience, but we made the best of it. I did take a glance or two to leeward, to see how the poor devils down that way were doing. They had to wait as we had, while the breeze dallied and thrust us on, before rescuing them.

By evening we were round Duart Point with its lovely, sombre, forbidding castle, and beating up the Sound of Mull. Night found us still at it, with a long way to go, and a foul tide. That was a night and a half.

With half a night's sleep behind us and before that none at all, we were faced with another all-night session. And so it proved. Through the short hours of summer darkness we beat to and fro, pinned between the rocky Mull shore, and the equally inhospitable Morven coast.

Chapter Seventeen

Just before Duart we had tacked and caught the genoa on the crosstree end. One of the far too many jobs I had not had time for was putting the soft padding on the ends of the crosstrees. Now we were faced with the prospect of an ever increasing rent in our brand new genoa. For us it was a novel experience to own a brand new head-sail. To tear it second time up, just when we looked like needing it, was a blow. But we had to change it, and even while Alan-L and I wrestled to get it down and the jib up with the minimum delay, the wind came in harder.

So that tear was in a way a blessing. It meant that we were not over-canvassed through the hard night's work. In the lulls we were undercanvassed, but in the squalls, and later there were some fizzers, we could manage. As darkness fell there were four boats in our group, with the leaders over 4 miles ahead, apparently in a bunch, and the rest of the fleet spread out for miles and miles astern.

As we entered the Sound of Mull, and before darkness settled in, I had to decide whether it was a justified risk to carry on. The Sound is not well lit for yachts beating through. Though there are some six lights in all, only two lay ahead of us by nightfall and one of these, Rudha nan Gall, was beyond Tobermory, our destination, so that it was of limited use. Tobermory lights would be little use apart from the final spurt. Already the weather was deteriorating. The boat was still untried, and Morag would obviously have to get a good night's sleep. If possible. The two Alans were apparently inexhaustible, but they were not used to cruisers, to racing, to sailing at night, to the *St Mary*. They were not navigators, had had little experience at the helm, and if they were not tired by then, they certainly ought to have been.

On balance it would have been sensible to give up. But I felt so exultant myself, the boat was going so well in spite of her handicaps, I honestly didn't feel tired, there were no good anchorages near that we could get into before darkness, there was never really any chance that we would give up.

We had a meal, then Morag and Alan-L turned in. Through rain-squalls and the increasing darkness Alan-H and I tacked and tacked again. We worked out a technique by which I put the helm over, then held the tiller (which was hinged, thank heaven) with my foot while both of us heaved with all our might to get the sheet in. It was hard work, but it kept us warm, for the rain lashed down then drizzled, then came on again, so we needed something to keep the blood circulating.

However, one feature of the *St Mary* now turned up trumps. We found that going to windward the aft end of the cabin top, which was designed to extend over the cockpit and make a little shelter, worked beyond our wildest hopes. It was so effective that we could stand in the cockpit, peering over the cabin top, just our eyes exposed, while the rest of us was under cover. It was not even necessary to wear oil-skin trousers. Clearly the *St Mary* was far ahead of her competitors in the matter of crew comfort.

She was not lacking in cunning, either. There was quite a lot of shipping about. Mostly fishing boats in small groups, with the occasional coaster and naval vessel. Every time one of these came along, one or two yachts round us flashed torches on their sails. They also used their cabin lights indiscriminately. As a result even in the rain squalls we could often tell where the opposition was, even when the rain was too heavy to let us see the navigation lights. As usual all the yachts in our group were using 'yacht size' navigation lights which only show up under ideal conditions at short range.

Knowing where the others were made a great deal of difference. We were tacking between dark, completely unlit shores. With no echo-sounder, and with water under us mostly too deep for a lead line, our only way of telling when to tack was to try and judge the distance we were off the shore. At times we would seem almost aground, would tack and in a few seconds would seem almost aground on the opposite shore. Actually at no point is the Sound less than half a mile wide, but after so little sleep, with rain pouring down the inside and outside of my glasses, and with shipping to dodge, it was sometimes very hard to judge how long we dared sail on. But if we saw someone on another yacht flash his torch on or put on a cabin lamp and they were inshore of us, we assumed they had water under their keel and stood on.

As a corollary, we used our own torch only when absolutely necessary. We had no cabin lights, and besides the watch below wanted to sleep. For navigating I used a carefully shrouded torch. If I thought there was no danger of a passing ship running us down I did not advertise my presence.

It was all very exciting. At times the pilotage was downright crude. When we reached Green Isle, the rain fairly thrashed down out of the inky black heavens. And naturally, but inevitably, this is the narrowest part of the Sound. Here too the tide was firmly against us so that we beat back and forth in that throttled channel a couple of dozen times before getting into wider waters.

There is a light on Green Isle itself, so all we had to do was judge how far away we were from it and we stood no risk of crashing ashore there. As some of my cousins were marooned there all night some years before, it has family connections. However, it was tacking away from the Isle that was the trouble. Theoretically all we had to do was judge our speed, say 4 knots, plot the distance, calculate the time we could stand towards Morven, and keep going that number of minutes. In practice it took a lot of nerve to sail straight at a shore that was often invisible, and never clearly seen.

By good fortune I worked out a useful technique at this stage which saved my sanity. I found that by standing at the chart table I could see virtually as well as when standing out in the cockpit. Our windows were so big, the all-round visibility from the cabin so excellent, that I could navigate without going on deck. This meant that I was no longer half-blinded by rain running down both inside and outside my glasses, nor did I have to spend so many minutes, quite half my time it seemed, trying to dry my glasses with damp handkerchiefs.

But when a small convoy of fishing boats trundled down the Sound as we zig-zagged wildly between Green Isle and the mainland, and when a particular full-bodied rain-filled squall slashed down at us, then I thought I'd never been involved in a more dangerous race. Or a more exciting one. Several times our nearby competitors sailed past close ahead or astern. Like us, their navigation lights were spasmodically efficient. The spasms depending largely on how much rain got in among the electrics. Once, another yacht thrashed past so close we could clearly see the crew huddled in their oilskins, peering ahead at the shore we had just left. They behaved as if they had not seen us, which was entirely possible.

Next time I come this way, especially if it's at night, I'm going to have an echo-sounder, I vowed. What's more I'm going to whip round the fleet and find out which boats have echometers. Then I'll know who I can trust to the nearest half fathom as I sail full pelt for the rocks two lengths behind them. By the time we left Green Isle behind, I was getting daring. After all, we'd not actually knocked any holes in anyone's property to date. So we made a long tack as soon as I gauged we could sail clear past the north side of the island, in towards the bay at Salen. This presented a new problem. The land here is lower lying. We could no longer depend on seeing the high hills against the cloud-slashed sky. Tentatively I got out the lead and line, thinking we might sail in till I felt bottom at say 4 fathoms, or maybe 2½ if my nerve was in good fettle, then tack off again. We'd done this a dozen nights along the Essex and Kent shores, but there the depth does not change half a fathom in half a mile. Here the depth could come up from 'no bottom' on our lead-line, to crash! all within a few feet, in such a short distance that we would not have time to tack offshore.

So we were back to our timed tacks and guess-work. Around this stage Alan-H, who'd been sailing the boat like an old hand, went below to sleep and the other Alan came up. As he wears glasses too, it was going to be a case of the blind leading the blind. However, the rain now stopped and we had a pleasant sail, doubly pleasant because the two other yachts that kept close to us through the night suddenly disappeared. We thought we'd left them behind.

Though we did not appreciate it at the time, our labour was largely over. The slight change of direction which the Sound has north of Green Isle meant we could now make long and short tacks. So when after an hour of almost dull sailing, and as we were getting near Tobermory, we saw a red flare, we fairly jumped to it. All the world over a red flare is the standard distress sign.

That looping trajectory of the red light swooped through the darkness, right in where we thought the rocky island of Ru Rea was. This island guards the Tobermory anchorage. I assumed the obvious: someone, a bit too keen, had cut the corner to get to the finishing line, and had impinged on a rock. There was no light or buoy to guard the island. If I had not been cautious, and mindful of the untried state of my boat, also our tiredness, and above all the impending baby, I might have been lunatically rock-dodging in there myself. Now it looked as if we would have to go in among the crags whether we liked it or not. And it was definitely not. For that hour was the darkest of all the night, just before the false dawn, when the morale is at a low ebb, when even on a summer night the cold strikes through layers of sweaters and woollen shirts. Hell and damnation, why couldn't people keep out of trouble when I had my hands already full and was rather tired?

'Alan-H,' I shouted down into the cabin, 'come up on deck quickly. You've time to put on oilies, but get a shift on. Some clots in trouble, close inshore.'

Then, very, very reluctantly: 'Morag. You better come up too. Put on lots of warm clothes.' I was far from keen about dragging her out of her bunk, but it looked as if we were all going to be in for a busy time.

I did not want to get to windward of whoever was in trouble. If I did I should have to bear away down to them, and arrive going too fast. The obvious thing was to get over as close as possible, sum up the situation, and then either go alongside if they were in deep water, or maybe anchor and either row down to them, or maybe stream the dinghy downwind on a long line. But I mistrusted our dinghy. It was called 'the bath' because it has the shape, proportions and size of a small bath. It was adequate for getting ashore in a protected harbour, but no good for deep-sea work.

As we bore off a little the wind came stronger, for we were now virtually clear of the protection of the island. At once the yacht accelerated, shooting forward eagerly. Straight for the sharp knobbly shore, still invisible in the thick blackness.

'Alan-L, get the mizzen off her. We're going too fast.' He jumped to it, and soon Alan-H joined him.

We tore along, shooting over the waves, throwing spray to leeward and even to windward, the motion of the whole boat exciting, thrusting forward. As we closed the coast the first searching fingers of light, the herald of the dawn reached across the sky. It was possible to pick out the land round Tobermory, see the hills and valleys. Our tired eyes blinked and strove to pick out details. After a few more minutes we saw the lights of yachts in Tobermory Bay. We could see no sign of anyone in trouble. Due to our alteration in course, also because a few minutes before it had been utterly dark, I was no longer certain exactly where we had seen the red flare. The more I thought about that flare the more perplexed I became. I couldn't visualize what sort of trouble to expect, and therefore was baffled to know what sort of precautions and preparations to make. Riddled with worry I luffed a fraction, towards the yachts' lights in the Tobermory anchorage. We were closing them fast, and none of us had seen any more red flares, nor could we pick out any sign of a vessel ashore, no wildly flashing torch, nothing. All very perplexing.

It was gusty here, almost under the shadow of the land. We talked in brief, fatigue-laden sentences:

'See anything?'

'Not a blind thing that means anything.'

'I'll swear I did see that red flare. I'm not that tired. Wonder if anyone else saw it?'

We sailed closer to the shore. Then ... THERE! Another red flare curved up, hesitated and looped down into the sea. RIGHT IN AMONG THE MOORED

YACHTS. I was absolutely staggered, and the two Alans too surprised to say anything. In utter disbelief I said:

'That's right in among the moorings. What in hell goes on?' and at that moment, in the pale uncertain light we saw a yacht sail past another, the second being moored and well lit up. For a moment my mind tried to fit the facts to a plausible pattern. Then, not knowing what to make of it all:

'They can't be finishing the race with red flares. They CAN'T, no one would. Not here especially, right by a shipping route. White flares perhaps. Blue even. But not red. If they'd run out of white and blue they'd know not to use red under any circumstances.' I just could not believe it.

Still utterly baffled, I decided that the only way to sort out the problem was to sail across the finishing line, close to the yacht taking the finishing times, and ask them if they'd seen someone sending out distress signals. We trimmed sheets:

'Morag. Pass up the cabin step, and the big torch.'

'Here, Ian, shall I hold it?'

'Yes. When we are close to the finishing line, hold the step and get one of the Alans to shine the torch on its under-side.'

Our racing number was painted in bold figures on the bottom of the portable step. We were going hard, then the wind began to fail as we got in the lee of the land. I pointed straight for the finishing yacht, which was well lit with a canvas awning rigged over the cockpit. We luffed to clear her by a safe berth and as we passed ... she fired out a red flare in the air, a finishing signal.

Too tired and amazed to do anything about it, and mindful that we were new boys in these waters, we turned away to find somewhere to moor. After all, it was now getting light, and red flares would not show up at any great distance in a few minutes, so it was fairly certain no coaster would come charging in to see who or what was in trouble.

We counted seven boats already moored which had been in the race with us, apart from others which we took to be local cruisers or visitors not racing. With one of the Alans at the helm we zig-zagged through the moorings, while we sounded with the lead-line. After carefully getting a picture of the depth at various points we selected a place to moor, spun round, nipped between two boats, round the stern of another, luffed into the wind, slid forward till the boat had lost way, and heaved the anchor over on the end of its terylene rope. Through a thickening haze of tiredness I was delighted with the way the yacht seemed capable of nipping in and out of a fairly crowded moorings, even though we had taken the mizzen down.

We should have piled into our bunks, but instead we looked over the fleet. Of the boats which were near us when darkness fell not one was in Tobermory before us. This cheered us a lot. We had no idea how long the others had been anchored, so could not tell whether we had done any good on handicap. While we discussed our prospects another yacht sailed in, rather a small one. She must have beaten us on corrected time, but she was in the small class. Without much energy we cleared up on deck, lashed the sails down, checked the depth under the keel, took a rough bearing in case we started to drag our anchor, checked the anchor rope to make sure it was properly made fast, purposely left the racing flag proudly fluttering at the masthead, and wearily went to our bunks.

It was early afternoon when we woke. The bay was well filled with boats. Plenty of those who came in after us had given up. Some motored through the night. A few had anchored and started again after dawn. Several crews talked about the rugged conditions the night before, and we learned that the leaders had, for a time, had very light winds just before crossing the finishing line.

Inevitably we soared between hope and disappointment about the results. In the end we went ashore to find the finishing order pinned up in a shop window. We were well down the list, seventh. A fair proportion of the yachts had given up, and we felt mixed satisfaction.

'Next year we'll have sheet winches ...'

'And halliard winches ...'

'Should we have a bigger crew?'

'There'll be our son ... or daughter.'

'At least we'll know the way.'

'An echo-sounder would make the world of difference.'

'It'd have made a difference if the genny hadn't torn.'

'Not really. We would never have been able to sheet it in. Especially with only two on watch.'

'At least we finished. Next year ...'

'Next year we'll all be more experienced, and the boat will be finished.'

'No boat of Ian's is ever finished.' From Morag.

'It's just that I like to try out new ideas.' I defend myself.

'I know. Remember the time you took the stanchions off to improve them? It was snowing and we worked all day, not even in a shed. In the open. I've never been so cold ...'

'We were engaged at the time ... Must have been madder than usual.'

'Even when we sold the *St Elizabeth* she was still being altered.'

'Looking at these race results again, they are not all that bad. A lot of people gave up. And a great many trailed in after us, either under power, or just cruising along. Several broke gear. Apart from the genny nothing on our boat carried away.'

'Next year we'll all be more experienced ...'

'Ah! Next year ...'

The following day we lazily got up, pottered about the boat, breakfasted at length, and it was midday before we hauled up the anchor. There was very little wind in Tobermory Bay, and yachts were anchored fairly close all round. But I determined to leave under sail, and so very slowly we slipped clear of the land.

Before our week's holiday we decided, at least I laid it down and the others agreed, that we would on no account go to windward after the race. There were good reasons for this:

1. We only had one week's holiday, so that we wanted to see something of the coastline in the limited time.

2. Going to windward is tiring and this was supposed to be a holiday, a rest from the intensive work of building the boat.

3. Windward work is harder on the boat, and we'd no wish to find defects while far from home. Admittedly the race was enough of a test to show up troubles.
4. Going to windward calls for sheet winches, and how!
5. We did not want to start up over a wave-crest with a crew of four, and land in the trough with a crash to find we were four plus a baby. And so on.

Our plan as we left harbour was to sail towards the island of Canna, but to turn round if it was going to be a beat all the way. It was.

For an hour we sailed with sheets tight in, pitching gently into an awkward sea. I tried to ease the boat along, worried that Morag would feel the motion. But it was one of the Alans who was first to feel 'off'. He went below, persuaded by us that the only thing to do is to lie down. We were now a strong crew, ample in numbers for gentle cruising. No point in all sitting around in the cockpit when there was little to do.

After a couple of tacks I took a cross-bearing. It was not so easy in this part of the world, where prominent objects seem less numerous than the navigator would wish. We were not making fast progress. At the current rate of progress it would be all day before we were anchored in the lee of Canna.

'I suggest we turn back to Loch Sunart.'

'That's over there, to the east?'

'Yes. It's downwind, and there's miles to explore.'

'It is a bit popply here.'

'Right, ready about, let the lee sheet stay slack when she's round.'

'OK. Ready.'

'Lee-oh, ease the main, and mizzen. We'll keep well to the north, it's lousy with rocks on the other shore. One buoy works overtime marking a whole bunch of nastiness.'

At once, we rounded downwind, the motion calmed right down. Someone went below to use the toilet bucket and was back in the cockpit when there was little to do.

'Oh, Ian! I've let the toilet bucket go.'

'Hell. NO? Gybe-oh. Leave the sheets. Morag, Alan-H, do nothing except just watch the bucket.'

'I see it, it's floating, but very low in the water.'

'Just watch it all the time. Alan-L, give a hand on the jib sheets. We'll beat up to the bucket as slowly as possible.'

'It's very hard to watch.'

'Alan-H, go forward. Take the boat-hook. You have first bash at hooking it. Alan-L you lie on the side-deck and try if Alan-H misses it. Trouble is the bow-wave will push it away from us.'

'Can you still see it?'

'Lucky we've got a spare bucket.'

'We MUST get that bucket back. It was a prize we won in the *St Elizabeth* in an all-comers race at Burnham. Besides it's a marvellous port navigation light. We shine the big torch through it and it glows like a large red steamer's light.'

'I've lost it.'

'Blast it, all you've got to do is WATCH!'

'There it is.'

'Where? How far? Oh, right, next tack. Ready about.'

We sailed as slowly as we could, just keeping steerage-way on, but even so our plunging bow came down close to the bucket and nudged it out of reach. It was obviously going to be hard to retrieve, as it was floating upside down. Though this trapped air under it, the handle was so far under water that there was little chance of grabbing it.

'We'll gybe again, get downwind, and come back at it. Slower this time if possible.'

But the second time I over-did it. Not used to the feel of the *St Mary*, and over confident after her fine performance in confined spaces, I brought her down to such a slow speed that we lost steerage-way. When we were near the bucket we stopped, drifted off the wind, picked up speed again, but were then too far off to reach the bucket and too close to tack and get it on the opposite board.

Learning from our mistakes we stood away again, rounded up, beat towards the bucket, and luffed smartly when the bow was past the bucket, so that the yacht ranged right alongside it.

'Missed it,' from the bow.

'Got it,' from amidships. And a good job too. That bucket had sailed several thousand miles with us, and was an old favourite.

Soon after this we were running into the narrowing neck of Loch Sunart changing first to the south shore, then the north, to avoid the unbuoyed rocks. The difficulty here was that the distances were quite small, much of the loch being well under half a mile wide. To take a couple of bearings, plot them, plot a new course from them and so on, conventional style was just not possible. It was a case of pilotage by eye, and very interesting too.

Chapter Eighteen

Our objective was Salen, a hamlet up a miniature loch on the north side of Loch Sunart. This Salen is known as Salen-Sunart, as there is a larger, much better known Salen halfway up the Sound of Mull. We beat into the anchorage, keeping well over to starboard as the chart showed very shoal ground on the west side. But even so, when the Alans went ashore later, a local told them we were too far into the centre of the loch, and might have touched if the tide had not been high.

Our anchor was put down exactly off the end of the stone jetty, just where recommended by that best of all pilot books, the *Clyde Cruising Club Sailing Directions*. It was one of those perfect days, quiet here in the completely sheltered waters, not particularly warm, but utterly peaceful. Ashore there was just, but only just, enough activity to show that there were other people alive. That evening the two Alans went to the local cinema ... hard benches and a film made a couple of decades previously, but fun for all that. Morag and I stayed aboard so that I could tinker with the engine and other parts of the boat, and listen to the radio.

It was late in the morning next day when we decided to get under way. Morag and I had been ashore for food. Instead of a sleepy half-dead village we found that there were a good number of holiday makers, plenty of local people, an atmosphere of activity everywhere. In the village shop we joined a sizeable queue to get fresh provisions, after getting water at the outside tap at the hotel. A new sun porch was being built onto the hotel, showing that our original idea about that part of the world needed revising. We had expected to find a wilderness of moss and rock with a few, a very few, sheep tended by shepherds spaced some 40 miles apart. Instead half of Glasgow apparently owned or was hiring a weekend cottage, caravan or tent.

Back on board it took no time to get ready to sail. Already we all knew our jobs, knew how to stow fresh food so that it would not slide into the bilge when we heeled, or get mixed up with the charts, or spill, slop, tip or insinuate itself into the sleeping bags. After four days aboard we could get under way within minutes. Or could we? The anchor seemed to be taking a lot of lifting. We had the mizzen set, the headsail ready for running up, and the main all ready to hoist once clear of the anchorage. In case of need in a hurry the engine was all set, with starting handle shipped, decompression levers aft, fuel pump setting at high. And now this unexpected trouble. The two Alans and I together tried to hoist the anchor:

'I've a horrid feeling we're fast round something. Let's try one more pull together. Ready? NOW!' and with straining muscles we hauled as if life depended on it.

'Gained an inch.'

'No more. What can have happened?'

'Must have got the anchor round a mooring chain. Funny thing, though. With three of us hauling we should be able to lift our anchor and the chain together. Can't be any big moorings here, there aren't any big ships for miles around. Nothing for them to come here to collect. Come on. One more try. Ok? NOW PULL!'

But it was no good, between us we could do nothing except pull our own bows down.

'Couldn't we try getting the anchor to let go some way?'

'We might try sailing it out. Alan-H you stand by the anchor, Alan-L give me a hand in the cockpit. I'll take the helm when the engine's going.'

Two tries to yank the anchor free failed. We stopped the engine, talked the problem over again, then had another try.

'There's nothing for it but to dive,' I decided. We knew we had a depth of 48 feet under us, and I was perfectly certain that I could never get to that depth without skin-diving gear. There was none aboard and we expected to find none nearer than Oban, over 55 miles away.

One of the Alans said: 'Without training the best anyone can do is get down to 30 feet. I remember reading that in a technical article recently.'

'We may be in luck. If we've lifted the anchor with whatever it's caught on about 18 feet off the bottom, then I may be able to touch it.'

'Do be careful Ian,' from Morag.

'Don't worry, there's no current here, and it's far too cold for prolonged partying below.'

'What's the plan?'

'Very simple. The anchor is hitched on to a chain or wire which is stretched along the sea bed. All I have to do is dive down, pass a rope round the chain, and get back to the surface. Then we haul the two ends of the rope at the same time. This lifts the cable, the anchor drops off, and we haul it up. Then we let go one end of the lifting rope and pull in the other. This will drop the cable, recover our rope and we're off. Dead easy, if it works.'

It was obviously going to be essential to get the rope round the chain on the first dive. We'd been far too busy boat building all year to go swimming. I had not been in at all the whole summer. While Morag put the kettle on and dug our towel out of the kit-bag I changed, thinking about the best way to get down the maximum depth. To dive or drop in was the first big question. Better go down feet first, and hand-over-hand down our anchor warp. That way there would be no waste of time looking for the anchor once I was below the surface. Also pulling myself down the anchor warp would be the quickest way to get to the anchor.

It was chilly on deck wearing only a bathing costume, and doubly so when I took my glasses off. One of the Alans stood by the bow, ready to pay out the light nylon line which I looped round my wrist. Our bows were high out of the water, and it seemed a long drop. Feeling grimly dreadful I slipped into the water. Its bitter icyness drove the breath from my lungs, like air from a pricked balloon. On the rebound I gulped in all the oxygen I could, reached down the terylene anchor line, and PULLED. Down and down and DOWN. The anchor rope was vertical, stretched perfectly taut and it made a fair bannister. Every fraction of a second the pressure mounted outrageously. I'd scarcely got down a few feet, it seemed, before my head was reeling, and there was no strength left in my arms for further effort. Mechanically I went on dragging myself down the anchor-warp, searching and probing the depths with my feet to try and touch the anchor and its ensnaring chain. At last I felt, no, feeling was long passed, I knew that if I went further down I'd be in a mess on the way back. With a despairing thrust of my foot I tried to plumb the depths a foot or two lower. Nothing solid touched my wildly seeking foot.

Dizzy and desperate I hauled myself back to the surface. It seemed an impossible distance, I JUST HAD TO BREATHE. But for solid seconds my head continued to bore on up through the cold green water. Hand over hand, feverishly trying to go faster, ears paining, throat throttled, I fought for the surface. When I did burst up, my lungs just could not grab the air in quick enough. I was like a baby snatching at its bottle after the purgatory of hunger which has lasted too long. For a time I just held weakly to the anchor warp, getting back enough strength to say:

'Sorry. No luck. Couldn't feel a thing. Seems blasted deep. Gi'me a hand getting back aboard.'

Both Alans grabbed one arm, and I struggled, panting and tired, to get up the slippery high sides. I knew that I had shot my bolt when I measured the amount of nylon line which I had pulled down with me. It came to 30 feet, and my foot would have been no more than 6 or 7 feet below that. So we were far from getting near the anchor.

As I went aft to change I saw there was a big motor yacht, around 90 feet long, anchored at the open end of the loch.

'They might have a frogman's suit on that yacht.'

'She's big enough. Often enough that type has water-skiing and skin-diving gear aboard.'

'They have to have some amusements aboard. She's like a block of mobile flats. Need binoculars to see the sea from the deck.'

'It's worth going to ask them.'

So Alan-L rowed off to see if he could get help. He had to go round the massive yacht three times, and yell like a coal-seller before he could attract any attention. After a time he came back, followed by a dinghy under outboard from the big yacht. There were two paid hands in the dinghy, tough experienced types. They brought a big purchase, a pair of blocks (pulleys) and a rope. We joined this to our anchor line and they, together with the two Alans and I, all tailed on to the fall of the purchase. We pulled! Heavens how we heaved! The anchor line went thin and rock hard with the strain. But the only effect was to pull the *St Mary*'s bow down.

We tried twice more. Then the two paid hands climbed back into their dinghy and tried to tow us clear. No luck. Next we ran a line, looped lightly, down the anchor warp. We let it slide down as far as it would go, till we hoped that the loop was round the stock of the anchor. Our two friends took the end of this light line away in their powered dinghy and tried to trip the anchor out. We tried hauling the anchor line tight and then dropping it quickly. Nothing worked. None of us could think up anything clever to try.

Very sadly I took out my knife, then realised that the terylene was iron hard, hauled taut as it was. So instead I got the bread-knife which has a serrated edge. Everything was made ready to get under way. One Alan stood at the helm, the other at the sheets. I leant over the bow as far as possible and cut through the brand new terylene line.

Sailing back out of Loch Sunart was fun. There are plenty of isolated rocks which have to be left alone. They are shown on the chart but not marked by buoys, so we had to pilot ourselves with care. At the entrance we turned sharp round to port and sailed inshore of Red Rock, Big Stirk and Little Stirk. The Alans, being new to cruising, were cool, calm and unworried, but I could not help fretting. This dodging around sharp and unyielding pieces of half-submerged rock takes practice. Morag and I were still suffused with the East Coast mentality as far as pilotage went. There the lead and line will take you up any back creek fairly safely, and if you do run aground no one is surprised, nor does it matter, except in very unusual circumstances. Here, running aground just was not to be contemplated.

Our next stop was to be at Loch Aline, and we arrived in the evening. Not to be caught again, we put the anchor down with a tripping line. Our small plastic water-can made a fine buoy for the tripping line. Being white, it showed up even at night. The handle is moulded into the body of the can, at the top. So when we tied on the tripping line there was no chance of it coming off. Also it held the can upside down, so even if the screw-on top did leak, air was trapped inside and the can would float. It was lucky that we had a second anchor aboard, otherwise we would have had to sail and sail and sail, like the *Flying Dutchman*, unable to stop. At least till we got to Oban where we could tie up alongside.

However, our second anchor was our bower, a massive job intended for riding out hurricanes. It weighs about twice as much as anyone wants to haul up more than once a lifetime. Thank heaven, when morning and departure came, the two Alans grabbed the anchor line and whipped it in swiftly.

We thought that Loch Aline, reputed to be one of the most beautiful anchorages on the west coast of Scotland, is rather spoilt by the silica sand mine deposits and tailings. Also the new houses have a rawness about them, they do not blend with the hills and heather the way a crofter's cottage does.

The silica sand deposit is mined for two special buyers. One puts it in a very well known brand of tooth-paste. The other uses it in an equally over-advertised make of saucepan and bath scouring powder. I've heard it said that the deposit was first worked during the early part of the war, or just before. Then the sand was used for optical instruments, since the previous source of supply in Belgium was not available. It's said that the vein of this remarkable, brilliant white powder extends right under the Sound of Mull and comes up the other side, in

Mull. When a block is mined it's very hard, compact, almost rock-like, but a blow with a hammer will shatter the lump into a heap of fine sand.

Among the minor items we had not had time to fit on the yacht was the water tank. We got along very well with a couple of plastic cans and a dozen ordinary bottles. These we filled every other day and we did not have to stint ourselves for water. As we did not go ashore at Loch Aline, we knew that the next day would be a watering one. We decided to head for Oban, since fresh bread was running out, and other fresh food would not last the weekend. None of us felt like falling back on a diet of tinned food. With a fair wind it was an easy sail towards Oban till someone thought of looking at the time. Then we realised we would be lucky to get there before the shops shut. Someone else looked into the appropriate page of the Clyde Cruising Club directions and came up with the gloom that it was early closing in Oban. Knowing this town is a holiday resort, we reckoned that there would be plenty of shops doing their damndest to net every farthing of the all-too transient prosperity. So we pressed on, at a breathless 2 knots. I was far from happy about the engine alignment still, and did not want to motor more than essential.

Our quickest route lay between Lismore lighthouse and Lady Rock. The gap is wide enough. The chart is clear enough. But in practice the passage is not without excitement. From 33 fathoms the bottom comes up very suddenly to 6½, then just as precipitately drops to 17 fathoms. It is, of course, the ridge of rock which forms Lismore Island, trailing off under the sea. We had a good tide under us, and as we approached, the glassy sea was boiling and bubbling in the gap between the Rock and the lighthouse. Under these conditions it's hard to trust the chart absolutely. All the evidence points to a lot of horror close under the surface, and with virtually no wind, dead astern too, a firm fair tide whisking the boat straight towards the turbulence, it's an iron-nerved navigator that does not consult and re-consult the chart before it's too late to turn back.

Naturally the chart was right, and though we peered intently into the depths we could see not even the suggestion of a shadow of rock far below. Plotting our position at short intervals made it clear that we were going to be late for the shops unless the engine did some work. As usual it started first swing, and at a low throttle setting we chugged into Oban.

As a yacht harbour it strikes the incoming crew as an unfriendly place. There is no obvious place to tie up or even anchor. The wind seems to have too easy a passage, and the sea heaves restlessly even on a calm day. This is in part due to the constant passage of all types of craft, especially fishing boats. With their heavy displacement and excess power, at least in many modern versions, the typical motor fishing vessel creates a great disturbance, to the discomfort of everyone aboard other vessels moored all round.

We tied up alongside a cadet ship, a converted motor fishing vessel. In a second the two Alans were ashore with a couple of canvas bags and a shopping list. I carried the water containers ashore to refill and found a long factory-like shed by the quay. It looked interesting inside, so I went in. In the dim light I made out rows and rows of large brick tanks. Every one was filled with lobsters, black, the essence of evil looks, slowly scrambling over each other, claws searching, antennae weirdly waving, they might have been tiny prehistoric beasts. Someone said that loads of lobsters were regularly flown south to victual the trans-Atlantic liners.

Back on board, Morag and I decided we would ask the Alans if they liked lobster, and if so we would buy enough for dinner that night. But by the time the Alans got back, laden with provisions in spite of early closing day, the lobstery was tight shut and locked. From the outside it looked just like any warehouse or dreary factory shed. Nothing betrayed the teeming life, the dozens of miniature monsters that were inside.

We had no wish to stay at Oban for the night, rolling and lolloping about.

As soon as the food was stowed we set off down Kerrera Sound, a delightful narrow waterway full of life, passing fishing boats, dinghies and a few yachts. We dropped the anchor in Little Horse Shoe Bay, carefully buoying the anchor because according to the pilot book there is a chain across the bay. Lobster rafts are moored to this chain, so the book says, but we saw none.

The bay is just small enough to make entry and departure by sail alone exciting. At least that's the way it struck this skipper. By now we were a team. One Alan stood on the foredeck with the anchor, as we approached. The other was on the jib sheets. At an interesting speed we reached down the Sound, at the red buoy marking the rocks which guard the north-east side of the buoy we luffed:

'Ready on the jib sheets.' The wind began to fail us, as we came under the shadow of the hills.

'Ready about. Get the anchor over the bow, but don't drop it yet. Lee-oh.' What a delight the *St Mary* seemed, the way she whipped round on her heel.

'We'll have to tack again at once.' We were close in to the shore already, a fraction too far north. The boat spun round again.

'Leave the jib sheets free. Free the main sheet.' We were now heading straight into the wind, losing way. As the yacht glided slower and slower:

'Right, let the anchor down. Check how much runs out. Stop at about 8 fathoms.' The jib flapped and rattled, the mainsail echoed it, but the mizzen, the fully-battened, hardworking, silent mizzen never made a sound. In fact one of its very minor disadvantages is that it is so silent it can be forgotten. Coming up to moorings it sometimes gets left sheeted in when the other sails have been freed off. This has the result that when the yacht should be slowing to a standstill she continues to forge ahead. For anyone not used to the mute hard-pulling sail aft, it's disconcerting to find the brakes apparently won't work.

After dinner the Alans went fishing. They scientifically quartered the surrounding area, working over each part of the Sound round us in turn, trolling from our dinghy. But the fish knew nothing of this scientific approach, they would not cooperate and nothing took the bait.

That night, after dark, a look round to make sure all was well gave the impression we were in for some fine weather. Up to now we'd had all the varieties of Highland weather except the hot sunny kind. Sure enough, when we reluctantly wriggled out of our terylene sleeping bags next morning the sky was clear. Over a comfortably lazy breakfast we discussed the day's run. A fair tide was essential to pass Fladda lighthouse, and we wanted it to carry us right to Crinan. That meant arriving by five o'clock in the afternoon, an easy day's sail provided there was wind.

By 11 a.m. we were under way, but using the engine because the wind was very light, and the mooring so confined. We had the mizzen and jib to help the engine, and as soon as we were clear the engine was switched off. The fair wind pushed us along fast enough, and we looked like being too early. So we left the main stowed, everyone rummaged in kit-bags for books, and soon enough not a word was heard. Even the helmsman stood, leaning against the cockpit coaming, glancing up every few minutes, but reading intermittently.

I laid a course to take us well clear of Sheep Island, and away out into the middle of the Firth of Lorne. Still full of caution, I couldn't get used to the idea of shaving along the coast. Besides, we wanted to relax. Away with the grindstone of constant navigational plots. For a change we just charged down the middle, flat out at 1½ knots. The tide was doing most of the work, no one aboard was doing a stroke.

Well clear of Kerrera we took in the jib and put up the spinnaker. It's a fine cruising rig, mizzen and spinnaker. The spinny appears to set better when there's no mainsail behind it. The main seems to make the wind twirl and wiggle so it cannot go smoothly into and out of the spinny. And of course our mizzen is perfectly behaved. Downwind it stands out flat as a board, due to its long fingers, its full length battens. No curled edges here to reduce the area and confuse the windflow over the sail.

As the day wore into afternoon the sun really beat down. Morag went below to sleep. The rest of us could not raise the energy to go below. As I had no sun-hat aboard I put a light sou'wester on backwards. Its long brim gave a superb shade. After a time even the spinnaker got tired of working in the hot sun. It flopped. We let it. Only the mizzen kept working, always gently urging us southwards.

Lunch came and went as we passed Sheep Island. In a lethargic way I looked for Fladda, couldn't see it, went back to my book. Two o'clock, and this is the life. Sweaters all off hours ago, shirt sleeves rolled up, apart from Alan-L who has his shirt off.

Suddenly. Something's wrong! We're not where we think we are. Hell's buttons, this is what comes from not keeping a constant navigation plot. Grab the hand-bearing compass, whirl round to pick up two, or better three prominent objects. Three quick bearings, and dive below to plot our position on the chart. We're too far south. While we have been taking life easy the boat has been going faster than we thought. And the tide has pushed us along too.

We are in danger of being swept by the tide past Fladda on the wrong side, the seaward side. Already we are beyond the red buoy which marks the entrance to the Sound of Luing. In a swirl of satiny smooth nylon we whip the spinnaker down and thrust it into the bag, starting the engine at the same time. It's at times like these that the instant starting is such a boon. I bring the boat round on the new course, across the tide, on a course which I hope will take us close round the top of Beul nan Uamh, the island at the north end of the Sound of Luing. One of the Alans takes the helm while I wrestle with the navigation because there's still something awry. Close by us are two tiny islets. At first I can't see them on one chart, then when I do, I find they're called Tighgeadh I. This is on the small scale chart. However we are just sailing on to the edge of a large scale chart. Here there are two islets named Dubh Pheith. Are they the same? It's all most annoying because it's absurd to miss a tide when up to now we've had so much time in hand. Serves me right for standing so far offshore, playing oversafe. To make life more difficult the red buoy proves extremely hard to pick out. I particularly want this to check my bearings, but the blasted thing sulks, sitting low in the water and merging, with malice aforethought, against the rocky shore.

Then we see it, and 20 minutes later we are in the grip of the tide hurrying us through the Sound of Luing. Going past Fladda the water is absolutely treacley, yet not flat. It boils and rolls under, cavorts and writhes as the tide drags masses of water over the rocky uneven sea bed.

As the afternoon wears on I work out average speeds and expected arrival times. We do not want to flog the engine till it is fully run in, and properly lined up. Just as much as we want to be through the narrow gap of Dorus More before the tide turns foul. If we are late, we may have to anchor for a whole tide. The sun blazes down. Not a breath of wind helps us, as we motor between the high deserted brooding Island of Scarba and the low farmlands of the friendly looking island opposite, Luing.

In the open stretch of water, where the Sound of Luing becomes the Sound of Jura there is a faint breeze. A magnificent sight comes towards us, an ex-12-metre, all plain sail set and turning slowly to windward, towering mast, pillars of sail, a thrilling rattle and chatter of sheet winches every time she tacks.

Again we find the navigation strange. We know where we are, know the course, yet we cannot pick out the gap in the rocks we have to dive through. Keeping carefully on course we try to identify where one island ends, and the next begins:

'That looks like the gap.'

'No. Too far south. It should be there.'

'I can't see any visible sign of a break in the shoreline.'

'Watch for boats coming out on the first of the tide. We're a few minutes late. Tide will be against us any minute now.'

'What about more speed?'

'Yes. Worth it to catch the tide. Just open the throttle a milligap,' and the Lister's throaty rumble deepens. Our swishing bow-wave steepens a trifle, the driftwood on the sheeny water goes past a fraction faster.

Then we see it, the rocky islets of Correasar and Ris an Vic Faden move aside to show us the Dorus More. As we turn through this gap, the tide is just beginning to turn foul. We edge away from the centre of the fairway and hope the swirls will not set us too much across towards the rocks. In a few minutes we are clear and into the bay that forms Loch Crinan. This is the perfect place to end a cruise, it's as beautiful as anywhere we've seen. On the north side stands a tiny castle, beautiful with the late afternoon sun warming it. Someone says:

'That's the perfect place to retire to. What's it called?'

'I'll look on the chart. Here it is. Duntroon Castle. And according to the chart there's a boathouse a few hundred yards to the west of it.'

'Perfect. Let's retire tomorrow.'

'Slow the engine, will you. Slow as it'll go without stalling. We'll circle off the lock entrance, till the gates open.'

'There's no one in sight.'

'They'll see us soon enough.'

'Or hear the engine.'

'Not necessarily. Standing at the bow it's hard to hear, and from even a few yards away it's difficult to tell it's running, especially on the opposite side to the exhaust outlet.'

'What happens if no one turns up to open the lock?'

'One of us'll have to be put ashore in the dinghy to open it.'

'Here are the fenders. Which side?'

'Port. We'll be going in alone. Get the bow and stern ropes ready too, please.'

'There's someone coming.'

'He's winding up a sluice.'

'When the lock gate opens we'll line up for the entrance, aim straight in, and cut the engine well before we get there.'

'Not using the reverse?'

'Not now. It twists the boat off course. And we still don't know enough about it to bring the boat to a standstill without slewing sideways.'

So when the gates opened we glided very slowly into the lock, made fast, and soon lay moored to the canal bank for the night. The Alans and I climbed the hill and took photos of the *St Mary*. In Barbados, or Brittany, Curaçao, Canada or California I don't think I've ever been in a better berth than at Crinan. It's reported to be cleggy (midge-ridden) but that evening it was just perfect.

It took us all next morning to work through the canal. At one point we met a 'puffer'. These maids-of-all work were originally designed to be the biggest freighters that could get through the Crinan and Forth–Clyde canals. They were made exactly the same length as the locks, less a very few inches. To get the maximum ship in the fixed length they all have vertical bows and sterns. Till recently all puffers were steam driven, with no condensers, so that as they chugged along they went 'puff-puff', emitting little white puff of steam from their high narrow funnels. This steam showed up in contrast to the inky thick black smoke caused by a rough hand stoking. Nowadays puffers are finding lorries take much of their trade. But they are keeping up with the times by fitting diesel engines. Sadly this means they no longer 'puff'.

Passing a puffer in a canal could be difficult. If it decided to stick plum in the middle, as it might to avoid grounding in the shallower part near the shore, then heaven help the yacht. She would have to knuckle under, and go to the edge of the canal even at the risk of bumping the bank or grounding. But the *Lascar*, the puffer we met, was skippered by a kindly man. When he saw that two yachts were coming towards him (we were in company with a 6-tonner) he stopped his ship, let her drift in the gentle breeze to one side to allow us to pass comfortably.

Late in the afternoon we sailed down Loch Fyne and into Tarbert, the finest little harbour. Here we lay alongside a fishing-boat, which meant we could jump ashore and not have to launch the dinghy. It also meant that we did not have to tend our warps with the rise and fall of the tide. As the sun set over the hills we relaxed aboard. Only one more day of the maiden cruise, and all of us felt somewhat triumphant. Not only did the *St Mary* float, she floated the right way up. She was comfortable, far ahead of most boats of her size and when she was finished she'd be clearly the best coastal cruising yacht I'd ever sailed aboard. Of course it's impossible to be satisifed:

'Next boat we build ...'

'You've not finished this one yet!'

'That's true, but she'll point the way to the next one. Faster. Yes, faster. But just now it's hard to see how we could improve on this one. More sheer next time. We couldn't put any sheer on this boat because the alloy cabin top had to have a straight bottom edge. We managed a false sheer by curving the top of the foot-rail round the deck. But now I've worked out how we can keep the super-simplicity of the straight cabin edge, and still have a sweeping sheer.'

'Who's for bed?'

'Back to Port Bannatyne tomorrow.'

'I'll just check the warps and fenders before we turn in.'

'Anyone brewing up tonight? No need to save water, we can top up the cans before leaving in the morning,' and so on, the pleasant quiet talk as darkness closed over the ideal berth for the night.

It was an effortless sail home next day. The *St Mary* rounded up to the moorings, one of the Alans leant over the bow, boathook in hand as we shot head to wind and coasted towards the buoy.

'Starboard a little,' comes the call from the bow. And a second later: 'Right, I have it,' as the boathook catches the buoy-ring and we are home.

20 minutes later I rowed the two Alans ashore, saying, 'Will you come again next year?'

'Yes. Definitely. There'll be five of us next year.'

'I hope our baby soon gets web-footed. An old lady once told me I'd never have children, they'd all turn out to be little dinghies!'

'She must have known you well.'

'Morag wants a boy. With black hair and blue eyes. She's sure that's what it'll be.'

And three months later she was proved exactly right.

Chapter Nineteen

During each winter we worked on the *St Mary* and we cruised her each summer. We also competed in the Clyde Cruising Club passage races and in the second full season we suddenly found form. With the same crew, race after race, with new sheet winches and some new sails, we were able to make our little ketch keep pace with sloops and cutters of our own size. When the weather breezed up we did especially well because while on other boats crews were battling with reefs, we just reduced sail area by dropping the mizzen. This was in the days before the modern style of jiffy reefing and it was common for a yacht to sag back in the fleet for 10 minutes, and sometimes much more, while the sweating, swearing, struggling crews fought to get the mainsail reefed. As the wind increased still further we had a fairly easy job reducing sail area because our mainsail was small and we could keep the aft end of the main boom steady, secured to the rugged permanent boom gallows.

For the annual race south from the Clyde to Belfast Lough, I left the family at home and filled the boat with an extra tough crew. One or two of them were very experienced and one was a famous pork butcher, who arrived on board with a cardboard box the size of a not-so-small suitcase. This was packed solid with sausages, chipolatas, chops, black puddings and all the other delicacies of his trade.

It was a rough race, to windward almost all the way. We hardly ate at all but took it in turns to be seasick and the only slight relief was when I said: 'I'm always alright after the third day at sea.' It was a cry from the heart as there is nothing so grim, so shattering and demoralising as seasickness. My comment raised a laugh because the race only takes a day and a half at the most.

Reaching the end of the race we beat into the wide entrance of Belfast Lough in a rising wind. Around us, ahead and astern, we saw plenty of bigger boats and we had that delicious feeling that we could be among the winners. The wind continued to strengthen and the *St Mary* was forced down with seas climbing up to the toerail. The mizzen had already been stowed and the genoa changed for the working jib by the time we could see the finish far ahead. We could just make out the biggest boats in the fleet crossing the line, rounding up and dropping sails, then motoring into the anchorage. Harder yet the wind came out of the Lough, but we could lay the finish in one tack. The strain on the rigging was nerve-wracking ... we still were not sure what our boat could take and anyone who has ever built a yacht knows that awful feeling that maybe there should be more fastenings here, or perhaps a thicker scantling there, or had every bolt in every part been properly tightened? A knowledge of a boat which is too intimate plays on the imagination.

It was the clew of the mainsail which started to go. The whole sail was under a ferocious strain, so that it looked and felt like sheet steel. In a frantic rush, with cold wet fingers, we put a lashing round the boom and the clew, then prayed that everything would hold for another half-hour. As we thundered in under the lee of the land conditions should have eased but they seemed to worsen. We should have eased the main but we had the bit in our teeth and drove hard, spurred by the sight of other boats coming into the Lough astern of us.

It was all worthwhile, as we found out when the committee worked out the finishing times and the handicaps. Standing round the yacht club bar we heard rumours, then incredulous remarks like:

'... that damned little blue ketch is first, though God knows how she can win a race to windward. Ketches don't sail to windward, do they? Here, have another drink ... She is supposed to be a family cruiser and she's as roomy as a church inside ... Besides the owner built her himself with the help of a pregnant wife ... Maybe I should get my wife pregnant again ... if that's what it takes to win to WINDWARD ... How *can* a ketch win? ... Here, have another drink ...'

It was true – we had won, though I was so tired and drained by seasickness it took time to filter through.

Race celebrations in Ireland are livelier and more cheerful, better lubricated and more hectic than anywhere else. It was a great night but we had finished the race in the evening and we had to sail for home not long after midnight. As we rowed offshore from the clubhouse, back to the *St Mary*, we had that cheerful feeling which comes from a first prize, a stern wind for home, a tough crew and a successful boat.

With so many hands aboard it was easy to haul up the anchor, even though we had no winch on the foredeck. As the chain rattled through the pipe into its locker and the sails stopped flapping when they filled, we bore off downwind for the Lough entrance.

Someone with more energy left than the rest of us (did he actually get some sleep on that bumpy beat south?) poured buckets of water over the foredeck to wash off the mud brought up by the anchor.

Aft, in the cockpit, we all sagged down hardly able to stay awake. In between trimming the sails we sat round-shouldered with fatigue and as I worked out the course for home the chart kept becoming blurred. Above the gurgle of the bow wave we heard the noises of continuing revelry ashore ... music and snatches of song. We slid through the darkness past other moored yachts ... on some of them the sails were going up for the journey home ... We called across and got quiet answers ... They were just as tired as we were, what with the hard race and the hectic celebrations ashore. In some ways the peace after a race is the best sailing time of all.

We were too tired to stay on deck long, so we worked out a watch system which ensured that there were always two people in the cockpit and the rest of us collapsed into our bunks. One of the two left on watch said, as I squirmed into my sleeping bag, 'What about food?'

'There's Billy's big box of pork chops and suchlike. It's all fresh food so if it's not eaten it might go off,' I said as I fell asleep and I thought I heard mutters of:

'There'll be no chance of that.'

When my turn came to go on watch I found I was skipper of a travelling restaurant. As soon as the frying pan was emptied of one lot of food, another was loaded in. We trailed a delicious smell of fried bacon, chops, black puddings, brown puddings, white puddings, kidneys, liver, steaks, more chops ... it went on all the way up the Irish Sea. As dawn broke the man who happened to be cook at the moment muttered: 'Thank God for daylight; now we can really start cooking.' All the food uneaten due to the rough conditions on the way south found its way into the frying pan; as watch succeeded watch the pan was filled and refilled.

Late Sunday night I got home. As I went through the front door Morag met me: 'Did you win?'

'Naturally!'

'You look tired. You must be starved. With all those men aboard and without me there to cook, I bet you hardly ate a thing all weekend.'

'Well, it wasn't quite like that.'

'Never mind now, you can tell me while you eat. I've got a lovely big dinner in the oven for you.'

Next year things went even better. With Morag and our little son aboard, we won the Tobermory Race. The stretch from Crinan north, round the headland dominated by Duart Castle and through the Sound of Mull was a reach and run. We had made ourselves a bright red spinnaker during the previous winter by hiring a church hall to cut it out and with this ecclesiastical background we always reckoned that sail had divine assistance. It certainly set and stayed full aloft when others were collapsing, so we naturally assumed that someone high above was holding it up. It was stitched together on an ordinary domestic sewing machine in a tiny room by a friend who had never sewn a sail before. She could only spread out the tiniest area at one time, so she sewed each seam with a lot of faith and hope. To make the job easier for her we had pinned each seam along its full length at close intervals. This job took hours and we had to borrow pins from half the county, but the end result was well worthwhile. All this was before I joined Dick Hughes to form a new Scottish sail loft, and I never dared tell him too much about the technical side of some of my sailmaking experiences.

As we rounded Duart we had the wind well aft and the spinnaker started to pull like wild horses. I'd been at the helm for hours and was tired. Our little boy was beginning to find the long race tedious ... he was not yet three and he had been cooped up below much of the time. So I handed over the helm and went down into the saloon. This cabin was designed to be roomy, with the furniture set well back and no central table, so the sole space is exceptionally large. Little David produced his miniature football and we played football in the saloon as we raced up the Sound of Mull while the crew in the cockpit won the race.

The year after that we had a daughter and two years later, another son. So the boat fulfilled her role as a floating nursery and when racing we used to say that we should get an enhanced handicap according to the number of nappies flying from the guardrails.

When we sold the *St Mary* she was bought by my sister and her husband who have five children, so the yacht continues to be what she was designed for – a true family cruiser. She has been to the Mediterranean, to France innumerable times, and with luck she will be doing her job happily for years to come.